Digital Color Management

ENCODING SOLUTIONS

Digital Color Management

ENCODING SOLUTIONS

Edward J. Giorgianni
Thomas E. Madden

ADDISON-WESLEY

An imprint of Addison Wesley Longman, Inc.

Reading, Massachusetts   Harlow, England   Berkeley, California
Menlo Park, California   Don Mills, Ontario   Amsterdam
Bonn   Mexico City   Sydney   Tokyo

The publisher offers discounts on this book when ordered in quantity for special sales. For more information, please contact:
Corporate & Professional Publishing Group
Addison Wesley Longman, Inc.
One Jacob Way
Reading, Massachusetts 01867

Library of Congress Cataloging-in-Publication Data
Giorgianni, Edward J.
  Digital color management : encoding solutions /
Edward J. Giorgianni, Thomas E. Madden ; foreword by R.W.G. Hunt
      p.   cm.
  Includes bibliographical references and index.
  ISBN 0-201-63426-0 (alk. paper)
    1. Image processing–Digital techniques. 2. Color. 3. Coding theory.
  I. Madden, Thomas E. II. Title.
  TA1637.G56 1997
  621.36′7–DC21   96-48149
                                                                        CIP

Text design by Pamela Yee
Text printed on recycled and acid-free paper
ISBN 0-201-63426-0
1 2 3 4 5 6 7 8 9 - DOC - 0100999897
First printing, December 1997

Contents

Foreword

Not many years ago, technical books on color were either printed entirely in black ink, or, if color was included at all, it was confined to a few color plates inserted as additions to the main text. *Digital Color Management: Encoding Solutions* is profusely illustrated with color throughout, and this demonstrates a revolution that has taken place in publishing. The graphic arts industry has developed color printing to the point where it is now economically possible to print textbooks in color and achieve very high quality. The availability of color in computer signals, in self-luminous display devices, and in printers has therefore led practitioners of desktop publishing to expect comparable results. But, in the printing industry, much technical development and human skill had to be used before consistently good results were obtained. Digital imaging currently faces the challenge of reaching a similar position. At first sight, it might seem that the endless flexibility provided by having signals in digital form should make all the problems easily solvable. That this is not so is illustrated by the plethora of different color management systems that have reached the market.

The complexity of the situation arises from the different input, monitoring, and output media involved, and the different objectives required for different applications. Thus the digital signals may originate from original artwork, from video cameras, from reversal films, from negative films, from *Photo CD* Discs, or from computer workstations. The final display may be a self-luminous monitor, a reflection print, a projected transparency, or a halftone graphic arts image. The application objective may be facsimile appearance, as in photocopying; or rendering like a conventional photographic system, as in working with color negatives; or re-rendering, as when making a reflection print from a transparency, or attending to the requirements of good portraiture.

Digital Color Management: Encoding Solutions addresses all these and many other issues. The diversity of the media is addressed by the use of appropriate profiles for both source and destination devices, and the provision of a suitable Profile Connection Space. This space is made effective by using a set of fully defined reference viewing conditions, colorimetric measures, and methods of allowing for subjective effects caused by chromatic adaptation, brightness adaptation, and the effect of surrounds on perceived contrast. Included in these operations are appropriate allowances for the flare occurring in different parts of the systems, and rendering intents that suit the particular applications. In certain areas, only approximate answers are possible. For instance, because most acquisition devices do not have spectral sensitivities that are a set of color-matching functions, the exact capture of original-scene colorimetry is not usually possible. In addition, reasonably accurate models of color appearance are still being developed, so that at present only approximate allowance can be made for some subjective effects.

Digital Color Management: Encoding Solutions tackles these topics at length, and in a tutorial manner. The authors write from much firsthand experience, and their account is both lively and personal. There is no doubt that the topic they cover is becoming increasingly important in imaging, and their text provides a much needed contribution to the literature on the subject.

R. W. G. Hunt

Preface

Digital color imaging is one of today's most exciting and fastest growing fields. As evidence, one only need consider that according to industry estimates, more digital color images were produced during the past year *alone* than the *total* number produced in all previous years!

The excitement and phenomenal growth in the field are not surprising, because digital technology offers unprecedented capabilities for editing, manipulating, storing, and displaying color images. But this technology is not without problems. In particular:

- Many current digital imaging systems do not produce predictable color results.
- Most systems will not work with all of the different types of imaging devices and media now available.
- It is often difficult or impossible to successfully exchange digital color images among different types of systems.

Although numerous solutions to these problems have been offered—generally in the form of color-management applications and image file format standards—none has been entirely successful. This is a most serious concern, because until these problems are solved, the full potential of digital color imaging cannot be realized.

We believe there is an underlying reason why these problems persist: The basic technology of *color encoding*—the representation of color in numerical form—is not widely understood.

While that is unfortunate, it also is understandable. The sciences of color and digital imaging are enormous in scope, and that has made it extremely difficult for equipment and media manufacturers, application developers, system designers, and others to find needed information.

That is why we have written this book. Our objective was to produce a single text containing all the essential information required for a solid understanding of the technology of representing and managing color in the digital domain. The book is intended for scientists, engineers, programmers, and others who are interested in developing that understanding. While we expect that most readers will have some scientific background and a basic familiarity with digital imaging, we have not assumed any specific prior knowledge of color. For that reason, we have provided background information as necessary, and we have included explanations of all required color science.

Among other benefits, a knowledge of digital color-encoding technology will allow the reader to comprehend fully such current topics as *Photo CD* System color, device-independent color, color interchange standards, and color-management systems. More generally, understanding the basic principles of numerically representing color is essential for anyone concerned with the successful input, storage, editing, interchange, and output of digital color images. We sincerely hope that those seeking information on this subject will find our book useful and interesting.

Acknowledgments

We wish to thank the following principal reviewers for their many helpful comments and suggestions: Paula J. Alessi, Ira A. Gold, H. Scott Gregory, Jr., Robert W. G. Hunt, John T. Keech, Thomas O. Maier, Elizabeth McInerney, Robert F. Poe, Michael R. Pointer, Charles Poynton, Chris Sears, John S. Setchell, Jr., and Michael Stokes.

We also wish to thank Paul L. Day, Jr., Timothy Harrigan, and Cynthia A. Pellow for their assistance in preparing the photographic images used in this book and Frank R. Brockler for preparing the three-dimensional figures.

Introduction

Until quite recently, digital color technology was available only on high-end color-imaging systems. Its use essentially was limited to professional applications, such as the production of graphic arts prints and motion picture special effects. Although high-end systems remain an important segment of the digital color-imaging industry, the overall field is rapidly changing.

Within the last few years, the cost of digital electronic cameras and scanners has been greatly reduced. The computational capabilities of moderately priced computer workstations have increased enormously, and relatively low-cost high-quality output devices, such as inkjet and thermal-transfer printers, have become widely available. As a result, digital color imaging is now practical for smaller scientific, commercial, and personal applications.

These developments have profoundly affected every aspect of digital imaging. In particular, they have generated the need to fundamentally change the way images are *color encoded,* i.e., the way the colors that make up images are numerically represented in digital form.

The color-encoding methods used on high-end systems typically have been quite simple. That has been possible because these systems generally have been "closed". For example, some electronic prepress systems always use a certain scanner to digitize images from a particular type of photographic film, and the digital images produced by these systems are used exclusively for graphic arts printing. Relatively simple color-encoding methods are successful in such systems because of the invariant nature of the input/output devices and media.

All of this is changing as more and more digital color images are being generated for various types of computer displays and applications, for display on conventional and high-definition television receivers, and for output to an ever increasing variety of hardcopy devices and media. The desire now is to move from "closed" systems to systems that are "open".

By definition, an "open" system is not restricted to using only certain inputs and outputs; it can make use of all available types of imaging devices and media. Also implied, by definition, is that if every digital color-imaging system were "open", digital image data could be exchanged freely among all systems, with predictable color results.

When the subject of "open" systems is discussed, particularly in computer magazines and at electronic-imaging conferences, the discussion invariably gravitates toward a concept widely referred to as *device-independent color*. "Device-independent" in this context means that color is expressed and exchanged in a way that does not depend on the particular characteristics of any given imaging device or medium.

To date, virtually all proposals for such "device-independent" color have been based on standard color-measurement techniques. However, our experience is that color-encoding methods based on these techniques *alone* are not sufficient for producing truly open systems.

This is not an obvious position to take. After all, standard methods of color measurement have been used successfully for more than half a century for any number of applications. It would seem reasonable that the use of these well-established measurement methods, along with some well-defined file format standards, should allow the open interchange of digital images among systems. Nevertheless, despite all the attention that such color-encoding methods have received, actual experience has shown that they work only in the most restricted applications. This does not mean, however, that it is *impossible* to design systems that are truly open. Nor does it mean that color measurement is not an important part of digital color encoding. What it *does* mean is that to work properly, open systems must be based on advanced color-encoding methods that go well beyond standard color-measurement techniques.

Our principal objective in this book is to describe these advanced encoding methods and other practical, successful, system-specific methods for digitally representing color. We believe that knowledge of these methods is essential to scientists, engineers, programmers, and others who are involved with digital color imaging.

We recognize that many who require this knowledge may not have backgrounds in color science or color imaging. For that reason, this book begins with a section called *Fundamentals,* which deals with color measurement and color imaging. We have tried to make this section as concise as possible by describing only what is necessary for understanding digital color encoding. (As a result, it may well be the only discussion of color science that does *not* include the seemingly mandatory cross-sectional diagram of the human eye!)

The second section, *The Nature of Color Images,* describes the color properties of color images produced on various types of imaging devices and media. Much of this information is not generally available, which has been unfortunate. We think the lack of factual information on this subject has been responsible for many common misconceptions regarding color imaging in general and color encoding in particular. Again, the discussion in this section is aimed towards our principal subject. Our objective is to explain why images from various types of devices and media *must* differ fundamentally in their basic color properties. These differences must be understood in order to appreciate the problems of encoding and managing color and to understand the solutions to those problems.

The final two sections cover our main topics: digital color encoding and the color-managed systems in which that encoding is used. These sections include the following:

- An explanation of the color-encoding method and *PhotoYCC* Space data metric we invented for the *Kodak Photo CD* System

- A discussion of various popular myths and misconceptions regarding device-independent color and other related topics

- A description of a Unified Color-Management Paradigm—a concept that offers the promise of a unified, color-managed environment for the color-imaging industry

- A description of a practical, appearance-based color-encoding method capable of supporting the Unified Color-Management Paradigm and providing unrestricted communication of color within and among all digital color-imaging systems

The book also contains a comprehensive glossary and an extensive series of appendices that provide additional information on selected subjects and detailed descriptions of various color calculations and transformations.

We suggest that this book be read straight through, even if the reader is familiar with most of the background material presented in the early sections. Each chapter builds on the preceding discussions, and most contain information that is not commonly available. If a chapter must be skipped, we would urge that at least the Summary of Key Issues given at the chapter's end be read.

PART I

Fundamentals

In this introductory section, some basic principles of color and color measurement will be examined in the context of color-imaging systems. This examination will provide the foundation required for later discussions on color images, color encoding, and color management.

The section begins with a review of the techniques of color measurement, which are the basis of all methods of numerically representing color. Color-imaging systems then will be described—not in terms of specific technology, but in terms of the basic functions they must perform. The focus here, and throughout the book, will be on systems for which the ultimate goal is to produce images that are high-quality color reproductions of original images.

Two very different types of original images will be dealt with in these discussions. In some cases, the original will be a live image, such as an outdoor scene being recorded with a digital still camera. In other cases, the "original" it-self will be a reproduction. For example, it might be a photographic print or slide that is to be reproduced *again* by an imaging system, perhaps for a catalog. As will be seen, each type of original has to be treated quite differently.

Regardless of the type of original being considered, however, one rule will remain constant throughout our discussions: *The assessment of color quality will be made according to the judgments of a human observer.*

In discussing and working with color imaging products and systems, it is easy to become so enamored with the technology that the real objective gets lost. It is important, then, not to forget that when it comes to images, a human observer—not a measuring instrument—is the ultimate judge of what is good or bad.

As obvious as that idea may seem, an experience of a colleague of ours shows that it is sometimes overlooked. He had called the manufacturer of a color-management program, purchased for his home computer, to report a problem: yellow colors always came out greenish on his monitor. The person with whom he spoke cheerfully informed him that there was no need for concern. Those greenish colors really *were* yellow, they just did not look that way because computer monitors have an overall bluish cast to them. He was told that if he were to measure those yellows, as they had done in designing the software, he would find that they were indeed yellow. His continued protests that he did not care how they *measured*, they still *looked* greenish, were to no avail!

Since human judgments are to be the basis for determining the success or failure of color encoding and color reproduction, the basic characteristics of human color vision must be understood. These characteristics are introduced in Chapter 1, which begins with a review of color-measurement techniques that are based on the responses of a representative human observer.

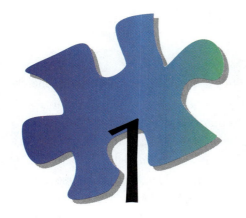

1
Measuring Color

Digital color encoding is, by definition, the numerical description of color in digital form. For example, on a *Photo CD* Disc, the set of digital values 40, 143, and 173 specifies a particular shade of red (the reason why will be explained later on). The fact that color can be digitally encoded implies that it somehow can be measured and quantified.

But color itself is a perception, and perceptions exist only in the mind. How can one even *begin* to measure and quantify a human *perception*? Vision begins as light reaches the eyes; thus, a reasonable place to start is with the measurement of that light.

Light Sources

In the color science courses we often teach, students are asked to list factors they think will affect color. There usually are quite a few responses before someone mentions light sources. But perhaps this should be expected.

It is easy to take light sources, such as the sun and various types of artificial lighting, for granted. Yet unless there is a source of light, there is nothing to see. In everyday language we speak of "seeing" objects, but of course it is not the objects themselves that we see. What we see is *light* that has been reflected from or transmitted through the objects. We "prove" this in the classroom by switching off all the room lights and asking if anyone can see anything at all! This usually gets a laugh (and most often results in one or two students taking a quick nap)!

Because color begins with light, the colors that are seen are influenced by the characteristics of the light source used for illumination. For example, objects generally will look redder when viewed under a red light and greener when viewed under a green light. In order to measure color, then, it first is necessary to measure the characteristics of the light source providing the illumination.

More specifically, the *spectral power distribution* of the source, i.e., the power of its electromagnetic radiation as a function of wavelength, must be measured. Spectral power distributions can vary greatly for different types of light sources. Figure 1.1 shows, for example, the spectral power distributions for a tungsten light source and a particular type of fluorescent light source. Note that the power values in the figure are expressed in terms of relative power, not absolute power. Such relative measurements generally are sufficient for most, although not all, types of color measurements.

The most common source of light is, of course, the sun. The spectral power distribution of daylight—a mixture of sunlight and skylight—can vary greatly depending on solar altitude and on weather and atmospheric conditions. Figure 1.2 shows three of many possible examples of daylight. The undulations in each of the spectral power distributions are the result of filtration effects due to the atmospheres of the sun and the earth.

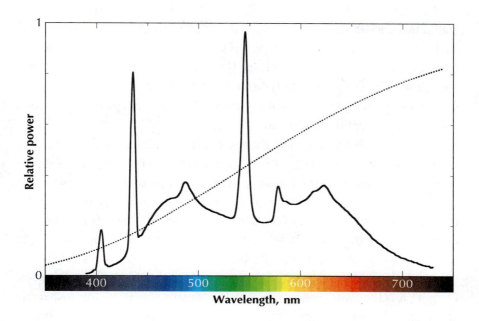

Figure 1.1
Comparison of the relative spectral power distributions for typical tungsten (dotted line) and fluorescent (solid line) light sources. The curves describe the relative power of each source's electromagnetic radiation as a function of wavelength.

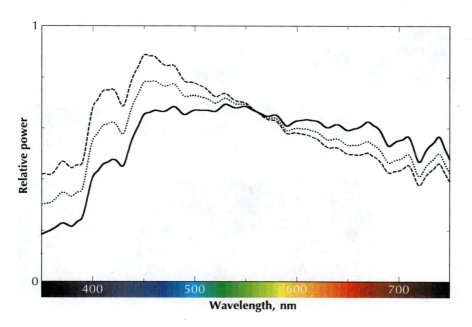

Figure 1.2
Relative spectral power distributions for three of many types of daylight illumination. The spectral characteristics of daylight can vary greatly depending on solar altitude, weather, and atmospheric conditions.

There can be a number of different light sources involved in a single digital imaging system, and each will affect the colors that ultimately are produced. For example, consider the system shown in Fig. 1.3. An original scene is photographed on a color slide film, and the slide is projected and also scanned. The scanned image is temporarily displayed on the monitor of a computer workstation, and a scan printer is used to expose a photographic paper to produce a reflection print that is then viewed.

There are six different light sources to consider in this system. First, there is the source illuminating the original scene. Another light source is used to project the slide for direct viewing. There is a light source in the slide-film scanner, which is used to illuminate the slide during scanning. The computer monitor also is a light source (the phosphors of its CRT emit light). The scan printer uses a light source to expose the photographic paper. Finally, a light source is used to illuminate the reflection print for viewing.

In later chapters, each of these uses of light sources will be discussed. For now, it is the measurement of color that is being discussed. Our immediate attention will be on the use of light sources to illuminate objects for viewing.

Figure 1.3
In this imaging system, there are six different light sources that contribute to the recording, reproduction, and viewing of colors.

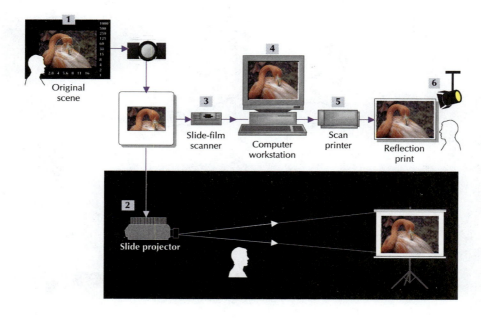

Objects

When light reaches an object, that light is absorbed, reflected, or transmitted. Depending on the chemical makeup of the object and certain other factors, the amount of light that is reflected or transmitted generally will vary at different wavelengths. For the purposes of color measurement, this variation is described in terms of spectral reflectance or spectral transmittance characteristics. These characteristics respectively describe the *fraction* of the incident power reflected or transmitted as a function of wavelength.

In most cases, an object's spectral characteristics will correlate in a straightforward way with the color normally associated with the object. For example, the spectral reflectance shown in Fig. 1.4 is for a red apple. The apple (generally) is seen as red because it reflects a greater fraction of red light (longer visible wavelengths) than of green light (middle visible wavelengths) or blue light (shorter visible wavelengths). Sometimes, however, the correlation of color and spectral reflectance is less obvious, as in the case of the two objects having the spectral reflectances shown in Figs. 1.5a and 1.5b.

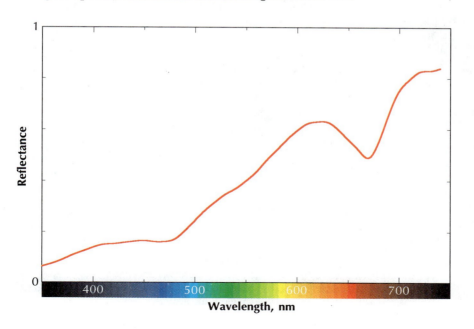

Figure 1.4
Spectral reflectance of a red Cortland apple. The apple generally is seen as red because it reflects a greater fraction of red light than of green light or blue light.

Figure 1.5a
Spectral reflectance of an ageratum. The flower appears blue, even though it seems to have more red-light reflectance than blue-light reflectance.

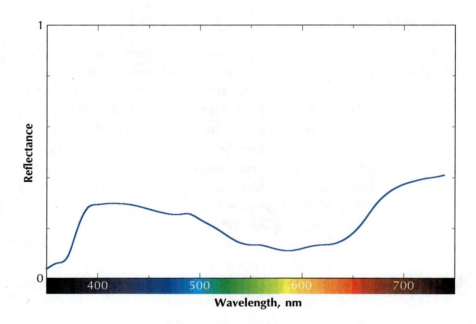

Wavelength, nm

Figure 1.5b
Spectral reflectance of a particular fabric sample. The fabric appears green, despite its having spectral characteristics that seem to indicate otherwise.

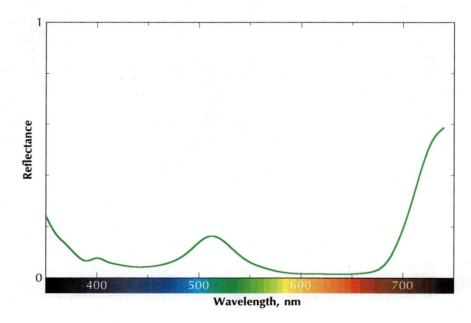

Wavelength, nm

The object in Fig. 1.5a is a particular type of flower (an ageratum). The flower appears blue to a human observer, even though it seems to have more red-light reflectance than blue-light reflectance. The object in Fig. 1.5b is a sample of a dyed fabric, which appears green to a human observer, despite its unusual spectral reflectance that would seem to indicate otherwise.

In a moment, human color vision will be discussed, and the reason why these objects have color appearances that might not seem apparent from their spectral reflectances will be given. But before that can be done, it is necessary to discuss the role that objects play in the formation of what are referred to in color science as *color stimuli*.

Color Stimuli

In color science, a "color" that is to be viewed or measured is called more correctly a color stimulus. A color stimulus always consists of light. In some cases, that light might come directly from a light source itself, such as when a CRT screen or the flame of a lighted candle is viewed directly.

But more typically, color stimuli are the result of light that has been reflected from or transmitted through various objects. For example, if the apple of Fig. 1.4 is illuminated with the fluorescent light source of Fig. 1.1, the color stimulus will have the spectral power distribution shown in Fig. 1.6. The spectral power distribution of this stimulus is the *product* of the spectral power distribution of the fluorescent source and the spectral reflectance of the apple. The spectral power distribution of the stimulus is calculated by multiplying the power of the light source times the reflectance of the object at each wavelength, as shown in Fig. 1.7.

It is important to emphasize that for a reflective or transmissive object, the color stimulus results from *both* the object and the light source. If another light source having a different spectral power distribution is used, the color stimulus will change. For example, if the apple of Fig. 1.4 is illuminated with the tungsten light source of Fig. 1.1, a color stimulus having the spectral power distribution shown in Fig. 1.8 will be produced.

Figure 1.6
Spectral power distribution for a Cortland apple, illuminated with a fluorescent light source. In color science, such power distributions are called *color stimuli.*

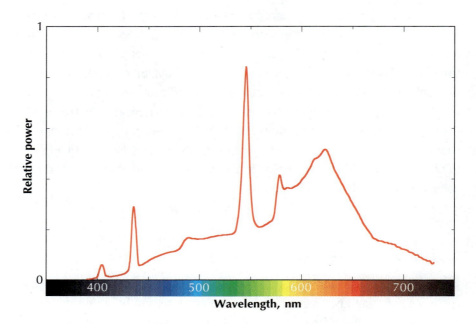

Figure 1.7
Calculation of the spectral power distribution of a color stimulus. The distribution is the product of the spectral power distribution of the light source and the spectral reflectance of the object.

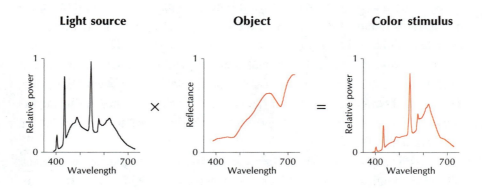

Light source   ×   Object   =   Color stimulus

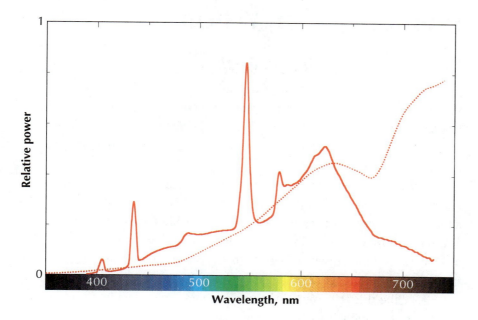

Figure 1.8

Comparison of the spectral power distributions for two stimuli—an apple illuminated by a tungsten light source (dotted line) and the same apple illuminated by a fluorescent light source (solid line).

As Fig. 1.8 shows, the stimulus is very different from that produced by fluorescent illumination of the same apple. What this means is that the color of an object is *not* invariant, nor is it determined solely by the object itself. A "red" apple can be made to appear almost *any* color (or even no color), depending on how it is illuminated.

The concept of the color stimulus is the foundation of all methods of representing color images in numerical form. Every individual point in a scene or image has a spectral power distribution. So any live scene, any image being scanned, any image displayed on a CRT, or any illuminated hardcopy reproduction can be treated as a collection of individual color stimuli. These stimuli can be measured by an instrument, and they can be detected by the sensors of an imaging device.

Most importantly, it is these color stimuli that are seen by a human observer. In order to make meaningful assessments of color stimuli, then, it will be necessary to examine how they are detected and interpreted by the human visual system.

Human Color Vision

Although instruments can measure color stimuli in terms of their spectral power distributions, the eye does not interpret color stimuli by analyzing them in a comparable wavelength-by-wavelength manner. Instead, human color vision derives from the responses of just three types of photoreceptors (cones) contained in the retina of the eye. The approximate *spectral sensitivities* of these photoreceptors—their relative sensitivity to light as a function of wavelength—are shown in Fig. 1.9.

Note that the sensitivity of the human visual system rapidly decreases above 650 nm (nanometers). That is why the blue flower discussed earlier appears blue, despite its reflectance at longer visible wavelengths (Fig. 1.10a). The human visual system also has very little sensitivity to wavelengths below 400 nm, so the fabric discussed earlier looks green despite its high reflectances in the shorter-wavelength and longer-wavelength regions (Fig. 1.10b).

While this trichromatic (three-channel) analysis might seem rather inelegant, it actually is the beginning of an exquisite process that is capable

Figure 1.9
Estimated spectral sensitivities, ρ, γ, and β, of the three types of photoreceptors of the human eye. (The curves, derived from Estevez, 1979, have been normalized to equal area.)

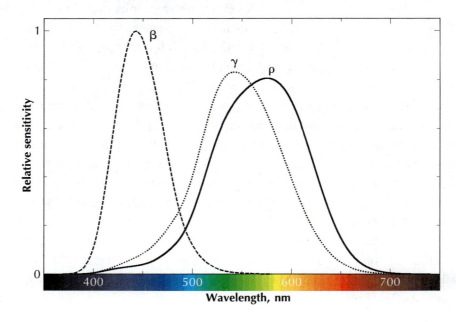

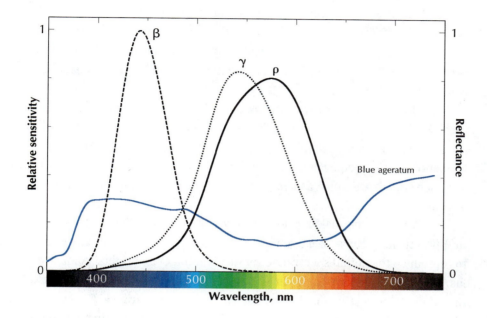

Figure 1.10a
Estimated human spectral sensitivities, co-plotted with the spectral reflectance from Fig. 1.5a. The sensitivity of the human visual system rapidly decreases above 650 nm, so the flower looks blue despite its reflectance at longer wavelengths.

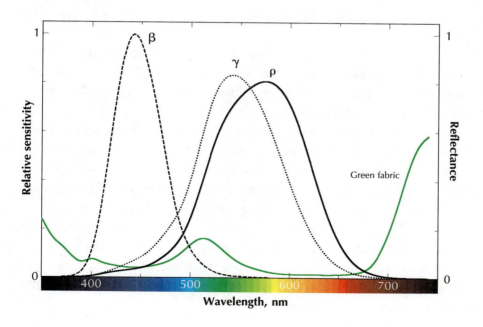

Figure 1.10b
Estimated human spectral sensitivities, co-plotted with the spectral reflectance from Fig. 1.5b. The fabric looks green despite its high reflectances at shorter and longer wavelengths.

of great subtlety. This process allows the human visual system to distinguish very small differences in stimulation of the three types of photoreceptors. In fact, it has been estimated that stimulation of these photoreceptors to various levels and ratios can give rise to about *ten million* distinguishable color sensations!

Because of the trichromatic nature of human vision, however, it is quite possible that two color stimuli having very different spectral power distributions will appear to have identical color. This can occur if the two color stimuli happen to produce equivalent stimulations of the photoreceptors (Fig. 1.11). Two such stimuli are called a *metameric pair,* and the situation is referred to as *metamerism*.

Metamerism makes color-imaging systems (and digital color encoding) practical. Because of metamerism, it is not necessary either to record or to reproduce the actual spectral power distribution of an original color stimulus. It is only necessary to produce a stimulus that is a *visual equivalent* of the original, i.e., a stimulus that produces the same appearance. For example, in Fig. 1.12 the color stimulus produced by the CRT is indistinguishable in color from the original, although its spectral power distribution obviously is very different.

As mentioned earlier, the spectral power distribution of a stimulus generally is a product of a spectral power distribution of a light source and a spectral reflectance of an object (self-luminous displays, such as CRTs, are an exception). It is important to emphasize that metamerism involves the matching of *stimuli,* not the matching of *objects*. The significance of this distinction is that two objects, having different spectral reflectances, may metamerically match under one light source, but not under another.

For example, a color copier may be capable of scanning original reflection images and producing copies that metamerically match those originals. However, if the spectral characteristics of the light source used for viewing the original images and the copies are changed, the stimuli involved will have changed, and it is likely that the copies will no longer match the originals. This is an important issue that will have to be revisited in later discussions on color-imaging systems and color-encoding methods.

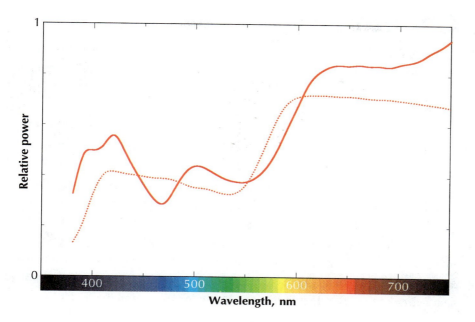

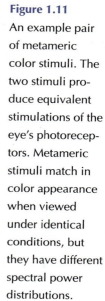

Figure 1.11

An example pair of metameric color stimuli. The two stimuli produce equivalent stimulations of the eye's photoreceptors. Metameric stimuli match in color appearance when viewed under identical conditions, but they have different spectral power distributions.

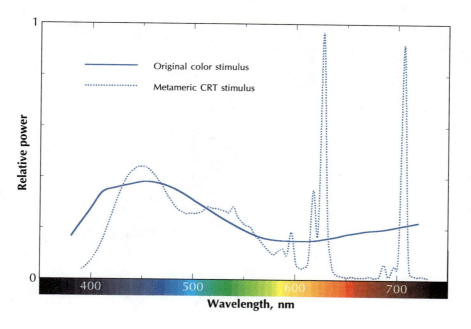

Figure 1.12

Spectral power distributions for an original color stimulus and a metameric (visually equivalent) color stimulus produced by a CRT.

Colorimetry

In the design of color-imaging systems and color-encoding schemes, it is important to be able to predict when two color stimuli will visually match. The science of *colorimetry* provides the basis for such predictions, and it is the foundation on which all color science is built.

Colorimetry provides methods for specifying a color stimulus by relating the measurement of its spectral power to the trichromatic responses of a defined standard observer. Doing so allows the prediction of metamerism. If two color stimuli produce the *same* trichromatic responses, those stimuli are, by definition, metameric. They will look the same (to a standard observer) if they are viewed under identical conditions.

Colorimetry is founded on a classic series of color-matching experiments that allowed the trichromatic properties of human vision to be studied and characterized. In a typical color-matching experiment, an observer views a small circular field that is split into two halves, as illustrated in Fig. 1.13.

Figure 1.13
A classic color-matching experiment. A test color illuminates one half of the circle, while the other half is illuminated by superposed light from three primaries. The intensities of the primaries needed to match a test color are called *tristimulus values.*

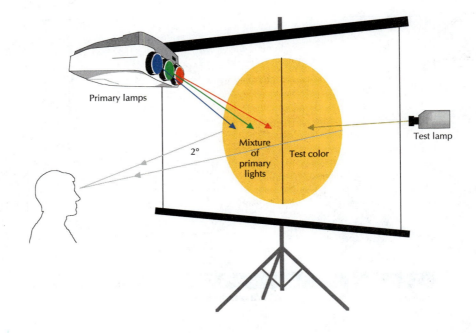

In the course of the experiment, light of a particular test color is used to illuminate one half of the circle. The other half is illuminated by the super-position of light from three independent sources. *Independent* in this context means that none of the sources can be matched by a mixture of the other two. The independent sources (which usually are red, green, and blue) are called color *primaries*.

In performing a matching experiment, an observer adjusts the amounts (*intensities*) of the three color primaries until their mixture appears to match the test color. The amounts of the primaries required to produce the match are called the *tristimulus values* of the test color, for that set of color primaries. If the experiment is performed using test colors of monochromatic light for each of the visible wavelengths (from about 380 nm to about 740 nm), a set of three curves called *color-matching functions* is obtained. Color-matching functions represent the tristimulus values (the amounts of each of the primaries) needed to match a defined amount of light at each spectral wavelength. Figure 1.14 shows a set of color-matching functions resulting from a matching experiment performed using a particular set of red, green, and blue primaries. The color-matching functions will be different for different sets of primaries, and they also may differ somewhat from observer to observer.

Notice that some of the tristimulus values of Fig. 1.14 are *negative*. These negative values result from the fact that when the color-matching experiment is performed using monochromatic test colors, some of those test colors cannot be matched by *any* combination of the three primaries. In these cases, light from one or more of the primaries is *added* to the light of the *test color* (Fig. 1.15). A match then can be achieved by adjusting the primaries in this configuration. Light that is added to the test color can be considered to have been *subtracted* from the mixture of the primaries. The amount of any primary added to the test color therefore is recorded as a negative tristimulus value.

It is very important to know that the color-matching functions for *any* set of physically realizable primaries will have *some* negative values. This fact will be of great significance in later discussions on a number of topics, including the signal-processing requirements of color-imaging systems and the ranges of colors that can be represented by various color-encoding schemes.

Figure 1.14
A set of color-matching functions resulting from a matching experiment performed using a particular set of red, green, and blue primaries (monochromatic light, wavelengths of 700, 546.1, and 435.8 nm).

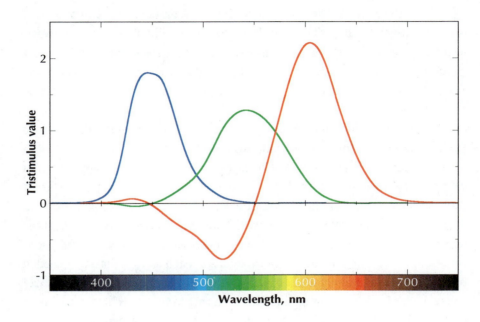

Figure 1.15
In this color-matching experiment, the test color of wavelength 520 nm cannot be matched by any combination of light from the three primaries. A match can be obtained, however, by adding light from the red primary to the test color.

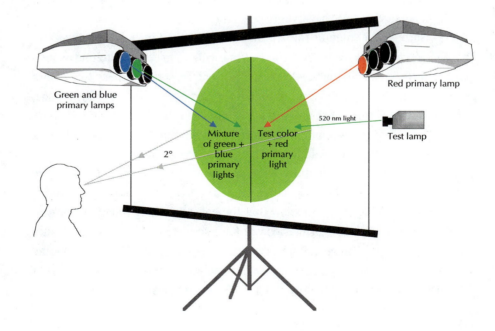

The number of possible sets of color primaries is, of course, unlimited. It follows, then, that there also must be an unlimited number of corresponding sets of color-matching functions. Yet it can be shown that *all* sets of color-matching functions for a given observer are simple linear combinations of one another. A matrix operation therefore can be used to transform one set of color-matching functions to another. For the example given in Fig. 1.16, the set of color-matching functions $\bar{r}_2(\lambda)$, $\bar{g}_2(\lambda)$, and $\bar{b}_2(\lambda)$ was derived from another set of color-matching functions $\bar{r}_1(\lambda)$, $\bar{g}_1(\lambda)$, and $\bar{b}_1(\lambda)$ by using the following linear matrix transformation:

$$\begin{bmatrix} \bar{r}_2(\lambda) \\ \bar{g}_2(\lambda) \\ \bar{b}_2(\lambda) \end{bmatrix} = \begin{bmatrix} 0.7600 & 0.2851 & 0.0790 \\ -0.0874 & 1.2053 & -0.1627 \\ 0.0058 & -0.0742 & 0.9841 \end{bmatrix} \begin{bmatrix} \bar{r}_1(\lambda) \\ \bar{g}_1(\lambda) \\ \bar{b}_1(\lambda) \end{bmatrix} \qquad \{1.1\}$$

As will be seen later, this type of matrix transformation is fundamental in color science, color signal processing, and color encoding.

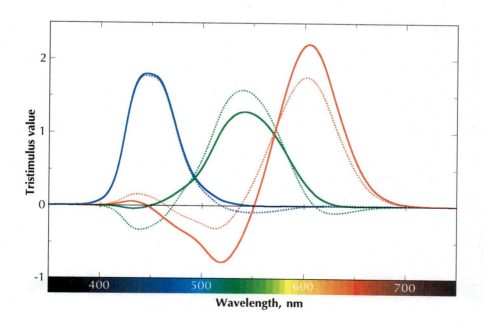

Figure 1.16

All sets of color-matching functions are linear transformations of all other sets. The set shown by the dotted lines $\bar{r}_2(\lambda)$, $\bar{g}_2(\lambda)$, $\bar{b}_2(\lambda)$ was derived from the set shown in solid lines $\bar{r}_1(\lambda)$, $\bar{g}_1(\lambda)$, $\bar{b}_1(\lambda)$ by using the linear matrix transformation given in Eq. {1.1}.

CIE Colorimetry

In 1931 the Commission Internationale de l'Éclairage (International Commission on Illumination), the *CIE*, adopted one set of color-matching functions to define a *Standard Colorimetric Observer* (Fig. 1.17) whose color-matching characteristics are representative of those of the human population having normal color vision. Although the CIE could have used any set of color-matching functions, including a set equivalent to average ρ, γ, and β cone-response functions, this particular set was chosen for its mathematical properties.

The CIE Standard Colorimetric Observer color-matching functions are used in the calculation of *CIE tristimulus values X, Y*, and *Z*, which quantify the trichromatic characteristics of color stimuli. The *X*, *Y*, and *Z* tristimulus values for a given object (characterized by its spectral reflectance or transmittance) that is illuminated by a light source (characterized by its spectral power distribution) can be calculated for the CIE Standard Colorimetric Observer (characterized by the CIE color-matching functions) by summing the products of these

Figure 1.17

A set of color-matching functions adopted by the CIE to define a Standard Colorimetric Observer.

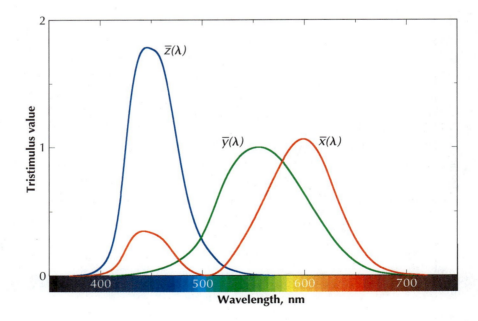

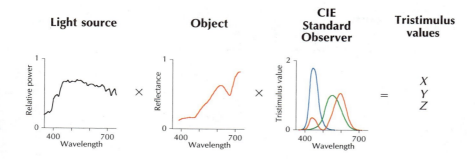

Figure 1.18
Calculation of CIE *XYZ* tristimulus values.

distributions over the wavelength (λ) range of 380 to 780 nm (usually at 5-nm intervals). This process is illustrated in Fig. 1.18. The calculations of *X*, *Y*, and *Z* are shown in the following equations:

$$X = k \sum_{\lambda=380}^{780} S(\lambda)R(\lambda)\,\bar{x}(\lambda)$$

$$Y = k \sum_{\lambda=380}^{780} S(\lambda)R(\lambda)\,\bar{y}(\lambda) \qquad \{1.2\}$$

$$Z = k \sum_{\lambda=380}^{780} S(\lambda)R(\lambda)\,\bar{z}(\lambda)$$

where *X*, *Y*, and *Z* are CIE tristimulus values; $S(\lambda)$ is the spectral power distribution of a light source; $R(\lambda)$ is the spectral reflectance of a reflective object (or spectral transmittance of a transmissive object); $\bar{x}(\lambda)$, $\bar{y}(\lambda)$, and $\bar{z}(\lambda)$ are the color-matching functions of the CIE Standard Colorimetric Observer; and *k* is a normalizing factor. By convention, *k* usually is determined such that *Y* = 100 when the object is a perfect white. A *perfect white* is an ideal, nonfluorescent, isotropic diffuser with a reflectance (or transmittance) equal to unity throughout the visible spectrum (Fig. 1.19). *Isotropic* means that incident light is reflected (or transmitted) equally in all directions. The brightness of a perfect white therefore is independent of the direction of viewing.

Figure 1.19
Spectral characteristic for a perfect white reflector or transmitter of light.

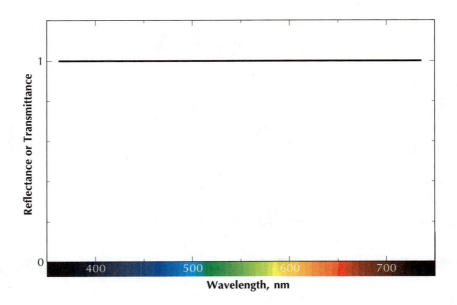

It was emphasized earlier that the color-matching functions for any set of physically realizable primaries will have negative values at some wavelengths. Yet the color-matching functions for the CIE Standard Colorimetric Observer (Fig. 1.17) have *no* negative regions. This was accomplished by first defining a set of *imaginary* primaries and then determining the color-matching functions for those primaries. *Imaginary primaries* correspond to hypothetical illuminants having negative amounts of power at some wavelengths. For example, the imaginary "green" illuminant of Fig. 1.20 has positive power in the green spectral region, but it has negative power in the blue and red regions.

While such primaries are not physically realizable, they nevertheless are very useful mathematical concepts. When they are chosen appropriately, their corresponding color-matching functions are positive at all wavelengths. Such functions are mathematically convenient because they eliminate negative values in the tristimulus calculations. (This may not seem very important now, but years ago people had to perform these calculations by hand!) Also, because the CIE Standard Observer color-matching functions are all-positive, it is possible to construct instruments called *colorimeters*. The *spectral responsivities*—relative response to light as a function of wavelength—of a colorimeter directly

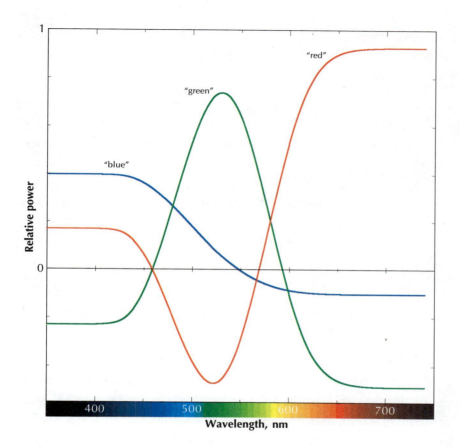

Figure 1.20
A set of spectral
power distribu-
tions correspond-
ing to a set of
imaginary "red,"
"green," and
"blue" primaries.
Imaginary pri-
maries correspond
to hypothetical
illuminants having
negative amounts
of power at some
wavelengths.

correspond to the color-matching functions of the CIE Standard Observer. A
colorimeter therefore can provide a direct measure of the CIE XYZ tristimulus
values of a color stimulus.

Another operational convenience of the CIE color-matching functions
is that the Y tristimulus value corresponds to the measurement of *luminance*.
The measurement of luminance is of particular importance in color-imaging
and color-encoding applications because luminance is an approximate correlate
of one of the principal visual perceptions—the perception of *brightness*. When
all other factors are equal, a stimulus having a higher measured luminance
value will appear to be brighter than an otherwise identical stimulus having a
lower measured luminance value.

Various mathematical normalizations, such as the scaling provided by the factor k in Eqs. {1.2}, are performed in colorimetric computations. The following normalizations and definitions specifically relate to the measurement of luminance values:

- The normalization may be such that Y tristimulus values are evaluated on an absolute basis and expressed in units of luminance, typically candelas per square meter (cd/m^2). Such values are properly referred to as *luminance values*. However, throughout this book there will be instances when it is particularly important to emphasize that absolute, not relative, amounts of light are being referred to. In these instances, the somewhat redundant expression *absolute luminance values* will be used to provide that emphasis.

- When the normalization is such that the Y value for a perfect white object is 1.00, normalized Y values are called *luminance factor values*.

- When the normalization is such that the Y value for a perfect white object is 100, normalized Y values are called *percent luminance factor values*.

Although the X and Z tristimulus values have no direct perceptual correlates, they are used in the calculation of tristimulus-value ratios called *chromaticity coordinates*. The chromaticity coordinates x, y, and z describe the qualities of a color stimulus apart from its luminance. They are derived from the tristimulus values as follows:

$$x = \frac{X}{X + Y + Z}$$

$$y = \frac{Y}{X + Y + Z} \qquad\qquad \{1.3\}$$

$$z = \frac{Z}{X + Y + Z}$$

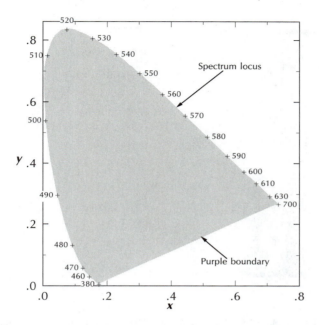

Figure 1.21a
CIE *x, y* chromaticity diagram. The chromaticity coordinates define the qualities of a color stimulus apart from its luminance. The chromaticity co-ordinates of *all* physically realizable color stimuli lie within the area defined by the spectrum locus and the purple boundary.

A plot of y versus x is called a *chromaticity diagram* (Fig. 1.21a). The horseshoe-shaped outline is the *spectrum locus,* which is a line connecting the points representing the chromaticities of the spectrum colors. In the figure, the ends of the spectrum locus are connected by a straight line known as the *purple boundary.* The chromaticity coordinates of *all* physically realizable color stimuli lie within the area defined by the spectrum locus and the purple boundary.

Figure 1.21b shows the locations of the chromaticity coordinates of the real primaries corresponding to the color-matching functions of Fig. 1.14. The triangle formed by connecting those locations encloses the chromaticity coordinates of all color stimuli that can be matched using positive (including zero) amounts of those real primaries. Also indicated are the locations of the chromaticities of the imaginary primaries corresponding to the color-matching functions of the CIE Standard Colorimetric Observer. Note that the triangle formed by connecting those locations encloses the entire area defined by the spectrum locus and the purple boundary. That is why all real color stimuli can be matched using positive amounts of those imaginary primaries.

Figure 1.21b
Chromaticity co-
ordinates of the
real primaries cor-
responding to the
color-matching
functions of Fig.
1.14, and those of
the imaginary pri-
maries corre-
sponding to the
color-matching
functions of Fig.
1.17. The triangle
formed by con-
necting the chro-
maticity coordi-
nates of a set of
primaries encloses
the chromaticity
coordinates of all
color stimuli that
can be matched
using positive
amounts of those
primaries.

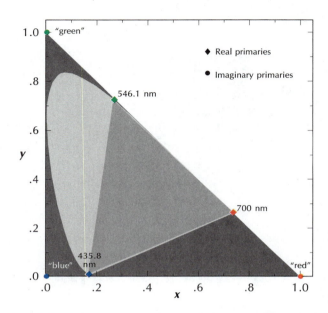

Figure 1.21b Chromaticity coordinates of the real primaries corresponding to the color-matching functions of Fig. 1.14, and those of the imaginary primaries corresponding to the color-matching functions of Fig. 1.17. The triangle formed by connecting the chromaticity coordinates of a set of primaries encloses the chromaticity coordinates of all color stimuli that can be matched using positive amounts of those primaries.

The CIE also has recommended the use of other color-coordinate systems, derived from *XYZ*, in which perceived differences among colors are represented more uniformly than they are on an *x*, *y* chromaticity diagram. These recommendations include the CIE 1976 *u′*, *v′* Metric Chromaticity Coordinates and the CIE 1976 *L* a* b** (CIELAB) and CIE 1976 *L* u* v** (CIELUV) color spaces. (Please refer to Appendix A for more details regarding these color spaces.)

All of the CIE coordinate systems are quite useful for specifying small color *differences* between color stimuli (CIE colorimetry was, in fact, developed specifically for that purpose); *but it is essential to understand that none of these systems specifies the appearance of those stimuli*. The reason for this will be discussed in Chapter 3. For now, the reader should be cautioned that this fact is commonly misunderstood and, as a consequence, CIE coordinate systems frequently are misinterpreted and misused as if they describe color appearance. The distinction between colorimetry and color appearance may seem subtle and of interest only to color scientists. In practice, however, failures to recognize that distinction have been responsible for the demise of numerous color-encoding methods, color-management systems, and entire color-imaging systems.

Other Color Measurements

In addition to CIE colorimetry, there are other types of color measurements that are relevant to color imaging and color encoding. Of particular importance in imaging applications involving hardcopy media is the measurement of *optical density*. Optical density values can be measured using instruments called *densitometers*. (Please refer to Appendix B for more details.)

Optical densities of color media generally are measured using three-channel (or sometimes four-channel) densitometers. The spectral responsivities for these instruments are defined by industry standards. Figure 1.22a, for example, shows the specified red, green, and blue spectral responsivities for an ISO Standard Status A densitometer.

Status A densitometers are widely used for measurements of photographic media and other types of hardcopy media that are meant to be viewed directly by an observer. That fact might seem to suggest that Status A density

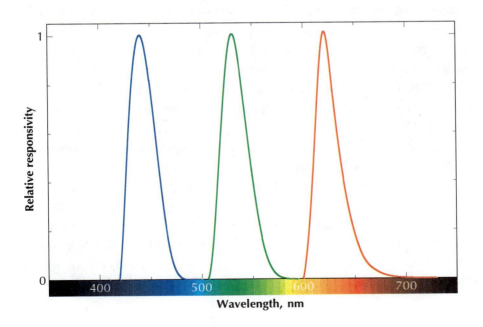

Figure 1.22a
Red, green, and blue spectral responsivities for an ISO Status A densitometer.

Figure 1.22b

Comparison of ISO Status A spectral responsivities to the color-matching functions of the CIE Standard Colorimetric Observer (normalized to equal area).

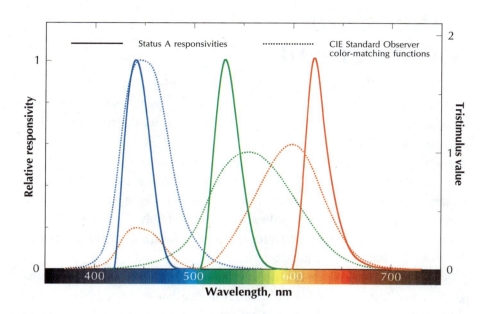

values must provide information equivalent to that provided by CIE colorimetric values, but that is not the case. Status A spectral responsivities do not correspond to those of a CIE Standard Observer, as shown in Fig. 1.22b, or to any other set of visual color-matching functions. As a result, two spectrally different objects that metamerically match under a particular illuminant (i.e., their stimuli have the same CIE XYZ values) are unlikely to have matched red, green, and blue Status A values.

For example, Fig. 1.23 shows the spectral reflectances of two objects. Although these objects metamerically match under a particular illuminant, their red, green, and blue Status A density values *differ* by $-0.61, 0.17$, and 0.03, respectively. The converse also is true: a pair of objects having the same red, green, and blue Status A values is unlikely to be a metameric pair. Figure 1.24 shows the spectral reflectances of two different objects. While these objects have identical Status A densities, their X, Y, and Z tristimulus values, under a particular illuminant, differ by $15.7, 14.6$, and -0.8, respectively.

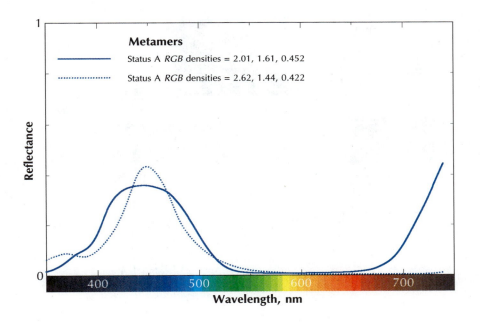

Figure 1.23
Spectral reflectances of two objects that metamerically match under a particular illuminant, but that have very different *RGB* Status A density values.

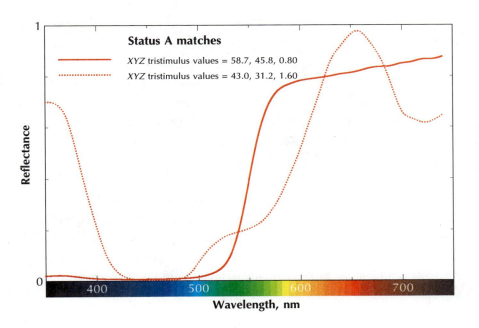

Figure 1.24
Spectral reflectances of two objects that have identical *RGB* Status A density values, but that do not match metamerically.

Figure 1.25

A film scanner and a reflection scanner. The spectral responsivities of most scanners do not correspond to a set of color-matching functions. Therefore, most scanners are densitometers, not colorimeters.

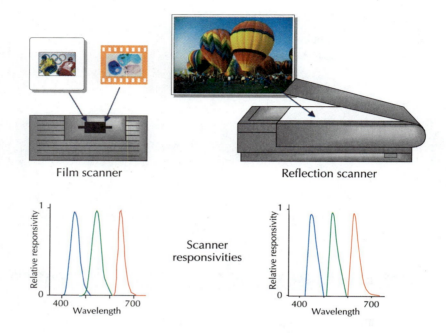

Film scanner   Reflection scanner

Scanner responsivities

Film scanners and reflection scanners (Fig. 1.25) are used for color measurement of hardcopy input images on digital color-imaging systems. While various sets of red, green, and blue spectral responsivities are used in different types of color scanners, those responsivities seldom correspond to a set of color-matching functions. Most scanners, therefore, are *densitometers;* they are *not* colorimeters. As will be shown later, that is a critical distinction that must be taken into account in the digital encoding of scanned colors.

Stimuli produced by self-luminous display devices, such as CRTs, often are measured in terms of light intensity. Three-channel instruments, which are somewhat similar to densitometers, can make simultaneous readings of red-light, green-light, and blue-light intensities. Various types of single-channel instruments also can be used in the measurement of self-luminous displays. When such instruments are used, separate red-light, green-light, and blue-light readings can be made by sequentially sending individual red, green, and blue signals to the display device that is to be measured.

Summary of Key Issues

- All vision is a response to light.

- Light sources are characterized by their spectral power distributions.

- Objects are characterized by their spectral reflectances or transmittances.

- Color stimuli generally are produced by a light source and an object; stimuli are characterized by their spectral power distributions.

- Scenes and images are collections of individual color stimuli.

- Human color vision is trichromatic.

- Metameric color stimuli are spectrally different but match in appearance.

- CIE colorimetry allows the prediction of metameric matching between color stimuli; metameric colors have the same CIE *XYZ* tristimulus values.

- CIE colorimetry was developed for specifying the trichromatic properties of color stimuli.

- CIE colorimetric values indicate how much the appearance of two stimuli will differ, if the differences in their trichromatic properties are sufficiently small.

- CIE colorimetric values such as CIE *XYZ* tristimulus values, CIE $L^* a^* b^*$ values, and CIE $L^* u^* v^*$ values do not describe color appearance.

- Densitometers are used to measure the optical densities of hardcopy media. Their spectral responsivities do not correspond to color-matching functions.

- A colorimeter directly measures CIE *XYZ* tristimulus values.

- Most image scanners are densitometers, not colorimeters. Their spectral responsivities do not correspond to color-matching functions.

2
Color-Imaging Systems

In Chapter 1 it was shown that, for the purposes of color measurement, scenes and other images can be characterized in terms of their color stimuli. In this chapter, the fundamental principles of how such color stimuli can be captured and reproduced by color-imaging systems will be discussed.

Color-imaging systems can be built using an almost unlimited variety of optical, chemical, and electronic components. But regardless of what technologies they incorporate, all imaging systems must perform three basic functions: *image capture, signal processing,* and *image formation* (Fig. 2.1). These functions are the building blocks of all color-imaging systems, from the simplest to the most complex.

Figure 2.1
These three basic functions are the building blocks of all color-imaging systems, from the simplest to the most complex.

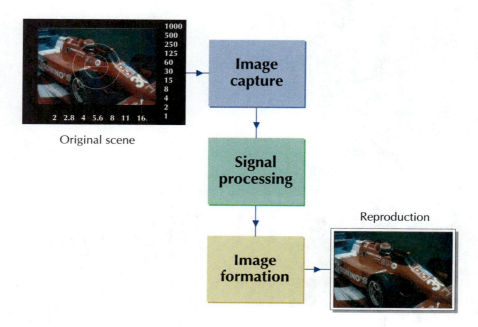

Original scene

Reproduction

Image Capture

To form a reproduction, an imaging system first must detect light from each original color stimulus and, from that light, produce a detectable image signal. This function, called *image capture*, can be realized in a number of ways, depending on the technology of the particular imaging system.

For example, a video camera, such as a digital still camera, might use a solid-state image sensor, such as a *charge coupled device* (CCD), to detect light. Image capture occurs as photons of light are absorbed by the sensor, resulting in the generation of electrons. These electrons are collected into charge packets, and an image signal is produced by a sequential readout of those packets.

In a photographic film, light is captured in the form of a *latent image*. The latent image, composed of small clusters of metallic silver, is produced by photons of light striking the light-sensitive silver halide grains of the film. This chemical signal is detected and amplified during subsequent chemical processing. (Please refer to Appendix C for more details on photographic media.)

Accurate color reproduction requires image capture that is, like the human eye, trichromatic. As part of the capture process, then, the spectral content of original color stimuli must be separated to form three distinguishable color signals. This generally is accomplished by some form of trichromatic capture. In some special applications, however, more than three color channels are captured and trichromatic color signals are subsequently derived.

In a video camera, trichromatic capture can be achieved using a single solid-state sensor, made up of a mosaic of light-sensitive elements. Individual sensor elements are overlaid with either red, green, or blue filters (Fig. 2.2a). Some high-end video cameras use three sensors (for higher spatial resolution) and an appropriate arrangement of beam splitters and color filters (Fig. 2.2b).

Trichromatic capture is achieved in photographic media by the use of overlaid light-sensitive layers. In the simplified film cross-section shown in Fig. 2.3, the top layer records blue light, the middle layer records green light, and the bottom layer records red light. A modern film actually may contain a total of 12 or more image-forming and other special purpose layers, but its behavior is fundamentally the same as that of a simple three-layer film.

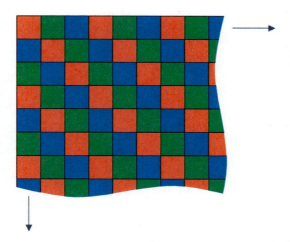

Figure 2.2a
Trichromatic image capture can be achieved using a CCD sensor with an integral mosaic of red, green, and blue filters.

Figure 2.2b

Use of three color separation filters for trichromatic image capture in a three-sensor video camera.

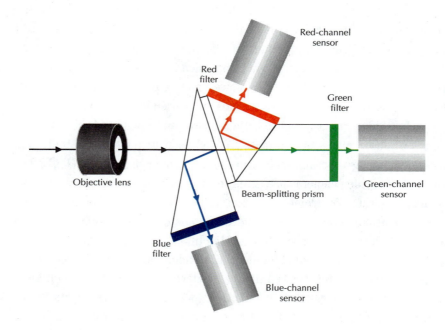

Figure 2.3

A simplified cross-section of a photographic film. Trichromatic image capture is achieved by the use of three layers sensitive to either red, green, or blue light.

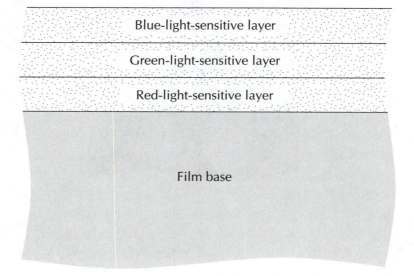

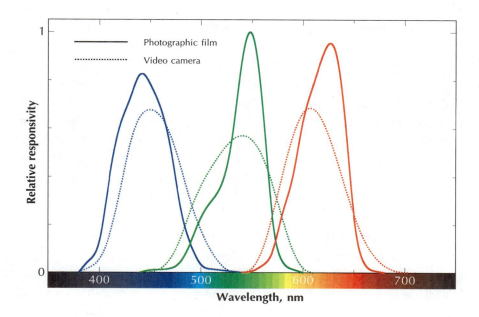

Figure 2.4
Spectral responsivities for a particular photographic film and video camera.

The color characteristics of the trichromatic capture are determined by the *spectral responsivities* of the system (its relative responses to light as a function of wavelength). These responsivities will differ among systems. For example, Fig. 2.4 compares the red, green, and blue spectral responsivities for a particular photographic film and one type of video camera.

The individual responses, called *exposures*, produced by a given set of spectral responsivities can be calculated using the following equations:

$$R_{exp} = k_{cr} \sum_{\lambda} S(\lambda)R(\lambda)r_c(\lambda)$$

$$G_{exp} = k_{cg} \sum_{\lambda} S(\lambda)R(\lambda)g_c(\lambda) \qquad \{2.1\}$$

$$B_{exp} = k_{cb} \sum_{\lambda} S(\lambda)R(\lambda)b_c(\lambda)$$

where R_{exp}, G_{exp}, and B_{exp} are red, green, and blue exposure values; $S(\lambda)$ is the spectral power distribution of the light source; $R(\lambda)$ is the spectral reflectance (or transmittance) of the object; $r_c(\lambda)$, $g_c(\lambda)$, and $b_c(\lambda)$ are the red, green, and blue spectral responsivities of the image-capturing device or medium; and k_{cr}, k_{cg}, and k_{cb} are normalizing factors. These factors usually are determined such that R_{exp}, G_{exp}, and B_{exp} = 1.00 when the object is a perfect white. This normalization is the equivalent of performing a *white balance* adjustment on a video camera, or *zeroing* a densitometer, where the red, green, and blue channels are adjusted such that equal *RGB* reference voltages are produced when a reference white object is imaged or measured. Because of these normalizations, the computed exposure values are *relative* values, which are referred to as *exposure-factor values*.

Equations {2.1} essentially are the same in form as those used for computing CIE *XYZ* tristimulus values (Chapter 1, Eqs. {1.2}). In fact, if the red, green, and blue spectral responsivities of the image-capture stage of an imaging system corresponded to the color-matching functions of the CIE Standard Colorimetric Observer, the resulting *RGB* exposure-factor values would be equivalent to CIE *XYZ* tristimulus values. In other words, the image-capture device or medium essentially would be a colorimeter.

This raises an interesting question. For accurate color reproduction, should the spectral responsivities of an imaging system *always* be designed to match those of a standard human observer? The answer is not as straightforward as it might seem. This question will be revisited in Part II, where a closer look will be taken at the second basic function performed by all imaging systems: *signal processing*.

Signal Processing

Signal processing modifies image signals produced from image capture to make them suitable for producing a viewable image. For example, an image signal produced by a broadcast video camera is electronically processed and amplified for transmission. A home television receiver performs further signal processing to produce signals appropriate for driving its CRT. In a photographic film, signal processing occurs as the film is chemically processed. (Chemical photographic processing sometimes is referred to as "developing." However, image development actually is just one of several steps in the chemical process, so the term is not strictly correct and will not be used here.)

Signal processing typically includes linear and nonlinear transformations of individual color signals. A linear transformation of an individual color signal is a simple amplification, which usually is required to produce a signal sufficiently strong to generate a viewable image. Nonlinear transformations of the individual color signals primarily are used to control the *grayscale* of the image produced by the system. The grayscale is a measure of how a system reproduces a series of *neutral* colors, ranging from black to white. In Part II, it will be shown that the grayscale characteristic is one of the most important properties of any imaging system, and the reasons why the signal processing associated with the grayscale must be highly nonlinear will be discussed.

Signal processing also is used to create linear and nonlinear interactions (*cross-talk*) among the individual color signals. For example, a modified red signal might be formed by taking portions of the green and blue signals and adding them to or subtracting them from the original red signal. In Part II, the reasons why such interactions are necessary will be discussed. Signal processing also may include spatial operations such as image compression, sharpening, and noise reduction. While spatial operations may not directly affect color, they are a factor that must be considered in developing the most appropriate form of digital color encoding for a given system.

Image Formation

The ultimate goal of a color-imaging system is, of course, to produce a viewable image. That is accomplished by the final stage of the system, *image formation*, where processed image signals are used to control the color-forming elements of the output medium or device. Although there are many types of color-imaging media, color-imaging devices, and color image-forming technologies, virtually all practical image-formation methods fall into one of two basic categories: *additive color* or *subtractive color*.

Figure 2.5
Additive mixing of
red, green, and
blue additive
color primaries.
Mixing red and
green forms yel-
low; mixing red
and blue forms
magenta; and
mixing green and
blue forms cyan.
Mixing the full
intensities of red,
green, and blue
forms white.

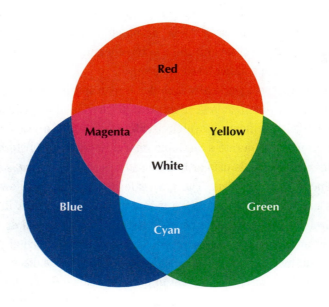

In the formation of most *additive color* images, processed image signals are used to directly control the intensities of lights that make up the displayed image. Colors are produced by additive mixing (Fig. 2.5). A three-beam video projector, for example, forms images by additively combining modulated intensities of red, green, and blue lights on a screen. This directly generates color stimuli, so no additional light source is required for viewing. Color CRTs also form images by generating red, green, and blue light. The addition of that red, green, and blue light takes place within the visual system of the observer.

In *subtractive color* image formation, processed image signals control the amounts of three or more *colorants* (dyes, inks, or pigments) that selectively *absorb* (subtract) light of different wavelengths (Fig. 2.6). Photographic media, for example, use *cyan*, *magenta*, and *yellow (CMY)* image-forming dyes to absorb red, green, and blue light, respectively. Some graphic arts printing processes use CMY inks plus an additional black ink (the *K* of *CMYK*). An image formed by subtractive colorants is an *object*. It requires a light source for viewing. As with any other object, the spectral characteristics of the color stimuli produced from a subtractive image will change if the spectral power distribution of the viewing light source is changed.

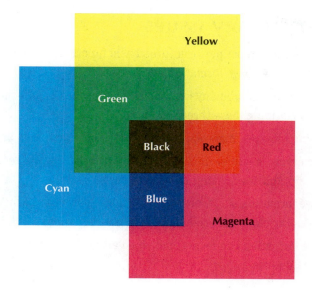

Figure 2.6
Subtractive mixing
of cyan, magenta,
and yellow color
primaries. Mixing
cyan and magenta
forms blue; mixing
cyan and yellow
forms green; and
mixing magenta
and yellow forms
red. Mixing maxi-
mum amounts of
cyan, magenta,
and yellow forms
black.

Complete Color-Imaging Systems

A complete imaging system can be defined as any combination of devices and/or media that is capable of performing the three basic functions of image capture, signal processing, and image formation. For example, the combination of a digital still camera, a computer workstation, and a video monitor forms a complete system. Somewhat less obvious is that, by this definition, photographic media—such as slide films and instant print films—also are complete imaging systems. That will be extremely important to remember later when the problems of color encoding in *hybrid systems,* which combine photographic media and various types of electronics, are addressed.

Summary of Key Issues

- All imaging systems must perform three basic functions: image capture, signal processing, and image formation.

- An imaging system can be any combination of devices and/or media that is capable of performing these three functions.

- Color imaging requires image capture that is (at least) trichromatic.

- Signal processing modifies image signals, produced by image capture, to make them suitable for forming a viewable image.

- In the image formation stage, processed image signals control the amounts of the color-forming elements produced by the output medium or device.

- Color image formation can be accomplished either by additive or by subtractive color techniques.

The Human Color-Imaging System

In Chapter 2, color-imaging systems were described in terms of three basic functions. In this chapter, those three functions will be used to examine the most important color-imaging system of all: the visual system of the human observer. In this discussion, and throughout the book, the visual system will be dealt with in the context shown in Fig. 3.1.

The figure is meant to illustrate that both the original and its reproduction are to be viewed, and that a human observer will judge the color quality of the reproduction. This is a common situation, and it conforms to the basic rule

Figure 3.1
An original scene
and its reproduc-
tion, where both
are viewed and
evaluated by a
human observer.

Original scene

Reproduction

established in the introduction to this section; but it does not seem like a very scientific method of assessing color quality. Wouldn't it be better to replace the observer with some type of objective measurement instrument? And, if so, what kind of instrument should be used?

Colorimeters directly measure CIE XYZ tristimulus values of color stimuli, so a colorimeter would certainly seem an obvious choice as a substitute for the observer. It could be used to measure the XYZ values of both the original and the reproduction (Fig. 3.2). The quality of the reproduction then could be quantified in terms of how well its XYZ values (or other colorimetric values, such as CIELAB $L^*a^*b^*$ values, derived from the XYZ values) match those of the original.

As logical as this approach might seem, it is fundamentally flawed. To understand why, one has to consider what goes on when an observer judges the quality of a reproduction. In most cases, color quality will be judged based on a comparison of the image that forms in the mind of the observer, when viewing the reproduction, to some reference mental image. This reference image may

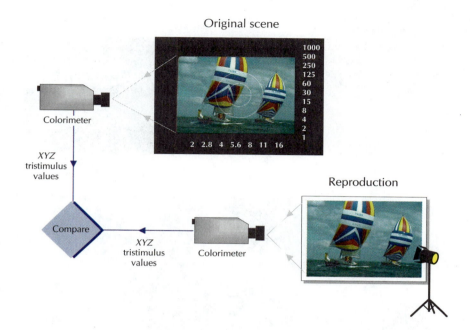

Figure 3.2
An original scene
and its reproduc-
tion. Both are
measured by a
colorimeter, and
the resulting col-
orimetric values
are compared.

derive from memory, if the observer actually saw the original at some time, or from the observer's conception of how the original should appear, based on his or her personal experience. In other cases, the observer may be looking at both the original and the reproduction at the same time, so the reference and repro-duction mental images will form simultaneously.

In any of these situations, the judgment will be based on a comparison of mental images that are the *end product* of the visual system. To produce these images, the human visual system must perform the same basic functions required of any other color-imaging system.

Figure 3.3 shows the human visual system in terms of those functions. The *image capture* process is performed by the trichromatic responses of the eye. The *image formation* process corresponds to the formation of a perception of a color image in the observer's mind. The formation of this mental image is influenced by intermediary visual *signal processing,* which can be broadly divided into two types: psychological and psychophysical.

Figure 3.3
The human visual system can be described in terms of the same basic functions used to describe all other color-imaging systems.

Psychological signal processing includes effects due to color memory, which generally is not colorimetrically accurate. It also includes color preference, which can be different from color memory, and various cognitive effects that cause the observer to perceive colors somewhat according to expectations and experience.

Psychophysical signal processing includes a variety of effects that are due to both physiological and mental processes. These effects result from various forms of visual adaptation, which are discussed next.

Adaptation

Adaptation refers to the process by which the visual mechanism adjusts to the conditions under which the eyes are exposed to radiant energy. The relationship between the physical characteristics of a color stimulus and the perception of its color is strongly influenced by effects produced by various forms of adaptation.

In the design of color-imaging media and systems, there are three adaptation effects of particular importance: *general-brightness adaptation, lateral-brightness adaptation,* and *chromatic adaptation*.

General-brightness adaptation refers to the adjustments of the visual mechanism in response to the overall level of the stimulus (or collection of stimuli) to which the eyes are exposed. For example, when the eyes are exposed for a sufficient length of time to a low level of illumination, the visual receptors compensate by becoming relatively more sensitive.

The human visual system, then, works on a *relative* basis, not on an absolute basis. This allows the recognition of objects under a wide range of illumination conditions. For example, a white flower likely will be seen as white whether it is viewed indoors or outdoors, even though the *absolute* amount of light reflecting from the flower is very different in the two viewing environments.

Despite this adaptation, visual perceptions still are affected somewhat by the *absolute* luminance levels of the stimuli being viewed. Stimuli having lower absolute luminance levels first of all are perceived as being somewhat lower in *luminance contrast*. This means that the light and dark *differences* among stimuli of higher and lower luminances are less apparent. In addition, stimuli having lower absolute luminance levels have less *colorfulness*. This means that color stimuli appear to have less of their particular hue.

For example, consider a reflection print viewed indoors, where the image luminances are low because of a low level of illumination, and also viewed outdoors, where a higher level of illumination results in higher image luminances. The print will appear quite different in the two environments, even to an observer who has become adapted to each of those environments. When the print is viewed indoors, areas of black will look less black, areas of white will look less white, and colors generally will look less colorful.

Lateral adaptation refers to changes induced in the sensitivities of adjacent areas of the retina. For example, the sensitivity of a particular retinal receptor may be increased or decreased depending on the amount of light being received by neighboring receptors. This important perceptual effect is called *lateral-brightness adaptation*. Lateral effects help the visual system to discriminate objects by making their edges more apparent.

Another manifestation of lateral-brightness adaptation is that the apparent luminance contrast of an image is lowered when areas immediately surrounding the image are relatively dark (Fig. 3.4). The figure shows two identical series of neutral squares, one series on a black background, the other on a white background. Note that each square on the black background appears to be lighter than its corresponding square on the white background. However, the effect is more evident for the darkest squares. As a result, the apparent luminance contrast—the perceived *difference* between the lightest and darkest squares—is diminished by the presence of the black background. A related effect, sometimes referred to as the *dark-surround effect,* occurs when an image, such as a photographic slide or motion picture, is projected in a darkened room and thus is surrounded by black.

Figure 3.4
One manifestation of lateral-brightness adaptation. The three gray squares on the white background are physically identical to those on the black background, but the luminance contrast of the black-background series appears lower.

Chromatic adaptation refers to adjustments of the visual mechanism in response to the average chromaticity of the stimulus (or collection of stimuli) to which the eyes are exposed. For example, when exposed sufficiently long to a reddish-yellow stimulus, such as a tungsten light, the eye's longer-wavelength-sensitive receptors become somewhat desensitized and its shorter-wavelength-sensitive receptors become relatively more sensitive. (The white-balance adjustment of a video camera, described earlier, is an approximate emulation of this process.) Chromatic adaptation helps the visual system interpret objects despite changes in the color of the illuminant. So a white flower generally will be recognized as white, regardless of the spectral composition of the illuminant under which it is viewed. The adaptation may not be *complete,* however, depending on the type of illumination that is used, the absolute level of that illumination, the extent to which the illumination fills the visual field, and certain other factors. For example, light from a dim tungsten lamp will continue to appear somewhat orange, even after the observer has had ample opportunity to adapt to it.

Colorimetry and Human Vision

From this discussion, it can be seen that the techniques of standard CIE colorimetry emulate the *first* stage of the human visual system—i.e., the *image capture* (trichromatic response) of the eye. Therefore colorimetry can be used to determine if two stimuli will produce the same trichromatic values, and this will predict whether those stimuli will visually match *if they are viewed under identical conditions.*

CIE colorimetry was developed specifically for that purpose. It is invaluable for determining metamerism and for specifying color-matching tolerances in a number of different industries. For example, it can be used to measure two paint samples to determine if they will match adequately under a specified illuminant. But CIE colorimetry does *not*—and was not designed to—emulate either the *signal-processing* or the *image-formation* functions of the human visual system.

By itself, then, standard CIE colorimetry is *not* a direct predictor of *color appearance*. In Part II, it will be shown how that fact has very important consequences on the colorimetric design of color-imaging systems and media. Part III will show how the distinction between colorimetry and color appearance also has important consequences for digital color encoding, which is based on the measurement and numerical specification of color.

To emphasize the latter point, we will close Part I with some cautionary words from one of our mentors, E. J. Breneman. When he worked at Eastman Kodak Company, Breneman would attach the following warning to any CIE chromaticity diagram he encountered that was printed in color:

WARNING!

Odysseus had to go to great lengths to keep his sailors from being bewitched by the sirens. Similarly, people who want to specify color appearance with numbers must be wary of chromaticity diagrams with lovely colors on them. Such illustrations as this tend to imply (or the viewer tends to infer) that a particular perceived color is associated with a particular point on the diagram. *This is false!*

The chromaticity diagram is a *stimulus* specification. A given *color perception* can be elicited by a stimulus represented by just about *any* point on the chromaticity diagram, depending on the nature of the visual field and the viewer's state of adaptation.

Although a colored rendition of a chromaticity diagram does, perhaps, help to indicate to a novice that with a common illuminant, blue paint will have a chromaticity in the lower left, etc., that novice is likely to jump to all the wrong conclusions and consequently find the world of color very confusing.

In short, the uses of such illustrations probably should be confined to making lovely wall decorations in places that never will be visited by budding color scientists and engineers.

Summary of Key Issues

- In most imaging applications, a human observer, not a measuring instrument, is the ultimate judge of color quality.

- The human visual system performs the same three basic functions—image capture, signal processing, and image formation—performed by all other color-imaging systems.

- CIE colorimetry emulates the first of these functions—trichromatic image capture.

- CIE colorimetry does not emulate the remaining functions—signal processing and image formation. Therefore, it does *not* measure color appearance.

- Color appearance is influenced by various psychophysical and psychological signal-processing effects.

PART II

The Nature of Color Images

Color images are the end product of color-imaging systems. In digital imaging systems, color images also are a source of *input*. In fact, in most digital systems, color images—and not original objects—are the principal source of the color information that will be encoded. However, at present these input images are made on color-imaging media that have been designed for purposes *other than* digital imaging.

For example, 35-mm photographic slides commonly are used as an input-image source on many digital imaging systems. Yet the slide films themselves are designed for an entirely different application: The images they produce are meant to be projected, using a particular type of projection lamp, in a darkened room. The imaging characteristics of these films are tailored specifically for that application. As a result, 35-mm color slide films have certain *colorimetric* color-reproduction characteristics, i.e., the characteristics measured according to standard colorimetric techniques, that are very different from those of all other media.

Other types of hardcopy color-imaging media, such as conventional photographic papers and negative films, also are designed for applications other than digital imaging. These media have their own particular colorimetric color-reproduction characteristics. When used as a source of input to a digital-imaging system, each provides a fundamentally different kind of color information.

Video cameras, especially digital still cameras, are another important input source for digital color-imaging systems. However, the colorimetric characteristics of most video cameras are designed to conform to standards that have been developed for another industry: broadcast video. Moreover, since video cameras typically are used to capture live scenes, rather than reproduced images, their signals represent yet another fundamentally different type of input color information.

The basic differences among the various types of input sources greatly complicate the process of digitally encoding color. In order to determine the exact nature of those complications, and to develop successful strategies for dealing with them, the fundamental colorimetric characteristics of each type of input source first must be examined.

One technique that can be used for examining the colorimetric color-reproduction characteristics of a device or medium is to measure how it records and reproduces an array of known color stimuli. In this section, that technique will be used to analyze the colorimetric characteristics of several types of imaging devices and media commonly used for input on digital color-imaging systems. The important consequences on digital color encoding that result from the unique colorimetric characteristics of each type of input source will be discussed. Understanding those consequences is essential for evaluating the capabilities and the limitations of existing color-encoding methods, which will be described later in Part III.

Video Images

Video cameras—particularly digital still cameras—are an important input source of color information in many digital color-imaging systems. But video cameras themselves do not produce color images; they only capture light and generate color signals. In order to understand the characteristics of those signals, and their consequences for color encoding, it is necessary to study how a camera and a video display work together to form a complete imaging system.

In this chapter, that will be done using an experimental system in which the characteristics of the video camera can be varied. The system will be analyzed in terms of its basic imaging functions (Fig. 4.1), and the image-capture and signal-processing requirements for the camera will be determined.

Figure 4.1

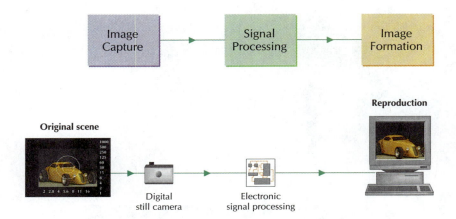

Figure 4.1

The basic imaging functions of image capture, signal processing, and image formation in a video system.

The video system will consist of a digital still camera, a computer, and a computer monitor. The system will be examined using a test target, composed of six spectrally nonselective neutral patches and six saturated color patches. Figure 4.2a shows the general layout of the target and the spectral reflectance characteristics of each of the test patches.

The test target will be illuminated by a light source simulating CIE Standard Illuminant D_{65} (Fig. 4.2b). The colorimetry for the target colors will be computed (using Eqs. {1.2}) from the spectral reflectances of the patches and the spectral power distribution of the light source. The colorimetry of the color stimuli reproduced on the monitor will be measured and compared to that of the original color stimuli of the illuminated test target (Fig. 4.3).

To get started, let us assume *for the moment* that the objective is for the system to produce a perfect *colorimetric* (metameric) match between the original test target and its reproduction on the monitor. This means that the *XYZ* tristimulus values measured from the monitor should exactly equal those computed for the D_{65}-illuminated test target.

What characteristics must the digital still camera have, and what kind of color signals must it produce, to achieve that result? For reasons that soon will become apparent, answering those questions requires that the characteristics of the *monitor* of the system first be examined.

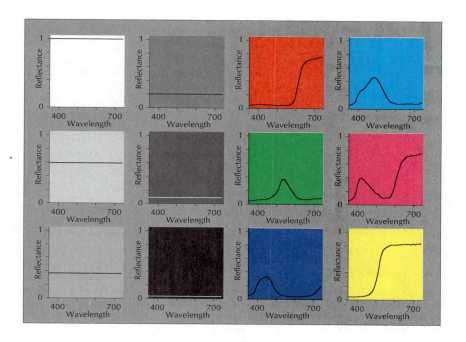

Figure 4.2a
General layout and spectral reflectances for the patches of the test target.

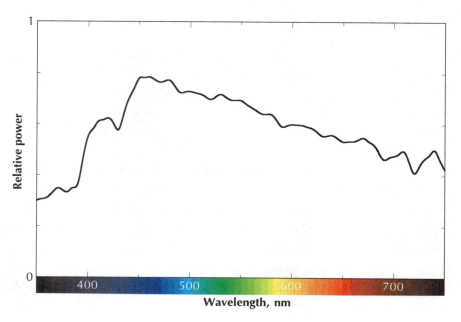

Figure 4.2b
Spectral power distribution for CIE Standard Illuminant D_{65}.

Figure 4.3
Arrangement of the test target, digital still camera, monitor, and colorimeter, as described in the text. In the experiment, the measured colorimetry of the monitor image is compared to the computed colorimetry of the illuminated test target.

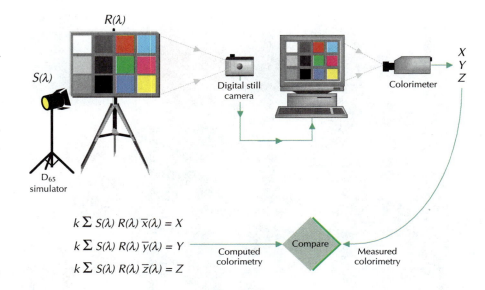

$$k \sum S(\lambda)\, R(\lambda)\, \bar{x}(\lambda) = X$$
$$k \sum S(\lambda)\, R(\lambda)\, \bar{y}(\lambda) = Y$$
$$k \sum S(\lambda)\, R(\lambda)\, \bar{z}(\lambda) = Z$$

Monitor General Characteristics

A video monitor is an additive color device. It displays color by producing various intensities of light from its three primaries, i.e., from light emitted by its red, green, and blue phosphors. Like all additive primaries, monitor primaries can be characterized in terms of their spectral power distributions. In the experimental system, the monitor has the primaries shown in Fig. 4.4, which are representative of those of many computer monitors.

Monitor colorimetric characteristics can be quantified by measuring the light emitted by the phosphors as a function of red, green, and blue control-signal voltages. On a computer monitor, these voltages are generated by digital-to-analog converters (DACs) from digital code values, $R'G'B'$, input to the DACs. (The prime sign in this designation is used to indicate values nonlinearly related to control voltages, as will be shown later.) A monitor can be characterized in terms of the stimuli generated as a function of those input $R'G'B'$ code values. In the characterization process, the generated stimuli can be measured

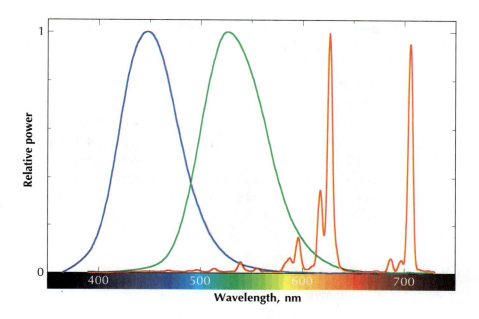

Figure 4.4

Spectral power distributions for light emitted by the red, green, and blue CRT phosphors of the computer monitor used in the experiment.

in terms of complete spectral power distributions, CIE colorimetric values, or *RGB* intensity values, depending on what characteristic is being studied.

In this experiment, a colorimeter will be used to measure the CIE *XYZ* values of monitor stimuli. Measurements will be made with the colorimeter and monitor arranged such that the measurement is *flareless*, i.e., the only light measured is that produced by the monitor itself, free of any stray room light.

Because the test target in the experiment is to be illuminated by D_{65}, the monitor white also has been set to the chromaticity of D_{65}. This means that the monitor has been adjusted electronically such that a white having chromaticity coordinates equal to those of D_{65} ($x = 0.3127$, $y = 0.3290$) is produced when maximum $R'G'B'$ input code values ($R' = 255$, $G' = 255$, $B' = 255$ in this 8-bit per channel system) are used. In addition, the absolute luminance of the monitor white has been adjusted to equal the absolute luminance of the illuminated perfect white (the first test patch) of the test target. Finally, the monitor has been adjusted such that its grayscale "tracks"; i.e., the chromaticity of the light it emits remains constant for any set of equal $R'G'B'$ code values.

Monitor Neutral Characteristics

Color monitors produce neutral color stimuli (and all other color stimuli) by emitting particular intensities of red, green, and blue light. For any given set of monitor red, green, and blue primaries, there is one and only one combination of *RGB* intensities that will produce a stimulus having a given set of CIE *XYZ* values. For example, Fig. 4.5 shows how certain intensities of the red, green and blue monitor primaries of Fig. 4.4 can be combined to form a stimulus having the *XYZ* values of a corresponding neutral in the D_{65}-illuminated test target. The spectral power distribution of the illuminated test target neutral is also shown in the figure.

Note that the monitor and test-target neutrals are *highly* metameric, i.e., although they have the same *XYZ* tristimulus values, their spectral characteristics are *very* different. As a result, some observers—even those having "normal" color vision—will disagree as to whether neutrals displayed on the monitor perfectly match the corresponding neutrals of the test target.

Such disagreements should be expected when highly metameric stimuli are involved. Recall that CIE colorimetry allows the prediction of matches *for the CIE Standard Observer;* but the color-matching functions of any particular observer are likely to differ somewhat from this standard. As a result, two stimuli having different spectral characteristics may appear identical to one observer but different to another. This is called *observer metamerism*.

Observer metamerism effects can have important consequences in practical imaging systems. For example, a video display may be used to provide a softcopy preview of hardcopy images to be produced by a system, and a human operator may perform color balance adjustments based on the video images. The operator's judgments will be influenced by the specific characteristics of his or her own visual system. If more than one operator makes these adjustments, the final output results may be quite inconsistent. This problem can be addressed by having each operator perform some type of visual matching to a reference output image. The results of that matching then can be factored into the adjustments subsequently made by each operator.

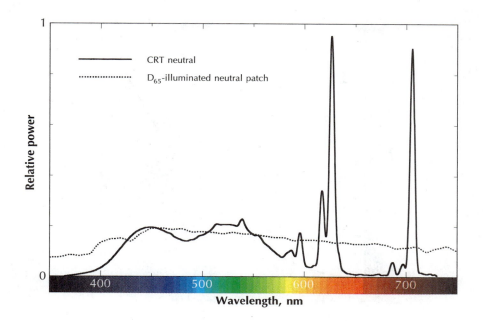

Figure 4.5
Relative spectral power distribution for a particular mixture of red, green, and blue light from a CRT. The *XYZ* values for this neutral stimulus are identical to those of the corresponding neutral patch of the test target, illuminated by D$_{65}$.

Monitor Grayscale Characteristics

As described earlier, a grayscale characteristic is a measure of how an imaging system reproduces a series of neutrals, ranging from black to white. The grayscale characteristic of an imaging system also plays a major role in how the luminances of non-neutral colors are reproduced.

Since the monitor in the experiment has been set up electronically such that the chromaticity produced from any set of equal $R'G'B'$ code values will not vary—it will always equal the chromaticity of D$_{65}$—the grayscale can be characterized simply by measuring monitor luminance-factor values for a series of equal input $R'G'B'$ code values. The measured characteristic of the monitor used in the experiment, which is shown in Fig. 4.6, is representative of many computer monitors. This characteristic is also representative of broadcast studio monitors adjusted according to industry recommendations.

Figure 4.6

The CRT grayscale
characteristic for
the monitor used
in the experiment,
expressed in terms
of luminance fac-
tor versus equal
monitor $R'G'B'$
input code values.

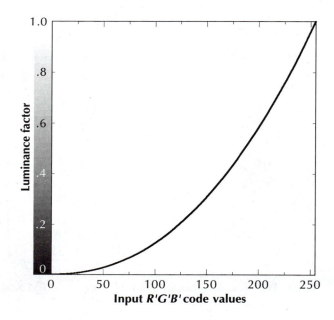

Figure 4.6

The CRT grayscale
characteristic for
the monitor used
in the experiment,
expressed in terms
of luminance fac-
tor versus equal
monitor $R'G'B'$
input code values.

The monitor grayscale characteristic can be described quite well by the following equation:

$$Y = k\left(\frac{C_{RGB}}{255}\right)^{\gamma} + Y_0 \qquad \{4.1a\}$$

where Y is the luminance factor of the light emitted by the monitor CRT; C_{RGB} is a code value of a set of equal $R'G'B'$ 8-bit code values input to the monitor; Y_0 is an offset value, i.e., the luminance factor when the R', G', and B' code values equal zero; and k is a normalizing factor determined such that $Y = 1.00$ when the R', G', and B' code values equal their maximum value of 255.

This type of characteristic would be expected. Cathode ray tubes inherently exhibit (more or less) a power law relationship between output luminance and control voltage. The relationship of monitor code values and control voltages essentially is linear, so an approximate power law relationship between output luminance levels and monitor code values should exist.

It is more straightforward to interpret grayscale characteristics if they are expressed in terms of logarithmic output values. That is because visual perceptions correlate more closely with logarithmic, rather than linear, luminance-factor values. For example, Fig. 4.7a shows the grayscale characteristics, expressed in terms of *linear* luminance-factor values, for two monitors. The curves suggest that these grayscale characteristics are virtually identical.

Figure 4.7b shows the same two grayscale characteristics expressed in terms of *logarithmic* luminance-factor values. The logarithmic values provide a much more meaningful description of the significant visual differences in the grayscale characteristics of the monitors. Note that the values used in Fig. 4.7b are *negative* logarithmic luminance-factor values, *relative to* the luminance-factor value produced at the maximum $R'G'B'$ code values. Use of these values will allow video grayscale characteristics to be compared later with those of hardcopy media, which will be measured in terms of *visual density*. The comparison is straightforward, because visual density is also the negative logarithm of the luminance-factor value. (Please refer to Appendix B for more details.)

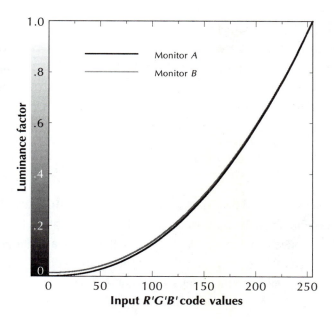

Figure 4.7a
CRT grayscale characteristics for two monitors, expressed in terms of luminance factor versus input equal $R'G'B'$ code values.

Figure 4.7b

CRT grayscale characteristics for the two monitors of Fig. 4.7a, expressed in terms of negative log luminance factor versus input equal $R'G'B'$ code values. These logarithmic values provide a more meaningful representation of the significant visual differences in the grayscale characteristics of the two monitors.

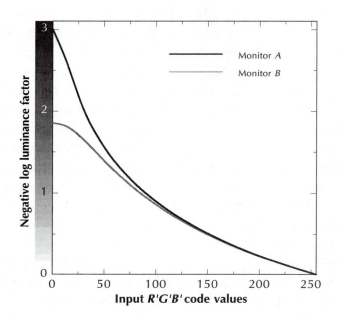

The grayscale characteristic of the particular monitor used in the experiment, expressed in terms of negative log luminance factor versus input equal $R'G'B'$ code value, is shown in Fig. 4.8. The measured value of the normalizing factor, k, is 0.999; the value of the exponent, γ (gamma), is 2.22; and the value of the offset, Y_0, is 0.001:

$$Y = 0.999 \left(\frac{C_{RGB}}{255} \right)^{2.22} + 0.001 \qquad \{4.1b\}$$

It should be noted here that some computer operating system software and some desktop-imaging applications load DAC lookup tables that alter the relationship of code values and control voltages. Such tables might be used for any number of reasons. For example, a set of tables might help to produce more satisfactory video images from image data derived from a particular input device or medium. In the experimental system, such tables are *not* present.

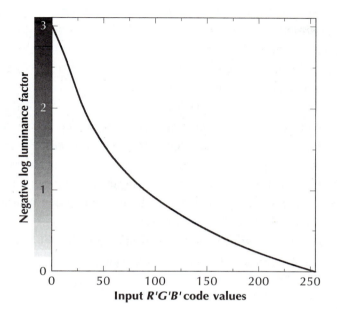

Figure 4.8
The CRT grayscale characteristic for the monitor used in the experiment, expressed in terms of negative log luminance factor versus equal input $R'G'B'$ values.

Camera Grayscale Characteristics

The grayscale of a digital still camera defines the $R'G'B'$ code values output by the camera in response to a series of neutral stimuli, i.e., stimuli having the chromaticity of the reference light source. The camera of the experimental system has been adjusted such that its grayscale "tracks"; it produces *equal* $R'G'B'$ code values for neutral stimuli of any given luminance. The grayscale therefore can be expressed in terms of equal $R'G'B'$ code values as a function of scene luminance-factor value (or scene exposure-factor value).

The appropriate characteristic for the camera grayscale can be determined based on the monitor grayscale characteristic. Since, for the moment, the goal for the experimental system is to have the colorimetry reproduced on the monitor equal that of the original test target, the grayscale characteristic of the digital still camera must be the *mathematical inverse* of the monitor characteristic. In other words, the characteristic must be such that when the camera is used together with the monitor, a one-to-one *overall system* grayscale characteristic—from the original illuminated test target to the final monitor reproduction—will be produced.

A camera grayscale characteristic that is the inverse of the monitor grayscale characteristic can be achieved by the use of appropriate camera signal processing. That signal processing often is referred to as *gamma correction,* because it includes a power function with an exponent that is the reciprocal of the monitor gamma. For example, in the experimental system, the monitor gamma is 2.22. Therefore, the exponent of the power function for the camera grayscale characteristic would be 1/2.22, or 0.45.

The actual monitor-inverse digital-camera grayscale characteristic for the particular monitor that was used in the experiment, and which is described by Eq. {4.1b}, is as follows:

$$C_{R'G'B'} = 255 \left(\frac{Y - 0.001}{0.999} \right)^{0.45} \qquad \{4.2\}$$

where $C_{R'G'B'}$ is a set of equal $R'G'B'$ camera output code values and Y is the luminance factor of the neutral stimulus being captured.

A plot of this monitor-inverse digital-camera characteristic is shown in Fig. 4.9a. The characteristic is expressed in terms of equal output $R'G'B'$ code values as a function of scene luminance factor. In Fig. 4.9b, the same camera characteristic is expressed in terms of equal output $R'G'B'$ code values as a function of *log* scene luminance factor.

Use of a camera having this particular characteristic, together with the monitor of the experimental system, will result in a one-to-one overall system grayscale characteristic. The basic steps involved in the formation of a system grayscale from camera and monitor grayscales are illustrated in Fig. 4.10a. A one-to-one system grayscale is shown in terms of linear values in Fig. 4.10b and shown again in terms of logarithmic values in Fig. 4.10c.

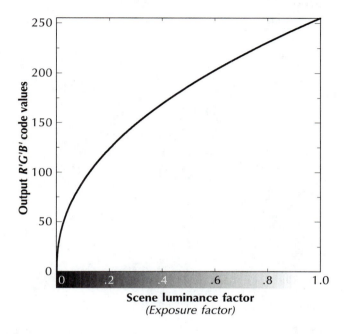

Figure 4.9a
Monitor-inverse digital camera characteristic, expressed in terms of equal output $R'G'B'$ code values as a function of linear scene luminance factor.

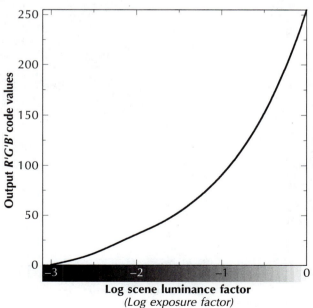

Figure 4.9b
Monitor-inverse digital camera characteristic, expressed in terms of equal output $R'G'B'$ code values as a function of log scene luminance factor.

Figure 4.10a
Formation of an overall video system grayscale. Scene luminances produce camera output code values. When these code values are input to a monitor, output luminances are produced.

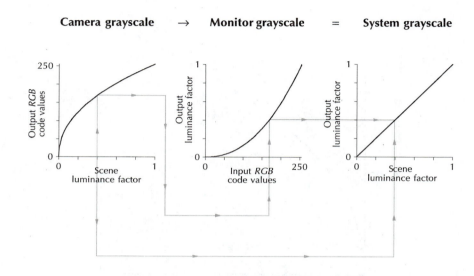

Camera grayscale   →   Monitor grayscale   =   System grayscale

Figure 4.10b
A one-to-one overall system grayscale characteristic, expressed in terms of reproduced luminance factor as a function of original scene luminance factor.

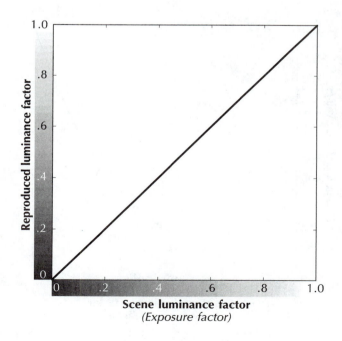

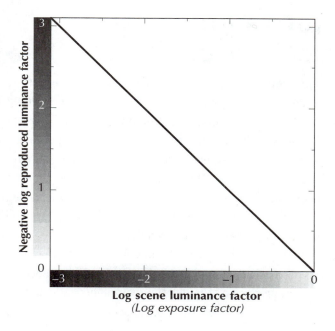

Log scene luminance factor
(Log exposure factor)

Figure 4.10c
A one-to-one overall system grayscale characteristic, expressed in terms of negative log reproduced luminance factor as a function of log original scene luminance factor.

The achievement of a one-to-one system grayscale reproduction is an important and necessary step toward achieving an overall colorimetric color-reproduction system. This system grayscale ensures that the measured output luminance-factor values of neutrals will equal the measured input luminance-factor values for those same neutrals. In addition, the video camera and monitor electronic setups described earlier ensure that the chromaticity values of the output neutrals will equal those of the corresponding input neutrals.

However, these conditions alone will not necessarily result in the chromaticities of output *non-neutral* colors being equal to the chromaticities of the corresponding input non-neutral colors. In order to also achieve that objective, the appropriate red, green, and blue spectral responsivities of the video camera first must be determined. In addition, any required color signal processing must be defined for the overall system. To do this, it is necessary to further investigate the characteristics of the system monitor. That process is described in the discussion that follows.

Monitor Color Characteristics

Because it is an additive device, a monitor can be used to perform a color-matching experiment similar to that described in Chapter 1. Doing so would generate the particular set of color-matching functions that correspond to the primaries of the monitor. In practice, it is not necessary to perform the experiment, because the monitor color-matching functions can be computed from the color-matching functions of the CIE Standard Colorimetric Observer and the chromaticity coordinates (x, y) of the monitor red, green, and blue primaries. The primaries of the monitor used in the experiment (Fig. 4.4) would generate the set of color-matching functions shown in Fig. 4.11.

The resulting monitor color-matching functions can be used to calculate the relative intensities of red, green, and blue light the monitor must generate in order to produce a stimulus that colorimetrically matches another given color stimulus. For example, Table 4.1 shows the relative red, green, and

Figure 4.11
Color-matching functions for the monitor primaries of Fig. 4.4.

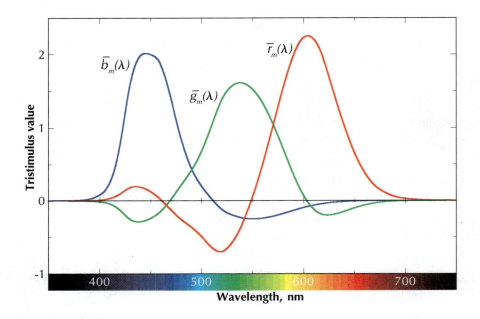

Test Target Color	Intensities Required for Colorimetric Matching		
	I_R	I_G	I_B
Neutral 1	1.0000	1.0000	1.0000
Neutral 2	0.5890	0.5890	0.5890
Neutral 3	0.3630	0.3630	0.3630
Neutral 4	0.2000	0.2000	0.2000
Neutral 5	0.0890	0.0890	0.0890
Neutral 6	0.0320	0.0320	0.0320
Red	0.3953	0.0156	0.0444
Green	0.0893	0.3209	0.0527
Blue	0.0313	0.0407	0.3322
Cyan	−.0010	0.2631	0.4038
Magenta	0.4598	0.0748	0.3290
Yellow	0.9037	0.6827	−.0400

Table 4.1

Monitor *RGB* relative intensity values, I_R, I_G, I_B, required to colorimetrically match the illuminated test target.

blue intensity values needed to match each illuminated patch of the test target. The equations used to calculate those values are as follows:

$$I_R = k_{mr} \sum_\lambda S(\lambda)R(\lambda)\bar{r}_m(\lambda)$$

$$I_G = k_{mg} \sum_\lambda S(\lambda)R(\lambda)\bar{g}_m(\lambda) \qquad \{4.3\}$$

$$I_B = k_{mb} \sum_\lambda S(\lambda)R(\lambda)\bar{b}_m(\lambda)$$

where I_R, I_G, and I_B are the red, green, and blue relative intensity values; $S(\lambda)$ is the relative spectral power distribution of the light source; $R(\lambda)$ is the spectral reflectance of the test patch; $\bar{r}_m(\lambda)$, $\bar{g}_m(\lambda)$, and $\bar{b}_m(\lambda)$ are the red, green, and blue color-matching functions for the monitor primaries; and k_{mr}, k_{mg}, and k_{mb} are normalizing factors determined such that I_R, I_G, and I_B = 1.00 for the first test patch (a perfect white reflector).

For colorimetric matching, the camera red, green, and blue signals for any test stimulus ultimately must result in the monitor red, green, and blue light intensities required to produce a stimulus having colorimetry identical to that of the test stimulus. Since signal processing already has been incorporated such that a one-to-one relationship of camera exposure-factor values and monitor intensity values has been achieved for neutral stimuli (Fig. 4.10b), all that remains is to determine the particular camera spectral responsivities that also will produce the exposure-factor values required for the colorimetric matching of non-neutral stimuli.

The spectral responsivities required to do that can be determined by setting the camera RGB exposure equations, Eqs. {2.1}, equal to the monitor RGB intensity equations, Eqs. {4.3}:

$$\begin{aligned}
R_{exp} &= I_R \\
G_{exp} &= I_G \\
B_{exp} &= I_B
\end{aligned}$$

{4.4a}

or

$$k_{cr} \sum_{\lambda} S(\lambda)R(\lambda)r_c(\lambda) = k_{mr} \sum_{\lambda} S(\lambda)R(\lambda)\bar{r}_m(\lambda)$$

$$k_{cg} \sum_{\lambda} S(\lambda)R(\lambda)g_c(\lambda) = k_{mg} \sum_{\lambda} S(\lambda)R(\lambda)\bar{g}_m(\lambda)$$

{4.4b}

$$k_{cb} \sum_{\lambda} S(\lambda)R(\lambda)b_c(\lambda) = k_{mb} \sum_{\lambda} S(\lambda)R(\lambda)\bar{b}_m(\lambda)$$

which reduces to

$$r_c(\lambda) = \frac{k_{mr}}{k_{cr}} \bar{r}_m(\lambda)$$

$$g_c(\lambda) = \frac{k_{mg}}{k_{cg}} \bar{g}_m(\lambda)$$

{4.5}

$$b_c(\lambda) = \frac{k_{mb}}{k_{cb}} \bar{b}_m(\lambda)$$

What this means, in general terms, is that colorimetric matching between the original and reproduction can be achieved if the red, green, and blue spectral responsivities, $r_c(\lambda)$, $g_c(\lambda)$, and $b_c(\lambda)$, of the *image-capture* device are *proportional* to the respective red, green, and blue color-matching functions, $\bar{r}_m(\lambda)$, $\bar{g}_m(\lambda)$, and $\bar{b}_m(\lambda)$, for the *output* device. The ratios k_{mr}/k_{cr}, k_{mg}/k_{cg}, and k_{mb}/k_{cb} define the appropriate proportionalities. A simpler way of saying this is that the red spectral-responsivity curve for the image-capture device should have the same "shape" as the red color-matching-function curve for the output device, and likewise for green and blue.

The digital still camera for the experimental system, then, should have relative red, green, and blue spectral responsivities that correspond directly to the red, green, and blue color-matching functions for the monitor (Fig. 4.11). The ideal spectral responsivities, white-balanced for D_{65}, are shown in Fig. 4.12. A camera having these responsivities would generate the *RGB* exposure-factor values shown in Table 4.2. Note that those values are *identical* to the required monitor *RGB* relative intensity values that were shown previously in Table 4.1.

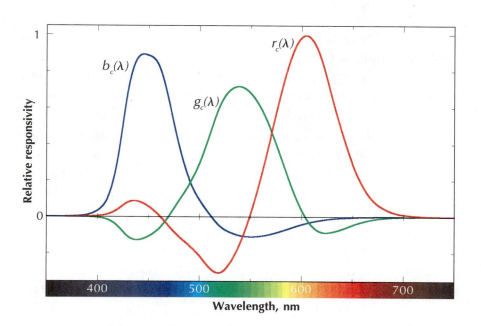

Figure 4.12

Ideal spectral responsivities for a digital still camera to be used with a monitor having the primaries of Fig. 4.4. The shapes of these responsivities equal the respective shapes of the monitor color-matching functions (Fig. 4.11).

Table 4.2
The *RGB* expo-sure-factor values, R_{exp}, G_{exp}, B_{exp}, for a digital cam-era having ideal spectral responsiv-ities, equivalent to the color-match-ing functions of the monitor RGB primaries, exactly equal the monitor *RGB* relative intensity values, I_R, I_G, I_B, required for colorimetric matching.

Test Target Color	Intensities Required for Colorimetric Matching			Exposures from Ideal Camera Spectral Responsivities		
	I_R	I_G	I_B	R_{exp}	G_{exp}	B_{exp}
Neutral 1	1.0000	1.0000	1.0000	1.0000	1.0000	1.0000
Neutral 2	0.5890	0.5890	0.5890	0.5890	0.5890	0.5890
Neutral 3	0.3630	0.3630	0.3630	0.3630	0.3630	0.3630
Neutral 4	0.2000	0.2000	0.2000	0.2000	0.2000	0.2000
Neutral 5	0.0890	0.0890	0.0890	0.0890	0.0890	0.0890
Neutral 6	0.0320	0.0320	0.0320	0.0320	0.0320	0.0320
Red	0.3953	0.0156	0.0444	0.3953	0.0156	0.0444
Green	0.0893	0.3209	0.0527	0.0893	0.3209	0.0527
Blue	0.0313	0.0407	0.3322	0.0313	0.0407	0.3322
Cyan	−.0010	0.2631	0.4038	−.0010	0.2631	0.4038
Magenta	0.4598	0.0748	0.3290	0.4598	0.0748	0.3290
Yellow	0.9037	0.6827	−.0400	0.9037	0.6827	−.0400

It would appear that achieving colorimetric color reproduction is quite simple. All that seems necessary is a one-to-one system grayscale characteristic and a camera having spectral responsivities like those just defined. However, if one were to attempt to *construct* a camera having such responsivities, a serious problem would be encountered: each of the monitor color-matching functions is *negative* for certain ranges of wavelengths. (As discussed in Chapter 1, *all* sets of physically realizable primaries have associated color-matching functions with at least some negative regions.) This means that the ideal camera would need to have "negative sensitivity" to light at certain wavelengths!

That is not possible, of course. One could, however, construct a camera having spectral responsivities that correspond to some *other* set of color-matching functions having *no* negative regions. For example, the camera could have spec-tral responsivities that correspond to the all-positive color-matching functions of the CIE Standard Observer. That essentially would make the camera a colorimeter, which certainly would seem a reasonable thing to do, given that the objective is to achieve colorimetrically accurate color reproduction.

Figure 4.13a illustrates the use of such a camera. The figure shows a color stimulus being captured according to the CIE Standard Observer color-matching-function spectral responsivities of the camera. The resulting exposure-factor values are then processed by the camera to form code values, which are then input to the monitor. The monitor then produces a color stimulus. However, except for a neutral color, the colorimetry of a stimulus produced on the monitor would *not* match the colorimetry of the original stimulus. The reason is that a video camera having CIE Standard Observer spectral responsivities would not generate *RGB* exposure-factor values equal to the required monitor *RGB* relative-intensity values. This is shown in Table 4.3.

The resulting colorimetric errors are shown in Fig. 4.13b. In this figure, the CIELAB a^*b^* coordinates for the stimuli of the illuminated test target are compared to those for the corresponding stimuli produced on the monitor. The coordinates for the monitor reproductions generally are closer to the neutral point at the center of the diagram. This means that the reproduced colors will have significantly lower *chromas* than the original colors, i.e., they will look less colorful. This can be seen in the test-target images of Fig. 4.14.

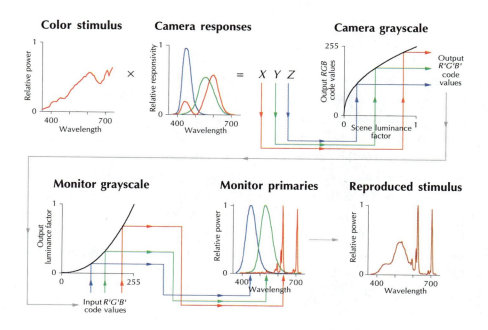

Figure 4.13a

Use of a video camera having spectral responsivities equivalent to the color-matching functions of the CIE Standard Observer.

Test Target Color	Intensities Required for Colorimetric Matching			Exposures from CIE Standard Observer Responsivities		
	I_R	I_G	I_B	R_{exp}	G_{exp}	B_{exp}
Neutral 1	1.0000	1.0000	1.0000	1.0000	1.0000	1.0000
Neutral 2	0.5890	0.5890	0.5890	0.5890	0.5890	0.5890
Neutral 3	0.3630	0.3630	0.3630	0.3630	0.3630	0.3630
Neutral 4	0.2000	0.2000	0.2000	0.2000	0.2000	0.2000
Neutral 5	0.0890	0.0890	0.0890	0.0890	0.0890	0.0890
Neutral 6	0.0320	0.0320	0.0320	0.0320	0.0320	0.0320
Red	0.3953	0.0156	0.0444	0.2104	0.1180	0.0514
Green	0.0893	0.3209	0.0527	0.1557	0.2380	0.0909
Blue	0.0313	0.0407	0.3322	0.0894	0.0620	0.2819
Cyan	−.0010	0.2631	0.4038	0.1568	0.2050	0.3710
Magenta	0.4598	0.0748	0.3290	0.3136	0.1970	0.2975
Yellow	0.9037	0.6827	−.0400	0.6597	0.6820	0.0900

There would seem to be a real dilemma here. Colorimetric matching apparently requires that a video camera have spectral responsivities shaped like the color-matching functions corresponding to the monitor primaries, but such responsivities are not physically realizable. On the other hand, a camera that has physically realizable spectral responsivities, such as responsivities that correspond to the color-matching functions of the CIE Standard Observer, produces large colorimetric errors when used with a real monitor.

There is a solution to this dilemma. Recall from Chapter 1 that all sets of color-matching functions are linear combinations of all other sets. This means that any set can be transformed to another set simply by the use of an appropriate three-by-three matrix-multiplication operation. It follows, then, that a matrix can be used to transform the tristimulus values of one set of color-matching functions to those of any other set of color-matching functions.

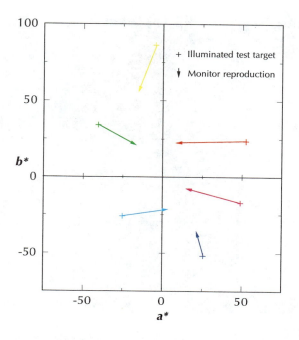

+ Illuminated test target

↓ Monitor reproduction

Figure 4.13b
The lengths of the vector arrows in this CIELAB *a**, *b** diagram indicate the magnitudes of the chromatic errors that result from using a video camera having the spectral responsivities of the CIE 1931 Standard Observer and a monitor having the primaries shown in Fig. 4.4.

This means that a real camera *can* have physically realizable spectral responsivities corresponding to the color-matching functions of the Standard Observer or to any of a virtually unlimited number of other sets of all-positive color-matching functions. In all cases, the all-positive color-matching functions will correspond to sets of *imaginary* primaries, but that is perfectly acceptable. A matrix can be used as part of the camera's signal processing to transform its *RGB* exposure signals (i.e., its *RGB* tristimulus values, which correspond to those of the imaginary primaries) to new $R_m G_m B_m$ exposure signals having the appropriate values for the actual monitor primaries (Fig. 4.15).

Because device spectral responsivities must be physically realizable, and because the color-matching functions corresponding to actual device primaries always have regions of negativity, it is *always* necessary to create interactions, such as those produced by a matrix, among the color signals of *any* real image-capture device having spectral responsivities equivalent to a set of color-matching functions.

Figure 4.14

The upper image approximates the appearance of the original test colors. The lower image approximates the appearance of a monitor image that results from using a video camera having the spectral responsivities of the CIE 1931 Standard Colorimetric Observer and a monitor having the primaries of Fig. 4.4.

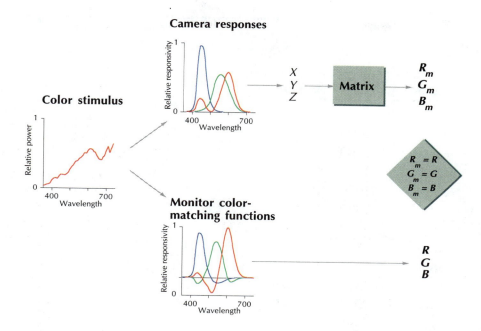

Figure 4.15
Use of a matrix in the signal processing of video camera signals. The $R_m G_m B_m$ values of the matrixed signals from the camera having spectral responsivities equivalent to a set of all-positive color-matching functions will exactly equal the *RGB* values of the signals from the camera having spectral responsivities equivalent to the actual color-matching functions of the monitor.

In the experimental system, where the camera spectral responsivities are equivalent to the color-matching functions of the CIE Standard Observer, the following matrix transformation can be applied to the *RGB* camera signals to form new signals, $R_m G_m B_m$:

$$\begin{bmatrix} R_m \\ G_m \\ B_m \end{bmatrix} = \begin{bmatrix} 2.654 & -1.182 & -0.472 \\ -1.078 & 2.040 & 0.038 \\ 0.080 & -0.297 & 1.217 \end{bmatrix} \begin{bmatrix} R \\ G \\ B \end{bmatrix} \qquad \{4.6\}$$

As shown in Table 4.4, the $R_m G_m B_m$ signal values are *identical* to those that would have been produced by a camera having ideal spectral responsivities, i.e., those equivalent to the monitor color-matching functions.

Table 4.4
The *matrixed* exposure-factor values R_m, G_m, B_m for a digital camera having spectral responsivities equivalent to the color-matching functions of the CIE Standard Observer exactly equal the monitor *RGB* relative intensity values I_R, I_G, I_B required for colorimetric matching. Use of the matrix produces exposure-factor values that are identical to those that would be produced by a camera having ideal spectral responsivities.

Test Target Color	Intensities Required for Colorimetric Matching			Matrixed Exposures from CIE Standard Observer Responsivities		
	I_R	I_G	I_B	R_m	G_m	B_m
Neutral 1	1.0000	1.0000	1.0000	1.0000	1.0000	1.0000
Neutral 2	0.5890	0.5890	0.5890	0.5890	0.5890	0.5890
Neutral 3	0.3630	0.3630	0.3630	0.3630	0.3630	0.3630
Neutral 4	0.2000	0.2000	0.2000	0.2000	0.2000	0.2000
Neutral 5	0.0890	0.0890	0.0890	0.0890	0.0890	0.0890
Neutral 6	0.0320	0.0320	0.0320	0.0320	0.0320	0.0320
Red	0.3953	0.0156	0.0444	0.3953	0.0156	0.0444
Green	0.0893	0.3209	0.0527	0.0893	0.3209	0.0527
Blue	0.0313	0.0407	0.3322	0.0313	0.0407	0.3322
Cyan	−.0010	0.2631	0.4038	−.0010	0.2631	0.4038
Magenta	0.4598	0.0748	0.3290	0.4598	0.0748	0.3290
Yellow	0.9037	0.6827	−.0400	0.9037	0.6827	−.0400

The experimental system, which now includes a digital still camera having spectral responsivities corresponding to the color-matching functions of the CIE Standard Observer, signal processing that implements the matrix given in Eq. {4.6}, and nonlinear signal processing that produces a one-to-one grayscale reproduction on a monitor having the primaries of Fig. 4.4, produces the results given in Fig. 4.16. These results show that, for the most part, the colorimetry of the illuminated test target has been reproduced exactly on the monitor. The colorimetry of the yellow patch, however, has not been reproduced accurately. That is because the monitor physically cannot generate a stimulus having that particular colorimetry; that stimulus is outside the monitor's *color gamut*. This can be seen in the required intensity values, I_R, I_G, I_B, given in each of the tables. The required blue intensity value for the yellow color is negative. To display this color, then, the monitor would have to produce *negative* amounts of blue light! Obviously it cannot do that, so the monitor cannot produce a colorimetric match to that particular yellow color.

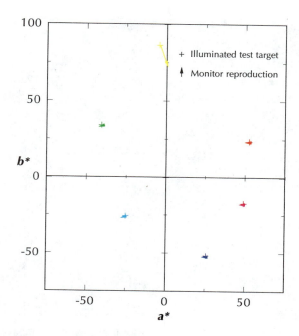

Figure 4.16
Most colorimetric
errors shown in
Fig. 4.13b can be
eliminated by the
inclusion of an
appropriate
signal-processing
matrix. The yellow
color is outside
the reproducible
color gamut of the
monitor.

Results of Colorimetric Matching

So far, the experimental camera/monitor combination produces a *perfect* colorimetric match of any color captured by the camera in the experimental setup, as long as that color is within the monitor's color gamut. It would seem, then, that this system should produce excellent images. The system does, in fact, make very good monitor images *of the test target*. It also makes good images when the camera is aimed at a *reproduction,* such as a reflection print. However, monitor images of *live* scenes, especially outdoor scenes, captured by the camera look quite "flat" (Fig. 4.17). Specifically, they appear too low in luminance contrast and too low in color saturation.

What is wrong? The monitor images, while colorimetrically accurate as measured by the colorimeter, are poor in color quality because several important factors have not yet been accounted for in the system. One of these factors is physical; the others are perceptual.

Figure 4.17
The upper image approximates the appearance of a monitor image that accurately matches the colorimetry of the original scene. The lower image approximates the appearance of a monitor image that is not colorimetrically accurate, but which generally would be judged to have improved color reproduction.

Viewing Flare

The physical factor not yet accounted for in the experimental system is *viewing flare*. When an image is viewed on a monitor, ideally the observer should see only the light emitted by the monitor itself. But in most practical viewing situations, the observer also will be seeing flare light (stray light) that is reflected from the monitor's glass faceplate. Flare light can come from ordinary light sources in the viewing environment (overhead lamps, window light, etc.). It also can come from the monitor itself—if, for example, the observer is wearing a white shirt that reflects monitor light back to the faceplate.

Flare light is added, more or less uniformly, to the light from the image being displayed on the monitor. Therefore, the luminance at each point in the system grayscale will be increased. This is shown, in terms of linear luminance units, in Fig. 4.18a. The representation in this figure might seem to imply that the effect of the flare light should be virtually undetectable. In reality, however, the effect will be very noticeable.

The visual impact of the effect is much better represented when the system grayscale is expressed in terms of negative log luminance-factor values (Fig. 4.18b). Again, such values are more consistent with the way the human visual system responds to variations in luminances. As Fig. 4.18b shows, the addition of flare light significantly brightens darker areas of an image, but it has a much less apparent effect on brighter areas. Therefore, the luminance contrast of a displayed image is reduced, particularly in the darker areas.

Because flare light generally is white, its addition also will reduce the saturation of colors, as shown in Figs. 4.19a and 4.19b. In Fig. 4.19a, the test colors have been photographed as if they were part of the *principal subject area* of the original scene, i.e., as if they were in the area used in determining the overall camera exposure. The test colors therefore are normally exposed. In Fig. 4.19b, the test colors have been photographed as if they were in a deeply shaded area of the same original scene. When photographed that way, the test colors are underexposed and effectively become darker. As the figures show, the desaturation caused by viewing flare is much greater for the darker test colors. (Please refer to Appendix E for more details on viewing flare.)

Figure 4.18a
Effect of flare light on the system grayscale characteristic, expressed in terms of linear reproduced luminance-factor values.

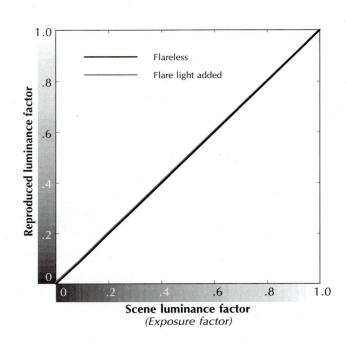

Figure 4.18b
Effect of flare light on the system grayscale characteristic, expressed in terms of negative log reproduced luminance-factor values. The visual impact of this effect is more appropriately represented by these logarithmic values. Note that the effect is greatest for blacks and dark grays.

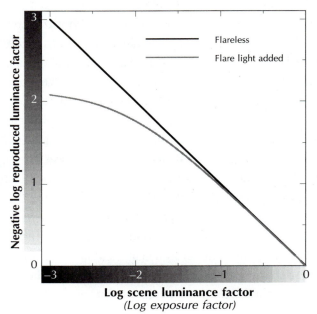

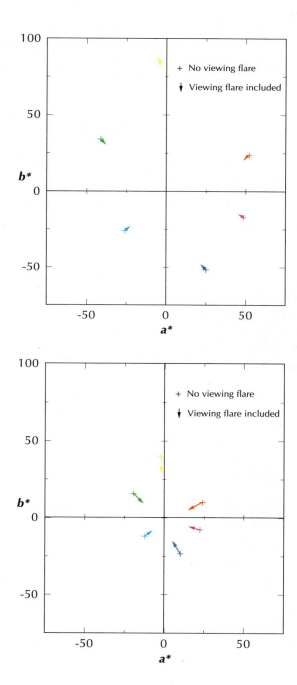

Figure 4.19a
Effect of flare light on color saturation. Since flare light essentially is white, its addition reduces the saturation of colors, i.e., it moves them toward white. In this figure, the test colors have been photographed as part of the principal subject area of an original scene.

Figure 4.19b
Effect of flare light on the color saturation of very dark colors. In this figure, the test colors have been photographed as if they were in a deeply shaded area of the original scene. The desaturation caused by viewing flare is much greater for these darker test colors.

In order to determine the proper compensation for viewing flare, the amount of flare light in the viewing environment must be measured. There are various methods that can be used. In one technique, illustrated in Fig. 4.20, an opaque white patch is attached to the monitor. The amount of light reflected from that patch is measured from the observer's viewing position. Since the patch is opaque, any light from it must be reflected flare light. The measurement can be made using an appropriate instrument, such as a telephotometer, that is designed to measure a small spot of light from a distance. The measured amount of flare light usually is expressed as a percentage of the light measured, using the same type of instrument, from a white area of a representative image displayed on the monitor.

Figure 4.20
One method for measuring viewing flare light.

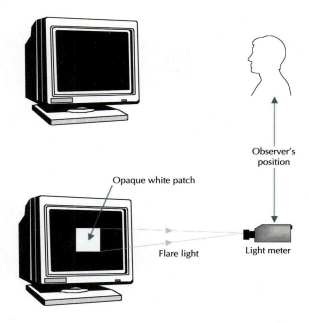

Observer's position

Opaque white patch

Flare light

Light meter

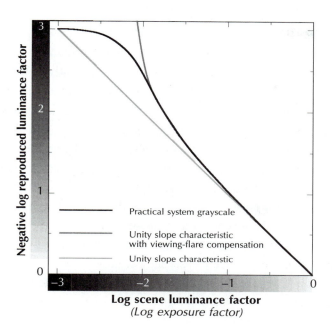

Log scene luminance factor
(Log exposure factor)

Figure 4.21
A practical system grayscale charac-teristic designed to compensate partially for the addition of 0.75% viewing-flare light. The repro-duced luminance-factor values were measured in the absence of flare light. Also shown for reference are a straight line of unity slope and a theoretical com-pensation for 0.75% viewing flare.

In video viewing environments where some care is taken to eliminate obvious sources of stray light, the intensity of the flare light generally will be equal to about 0.5 to 1.0% that of a displayed image white. Although that might sound like a small amount, the effect of that much flare light is *very* significant. It *must* be compensated for if high-quality images are to be produced.

Signal processing can be used to compensate, at least partially, for the effects of flare light. The compensation, shown in Fig. 4.21, has an exponential increase in the darker regions. That should be expected. Flare is an addition of light, which requires a subtraction of light for compensation. When plotted on a logarithmic scale, the linear subtraction will be an exponential increase.

With appropriate signal processing, *RGB* image signals can be adjusted such that colorimetric measurements made *from the observer's position* (as shown in Fig. 4.20) have a one-to-one relationship to measured original-scene luminance-factor values. This result can be achieved except for the darkest colors. When that signal processing is applied, the practical system grayscale *measured in the absence of flare light* will be similar to that shown in Fig. 4.21.

Perceptual Factors

With the addition of flare-compensating signal processing in the experimental system, monitor images from live scenes are improved greatly. However, to most observers, the monitor images still appear somewhat low in luminance contrast and color saturation. This result might seem surprising, because measurements made from the observer's position confirm that colorimetric matching has been achieved. Nevertheless, as stated earlier, when such discrepancies arise, the judgments of the observers must prevail. So despite the fact that colorimetric matching has been achieved in the system, the remaining problems with the appearance of images must be addressed. If these problems are not due to physics, they must be due to perceptual phenomena.

There are several possible factors that might contribute to the apparent discrepancy between color measurements made of the images and their color appearance. A monitor image is somewhat less sharp than the original, and it is known that a reduction in image sharpness can produce a corresponding reduction in perceived image luminance contrast. A reduction in image sharpness also can produce a reduction in perceived image color saturation.

In addition, the *absolute* luminances produced by the monitor generally will be significantly less than those of the original scene. For example, the absolute luminances of an outdoor scene may be hundreds of times greater than those that can be produced by a reproduction of that scene on a typical high-resolution computer monitor. As discussed in Chapter 3, images having lower absolute luminances are perceived to be lower in luminance contrast, and they also are perceived to be lower in colorfulness.

Another factor is that, in most cases, the monitor is not viewed simultaneously with the original scene. The monitor image therefore will be judged according to the observer's *memory* of the original, and colors generally are remembered as being somewhat more saturated than they really were. Finally, many observers *prefer* colors to be reproduced even *more* saturated than they remember them being. For example, the preferred reproduction of the color of the sky near the horizon closely corresponds to the much more saturated color of the actual sky directly overhead.

There are a number of factors, then, to suggest that the color signals of a video camera should be modified somewhat in a way that will increase both the luminance contrast and color saturation of images produced on the monitor. But how should these modifications be made, and by how much?

Video Signal Corrections

There are several techniques that could be used to determine, from first principles, the video signal processing required to compensate for the perceptual factors described above. Another approach would be to examine, or "reverse engineer," a successful existing video system to see how such modifications are performed in actual practice. That is the approach that will be taken here.

A television broadcast system is a reasonable choice for examination, since broadcast specifications and practices are based on decades of industry experience. Our own experience also supports this choice. We have found that although some improvements certainly can be made, the color quality of video images generally is quite high when the relationship between original and reproduced colorimetry is essentially that produced by conventional broadcast video systems.

Figure 4.22 shows the measured grayscale characteristic for a representative broadcast video system. Both the camera and the monitor have been adjusted according to broadcast industry recommendations. The grayscale characteristic results from the use of a monitor similar to that of the experimental system and a video camera employing signal processing corresponding to the following equations:

$$\text{for } 1.0 \geq Y \geq 0.018 \quad V = 1.099\, Y^{0.45} - 0.099 \qquad \{4.7a\}$$

$$\text{for } 0.018 > Y \geq 0.0 \quad V = 4.50\, Y \qquad \{4.7b\}$$

where V is the camera output signal or voltage, and Y is the scene luminance-factor value.

Figure 4.22

Measured system grayscale characteristic for a broadcast video system.

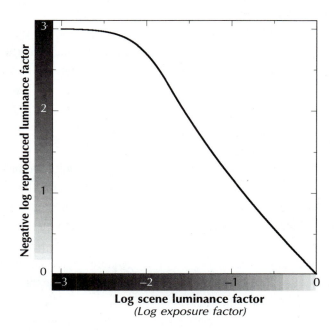

These equations, which are from ITU-R BT.709, *The HDTV Standard for the Studio and for International Programme Exchange,* originally were derived from analog measurements made of broadcast video cameras that had been adjusted by skilled camera operators such that excellent quality video images were produced on studio monitors set up according to broadcast recommendations.

The grayscale characteristic of a video camera having signal processing corresponding to these equations is *not* simply a mathematical inverse of the monitor characteristic. This is shown in Figs. 4.23a and 4.23b, which compare the grayscale characteristics for two digital still cameras. The signal processing of one camera is an exact mathematical inverse of the monitor characteristic, while that of the other camera corresponds to the ITU equations. The camera characteristics are normalized for white and expressed in terms of output code values as a function of linear scene luminance-factor value (Fig. 4.23a) and log scene luminance-factor value (Fig. 4.23b).

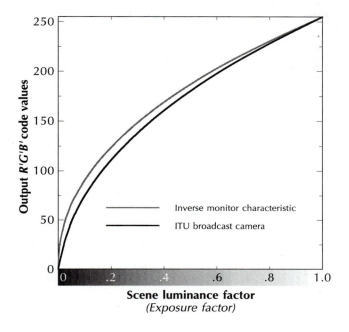

Figure 4.23a
Digital camera characteristics. The signal processing of one camera is a mathematical inverse of the monitor characteristic. The signal processing of the other corresponds to the ITU broadcast camera equations.

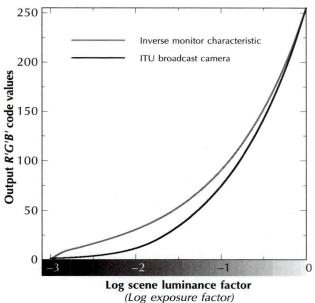

Figure 4.23b
Characteristics for the cameras of Figure 4.23a, expressed in terms of output $R'G'B'$ code values as a function of log scene luminance-factor value.

Figure 4.24

Overall system grayscale characteristics resulting from the use of the cameras of Fig. 4.23a (and Fig. 4.23b), and the monitor of the experimental system.

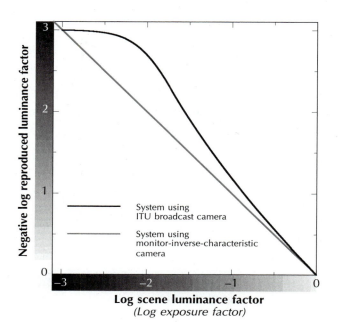

The overall system grayscales produced by these cameras, when used with the monitor of Fig. 4.8, are shown in Fig. 4.24. As would be expected, the camera having the monitor-inverse characteristic produces a straight-line overall system grayscale of unity slope. The camera corresponding to the ITU equations produces a system grayscale consistent with broadcast video.

In the experimental system, the monitor images are significantly improved by the use of camera signal processing corresponding to the ITU equations. This improvement is illustrated in the images of Fig. 4.25. There are several factors that contribute to this improvement.

First, the use of signal processing corresponding to the ITU equations produces a system grayscale characteristic that compensates partially for about 0.75% viewing flare (Fig. 4.26a). That amount of flare corresponds well with the experimental conditions, and it is typical for many video-viewing environments . The figure also shows that, in addition, the camera signal processing increases the overall slope of the system grayscale by about 15%.

Figure 4.25
Approximate appearances of monitor images corresponding to the overall system grayscale characteristics shown in Fig. 4.24. The upper image has a straight-line system grayscale of unity slope. The lower image has a system grayscale consistent with broadcast video practices.

Figure 4.26a

Video system grayscale characteristic resulting from ITU camera signal processing. Also shown are a unity slope characteristic, a 1.15 slope characteristic, and a 1.15 slope characteristic with 0.75% viewing-flare compensation.

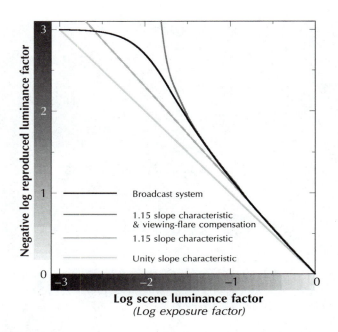

It was this slope increase that was lacking in the system grayscale characteristic examined earlier (Fig. 4.21). That grayscale provided flare compensation only. The two system grayscale characteristics are compared in Fig. 4.26b. The slope increase in the broadcast system is desirable because it helps compensate for the reduction in perceived luminance contrast resulting from the relatively low absolute luminance levels of the monitor.

Because the camera signal processing is applied to camera *RGB* signals (not just to a separate achromatic signal), the slope increase and flare compensation also affect overall color reproduction. The reason for this, as shown in Fig. 4.27, is that in an additive system, a grayscale is formed by the addition of red, green, and blue color scales. The signal processing used to alter the grayscale does so by altering these individual color scales, and the higher color contrasts produced by these alterations result in higher overall color saturation (Fig. 4.28). That is desirable, because higher saturation is needed in order to compensate for the color saturation decreases associated with viewing flare and with the various perceptual factors described earlier.

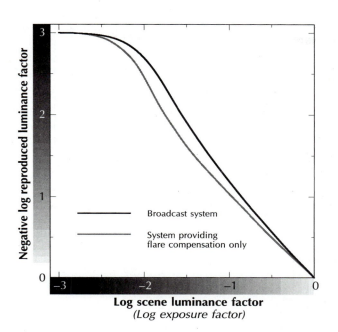

Log scene luminance factor
(Log exposure factor)

Figure 4.26b
Comparison of video system grayscale characteristics.

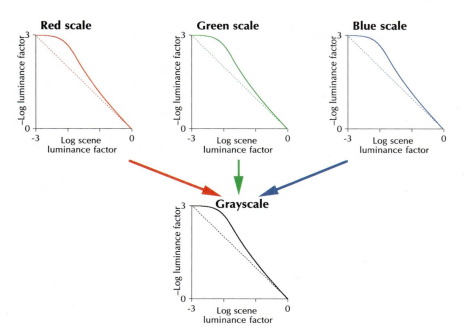

Figure 4.27
A monitor grayscale is comprised of red, green, and blue light. If the grayscale shape is altered (e.g., from the dotted unity line to the solid curve) using *RGB* signals, the individual red, green, and blue scales also are affected.

Figure 4.28
Chroma increases
associated with
the 15% slope in-
crease and view-
ing flare compen-
sation resulting
from the use of
ITU signal pro-
cessing. The *a* b**
values are based
on measurements
made in the
absence of flare
light.

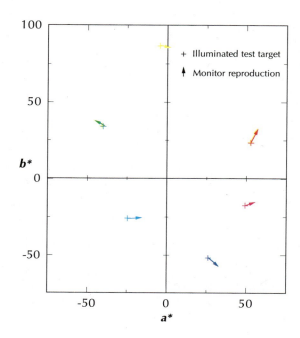

Some video texts suggest that the greater-than-unity slope—often called *system gamma*—of a video grayscale characteristic is required because video displays generally are viewed in a dim-surround viewing environment, i.e., an environment in which the displayed image is somewhat brighter than the areas immediately surrounding the display. However, our experience is that when the original is a live scene, red, green, and blue slope increases of 15 to 20% (in addition to any slope increases required for viewing-flare correction) are desirable on all video-display systems, including systems where the display is viewed in *average-surround* conditions. This is particularly true when the original is a highly illuminated outdoor scene.

Furthermore, if these desirable slope increases were related only to a dim-surround effect, then only luminance values would need to be altered. (The dim-surround has been shown to affect perceived luminance contrast almost exclusively.) However, our experience is that higher-quality images invariably are produced when the increase is applied to each of the *RGB* signals, rather than to just a luminance signal. Increasing the slope of the *RGB* signals results in increases in luminance contrast *and* color saturation, which suggests that the adjustment is required for reasons other than dim-surround correction. As discussed earlier, the possible reasons include compensation for the relatively low absolute luminances of the monitor, lack of image sharpness, color memory effects, and color reproduction preferences.

What is true, however, is that in some viewing conditions, including most home television viewing, an *additional* increase in luminance contrast (but not color contrast) is required in order to compensate for dim-surround viewing. That additional luminance contrast requirement is consistent with the higher-slope grayscale characteristics, compared to those of broadcast studio and computer monitors, measured on home receivers. In television systems, this increase can be made conveniently at the receiver, where the signal processing is arranged such that luminance contrast can be increased without increasing the chromas of colors.

An Ideal Video System

From this analysis, it can be seen that in an ideal video system (Fig. 4.29), the camera would have spectral responsivities equivalent to an all-positive set of color-matching functions. The ideal camera would contain a signal-processing matrix to transform its linear color-signal values to those that would have been formed if the camera had spectral responsivities equivalent to the particular color-matching functions for the monitor primaries. Nonlinear signal processing also would be used in the ideal video camera to produce color signals that, when used by the monitor, would produce desirable colorimetric departures from a one-to-one colorimetric reproduction of the original scene.

Although the responsivities shown in Fig. 4.29 are equivalent to the color-matching functions of the CIE 1931 Standard Colorimetric Observer, it generally is more appropriate to use responsivities equivalent to other sets of all-positive color-matching functions. Appropriately chosen responsivities, such as those shown in Fig. 4.30, can reduce the magnitudes of the signal-processing matrix coefficients. This is important, because most forms of electronic noise increase significantly as the magnitudes of the matrix coefficients increase.

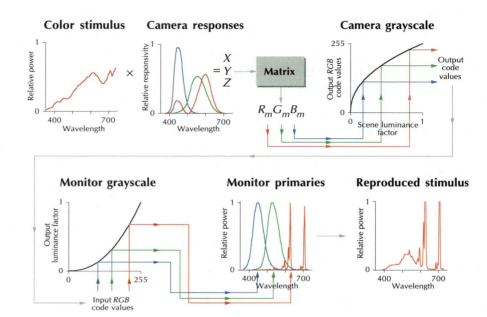

Figure 4.29
An ideal video system. The system includes a camera having spectral responsivities equivalent to a set of all-positive color-matching functions. It also includes appropriate signal processing of the camera *RGB* exposures.

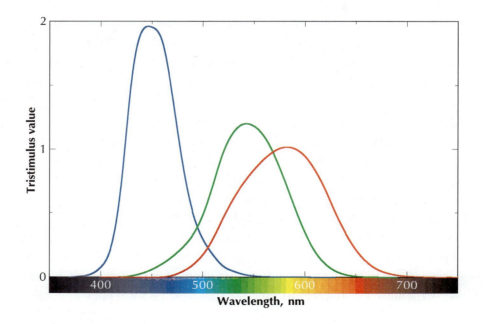

Figure 4.30
These spectral responsivities are equivalent to a set of color-matching functions different from those that define the CIE 1931 Standard Observer. Use of spectral responsivities such as these can reduce the magnitudes of the signal-processing matrix terms.

Actual digital still cameras and other types of video cameras conform to this ideal to varying degrees. While perhaps no camera has spectral responsivities that are exactly equivalent to a set of color-matching functions, some come reasonably close. Most video cameras incorporate matrices to transform their linear signals according to reference color primaries defined by industry standards. Virtually all produce nonlinear output signals, again in accordance with industry standards, which, when used with an appropriately set-up monitor, produce an overall system grayscale characteristic closely approximating that previously shown in Fig. 4.22.

Color-Encoding Considerations

This analysis has produced two important outcomes that directly relate to color encoding. First, it has shown that the optimum video reproduction of a live original scene is *not* a one-to-one reproduction of the scene colorimetry. That result is not unique to video systems. It is just one illustration of the fact that in order to produce a visual match under most circumstances, the colorimetry of the reproduction must differ from that of the original.

The analysis also has shown that video camera output signal values themselves do not correspond directly to original scene colorimetric values, nor do they correspond directly to reproduced colorimetric values. However, camera signal values can be color encoded in terms of colorimetric values if their relationships to original-scene colorimetry or to colorimetry reproduced on a video display are determined. This can be done in a number of ways. For example, the relationship between original-scene colorimetry and a particular digital video camera's output code values can be defined from a knowledge of that camera's spectral responsivities and its signal processing. The relationship also can be determined empirically using various calibration procedures. Such procedures generally include the use of color test targets and measurement methods that are similar to those described in this chapter.

The relationship between a video camera's $R'G'B'$ signal values and the colorimetry that is produced on a video display also can be defined using various calibration procedures. For example, arrays of camera output code values can be input to a monitor, and the colorimetry of the resulting stimuli can then be measured directly. Alternatively, the relationship can be determined based on knowledge of the output signal processing and the chromaticities of the monitor phosphors. A similar relationship between video camera signal values and output colorimetry can be derived based on the properties of a mathematically defined reference monitor.

The techniques that have just been described make it possible to color encode video camera signals either in terms of the colorimetry of the original scene captured by the camera or in terms of the colorimetry that would be produced if those signals were sent to an actual or reference monitor. Another alternative, of course, is simply to encode video signals directly in terms of their $R'G'B'$ signal values, without applying transformations to colorimetric values. Video signal values also can be transformed to those that would have been formed by a specified reference camera, and the reference camera signal values can be used in the encoding process. Each of these types of color encoding can be valid, depending on the particular application.

The decision as to which type of color encoding should be used for a given color-imaging system is not always a simple one to make, as will be discussed in later sections. One important factor in that decision is the nature of any hardcopy (nonvideo) input sources the particular system also might support. Those sources are discussed in the next three chapters.

Summary of Key Issues

- An ideal video camera would have spectral responsivities equivalent to the color-matching functions of the system monitor primaries.

- Because the color-matching functions of monitor primaries, and all other real output devices, have negative values at some wavelengths, the equivalent spectral responsivities are not physically realizable.

- Signals equal to those that would be produced from physically unrealizable spectral responsivities can be achieved by applying an appropriate matrix transformation to signals produced by a camera having spectral responsivities equivalent to a set of all-positive color-matching functions.

- Matrixed signals will have positive values for colors that are within the color gamut of the monitor. Colors outside this gamut will produce negative values in at least one of the color signals. Negative signal values will be clipped at a typical display device, such as a CRT.

- The optimum video reproduction of a live original scene is not a one-to-one reproduction of the scene's colorimetry.

- A video system grayscale must depart from a one-to-one colorimetric relationship with the original scene in order to compensate appropriately for viewing flare and to account for the effects resulting from various perceptual factors.

- Video camera signals themselves do not correspond directly to original scene or reproduced colorimetric values.

- For color encoding purposes, the relationships among scene colorimetry, video camera signals, and reproduced colorimetry must be defined.

5 Reflection Images

Scans of hardcopy images—such as reflection prints, photographic slides, and negatives—are the principal input source of color information in many color-imaging systems. This chapter begins an analysis of the nature of hardcopy images with an examination of the colorimetric characteristics of images on reflection media.

Reflection images can be produced by conventional and instant photography, graphic arts printing, thermal dye transfer, inkjet printing, and by a number of other technologies. However, regardless of the exact technology employed in their production, most high-quality reflection images share certain fundamental characteristics and colorimetric relationships to original

Figure 5.1

Image capture,
signal processing,
and image forma-
tion in an experi-
mental reflection-
print system.

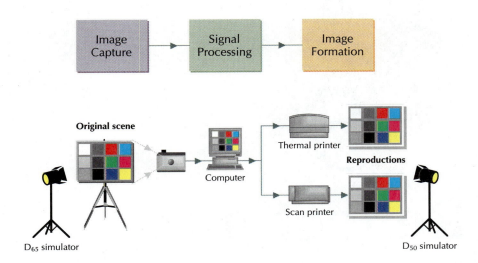

Figure 5.1

Image capture, signal processing, and image formation in an experimental reflection-print system.

scenes. Those characteristics and relationships will be examined in the context of an experimental color-imaging system (Fig. 5.1) consisting of a digital still camera, a computer, a thermal-transfer printer, and a scan printer that writes directly onto a conventional photographic paper. The system produces very high quality images on both thermal and photographic reflection media.

The test target that was described in Chapter 4 will again be used in the analysis of the system. As before, the target will be illuminated by a light source simulating CIE Standard Illuminant D_{65}. The test target colorimetry will be computed from the measured spectral reflectances of its patches and the spectral power distribution of the light source. Images reproduced on the reflection media will be illuminated by a different light source—one simulating CIE Standard Illuminant D_{50} (Fig. 5.2), which is an industry standard for indoor viewing of reflection images. The situation is both realistic and common; it corresponds, for example, to photographing scenes outdoors and subsequently viewing the reproduction indoors.

The illuminated reproductions will be measured using a colorimeter placed such that the measurements are free of flare light. The measured colorimetric values of the illuminated reproductions then will be compared to those computed for the illuminated test target.

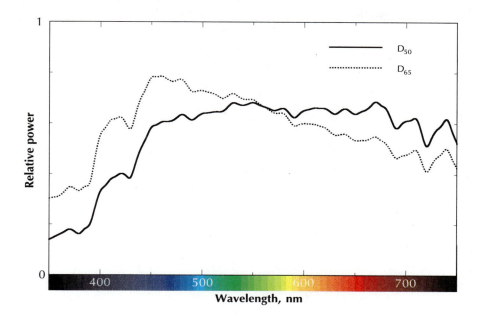

Figure 5.2
Relative spectral power distributions for CIE Standard Illuminants D_{50} and D_{65}.

Reflection Media: General Characteristics

Figure 5.3 illustrates the basic light-modifying properties of a reflection medium consisting of a colorant (dye, ink, or pigment) and a reflective support. Light incident on the medium is absorbed at least twice by the colorant: once as that light passes through the colorant to the support, and a second time after it reflects from the support and passes through the colorant again. Light reflecting from the support generally will be scattered in all directions, so some of that light will be subject to various types of internal reflections before leaving the medium. Some incident light may be reflected from the front surface of the medium without passing through the colorant. Such front surface reflections cause flare in reflection-image viewing, and that flare must be accounted for in the design of the imaging system.

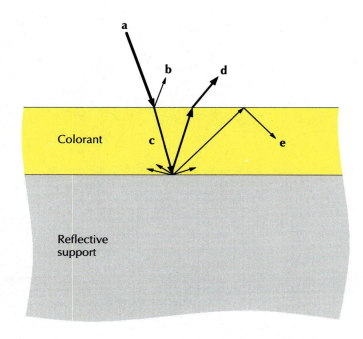

Figure 5.3

Reflection optics. A fraction of the light (a) incident on a reflection medium may reflect from the front surface (b). Most incident light will pass through the colorant to the support (c), where it will be scattered in all directions. Light reflected from the support will again pass through the colorant to the surface, where it may exit (d) or be internally reflected (e). Depending on the nature of the medium, other types of internal reflections also may occur.

Color reflection media use multiple colorants to selectively absorb particular wavelengths of light. In the three-colorant media that will be discussed here, a cyan dye is used to absorb red light, a magenta dye to absorb green light, and a yellow dye to absorb blue light. In a thermal printer, these image-forming dyes are transferred sequentially from a donor to a reflective support (Fig. 5.4a). The amount of each dye that is transferred is determined by the red, green, and blue image signals sent to the printer.

Conventional photographic papers also use cyan, magenta, and yellow image-forming dyes to absorb red light, green light, and blue light, respectively. These dyes are formed within three separate layers that are coated on a reflective support (Fig. 5.4b). The amount of each dye that is formed is determined by the amount of exposure received in each layer. The exposing light may come from an optical device, such as an enlarger used in printing photographic negatives. In the experimental system described here, the exposure is provided by a scan printer. The amount of each dye that is formed is controlled by the red, green, and blue image signals sent to the printer.

Side view

Top view

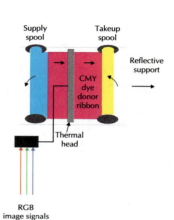

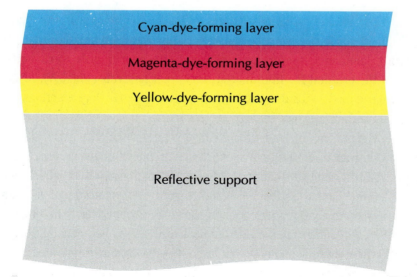

Figure 5.4a
In a thermal printer, cyan, magenta, and yellow dyes are transferred sequentially from a donor to a reflective support.

Cyan-dye-forming layer

Magenta-dye-forming layer

Yellow-dye-forming layer

Reflective support

Figure 5.4b
In a photographic paper, cyan, magenta, and yellow dyes are formed within light-sensitive layers coated on a reflective support.

Reflection Neutrals: Colorimetric Considerations

In the video system examined in the previous chapter, neutrals were defined as stimuli having chromaticity coordinates identical to those of the original-scene illuminant. That is why the CRT white point was set to those chromaticities. However, the experimental reflection-print system being studied here is different in two respects.

First, unlike a self-luminous CRT display, a reflection image alone cannot generate color stimuli. A reflection image is an *object* that forms stimuli only when illuminated. A viewing illuminant therefore is required, and the spectral power characteristics of the resulting stimuli will be influenced directly by the spectral power characteristics of that illuminant.

Second, there are *two* illuminants used in the experimental system: a D_{65} source for illuminating the original scene, and a D_{50} source for illuminating the reflection image. The chromaticities of the two illuminants are different ($x = 0.3127, y = 0.3290$ for D_{65}; $x = 0.3457, y = 0.3585$ for D_{50}). This chromaticity difference, and the effect that difference will have on the observer, must be taken into account when evaluating neutrals reproduced by the system.

For example, suppose the spectral reflectances of the system's reproduced neutrals were such that when they were illuminated by D_{50} their resulting luminance factors and chromaticity coordinates were equal to those of the original D_{65}-illuminated test-target neutrals (Fig. 5.5). Although such reproduced neutrals would be exact *colorimetric* reproductions of the target neutrals, they would *appear* too blue.

The reason for this is that an observer's state of chromatic adaptation will be different in the original-scene and reproduced-image viewing environments. As described in Chapter 3, chromatic adaptation is an adjustment of the visual mechanism in response to the average chromaticity of the stimuli being viewed. An area of a reflection image generally must have the same chromaticity *as that of the viewing illuminant* in order to appear neutral. To appear neutral when viewed in the D_{50}-illuminated viewing environment, then, the reproduced neutrals must have the chromaticity of D_{50}, not of D_{65} (Fig. 5.6).

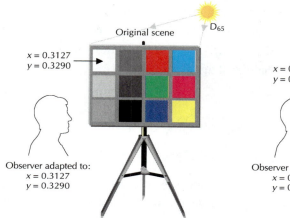

Original scene

$x = 0.3127$
$y = 0.3290$

D_{65}

Observer adapted to:
$x = 0.3127$
$y = 0.3290$

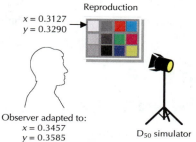

Reproduction

$x = 0.3127$
$y = 0.3290$

Observer adapted to:
$x = 0.3457$
$y = 0.3585$

D_{50} simulator

Figure 5.5
Under these view-
ing conditions, a
colorimetric
reproduction of a
D_{65}-illuminated
test-target neutral
would *not* appear
neutral.

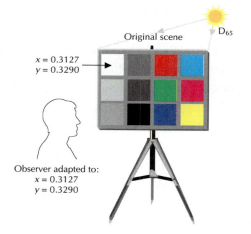

Original scene

$x = 0.3127$
$y = 0.3290$

D_{65}

Observer adapted to:
$x = 0.3127$
$y = 0.3290$

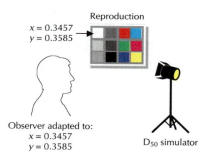

Reproduction

$x = 0.3457$
$y = 0.3585$

Observer adapted to:
$x = 0.3457$
$y = 0.3585$

D_{50} simulator

Figure 5.6
To appear neutral
under a D_{50} view-
ing illuminant, a
reproduction of a
test-target neutral
must have a chro-
maticity equal to
that of D_{50}.

In the experimental system, reflection reproductions of the test target neutral patches are made such that they appear neutral when viewed in the D_{50} environment. Colorimetric measurements of those neutrals confirm that they have a chromaticity equal to that of D_{50}. The characteristics the reproduced neutrals must have to achieve that result are discussed next.

Reflection Neutrals: Spectral Characteristics

Neutrals, and other colors, are produced on three-dye reflection media from combined appropriate amounts of cyan, magenta, and yellow dyes. For any given set of CMY dyes, reflective support, and viewing illuminant, there is one and only one combination of dye amounts that will produce a visual neutral of a given luminance-factor value.

For example, Fig. 5.7a shows the spectral characteristics for the dyes and paper support of the photographic paper used in the experimental system. The dye characteristics are expressed in terms of spectral reflection density, which is the negative logarithm of spectral reflectance. Reflection density values, rather than reflectance values, are used here and throughout this discussion because changes in density values correlate more closely with changes in appearance. Figure 5.7b shows the relative amounts of those dyes required to form a neutral of visual reflection density 1.00 (a luminance-factor value $Y = 0.10$) when a D_{50} viewing illuminant is used. Also shown are the spectral reflection densities for that neutral and a spectrally nonselective neutral of 1.00 reflection density.

Notice that the neutral formed by the CMY dyes is somewhat spectrally selective, i.e., it does not absorb or reflect light equally at each wavelength. The neutral therefore is a *metameric* match to a spectrally nonselective neutral. As was discussed earlier, objects that are metameric matches under one illuminant may not match under another illuminant. Therefore, different spectral reflectances may be required in order to produce metameric neutral stimuli under different illuminants. For spectral reflectances to be made different, the amounts of the CMY dyes forming those reflectances must be adjusted.

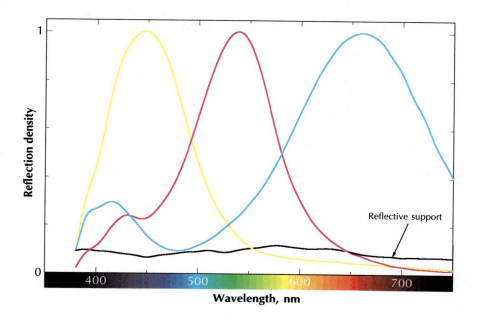

Figure 5.7a
Spectral reflection density characteristics for a set of photographic cyan, magenta, and yellow dyes and a reflective support.

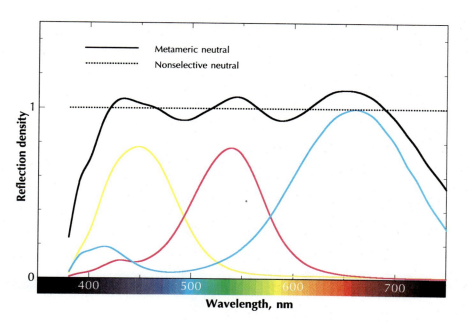

Figure 5.7b
Spectral reflection densities for a nonselective neutral and a metamerically matching neutral formed using the cyan, magenta, and yellow dyes of Fig. 5.7a. Also shown are the relative amounts of the CMY dyes needed to form the metameric neutral.

Media in which the relative amounts of colorants must be changed significantly in order to form visual neutrals under different viewing illuminants are said to be viewing illuminant sensitive. Reflection media can differ greatly in this characteristic, depending on the spectral absorption properties of their colorants. In the following figures, the degrees of viewing illuminant sensitivity of the two reflection media of the experimental system and one hypothetical medium will be compared.

Figure 5.8a shows the spectral reflection densities for a set of CMY *block dyes* used in the hypothetical medium, and Fig. 5.8b shows the spectral reflection densities for two neutrals formed by those dyes. The neutrals are those determined for two different viewing conditions. In one, the light source simulates CIE Standard Illuminant D_{50}; in the other, the light source is a particular type of fluorescent lamp. The spectral reflection densities of the two neutrals are *identical,* as would be expected. Since a neutral produced from these dyes absorbs (and reflects) light equally at each wavelength, it *always* will have the same chromaticity as the light source itself. If, as has been assumed, the observer

Figure 5.8a

Spectral reflection density characteristics for a set of hypothetical cyan, magenta, and yellow block dyes.

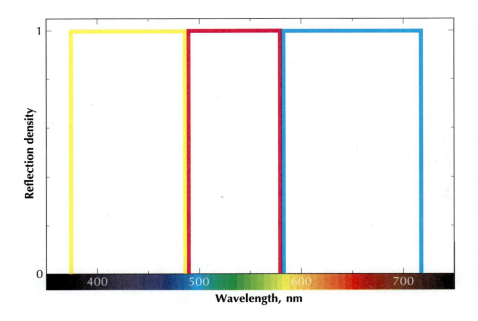

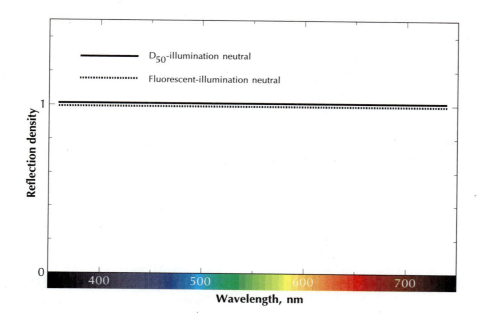

Figure 5.8b
The neutrals of a reflection medium having block dyes are not viewing-illuminant sensitive. The spectral densities of the neutrals are identical for the two viewing conditions.

chromatically adapts to the chromaticity of each light source, then an area that appears neutral on this medium under one light source also will appear neutral under any other light source. Neutrals formed on this medium therefore are not at all viewing-illuminant sensitive. That is a very desirable feature for a reflection medium to have, because a given reflection image is likely to be viewed under a variety of different illumination conditions.

The situation is somewhat different when the dyes of the photographic paper of the experimental system are used. The spectral characteristics of these dyes are shown in Fig. 5.9a. Figure 5.9b shows that different spectral reflection densities are required in order to produce visual neutrals under each of the two previously described viewing conditions. However, although the spectral density characteristics of these neutrals are different, their basic similarities indicate that the photographic paper may not be highly viewing-illuminant sensitive. An area of this medium that appears neutral when viewed under one light source likely will appear neutral, or at least nearly neutral, when viewed under most other light sources. In practice, that is the case.

Figure 5.9a

Spectral reflection density character-istics for a set of cyan, magenta, and yellow photo-graphic paper dyes.

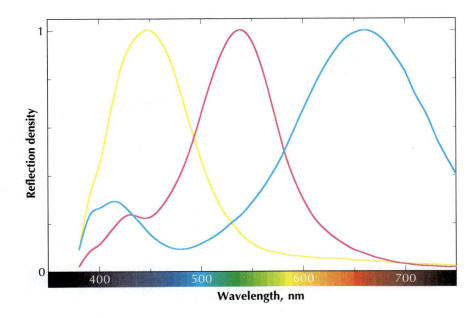

Figure 5.9b

The neutrals of a reflection medium using the photo-graphic paper dyes have rela-tively little view-ing-illuminant sensitivity.

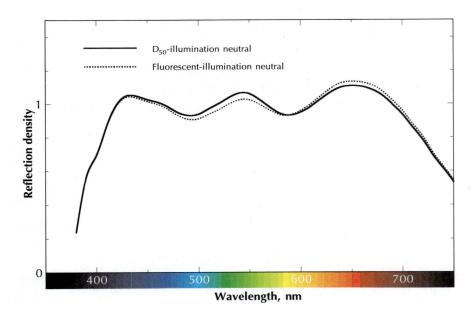

Figure 5.10b shows comparable spectral reflection densities for the neutrals of the thermal dye-transfer medium used in the experimental system. The spectral characteristics of these dyes are shown in Fig. 5.10a. Note that the neutrals of this medium are much more spectrally selective than those of the photographic paper. Moreover, note that quite different spectral reflection densities are required in order to produce neutrals under each of the two light sources. These are strong indications that the thermal medium is quite viewing-illuminant sensitive, which indeed it is.

The appearance of images produced on a viewing-illuminant-sensitive medium can be very different under different light sources. For example, if a typical thermal dye-transfer image is viewed under a variety of illumination conditions, such as by window light, fluorescent light, and tungsten light, the overall color balance of the image and the appearance of neutrals and other specific colors within the image will change significantly. For critical imaging applications, it may be necessary to produce custom images designed specifically for the particular illuminant that will be used for viewing.

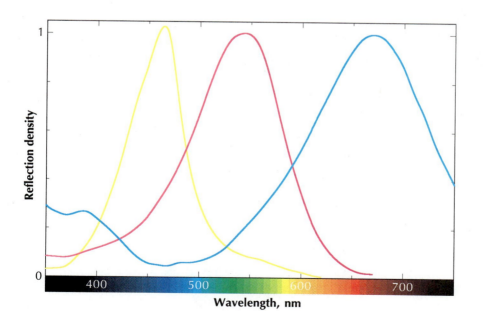

Figure 5.10a
Spectral reflection density characteristics for one set of cyan, magenta, and yellow thermal transfer dyes.

Figure 5.10b
Figure 5.10b
The neutrals of a reflection medium using the thermal transfer dyes are viewing-illuminant sensitive.

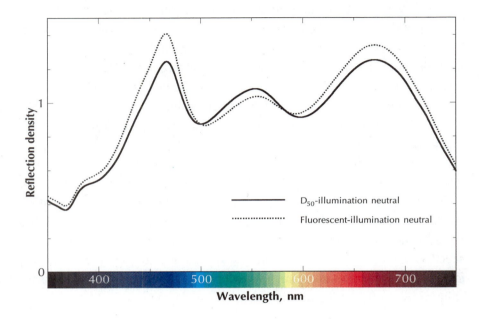

Reflection Neutrals: Grayscale Characteristics

The overall system grayscales—from the original scene to the reflection print—for each of the outputs of the experimental system can be characterized by photographing the test target and measuring the neutrals of the resulting prints. In this discussion, system grayscales will be specified in terms of reproduced visual densities (negative log luminance factor) as a function of original scene log luminance factor.

When the signal processing of the experimental system is adjusted such that high-quality reflection images of live scenes are obtained, the system grayscale characteristic (on either the photographic or the thermal medium) is substantially that shown in Fig. 5.11. Similar results would be obtained from almost any high-quality reflection-print system used for reproducing live scenes, such as a system consisting of a color photographic negative film and a color photographic paper.

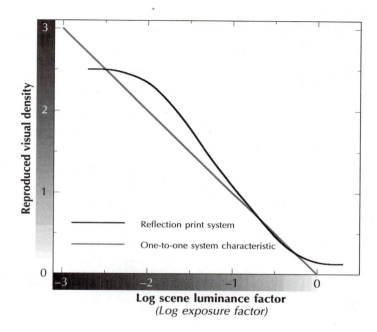

Figure 5.11
Grayscale char-
acteristic for a
high quality reflec-
tion-print system,
expressed in terms
of reproduced
visual density as
a function of log
scene luminance
factor. A one-to-
one system char-
acteristic is shown
for reference.

The shape of the grayscale characteristic reveals that the system does not simply generate images that are one-to-one colorimetric reproductions of original scenes. As was the case for the video system discussed previously, a one-to-one colorimetric reproduction of an original is appropriate only when the original *itself* is a reproduction, and only when the original and its reproduction are to be viewed under identical conditions.

Note that the grayscale characteristic for the reflection-print system is similar in many respects to that of a video system (Fig. 4.22). That similarity is not unexpected, since many of the factors that required departures from one-to-one colorimetric reproduction in the video system are present in a reflection-print system as well. One of those factors is viewing flare.

In reflection-image viewing, viewing flare occurs when incident light is reflected directly from the front surface of the medium. The amount of flare will vary, depending on the surface texture of the medium and other factors. As in the video system, the system grayscale must be designed such that it provides compensation for the anticipated amount of viewing flare.

Figure 5.12 shows three practical reflection-print system grayscales that incorporate compensation for different levels of viewing flare. Note that as more viewing-flare compensation is included, the higher-density portions of the grayscales are increased in density. However, these densities cannot exceed the maximum density achievable by the medium. Therefore, the compensation is less successful as the required amount of that compensation is increased.

Another factor affecting the departure from a one-to-one grayscale reproduction is that reflection images generally are viewed indoors, where the level of illumination is much lower than is typical outdoors. The absolute luminances of images viewed indoors therefore will be relatively low. As discussed previously, images having lower absolute luminances will be perceived to have lower luminance contrast.

Compensation for this contrast effect can be achieved by increasing the overall *slope* of the grayscale characteristic (Fig. 5.13). In photographic terms, that slope is referred to simply as gamma. However, to avoid confusion with the previously described gamma (the exponent used in CRT equations),

Figure 5.12

Reflection-print system grayscales incorporating compensation for three different levels of viewing flare. The black curve provides the most compensation of the three, the light-gray curve the least.

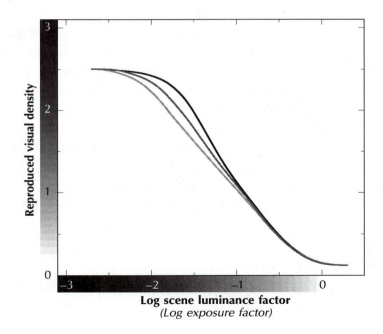

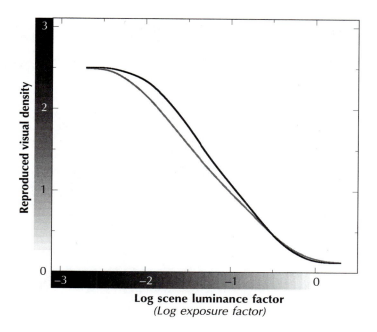

Figure 5.13
Increasing the photographic gamma of a system grayscale characteristic can provide compensation for a reduction in apparent luminance contrast. Both characteristics shown in the figure also include compensation for 0.75% viewing flare.

the expression *photographic gamma* will be used from this point on when referring to measurements of hardcopy media.

Although the photographic gamma of any successful reflection-print system in which the originals are live scenes will be greater than unity, that of any given system will depend somewhat on its intended application. For example, reflection-print systems designed for portraiture generally are somewhat lower in photographic gamma, while those intended for amateur applications and some types of commercial advertising generally are higher. The grayscale characteristics of different reflection-print systems also may differ because of the particular capabilities and limitations of their reflection media. For example, each medium has a minimum density, which depends on the reflectance of its support and the density of any overcoated layers. Each medium also has a maximum density, which is limited by how much colorant can be formed or deposited in any given area and by certain other factors. The overall shape of the grayscale characteristic must be consistent with those density limits, as has been the case for all of the practical grayscale characteristics shown thus far.

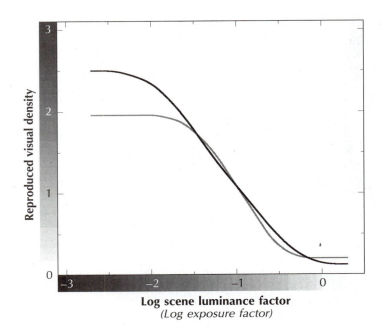

Figure 5.14

Grayscale characteristics for two reflection-print media having different minimum and maximum densities. The medium with the lower maximum density and higher minimum density (shown in gray) requires a higher photographic gamma in order to produce both whites and blacks at acceptable density levels.

In general, media having lower maximum densities and higher minimum densities must have somewhat higher mid-scale photographic gammas in order to produce whites and blacks at acceptable densities. This is illustrated in the grayscale characteristics of the two media shown in Fig. 5.14.

Note that there is a significant amount of nonlinearity (beyond that required for flare compensation) in all of the reflection system grayscale characteristics that have been shown thus far. These nonlinearities are essential. They compress information from the high and low ends of the scene exposure range. That compression makes it possible for the reflection medium to display as much of the original exposure information as possible, given the minimum and maximum density limits of the medium itself.

Attempts sometimes are made to "correct" these grayscale nonlinearities by various means, particularly in digital-imaging systems where grayscales can be linearized easily by the use of digital signal processing. However, when this is done, the resulting images inevitably are poor because they fail to reproduce visually important details in highlight and shadow areas.

Reflection Colors: Colorimetric Considerations

A meaningful evaluation of reproduced colorimetry from a color-imaging system must take into account effects due to the observer's state of chromatic adaptation. This is a particularly important consideration for reflection-print systems, because reflection images typically are viewed under conditions where there are numerous other visual cues—such as white objects and specular reflections of light from the viewing illuminant—that cause the observer to chromatically adapt to the conditions of the viewing environment rather than to the color reproduction properties of the images themselves.

When the observer's state of chromatic adaptation is different in the original-scene and reproduced-image viewing environments, reproduced colorimetric values should be compared to original colorimetric values that have been *transformed* appropriately to visually equivalent colorimetric values. The transformed values describe a color stimulus that would produce, for an observer chromatically adapted to the reproduced-image viewing illuminant, a visual match to the original color stimulus viewed by an observer who is chromatically adapted to the original-scene illuminant.

That last sentence may warrant rereading; the idea is not easy to grasp. But it is critical that the concept of chromatic adaptation be understood before proceeding. The appropriate use of chromatic adaptation transforms is essential for evaluating color-imaging systems, as is being done here. In addition, such transforms play a major role in the appearance-based color-encoding methods that will be discussed later.

A number of different transformation techniques can be used to determine visually equivalent colorimetric values. At present, the CIE is seeking an agreed upon model of color vision that will include a process for performing highly accurate chromatic adaptation transformations. Of the existing techniques, a von Kries matrix transformation, which is described in Appendix D, is one of the simplest. The method is used widely, and it generally works quite well, especially in situations where the differences in adaptation chromaticities are relatively small.

The matrix equation below is an example of a von Kries transformation of CIE XYZ values for D_{65} chromatic adaptation to visually equivalent CIE XYZ values for D_{50} chromatic adaptation.

$$\begin{bmatrix} X_{D50} \\ Y_{D50} \\ Z_{D50} \end{bmatrix} = \begin{bmatrix} 1.0161 & 0.0553 & -0.0522 \\ 0.0060 & 0.9956 & -0.0012 \\ 0.0000 & 0.0000 & 0.7576 \end{bmatrix} \begin{bmatrix} X_{D65} \\ Y_{D65} \\ Z_{D65} \end{bmatrix} \qquad \{5.1\}$$

The XYZ_{D50} values describe a color stimulus that would produce, for an observer chromatically adapted to the chromaticity of D_{50}, a visual match to the original XYZ_{D65} stimulus viewed by an observer who is chromatically adapted to the chromaticity of D_{65}. Note that if the XYZ values for CIE Standard Illuminant D_{65} ($X = 95.04$, $Y = 100.00$, $Z = 108.89$) are transformed using this matrix, the resulting values ($X = 96.42$, $Y = 100.00$, $Z = 82.49$) will be those for CIE Standard Illuminant D_{50}. This is consistent with the assumption that the observer is chromatically adapted to the chromaticity of the viewing illuminant.

Table 5.1 lists the original and transformed colorimetric values for each of the patches of the test target. The chromaticity coordinates for the two sets of tristimulus values are compared graphically in Fig. 5.15. The chromaticities are plotted in terms of CIE u', v' coordinates, rather than CIE x, y coordinates, to better illustrate the magnitudes of the colorimetric transformations.

Reflection Colors: Other Characteristics

In the experimental system, grayscale modifications required to compensate for viewing flare and low absolute luminances are accomplished by adjusting RGB, rather than luminance, signal processing. Doing so has the effect of altering the characteristics of the cyan, magenta, and yellow scales that make up the grayscale (Fig. 5.16). This results in higher overall reproduced color saturation, which is desirable because it helps compensate for the color saturation decreases associated with viewing flare and with the relatively low absolute luminance levels of the reflection images (Fig. 5.17).

Test Target Color	D$_{65}$-Illuminated Test Target Values			Visually Equivalent D$_{50}$ Viewing Environment Values		
	X_{D65}	Y_{D65}	Z_{D65}	X_{D50}	Y_{D50}	Z_{D50}
Neutral 1	0.9504	1.0000	1.0889	0.9642	1.0000	0.8249
Neutral 2	0.5598	0.5890	0.6414	0.5679	0.5890	0.4859
Neutral 3	0.3450	0.3630	0.3953	0.3500	0.3630	0.2995
Neutral 4	0.1901	0.2000	0.2178	0.1929	0.2000	0.1650
Neutral 5	0.0846	0.0890	0.0969	0.0858	0.0890	0.0734
Neutral 6	0.0304	0.0320	0.0348	0.0308	0.0320	0.0264
Red	0.2000	0.1180	0.0560	0.2068	0.1186	0.0424
Green	0.1480	0.2380	0.0990	0.1584	0.2377	0.0750
Blue	0.0850	0.0620	0.3070	0.0738	0.0619	0.2326
Cyan	0.1490	0.2050	0.4040	0.1416	0.2045	0.3061
Magenta	0.2980	0.1970	0.3240	0.2968	0.1975	0.2455
Yellow	0.6270	0.6820	0.0980	0.6697	0.6826	0.0742

Table 5.1
Comparison of test target XYZ tristimulus values for D$_{65}$ illumination and visually equivalent XYZ tristimulus values based on D$_{50}$ chromatic adaptation. The values were computed using a von Kries transformation matrix.

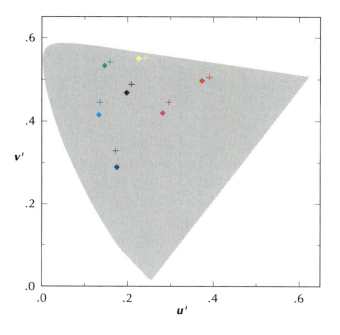

Figure 5.15
CIE u', v' diagram showing a comparison of test target chromaticities for D$_{65}$ illumination (♦) and visually equivalent chromaticities based on D$_{50}$ chromatic adaptation (+). The equivalent values were computed using a von Kries transformation matrix.

Figure 5.16

A subtractive grayscale and its component cyan, magenta, and yellow dye scales.

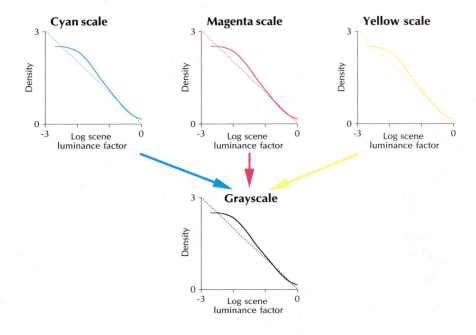

Figure 5.17

The vector arrows indicate the chroma increases associated with the photographic gamma increase and viewing flare compensation described in the text. The *a* b** values are based on measurements made in the absence of flare light.

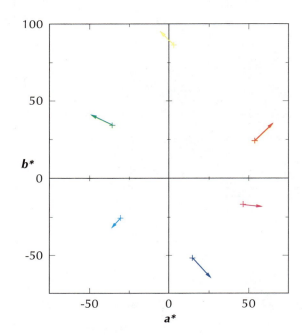

In most reflection-print systems, additional signal processing is used to further modify color reproduction. Color reproduction may be altered to compensate for color memory effects, to account for various color preferences, or to adjust the overall color saturation to best meet the goals of the intended application. The exact methods used by manufacturers to adjust and optimize the color reproduction of their media and systems vary, and such methods usually are proprietary. However, the general ideas behind these methods, and their relationship to the concepts that have been discussed, can be illustrated for the experimental system.

Figure 5.18 shows that in the experimental system, the video camera has spectral responsivities equivalent to a set of all-positive color-matching functions. A matrix is used to transform the linear RGB color signal values produced by the camera to CIE XYZ_{D65} values. This is followed by a chromatic adaptation matrix to transform the D_{65} colorimetric values to visually equivalent D_{50} colorimetric values. A third matrix, which is a function of the particular cyan, magenta, and yellow dye set used in the output medium, then is used to transform from XYZ_{D50} values to RGB_m values.

Appropriate nonlinear processing then is used such that the overall system grayscale characteristic corresponds to that shown in Fig. 5.11. Finally, a fourth matrix, or some other form of three-dimensional signal processing, is used to create desirable interactions among the nonlinear color signals. These interactions are used to control overall color saturation and to produce other desirable colorimetric alterations. The determination of these nonlinear interactions is well beyond the scope of this book, but it is important to know that variations in their use produce very significant differences in the color-reproduction properties of different reflection-print systems.

When appropriate signal processing is used, a reflection-print system based on the experimental system will produce excellent quality images. The colorimetric results of the system are shown in Fig. 5.19. These results show that the reproduced colorimetry matches the modified colorimetry of Fig. 5.17 for all colors within the gamut of the output medium. These results also show once again that high-quality reproductions of original scenes are not simply one-to-one reproductions of the original colorimetry.

Figure 5.18

Signal processing in the experimental reflection-print system. The output is shown both in terms of reflection density and linear reflectance.

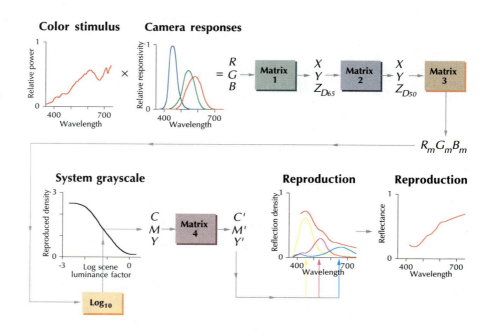

Figure 5.19

Colorimetric results of an actual reflection-print system based on the experimental system. The **+** marks indicate equivalent (chromatically adapted) D_{50} values for the D_{65}-illuminated test target. The vector arrowheads indicate the overall system reproductions.

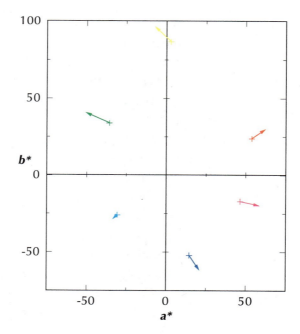

The colorimetric behavior of other actual reflection-print systems corresponds to that of this experimental system to various degrees. As mentioned earlier, some differences are deliberate and are based on the specific application for which the system is designed. Other differences are unavoidable, due to limitations of the particular devices and media that are involved. For example, implementing all of the color signal processing that has been described for the experimental system can be quite difficult in a conventional photographic system where that processing must be accomplished using chemistry alone.

Color-Encoding Considerations

This analysis has raised several issues that have consequences related to the scanning and color encoding of reflection images. The fact that reflection images are objects that produce stimuli only when illuminated means that the colorimetry they ultimately will produce cannot be determined and numerically represented unless the spectral power distribution of the intended viewing illuminant is specified. Meaningful interpretation of the resulting colorimetric values requires that the amount of flare in the viewing environment and the observer's state of chromatic adaptation also be known.

Viewing illuminant sensitivity was discussed in terms of changes in image appearance with changes in viewing illuminant, but such sensitivity also is an important consideration for input scanning. Viewing-illuminant-sensitive media are problematic input sources. The values that are measured from such media are strongly affected by variations in the spectral properties of the scanner, such as the spectral power distribution of its illuminant and the spectral sensitivities of its sensor.

This analysis has also described some of the reasons why different reflection-print systems and media have unique and distinctive appearances. Whether such distinctions should be retained fully, modified, or removed entirely during the color-encoding process is an important issue that will need to be revisited in later discussions.

Summary of Key Issues

- Reflection images are objects that produce stimuli only when illuminated. Their colorimetry is directly affected by the spectral characteristics of the illuminant.

- Reflection media differ greatly in their sensitivity to changes in viewing illuminant spectral power distribution.

- Reflection images are perceived as objects within a viewing environment. The observer's state of adaptation is determined by that environment. There is little or no adaptation to the image itself.

- Differences in the observer's adaptive state in the original and print viewing environments must be accounted for in the design of a reflection-print system.

- A chromatic adaptation transformation can be used to determine visually equivalent tristimulus values for two states of observer adaptation.

- An optimum reflection-print system must depart from a one-to-one colorimetric relationship with the original scene in order to compensate appropriately for viewing flare and to provide desirable colorimetric alterations.

- Different reflection-print systems and media have distinctive appearances that result from their particular capabilities and limitations and from differences in the applications for which they were designed.

6
Photographic Transparencies

Photographic transparencies, such as 35-mm slides and large-format sheet films, presently are the most commonly used form of input for high-end color-imaging systems. There are good reasons for this. Photographic transparency films are capable of extraordinary image quality—high sharpness, low noise—and they can record and reproduce a wide range of colors. Because they can be viewed directly for evaluation and selection, photographic transparencies are the favorite medium of most magazine and catalog editors. Photographic transparency media have certain unique colorimetric characteristics, however, that must be taken into account when transparencies are to be scanned and color encoded.

General Characteristics

Figure 6.1 shows a simplified cross-section of a photographic transparency film. The film has a blue-light-sensitive layer, a green-light-sensitive layer, and a red-light-sensitive layer, which are coated on a clear support. Because both the green-light-sensitive and red-light-sensitive layers also are inherently sensitive to blue light, a yellow filter layer is coated above these layers to prevent any blue light from reaching them.

Photographic transparency films are designed to be used with specific image-capture illuminants. For example, some films are designed for daylight-illumination photography, while others are designed for tungsten-illumination photography. In the manufacturing of a photographic transparency film, the relative sensitivities (*speeds*) of the red-light-sensitive, green-light-sensitive, and blue-light-sensitive layers are balanced such that properly color-balanced images result when scenes illuminated by the reference scene illuminant are photographed. Use of any other type of scene illuminant most likely will result in images having an overall color-balance shift.

Figure 6.1
Simplified cross-section of a photographic transparency film (prior to chemical processing).

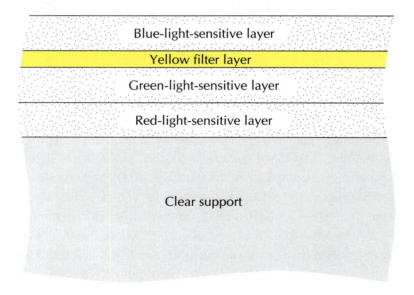

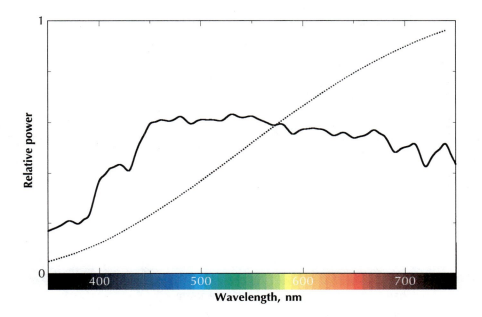

Figure 6.2
Spectral power
distributions of
CIE Standard
Illuminant D_{55}
(solid line) and a
tungsten light
source (dotted
line).

For example, Fig. 6.2 shows the relative spectral power distributions for CIE Standard Illuminant D_{55} and a tungsten light source. Figure 6.3 shows the red, green, and blue spectral sensitivities of a representative *daylight* transparency film, which is balanced for D_{55} scene illumination. If this film were used to photograph a scene illuminated by a *tungsten* light source, the resulting slides would have an overall orange (red-yellow) color balance due to the relatively high red power and low blue power of the tungsten source.

Figure 6.3 also shows the red, green, and blue spectral sensitivities for a representative photographic transparency film that is balanced specifically for tungsten-illumination photography. Note that its red sensitivity is relatively low, and its blue sensitivity is relatively high, compared to the respective sensitivities of the daylight film.

When an exposed area of photographic transparency film is chemically processed, yellow, magenta, and cyan image dyes are formed in the blue-light, green-light, and red-light-sensitive layers, respectively (Fig. 6.4). A *positive* image results, i.e., the *maximum* amount of dye forms at the *minimum* exposure;

Figure 6.3

Red, green, and blue spectral sensitivities of representative daylight-balanced and tungsten-balanced photographic transparency films.

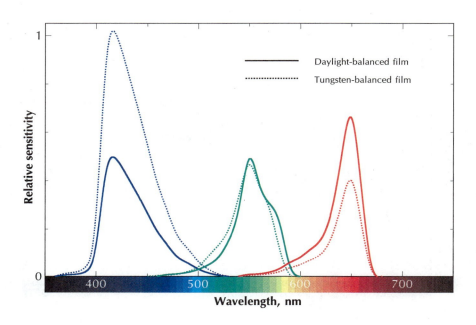

Figure 6.4

Simplified cross-section of a photographic transparency film (after chemical processing). Yellow, magenta, and cyan image dyes are formed in the blue-light, green-light, and red-light sensitive layers, respectively.

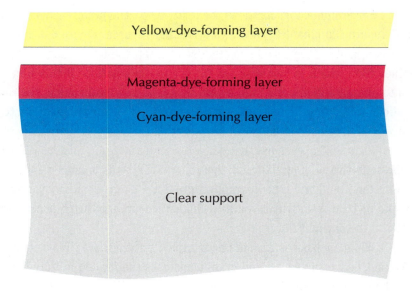

the *minimum* amount of dye forms at the *maximum* exposure. Also during chemical processing, the yellow filter layer is made colorless. (Please refer to Appendix C for more details on photographic media.)

Figure 6.5 shows the spectral transmission densities of the cyan, magenta, and yellow image-forming dyes of a representative photographic transparency film. Note that these dyes seem to be purer than those of the photographic paper, which are also shown in Fig. 6.5. *Purer* means that each dye more nearly absorbs light of just one primary color, and each has less unwanted absorption of light of the other two primary colors. For example, the cyan dye of the photographic transparency film absorbs mostly red light and relatively little green or blue light. In addition to absorbing red light, however, the cyan dye of the photographic paper significantly absorbs green and blue light.

This apparent difference in purity is not due to differences in the inherent qualities of the dyes that are used. It is due to the different optical characteristics of transmission and reflection media. The internal reflections of light within a reflective-support medium, previously shown (Fig. 5.3), effectively increase the unwanted spectral absorptions of its image-forming dyes.

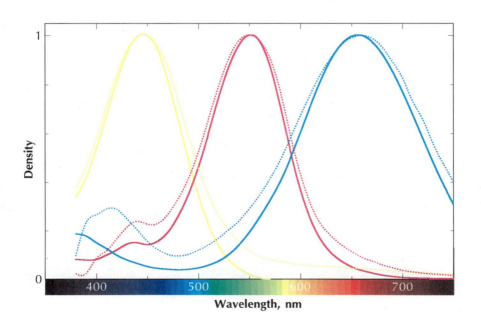

Figure 6.5
Spectral densities of the cyan, magenta, and yellow image-forming dyes of a representative photographic slide film (solid lines) compared to those of a representative photographic paper (dotted lines).

For example, a dye that appears to be a pure yellow on a transmissive support may appear quite orange on a reflective support because the reflection optics magnify any unwanted green-light absorption the dye might have. This is shown in Figs. 6.6a and 6.6b. In Fig. 6.6a, the spectral transmission-density characteristics and the spectral reflection-density characteristics for the same yellow dye are compared. Note that the dye exhibits greater unwanted absorption of green light (at 530 nm, for example) when used on a reflective support. Figure 6.6b shows the effective hue change of the yellow dye. The vector in the figure shows a clockwise rotation, which corresponds to a move from a purer yellow to a redder (more orange) yellow.

As a result of this effect, when all other factors are equal, a transmission medium will have a larger color gamut than that of a reflection medium that uses the same CMY image-forming dyes (Fig. 6.7). Also as a result of this effect, again when all other factors are equal, an imaging system using a transmission medium for output will require less signal processing (color correction) than an otherwise comparable system using a reflection output medium.

Figure 6.6a

Spectral transmission density and spectral reflection density for the same yellow dye. The dye amounts used are adjusted such that the peak reflection densities and peak transmission densities are equal.

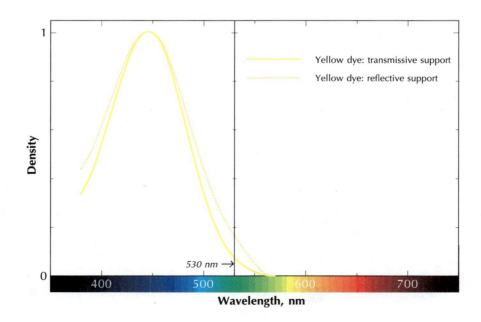

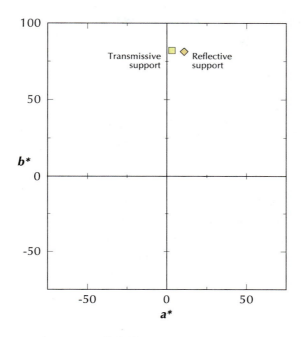

Figure 6.6b
Hue change, from yellow toward orange, which results when the same yellow dye is used on a transmissive support and on a reflective support.

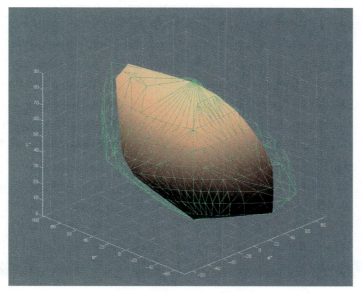

Figure 6.7
Comparison of the resulting color gamuts when the same set of CMY image-forming dyes is used on a transmissive support (the gamut boundary shown by the wire frame) and a reflective support (gamut boundary shown by the solid).

Neutral Characteristics: Viewing Illuminant Sensitivity

Like reflection images, images on photographic transparency media are objects that produce color stimuli only when illuminated. The colorimetry of a transparency film neutral, therefore, will be affected directly by the spectral power characteristics of the viewing illuminant.

Figure 6.8 shows the spectral characteristics for a colorimetric neutral produced by the CMY image-forming dyes of a representative photographic transparency film. The neutral, which has a visual density of 1.00, was determined for a particular viewing illuminant. Note that the neutral is quite spectrally selective. This suggests that it will be viewing illuminant sensitive, which indeed is the case.

Figure 6.8

Colorimetric neutral produced by the CMY image-forming dyes of a representative photographic transparency film. The viewing illuminant is a tungsten-halogen projection lamp.

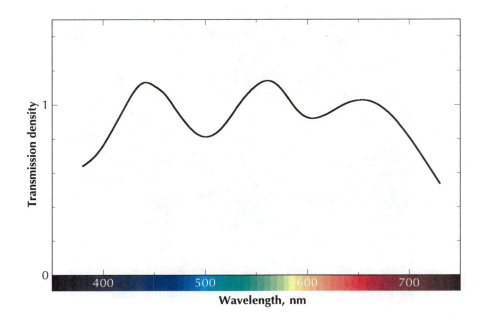

A comparable degree of viewing illuminant sensitivity would be a very serious problem for a reflection medium, because reflection images are likely to be viewed under a wide variety of conditions. However, a given transparency film, in addition to being designed for a specific reference *scene* illuminant, also is designed for a specific reference *viewing* illuminant.

For example, 35-mm slide films are designed to be projected using a particular type of tungsten-halogen projection light source. Larger sheet films are designed to be viewed on a light box having an artificial D_{50} light source. In the engineering of most transparency films, therefore, illuminant sensitivity is of lesser concern, and it generally is traded for other features. In particular, CMY image-forming dyes having a larger color gamut can be used when viewing illuminant sensitivity is not a major concern.

This type of trade-off is illustrated in Figs. 6.9a, 6.9b, and 6.9c. These figures show that although dye set *A* has greater viewing illuminant sensitivity than does dye set *B,* it also has lesser amounts of unwanted absorptions. Thus it has a somewhat larger color gamut, and it requires less color correction.

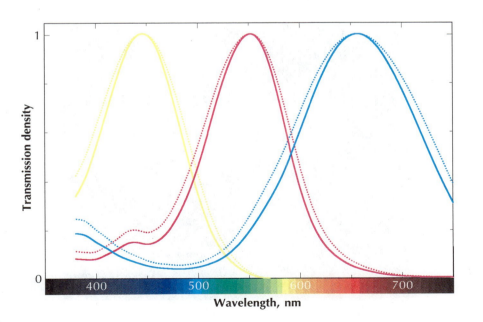

Figure 6.9a

Spectral transmission density characteristics of two sets of cyan, magenta, and yellow image-forming dyes. The dyes of set *A* (solid lines) have much lesser amounts of unwanted absorptions than do the dyes of set *B* (dotted lines).

Figure 6.9b
Neutrals formed by dye set *A* are more spectrally selective, and therefore more viewing illuminant sensitive, than those formed by dye set *B*.

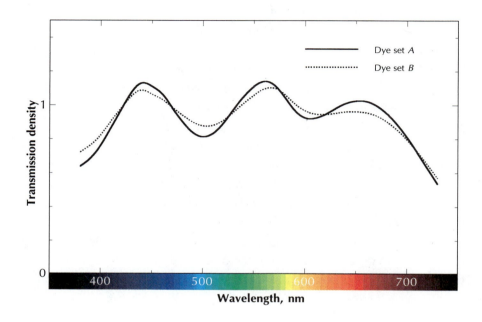

Figure 6.9c
The color gamut of dye set *A* (indicated by the wire frame) is greater than that of dye set *B* (indicated by the solid).

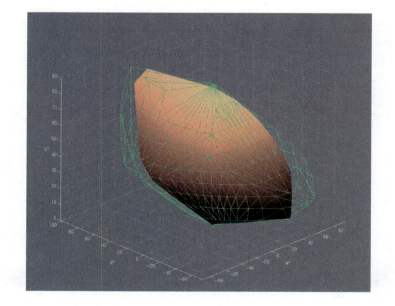

Neutral Characteristics: Color Balance

The neutral previously shown in Fig. 6.8 is a colorimetric neutral, i.e., the CIE *x, y* chromaticity coordinates of that neutral are identical to those of the projection light source itself. In Fig. 6.10, the colorimetric neutral is compared to an *actual* neutral produced by a representative commercially successful photographic slide film having the same set of CMY dyes. The actual neutral is a reproduction of a spectrally nonselective neutral patch of the test target, which was photographed using the reference scene illuminant.

The figure would seem to suggest that the actual neutral produced by the slide film is cyan-blue, since it has relatively more density to red light (more cyan dye) and relatively less density to blue light (less yellow dye). In fact, density measurements, colorimetric measurements, dye-amount measurements, or any other physical measurements that could be made, all would indicate that

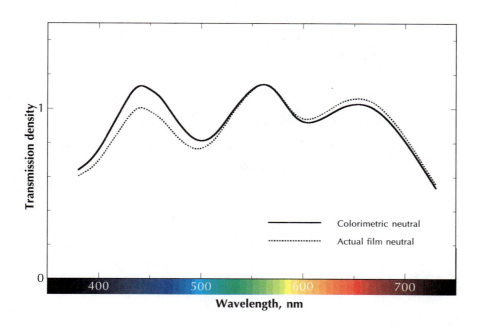

Figure 6.10

A colorimetric neutral and the actual neutral produced by a representative photographic slide film. Slides made by this film are designed to be viewed using a tungsten-halogen projection lamp.

the actual film neutral is indeed cyan-blue. The only disagreement on this point would come from one source: human observers.

When observers view the projected "cyan-blue" film neutral, they judge it to be neutral. And when observers view the projected *colorimetric* neutral, they judge it to be somewhat reddish-yellow. Why? Since other visual cues are absent in a darkened room, an observer will tend to adapt to a projected image itself. If that adaptation were *complete,* then *either* projected neutral, viewed individually, would appear neutral.

However, a tungsten-halogen projection lamp is quite reddish-yellow, the absolute luminance of a projected image is fairly low, and a projected image fills only a portion of an observer's field of view. As a consequence of these three factors, the observer's chromatic adaptation to a projected image will *not* be complete. So although a projected colorimetric neutral matches the illuminant in *chromaticity,* it will still appear somewhat reddish-yellow.

Projection slide films therefore are built to have an overall color balance that *measures* somewhat cyan-blue. This color bias, when combined with the observer's partial chromatic adaptation to the reddish-yellow projection conditions, produces images that appear to be optimally color balanced. This means that they *are* optimally color balanced, given our frequently stated rule that the human observer is the ultimate arbiter of image quality.

Grayscale Characteristics

Figure 6.11 shows the grayscale characteristic, in terms of visual density, of a representative high-quality 35-mm photographic transparency film designed for projection. The figure also shows the grayscale of a representative reflection-print system for comparison.

Like those of the other media examined earlier, the grayscale of this commercially successful film is not one-to-one with the original scene. It is apparent from the nonlinear shape—particularly from the exponential increase in visual density as the characteristic approaches higher densities—that the grayscale characteristic has been designed to compensate for viewing flare. In an otherwise darkened projection-viewing environment, viewing flare can

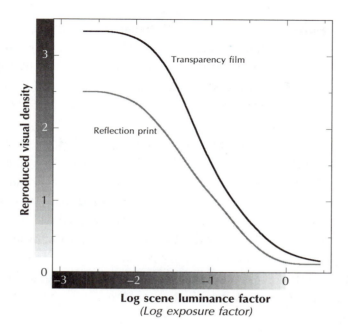

Figure 6.11
Grayscale characteristic of a high-quality photographic transparency film. The grayscale of a high-quality reflection-print system is shown for comparison.

result from stray projector light. Flare also can result from projected image light that first reflects from the projection screen to surfaces in the room and then reflects back to the screen. The amount of flare light in the room, and the amount of that light that reaches the image on the projection screen, will vary depending on the type of screen and the characteristics of the room. In most cases, the relative amount of flare is approximately the same as, or somewhat lower than, that encountered in video and reflection-image viewing.

The absolute luminance of a projected image is quite low relative to that of most original scenes. As discussed previously, this will result in the image being perceived as having lower luminance contrast and less colorfulness. The very high photographic gamma of the grayscale can be explained, in part, as a compensation for both of these effects. A higher grayscale photographic gamma directly increases reproduced luminance contrast. In addition, because a higher grayscale photographic gamma generally is accomplished by raising the photographic gammas of the individual cyan, magenta, and yellow dye-forming layers, reproduced color saturation also is increased.

But even if a photographic gamma increase of about 15% (an amount comparable to that used in video and reflection-print systems) is assumed to compensate for low absolute luminance level, and if correction for about 0.75% viewing flare (a reasonable average) also is assumed, the high photographic gamma of the transparency grayscale still is not fully explained (Fig. 6.12). In particular, the transparency grayscale is still higher in photographic gamma and higher in overall density.

Both of these characteristics of a photographic transparency grayscale are related to perceptual phenomena. The higher photographic gamma of the grayscale is required as a consequence of the viewing environment and observer *lateral-brightness adaptation,* which was described previously in Chapter 3. When a transparency image is projected in a darkened room, it essentially is surrounded by black. The black surround will cause the observer to perceive the image as having somewhat lower luminance contrast than if the image were viewed with a normal surround. That effect must be counteracted by a corresponding increase in the photographic gamma of the transparency grayscale.

Figure 6.12

Compensations for absolute luminance level and viewing flare do not fully explain the grayscale characteristics of a photographic transparency film.

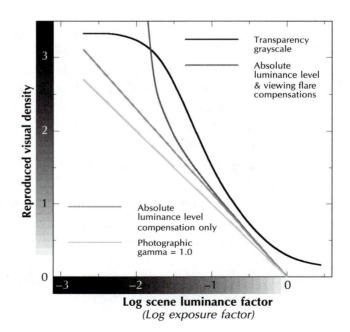

The relatively high overall density is related to another perceptual phenomenon described earlier: *general-brightness adaptation*. In this case, however, the design of the medium does not *compensate* for the perceptual effect; it takes *advantage* of it.

When a transparency is projected in a darkened room, there are few (if any) other visual references. As a result, the observer will adapt to a considerable extent to the absolute luminance level of the image itself. This can be demonstrated by sequentially projecting a series of slides that are identical except for their overall density. For example, the series might consist of seven slides that are identical, except that each has 0.05 greater overall density than the preceding. Most observers, if given a brief amount of time to adapt to each image, will not detect any change in the appearances of the images from the beginning to the end of the series, even though the absolute luminance of the final projected slide is only *half* that of the first. Photographic engineers take advantage of this general-brightness adaptation effect to increase the ability of a projection slide film to record and display original-scene information.

How this is done is shown in Fig. 6.13, which compares the grayscale of a photographic transparency film to that of a photographic reflection-print system. The figure shows that for the reflection-print system, a perfect white is reproduced very nearly at the minimum density of the print medium. Reflection images *must* reproduce whites at low densities because the typical environments in which such images are viewed contain white objects and other visual cues that essentially control the general-brightness adaptation of the observer. A reflection image with darker whites would look unacceptably dark.

However, because an observer will partially adapt to a projected image, it is acceptable to reproduce a perfect white at a relatively high density on a photographic transparency film (also shown in Fig. 6.13). This makes it possible to use some of the density range of the film to reproduce highlight information corresponding to very high scene luminance-factor values. This is important, because in a typical scene, a considerable amount of important information is present at high luminance levels, including levels that are well above the luminance of a perfect white object in the scene. Specular highlights, such as those produced by sunlight reflecting from water or polished surfaces, are one source of such information. Regions of highly illuminated diffuse highlights, such as

Figure 6.13
Densities of the
reproductions of a
perfect white on
the grayscales of a
photographic
transparency film
and a photo-
graphic reflection-
print system.

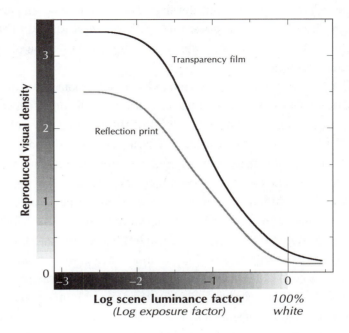

those that will be present in certain areas of a wedding dress illuminated from above the camera angle, represent another important source of scene information above perfect white.

In addition, some areas of a scene may be more highly illuminated than the principal subject area. For example, the principal subject may be a person standing in the shade of a tree, but the scene may also include other subjects standing in direct sunlight. These sunlight-illuminated areas easily can have luminance levels above that of a perfect white within the shaded principal subject area of the scene. Similarly, a cloudy sky may contain areas with luminances well above the luminance of a white object in the principal subject area of a scene. Fluorescent colors also may produce, at certain wavelengths, light levels greater than those reflected from a perfect white. Therefore, they too may have very high luminances. The ability of photographic transparency films to record and display such information greatly adds to the brilliance, fidelity, and the almost three-dimensional appearance of images on these media.

Color Characteristics

A photographic transparency film is one of the best illustrations of a point made in Chapter 2: Some imaging media are complete imaging systems in themselves. Each of the basic imaging-system functions—image capture, signal processing, and image formation—is performed entirely within the transparency film itself (Fig. 6.14). The exact manners in which these basic functions are implemented determine the particular colorimetric characteristics of the film.

The colorimetric characteristics of the *image-capture* function of a transparency film are determined by the spectral sensitivities of that film. These sensitivities can differ somewhat from product to product, as shown in Fig. 6.15. Such differences are responsible for some of the color reproduction differences that exist among commercially available films. Fig. 6.16 shows, for example, the color reproduction properties of two photographic transparency film products that are identical except for their spectral sensitivities. The design of film spectral sensitivities is a complex process that involves the optimization of other properties, such as noise, in addition to color reproduction.

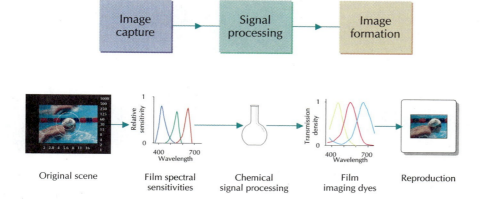

Figure 6.14

A photographic transparency film is a complete imaging system.

Figure 6.15

Comparison of the red, green, and blue spectral sensitivities of two photographic transparency films.

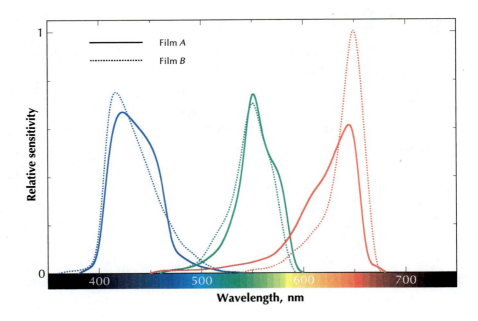

Figure 6.16

Comparison of test target colors, as reproduced by the two films of Fig. 6.15. The two films are identical except for their red, green, and blue spectral sensitivities.

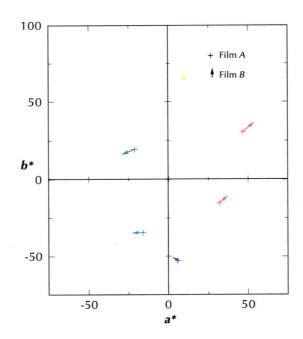

The *signal-processing* function of a transparency film can be thought of as two sequential operations (although both actually occur simultaneously during chemical processing). First, the latent images, formed by exposure of the red-light, green-light, and blue-light-sensitive layers of the film, are chemically amplified. That amplification must be highly nonlinear (with exposure) in order to produce the desired transparency grayscale characteristic shown in Fig. 6.11. This grayscale characteristic, measured in terms of visual density, will result if the density values for the cyan, magenta, and yellow dye scales match those shown in Fig. 6.17. The CMY density values of that figure are expressed in units such that *equal* CMY density values would produce a *colorimetric* neutral for the viewing illuminant. The actual, unequal density values shown produce the desirable cyan-blue colorimetric shift discussed earlier, i.e., at a given scene luminance-factor value, there is greater cyan density and less yellow density.

The second chemical signal-processing operation creates desirable interactions among the color records. The need for such interactions was explained in Chapter 5. In photographic transparency films, as well as in other

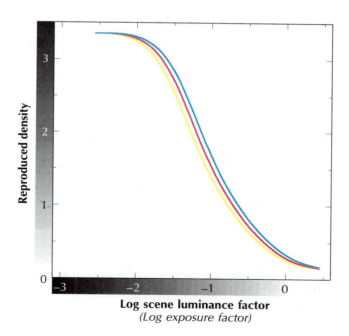

Figure 6.17
CMY density scales for a particular photographic transparency film. Note the overall cyan-blue color balance.

Log scene luminance factor
(Log exposure factor)

silver-halide-based photographic media, *interlayer effects* are used to produce these desirable color interactions. In modern films, a variety of chemical techniques are incorporated such that image-dye formation in one film layer influences the amount of image dye that forms in one or both of the other two layers. (Please refer to Appendix C for more details.)

In photographic media, chemical interactions generally behave proportionally to the *logarithm* of the exposure, rather than to the exposure itself. Logarithmic interactions are well suited for imparting application-specific alterations in color reproduction. For example, logarithmic interactions can be used to increase the overall color saturation of a film designed for advertising or to decrease the overall color saturation of a film designed for studio portraiture.

However, the transformation of captured exposure values to those that are appropriate, based on the spectral characteristics of the image-forming colorants, requires interactions that are *linear* with exposure. Chemical interactions that are linear with exposure are extremely difficult to achieve in photographic media. Film spectral sensitivities therefore are designed such

Figure 6.18

Spectral sensitivities of a representative photographic transparency film, compared to a set of all-positive color-matching functions.

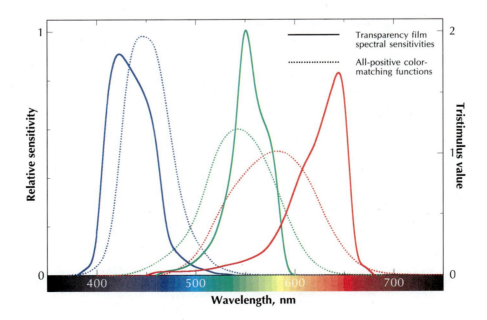

that the *need* for these interactions is minimized. This can be accomplished by the use of spectral sensitivities that differ somewhat from visual color-matching functions. For example, Fig. 6.18 compares the sensitivities of a representative photographic transparency film to a set of color-matching functions. The film sensitivities are spectrally narrower and more separated than this set, or any other set, of all-positive color-matching functions.

These departures from color-matching functions must be designed very carefully in order to optimize the overall color reproduction of the film. Particular attention has to be paid to the reproduction of important memory colors, such as human skin tones, foliage, and sky. The reproduction of metameric pairs also is an important consideration in the design of film spectral sensitivities. Important metameric pairs should produce matched reproductions.

Color-Encoding Considerations

The colorimetric characteristics of a photographic transparency film result from a complex relationship involving the characteristics of spectral sensitivities, grayscale signal processing, color signal processing, and image-forming dyes. One consequence of this complexity is that each transparency film product tends to have its own distinctive appearance. Sometimes the color-reproduction characteristics that contribute to that particular appearance are created deliberately, and sometimes they are a result of various design compromises. Regardless of their origin, the color-reproduction differences among transparency films are significant, and they must be taken into account in any digital color-encoding method that uses these films as a source of input.

This analysis of the colorimetric characteristics of photographic transparencies has uncovered several other factors related to color encoding. Photographic transparency films are designed for specific scene illuminants; yet in practice they may be used under a variety of different scene-illumination conditions. This results in color-balance shifts in the photographic image that may require correction during the encoding process.

Photographic transparency films have very large color gamuts, in part because their image dyes are formed on a transmissive, rather than reflective, support. Successful color encoding of these media therefore must be capable of numerically representing large color gamuts. In addition, the image-forming dyes used in most transparency media are very illuminant sensitive, and the media are designed for a particular viewing illuminant. This is a consideration for scanning, in that the measured colorimetry will be strongly affected by the spectral properties of the scanner illuminant.

Of particular importance for color encoding is the fact that because photographic transparencies are viewed in a dark environment, the relationship between their colorimetric measurements and their visual appearance is not straightforward. For example, standard colorimetric measurements would indicate that photographic transparencies intended for projection are too dark, too high in luminance contrast, and cyan-blue in overall color balance compared to an original scene or a reflection image—yet they do not *appear* that way at all. This discrepancy between colorimetric measurement and color appearance is a *very* significant complication that will have to be dealt with later, when several alternative methods for encoding color information from these important media are discussed.

Summary of Key Issues

- Photographic transparency films are designed for use with specific scene illuminants.

- Like reflection images, images on photographic transparency media are objects that produce color stimuli only when illuminated.

- Photographic transparency media are quite sensitive to changes in viewing illuminant spectral power distribution. They generally are designed for use with one specific viewing illuminant.

- When a photographic transparency is viewed in an otherwise darkened environment, the observer's state of adaptation is influenced by the image itself, and the appearance of the image is influenced by its dark surround. Under such conditions, the relationship between standard colorimetric measurements and visual appearance is not straightforward.

- Photographic transparency films must depart significantly from a one-to-one colorimetric relationship with the original scene in order to compensate appropriately for viewing flare and for observer general-brightness adaptation, lateral-brightness adaptation, and incomplete chromatic adaptation.

- Different photographic transparency media have different characteristic appearances that result from their particular capabilities and limitations. Other differences are created deliberately, based on the specific applications for which the media are intended.

- Photographic transparency films are color balanced for one scene illuminant, yet they are often used under different illuminants. This results in color-balance shifts that may require correction during the encoding process.

- Photographic transparency films have very large color gamuts, in part because their image dyes are formed on a transmissive, rather than reflective, support. Successful color encoding of these media therefore must be capable of numerically representing large color gamuts.

7
Photographic Negatives

Although they are generally designed for a different purpose—to be optically printed onto photographic papers and other media—photographic negative films have inherent properties that make them well suited for input to digital color-imaging systems. In particular, they can record, and make available to a scanner, color information recorded from an extremely wide range of exposures. On many photographic negative films, the dynamic range of recorded exposures can easily exceed a ratio of 10,000 : 1 (a 4.0 log exposure range).

Negative films are low in photographic gamma. So despite their extensive exposure dynamic range, they produce relatively low optical densities. For example, a 100:1 ratio of exposures (a 2.0 log exposure range) would result in a density range of approximately 3.0 on a representative photographic transparency film; but that same ratio of exposures would result in a density range of only about 1.1 on a representative photographic negative film (Fig. 7.1). This is a desirable characteristic for scanning, particularly in cases where the dynamic range of the scanner's sensor is somewhat limited and/or there are signal-to-noise problems. In certain CCD-based scanners, for example, it is quite difficult to derive meaningful information from areas of very high densities.

Color photographic negatives do have one important disadvantage: they are not easily "human readable." Their low contrast and overall orange color cast make them difficult to evaluate visually. Even more troublesome is that they produce images that are "backwards." They reproduce whites as blacks, blacks as whites, reds as cyans, greens as magentas, blues as yellows, and so on. It requires a great deal of experience and skill to judge negative images by direct viewing.

Figure 7.1

Comparison of log exposure ranges and density ranges of negative and transparency photographic films.

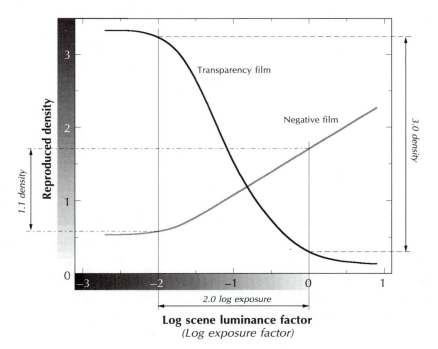

Log scene luminance factor
(Log exposure factor)

This is an important concern in applications where large numbers of images must be evaluated. In the production of catalogs, for example, perhaps a hundred photographic images might be examined for each one that is actually used. In some national magazines, the ratio of images examined to those used can be more than a *thousand* to one.

Until quite recently, the scanning of photographic media was slow and expensive, making it impractical to scan large numbers of images for evaluation. Image selection therefore had to occur *prior* to scanning. That is one of the principal reasons why transparency films, which are designed for direct viewing, generally have been favored over negative films for input in the majority of digital-imaging applications.

That situation is beginning to change, however. High-quality scanning is becoming faster and less expensive, and many digital imaging systems provide accurate video previews of scanned images. This essentially eliminates the need to print negatives for evaluation. As a result, negatives now are used widely for input on systems such as the *Photo CD* System; and within the last year or so, there has been a very significant increase in the use of negatives in high-end electronic prepress applications. That trend no doubt will continue as more and more users of digital imaging systems become aware of the unique properties of these "backwards" media.

General Characteristics

Figure 7.2 shows a simplified cross-section of a photographic negative film. The basic structure is identical to that of a photographic transparency film: a blue-light-sensitive layer, yellow filter layer, green-light-sensitive layer, and red-light-sensitive layer coated on a clear support. When the exposed film is chemically processed, yellow, magenta, and cyan dyes are formed in the blue-light, green-light, and red-light-sensitive layers, respectively. Unlike a photographic transparency film, however, a photographic negative film produces its *maximum* amount of image dye from a *maximum* exposure and its *minimum* amount of dye from a *minimum* exposure.

Figure 7.2

Simplified cross-section of a color negative photographic film (prior to chemical processing).

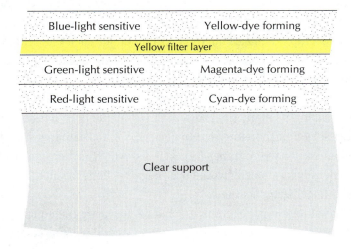

If their structures are the same, why does a photographic transparency film produce a positive image and a photographic negative film produce a negative image? It is a common misconception that this happens because photographic negative films somehow "see" the world backwards. But that is not the case.

Photographic negative and transparency films actually "see" the world in much the same way. In other words, their sets of red, green, and blue spectral sensitivities are not fundamentally different. The sensitivities may, in fact, be virtually identical for a given pair of negative and transparency films. In terms of basic imaging-system functions, then, these two media are not fundamentally different in their *image-capture* characteristics. Both types of media form cyan, magenta, and yellow dyes, so they also are not fundamentally different in their *image-formation* characteristics.

That leaves just one imaging-system function—*signal processing*—that must be responsible for making a photographic film produce either a negative or a positive image. That can easily be demonstrated with a simple experiment: If a transparency film is exposed and then processed in a chemical process intended for negative films, its images will come out *negative,* not positive. Likewise, if a negative film is exposed and then processed in a transparency-film chemical process, its images will come out *positive,* not negative.

Neutral Characteristics

Figure 7.3 shows the spectral transmission densities of the cyan, magenta, and yellow image-forming dyes for a representative photographic negative film. Note that the spectral characteristics of these dyes, particularly the cyan dye, are somewhat different from the spectral characteristics of the dyes of a representative photographic transparency film. That negative and transparency media form somewhat different dyes might be expected, since transparency films are designed to be viewed by humans, but negative films are not. This fact raises an interesting issue.

In previous system examinations, standard colorimetric measurements were used to quantify the trichromatic characteristics of color stimuli produced by the output media. It was logical to make such measurements because the media involved formed positive images intended for direct viewing. But since negatives are not meant to be viewed directly, it would not seem logical to also measure them using methods based on the responses of a human observer.

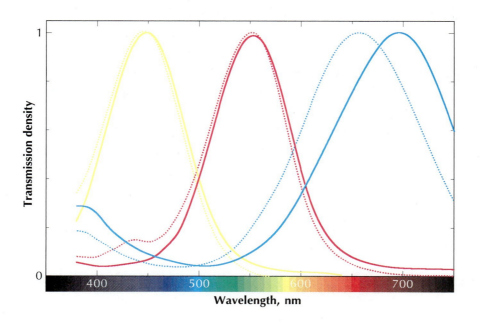

Figure 7.3

Comparison of the cyan, magenta, and yellow image-forming dyes of a representative photographic color negative film (solid lines) and a transparency film (dotted lines).

If standard CIE colorimetry is ruled out, how else can images on negative films be measured? Is there a different type of "standard observer" that would be more appropriate for negative images? Answering these questions requires a closer look at how photographic negative films are designed and how they are used in practice.

In typical applications, photographic negatives are optically printed onto a second negative-working photographic medium (Fig. 7.4). The second medium might be a photographic paper, in which case the final image is a reflection print. Negatives also can be printed onto special clear-support films, such as those used to make motion picture projection prints from motion picture negatives. In either case, the resulting print is a directly viewable positive image.

What is important to appreciate is that each photographic negative film is designed to be optically printed onto one or more *specific* print films or papers, using *specific* printer light sources. That fact provides the key to making meaningful measurements of color negative images.

Optical printing is an image-capture process that is quite similar to several others discussed earlier. As shown in Fig. 7.5, there is an object (the negative image) that is illuminated (by the printer light source) being "viewed" by an "observer" (in this case, a print medium). The print medium for which the negative film is intended, then, should be considered the "standard observer" for that film, and measurements should be made *according to the particular red, green, and blue spectral responsivities of the intended print medium*. In other words, measurements should be made based on what the intended print medium will "see" and *capture* when it "looks" at the illuminated negative in the printer.

What the print material will capture, i.e., the red, green, and blue *exposures* it will form, can be computed using the following equations:

$$R_{exp} = k_r \sum_{\lambda} S(\lambda)T(\lambda)r(\lambda)$$

$$G_{exp} = k_g \sum_{\lambda} S(\lambda)T(\lambda)g(\lambda) \qquad \{7.1\}$$

$$B_{exp} = k_b \sum_{\lambda} S(\lambda)T(\lambda)b(\lambda)$$

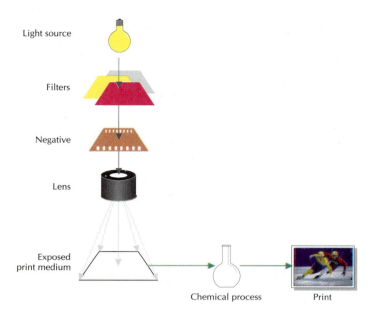

Light source

Filters

Negative

Lens

Exposed
print medium

Chemical process   Print

Figure 7.4
Optical printing of
a photographic
negative onto a
photographic print
medium. The
negative is illumi-
nated by a printer
light source. Color
filters are used to
control the overall
density and color
balance of the
print by altering
the spectral power
of the printer light.
Filtered light
passes through the
negative and is
focused onto a
photographic print
medium. Finally,
the exposed print
medium is chemi-
cally processed to
form a directly
viewable image.

where R_{exp}, G_{exp}, and B_{exp} are the print-medium red, green, and blue exposure-factor values; $S(\lambda)$ is the spectral power distribution of the printer light source; $T(\lambda)$ is the spectral transmittance of the negative "object"; $r(\lambda)$, $g(\lambda)$, and $b(\lambda)$ are the red, green, and blue spectral sensitivities of the print medium; and k_r, k_g, and k_b are normalizing factors. These factors usually are determined such that R_{exp}, G_{exp}, and B_{exp} = 1.00 for a theoretical 100% transmission (zero optical density) negative.

The negative logarithms of the red, green, and blue exposure-factor values are called *printing densities:*

$$PD_r = -\log_{10}(R_{exp})$$

$$PD_g = -\log_{10}(G_{exp})$$ {7.2}

$$PD_b = -\log_{10}(B_{exp})$$

Figure 7.5

Figure 7.5

The optical printing of a photographic negative film onto a photographic print medium is an image-capture process involving an object, an illuminant, and an "observer."

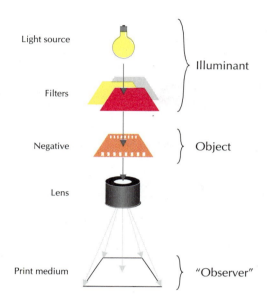

Light source

Filters

Illuminant

Negative

Object

Lens

Print medium

"Observer"

where PD_r, PD_g, and PD_b are the red, green, and blue printing-density values, and R_{exp}, G_{exp}, and B_{exp} are the red, green, and blue exposure-factor values that were calculated from Eqs. {7.1}.

The neutral and color characteristics of all color negative films are *designed* in terms of computed printing densities; therefore, printing densities are the most meaningful density measurements that can be made from color negative films. One way to conceptualize the measurement of printing densities is to imagine a densitometer having a light source that is spectrally identical to the printer light source, and red, green, and blue light sensors having spectral sensitivities identical to those of the print material (Fig. 7.6a). A densitometer meeting those criteria would *directly* measure printing densities.

In practice, such specialized densitometers generally are not used. Instead, printing-density values are computed from spectral transmission data, as in Eqs. {7.1} and {7.2}. Printing density values also can be determined from appropriate mathematical transformations of density values measured with an ISO Status M densitometer, as shown in Fig. 7.6b.

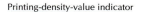

Printing-density-value indicator

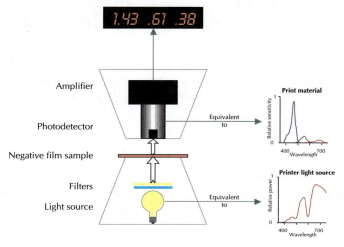

Amplifier

Photodetector

Negative film sample

Filters

Light source

Equivalent to

Equivalent to

Print material

Relative sensitivity

400 Wavelength 700

Printer light source

Relative power

400 Wavelength 700

Figure 7.6a
This specialized densitometer would directly measure printing densities for the specified printer and print material.

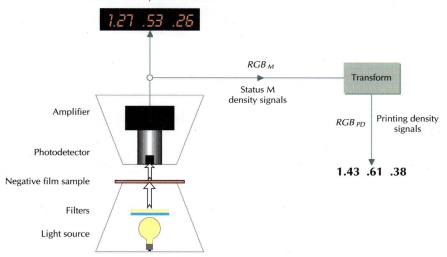

Status M density-value indicator

Amplifier

Photodetector

Negative film sample

Filters

Light source

RGB_M

Status M density signals

Transform

RGB_{PD} Printing density signals

1.43 .61 .38

Figure 7.6b
Printing density values also can be measured using an ISO Status M densitometer and an appropriate mathematical transformation. A different transformation is required for each different negative film, printer, and print material.

Just as it is possible to have metameric neutrals for human observers, it is possible to have metameric neutrals as "seen" by print materials. If color areas on two negative films have *the same printing densities* (determined for a particular print material and printer light source), both areas will produce *the same color* on the final print when the negatives are printed identically, using that particular printer light source and print material. This will be true even if the spectral density characteristics of the image-forming dyes of the two films, and thus the spectral characteristics of all color areas formed by the two films, are different. For example, Fig. 7.7 shows the different spectral characteristics of metameric color areas from two different negative films.

Printing-density metamerism makes it possible for manufacturers to design negative films with different sets of CMY image-forming dyes for use with the same print medium. Figure 7.8, for example, shows the dye sets used in two different color negative films. Despite these differences in their dye sets, both films will print satisfactorily onto the same photographic paper medium because each was designed in terms of printing density values based on that medium and a specified printer light source.

Figure 7.7

Printing-density metamerism. The spectral density characteristics of two areas on two different color negative films are quite different. However, they have the same red, green, and blue printing densities for a particular print medium and printer.

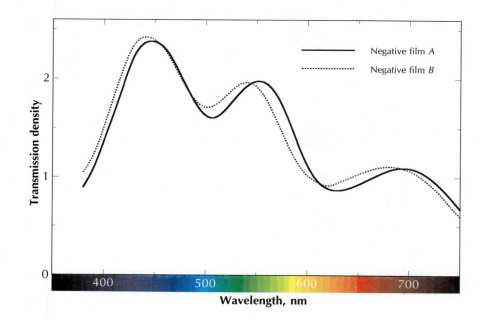

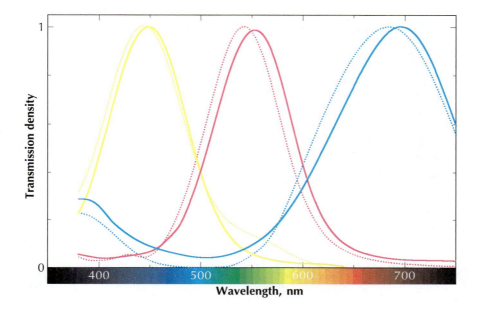

Figure 7.8
Image-forming
dye sets used in
two different color
negative films.

Grayscale Characteristics

Figure 7.9a shows, in terms of printing densities, the grayscale characteristic for a representative photographic negative film. The curves show the basic negative characteristic of the film: greater exposure levels result in more density in the processed film. The curves also show the extensive exposure dynamic range and low photographic gamma of the film. The somewhat higher overall densities of the blue and green printing density curves are indicative of the orange cast of negative films. That overall cast, which is part of the color correction built into the film, is compensated for in the printing process. (Please refer to Appendix C for a more detailed explanation of the purpose of this orange cast.)

Note that the red, green, and blue printing density curves of Fig. 7.9a are perfectly parallel to one another. They differ only in terms of overall printing density value. This means that when the negative is printed properly onto an appropriate print medium, a printed grayscale will be perfectly neutral from one end of the scale to the other (Fig. 7.9b).

Figure 7.9a
Grayscale characteristic, in terms of printing densities, for a representative photographic negative film. Note that the log exposure-factor range is 4.00 (a 10,000:1 ratio of linear exposure-factor values).

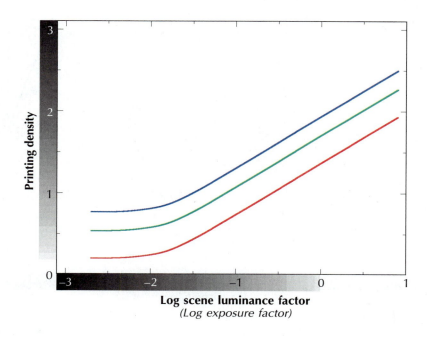

Figure 7.9b
The grayscale printing density curves for the film of Fig. 7.9a are perfectly parallel to each other. This means that when the negative is printed properly, a printed grayscale will be perfectly neutral throughout the scale.

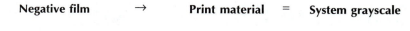

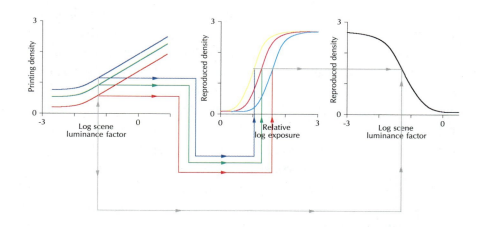

The use of metrics other than printing density for the measurement of photographic negatives can be misleading. For example, Fig. 7.10a compares red, green, and blue printing density curves to Status M density curves for the same negative film grayscale. In terms of Status M density values, the grayscale curves are no longer parallel. The Status M measurements therefore incorrectly imply that when the negative is printed properly onto an appropriate print medium, a printed grayscale will *not* be perfectly neutral throughout the scale. As shown in Fig. 7.10b, the Status M measurements incorrectly imply that the print grayscale will be yellow-red at higher densities and cyan-blue at lower densities. For proper interpretation, then, Status M density values should be transformed to printing density values.

Like photographic transparency films, negative films generally are color balanced for use with particular reference scene illuminants. However, the optical printing process provides an opportunity to adjust the density and color balance of the final print made from a negative. The optical printing step thus allows greater flexibility in the design of the film.

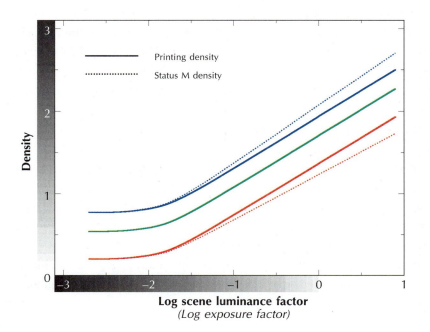

Figure 7.10a
Grayscale characteristic for a color negative film, measured in terms of printing density values and in terms of Status M density values.

Figure 7.10b
The Status M density grayscale curves shown in Fig. 7.10a are not parallel to each other. This incorrectly implies that if the negative were printed, the printed grayscale would *not* be perfectly neutral throughout the scale.

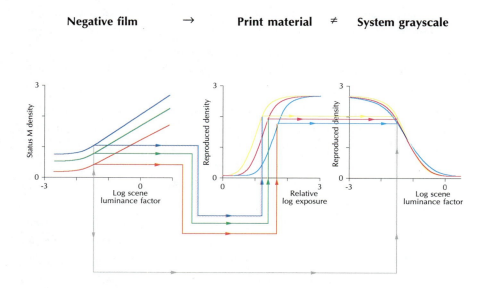

Negative film → **Print material** ≠ **System grayscale**

For example, if a negative photographic film is overexposed, the overall density of the resulting processed negative will be too high. But when that negative is printed, more printer light can be used (by increasing the intensity of that light and/or by increasing the printing time). This will result in a print that is properly balanced in overall density. Similarly, if a negative is exposed using a light source that is too blue, the overall blue density of that negative (the amount of yellow dye formed) will be too high. But if more blue light is used in printing, a properly color-balanced print will be produced.

Because color-balance corrections can be applied during the output printing process, the color balance of a negative-film grayscale is far less critical than that of a film—such as a photographic slide film—that is not printed, but is instead viewed directly. Since their color balance is not particularly critical, negative films can be designed with grayscales that are color balanced such that good results are produced when the films are used to capture images in any of a variety of scene-illumination conditions. For example, a photographic negative film that is labeled "daylight balanced" actually may be designed with extra sensitivity to blue light (Fig. 7.11a).

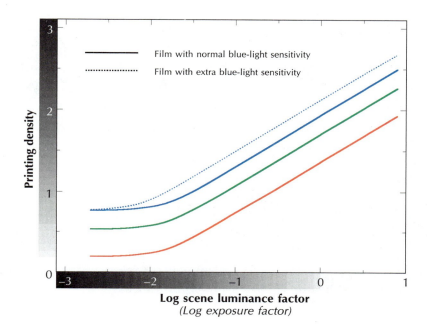

Film with normal blue-light sensitivity

Film with extra blue-light sensitivity

Log scene luminance factor
(Log exposure factor)

Figure 7.11a
A "daylight balanced" negative film may be designed with extra sensitivity to blue light. The extra blue sensitivity helps prevent blue-light underexposure when the film is used to photograph tungsten-illuminated scenes.

This additional blue sensitivity will result in too much blue-light exposure when the film is used to photograph daylight-illuminated scenes. But it also helps to prevent blue-light underexposure when the film is used to photograph tungsten-illuminated scenes. This is a sensible compromise. While a negative film can record information that is considerably overexposed, and an overexposed negative can be corrected for in printing, underexposure results in an unrecoverable loss of scene information (Fig. 7.11b).

The grayscale characteristics shown thus far are representative of those of many color negative films. However, the characteristics of individual products will differ somewhat, based primarily on their intended application. For example, negative films intended for studio portraiture generally are lower in photographic gamma. Films intended for amateur systems tend to be higher in photographic gamma, in part to help compensate for the higher flare and lower sharpness of lower-cost cameras. In addition, it has been found that many amateurs tend to prefer higher contrast, "snappier" looking prints.

Figure 7.11b
Figure 7.11b

A negative film can record information that is considerably overexposed, but underexposure results in an unrecoverable loss of original scene information.

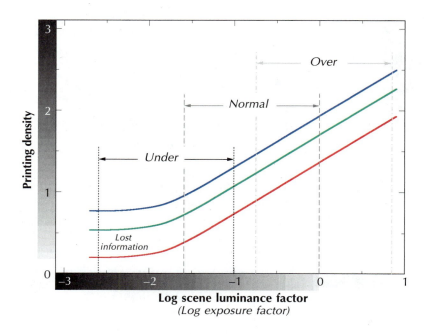

When a typical color photographic negative is printed onto a typical photographic reflection-print material, the resulting overall system grayscale characteristic, relating the original scene and final print, will be similar to that described in Chapter 5 and shown again here in Fig. 7.12. When a typical color negative is printed onto a typical photographic transmission print material, the resulting system grayscale characteristic will be similar to that described in Chapter 6 and also shown here in Fig. 7.12.

The basic relationships of the grayscale characteristics for a negative, a print medium, and an overall system were shown previously in Fig. 7.9b. Achieving system grayscales like those of Fig. 7.12 requires proper design of both the negative and print medium. The photographic gamma of the system grayscale characteristic is simply the product of the photographic gammas of the negative and the print medium. However, because negative grayscales are straight lines when plotted in terms of density versus log exposure-factor, the desirable nonlinear characteristics for the overall system grayscale, plotted in those terms, must be designed into the print medium rather than the negative.

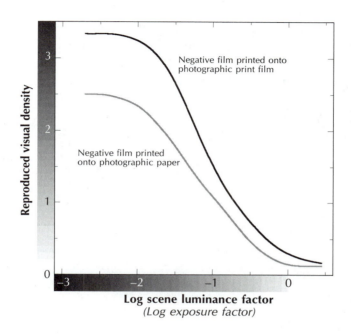

Figure 7.12
System grayscales that result from printing a photographic negative onto a photographic paper and a photographic print film.

Color Characteristics

A negative image, while not aesthetically pleasing to look at, nevertheless is a viewable image. A photographic negative film, then, like a photographic transparency film, is a complete imaging system. Each of the three basic imaging-system functions takes place within the film itself (Fig. 7.13).

In addition, a negative film is the first *half* of a two-stage imaging system composed of the negative film and a print medium (Fig. 7.14). In this and any other two-stage imaging system, the output image formed by the first stage becomes the input to the second stage.

It is often useful to analyze an imaging system having two or more stages in terms of a single *compound* system (Fig. 7.15). If that is done for this example, it can be seen that the spectral characteristics of the *image capture* stage of the compound system are determined solely by the red, green, and blue spectral sensitivities of the negative film. It also can be seen that the spectral characteristics of the *image formation* stage are determined solely by the

Figure 7.13

A photographic negative film is a complete, single-stage color-imaging system.

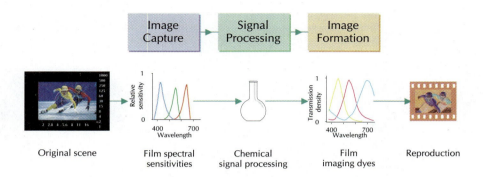

Figure 7.14

A photographic negative film is the first stage of a two-stage imaging system. In multi-stage imaging systems, an output image formed by one stage then becomes the input to the next.

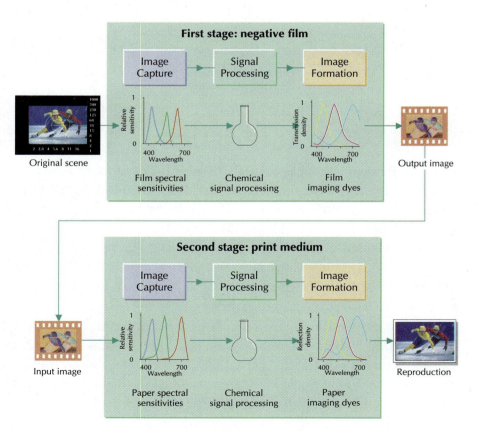

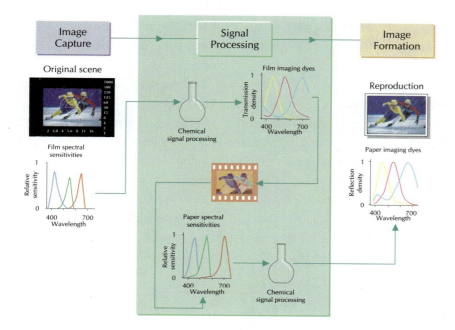

Figure 7.15
A two-stage imaging system can be analyzed in terms of a single *compound* system.

cyan, magenta, and yellow image-forming dyes of the print medium. Everything else within the compound system can be classified as *signal processing.* In other words, everything else serves to influence the *output* of the compound system (how much of each image dye forms on the print medium) as a function of system *input* (the amounts of red, green, and blue exposure recorded at the original scene by the negative film).

The total signal processing of the compound system includes chemical signal processing that occurs within the photographic negative film and within the print medium. In addition, the *transfer of information* between the two stages—the way the print medium stage "sees" the color information recorded on the negative—is a form of color signal processing. The signal-processing consequences of the transfer process are illustrated in Figs. 7.16 and 7.17.

Figure 7.16 shows an idealized example of the information transfer. In this example, the image-forming dyes of the negative film are hypothetical "block dyes." The spectral responsivities of the print medium are very narrow, they are completely separated from each other, and they are perfectly aligned with the spectral absorptions of the corresponding negative dyes. As a result, the cyan dye of the negative uniquely controls the red-light exposure to the print medium. Therefore, that cyan dye has only red printing density and has no green or blue printing density.

Similarly, the magenta dye of this idealized example uniquely controls green-light exposure to the print medium, so it has only green printing density and has no red or blue printing density; and the yellow dye uniquely controls blue-light exposure to the print medium, so it has only blue printing density and has no red or green printing density. In this example, then, there is *no* cross-talk in the transfer of color information from the negative to the print medium.

Figure 7.17 shows a more realistic example. In this case, the cyan dye of the negative absorbs not only red light, but also some green and blue light (as "seen" according to the spectral responsivities of print medium). The cyan dye therefore has *unwanted absorption* of green and blue light. In other words, it

Figure 7.16

There is no cross-talk in the transfer of information from a negative to a print medium if the spectral absorptions of each image-forming dye in the negative uniquely align with the corresponding spectral responsivities of the print medium.

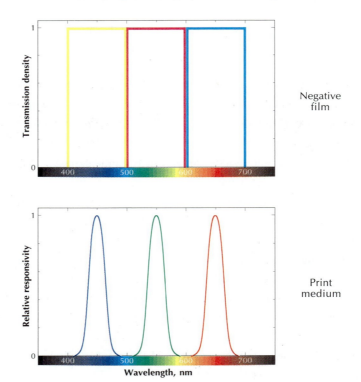

not only has red printing density, it also has green and blue printing density. The other dyes also have some unwanted absorptions. In particular, the magenta dye absorbs not only green light, but also some blue light. As a result of these unwanted absorptions, cross-talk is introduced in the transfer of color information from the negative to the print material.

This type of cross-talk must be counteracted by the use of appropriate color-correction mechanisms that create compensating cross-talk (interactions) among the color layers of the negative. Color correction can be provided by chemical interlayer effects, as is done in photographic transparency films. Because color negative films are not viewed directly, another color correction mechanism also can be used. It is this second mechanism—the incorporation of what are called *colored couplers*—that gives negative films their distinctive overall orange color cast. (Please refer to Appendix C for more details on photographic media, chemical interlayer effects, and colored couplers.)

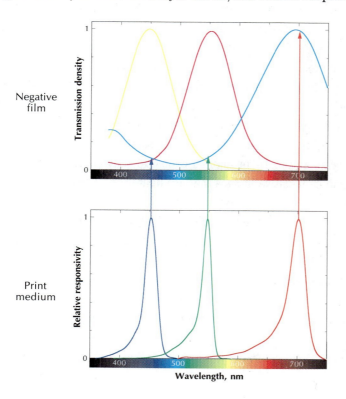

Figure 7.17

In most real cases, there is some cross-talk in the transfer of information from a negative to a print medium. For example, the cyan dye of the negative will modulate not only red light, but also some green and blue light as "seen" by the print medium.

Color-Encoding Considerations

Several important issues related to color encoding have been uncovered in this analysis of color photographic negative films. First, the analysis has shown that the spectral sensitivities of color negative and transparency films are not basically different, which means that color images on positive and negative photographic media are fundamentally the same *at the image-capture stage*. This is an extremely important finding; it will be shown later that it provides the key to successful color encoding in the *Photo CD* System.

The analysis also has shown that negatives having different sets of image-forming dyes can be metameric to a print medium, i.e., they can have the same printing densities. Printing-density metamerism has important implications for scanning and color encoding. Very few scanners measure negatives in terms of printing densities; most measure values that are closer to Status M densities. As a result, *RGB* scanned values alone are not accurate predictors of printing-density metamerism. For example, areas on two different negative films might have identical printing densities, but their *RGB* scanned values might indicate that the two areas are different.

Negative films frequently are used under circumstances that lead to significant variations in overall exposure. For example, they often are used in cameras having no automatic or manual exposure control. The resulting exposure errors produce negative images that are lighter or darker than they would be if properly exposed. In addition, negative films typically are used under a wide variety of scene illumination conditions. This results in considerable color-balance and density variations among negative images, even among images on the same roll of film.

While such variations ordinarily are compensated for in the optical printing process, they introduce a basic *ambiguity* into the meaning of values scanned directly from negatives. For example, consider three negative images taken of the same scene. One image is normally exposed, one is somewhat underexposed, and one is considerably overexposed (Figs. 7.18a, 7.18b, and 7.18c).

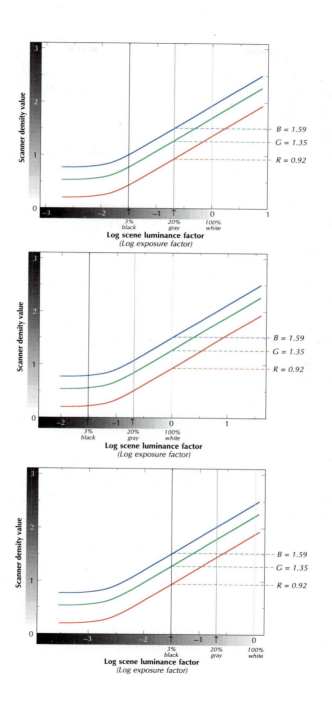

Figure 7.18a
Placement of
scene information
on a normally
exposed negative.
The indicated
RGB values corre-
spond to a 20%
reflectance gray in
the original scene.

Figure 7.18b
Placement of
scene information
on an under-
exposed negative.
The same *RGB*
values now corre-
spond to a 100%
reflectance white
in the original
scene.

Figure 7.18c
Placement of
scene information
on an over-
exposed negative.
The same *RGB*
values now corre-
spond to a 3%
reflectance black
in the original
scene.

As the figures show, the values $R = 0.92$, $G = 1.35$, and $B = 1.59$, measured by a film scanner, would represent a medium gray (20% reflectance) in the original scene, if the negative being scanned were normally exposed. However, the *same* set of *RGB* values might represent a scene perfect white (100% reflectance) if the negative were underexposed, or a scene dark black (3% reflectance) if the negative were overexposed. There is a basic ambiguity, then, in any set of *RGB* values measured from a negative by a scanner.

Another challenge for digital-imaging applications is that negative images are *intermediary* images. Color values measured from the film itself do not correspond directly to original-scene colorimetric values, because the formation of a negative image involves a significant amount of chemical signal processing. On the other hand, color values measured from a negative do not correspond directly to colorimetric values of the image that ultimately will be produced from that negative, because those values will vary depending on the characteristics of the printer, print medium, and viewing illuminant.

All of this raises some serious problems for color encoding. The color-encoding process will have to deal both with the ambiguity associated with values measured directly from negatives and with the intermediary nature of color negative images. This suggests that a successful color-encoding process is going to have to do more than just *measure* color values from negatives. Specifically, in order to represent color in a meaningful way, the encoding process will have to *interpret* color measurements.

In Part III, it will be shown that interpretation of measured values is required not just for input from negative images, but for images from *all* input media and from *all* input devices. *It will be shown, in fact, that the concept of interpretation is the key to all successful digital color encoding.*

Summary of Key Issues

- The low photographic gamma, extensive exposure dynamic range, and straight-line grayscale characteristic of color photographic negative films make them well-suited for input to digital color-imaging systems.

- At the image-capture (latent image) stage, images on positive and negative photographic films essentially are the same.

- The neutral and color characteristics of all color negative films are designed in terms of printing densities.

- Printing densities are the densities that the print material "sees" when it "looks" at the negative film, as illuminated by the printer light source.

- Negative films having different sets of image-forming dyes may have areas that are spectrally different but identical in terms of their printing densities. Such areas are metameric to the print material. If printed identically, they will produce the same color in the final print.

- Negative films are part of a two-stage system. The linkage between the two stages—the way information recorded on the negative is transferred to the print medium—is a form of color signal processing.

- Colored couplers are one mechanism used in color negative films to compensate for certain unwanted absorptions of their image-forming dyes. They are responsible for the orange color cast of unexposed areas of the film.

- Negative films often are used under circumstances that lead to significant variations in exposure, which results in corresponding variations in density. Density measurements alone therefore are ambiguous.

- Negative films produce intermediary images. Values measured from these images do not correspond directly to the colorimetry of the original scene, nor do they correspond directly to the colorimetry of the final print.

- Measurements made directly from color negative films must be interpreted appropriately in order to be meaningful.

PART III

Digital Color Encoding

Most discussions of digital color encoding focus on two areas: image file formats and color spaces. The underlying assumption of such discussions is that if the industry could define file format standards and then agree to use the same "device-independent" colorimetric color space(s), the problems of representing color in digital form and interchanging images among color-imaging systems would be solved.

The discussion presented in this section will be quite different, primarily because we do not concur with that basic assumption. Our experience instead has shown that the current problems of color encoding and interchanging digital images cannot be eliminated simply by file format standards and an industry-wide adoption of *any* standard colorimetric color space.

The basic reasons for this were introduced in Part II, where it was shown that different types of imaging media *do* have, and *must* have, fundamentally different colorimetric properties. Using the same colorimetric color space to encode images from these media, and doing nothing more, will in no way account for such differences. All it will do is quantify those differences in terms of the agreed-upon color space!

In this section, strategies will be devised to deal appropriately with the basic colorimetric differences that exist among various combinations of input imaging media and devices. First, some basic color-encoding concepts will be described. Several encoding methods that have been used successfully in commercial color-imaging systems then will be examined. These examinations will show why some current methods work well in certain situations and why they fail in others. Particular attention will be paid to the *Photo CD* System color-encoding method, because, at the moment, it is the only method demonstrated to work well with all forms of input and output.

Much of the discussion in this section will focus on a concept that we refer to as *input compatibility*. We believe this concept to be the key to all successful color encoding. Also in this section, the concept of "device-independent color" will be critically examined.

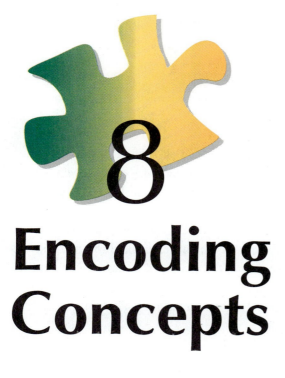

8

Encoding Concepts

The basic function of digital color encoding in imaging systems is to provide a digital representation of colors for image processing, storage, and interchange among systems. Within a given system, encoding provides a digital link between the system's inputs and outputs.

In a simple system, having just one type of input and one type of output, color encoding can be performed prior to any signal processing (Fig. 8.1). The encoding therefore is a direct representation of the color values measured by the system's input device.

Figure 8.1

A simple color-imaging system.

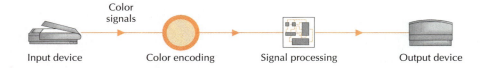

Input device   Color signals   Color encoding   Signal processing   Output device

In more complex systems, supporting multiple types of inputs and outputs, such an arrangement is impractical because each and every *combination* of input and output would require a separate signal-processing transform. For example, a single output device would require two different transforms in order to process color values measured by one input device that scans photographic negative films and another that scans reflection prints. The number of required system transforms in this arrangement equals the *product* of the number of inputs and outputs. That can get to be a sizable number of transforms. A system having four inputs and eight outputs, for example, would require 32 different transforms (Fig. 8.2).

Figure 8.2

A system with four inputs and eight outputs. In this arrangement, 32 signal-processing transforms are required.

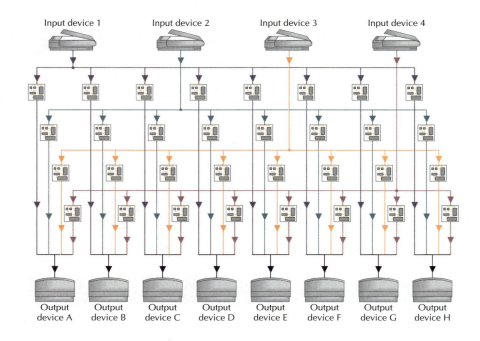

Input device 1   Input device 2   Input device 3   Input device 4

Output device A   Output device B   Output device C   Output device D   Output device E   Output device F   Output device G   Output device H

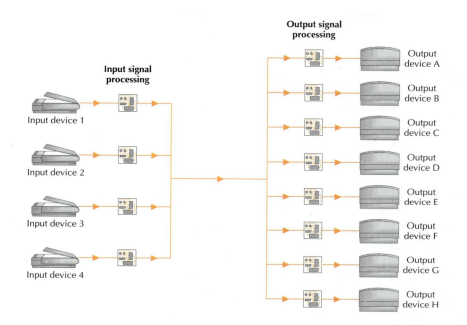

Figure 8.3
In this arrangement, only 12 signal-processing transforms are required.

A much more efficient system results if the color signal processing is split into two parts—input signal processing and output signal processing. In this arrangement, shown in Fig. 8.3, each input and each output has its own associated transform. The number of system transforms then equals the *sum,* rather than the product, of the number of inputs and outputs. Only 12 signal-processing transforms, instead of 32, would be required for four inputs and eight outputs.

The signal-processing arrangement has other advantages that can best be described by looking at one very successful system in which it is used—the audio compact disc (CD) system (Fig. 8.4a). This system is an excellent example of good multiple input/output design. One of the most important features of the overall system is that it supports input from a wide variety of sources. For example, a single CD may store digital information from sounds previously recorded on such different media as wax cylinders, lacquer discs, wire, vinyl discs, or tape. Some input sources, especially audio tapes, may have been recorded using either analog or digital technology, and any of a number of different noise suppression and frequency pre-emphasis techniques may have been included in the original recording process.

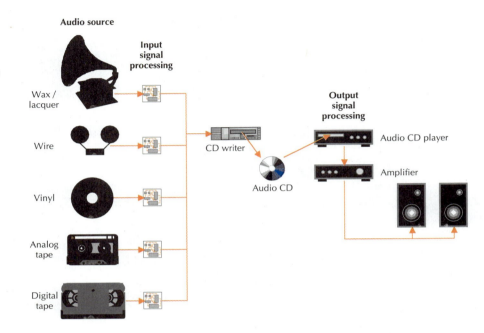

The system works well, despite the disparities of the input media, because appropriate signal-processing transforms are used on all input signals. As a result, data stored on an audio CD represent processed signals that have been digitally encoded and stored in an efficient and standardized way. Moreover, all stored data essentially are *independent* of the original audio source.

Without that independence, the original audio source would have to be identified, and the signal processing of the CD player would have to be altered accordingly (a situation essentially corresponding to Fig. 8.2). This would greatly increase the cost and complexity of the CD player. It also would preclude the future addition of different types of input sources to the overall system, because existing players would not have the corresponding signal processing required to properly play back discs made from those sources.

Note, however, that the use of standardized encoding does not mean that the system *output* necessarily is fixed or restricted. Additional output signal processing—in the form of volume and tone controls, graphic equalizers, digital signal

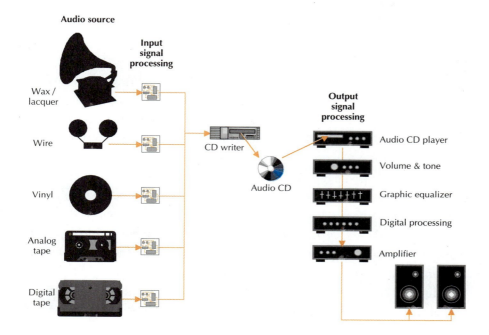

Figure 8.4b
Some output signal processing options in an audio CD system.

processors, etc.—can be used by the listener to optimize the output sound ultimately produced by the system (Fig. 8.4b). Factors such as listener preferences and listening environment characteristics will affect this optimization process.

From this examination, it can be seen that the audio CD system incorporates a number of important features: The system provides for input from a wide variety of different sources; it has a means for encoding, storing, and exchanging data in an efficient and standardized way; its basic output signal processing is independent of the original input source; and additional output signal processing can be used to optimize the final output of the system.

All of these features would be very desirable in a multiple input/output color-imaging system. Providing them requires that a suitable signal-processing arrangement be used and that careful attention be paid to the encoding of color.

Multiple Input/Output Color-Imaging Systems

Figure 8.5 shows a signal-processing arrangement for a multiple input/output color-imaging system. As in the audio CD system, this arrangement uses a standardized input/output interface at the center of the system. The interface must provide a standardized representation of color, defined in terms of what we will refer to as a *color encoding specification (CES)*.

A color encoding specification must define two principal attributes of the color representation: a *color-encoding method* and a *color-encoding data metric* (Fig. 8.6). The distinction between these attributes is extremely important.

The *color-encoding method* determines the actual *meaning* of the encoded data, while the *color-encoding data metric* defines the *color space* and the *numerical units* in which encoded data are expressed. For example, the encoding method might be such that the color data represent standard CIE colorimetric measurements of reproduced images. (Whether that method will

Figure 8.5

Use of a color encoding specification (CES) in a multiple input/output color-imaging system.

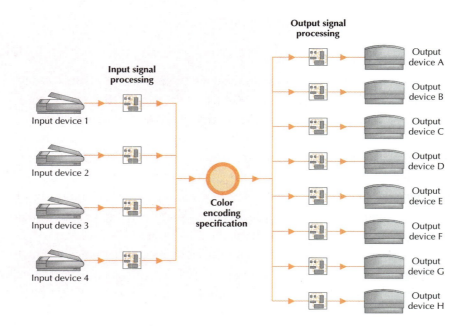

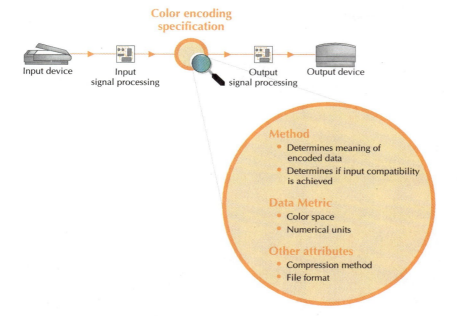

Input device · Input signal processing · Color encoding specification · Output signal processing · Output device

Method
- Determines meaning of encoded data
- Determines if input compatibility is achieved

Data Metric
- Color space
- Numerical units

Other attributes
- Compression method
- File format

Figure 8.6

A color encoding specification must define two principal attributes: a color-encoding method and a color-encoding data metric. Other attributes also may be defined.

work or not will be discussed later.) Those measurements then can be expressed in terms of various *data metrics* without changing their basic meaning. For example, any of several different *color spaces,* such as CIELAB or CIELUV, could be used. Color space values in turn can be digitally encoded in various ways, again without changing the basic meaning of that data. For example, CIELAB values might be scaled in a particular way and represented by three 8-bit numbers (Figure 8.7).

The selection of a data metric is one of many important engineering decisions that must be made for any color-imaging system. The choice will affect the efficiency of the color encoding, and it will directly affect factors such as image compression, as will be shown in Chapter 12. But the color-encoding method is much more fundamental. It defines the entire basis for the standardized representation of color within the system. The critical point is this: *If the encoding method is inappropriate, the system will fail, regardless of which data metric is chosen.*

Figure 8.7

An example of a
color encoding
specification.

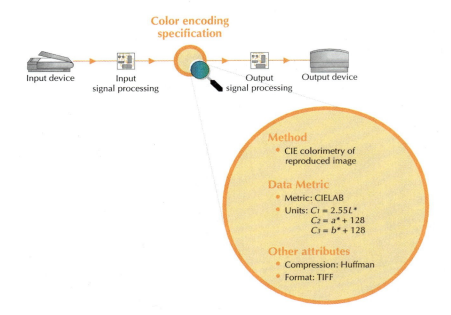

Color encoding specification

Input device   Input signal processing   Output signal processing   Output device

Method
- CIE colorimetry of reproduced image

Data Metric
- Metric: CIELAB
- Units: $C_1 = 2.55L^*$
  $C_2 = a^* + 128$
  $C_3 = b^* + 128$

Other attributes
- Compression: Huffman
- Format: TIFF

The reason for this is that the encoding method determines *what will be represented* by the encoding, whereas the data metric determines only *how the representation will be numerically expressed*. As an analogy, the selection of a method is equivalent to determining whether something will be measured in terms of its volume, weight, or mass. Once that is determined, various data metrics then can be used to express the measurement without changing its basic meaning. For example, the method might determine that volume will be measured. That measurement then can be expressed in cubic inches, cubic centimeters, or various other units without changing its meaning.

In addition to a color-encoding method and a color-encoding data metric, a color encoding specification also may include other attributes, such as a data compression method and a data file format. Although they are not strictly part of the color representation, those attributes must be completely defined so that images encoded according to the specification can be interchanged among various imaging systems and applications. Some of those attributes, as they relate to color, will be discussed in later chapters. For now, our focus will be on color-encoding methods.

The Concept of Input Compatibility

The most effective color encoding specification for a given system will depend on the particular requirements for that particular system. Nevertheless, there is one rule that *always* must be obeyed: To be successful, a color encoding specification must be based on a color-encoding method that creates a condition that we call *input compatibility.*

A system in which the inputs have been made compatible will have a number of important system features, similar to those of the audio CD system:

- Each output device can produce images from any image encoded in terms of the color encoding specification, regardless of the type of input medium or device that was used to produce the encoded image data.

- Image data encoded from one medium can be intermixed with image data encoded from another. For example, image data encoded from two different types of media can be merged (cut and pasted) to produce a seamless composite image.

- The number of signal-processing transforms required by the system is minimized.

- New input sources can be added to the system without requiring the addition of new corresponding output transforms. Each new input source requires only a transform from that input to the color encoding specification.

- Similarly, new output devices and media can be added to the system without requiring the addition of new corresponding input transforms. Each new output requires only a transform from the color encoding specification to that output.

Creating input compatibility requires that—at a minimum—all fundamental differences, such as those that exist between negative and positive input media, be eliminated as part of the encoding process. In addition, image data from all input sources must be encoded on some *common basis.*

When this is done appropriately, interpretation of encoded color values does *not* require knowledge of the input image medium that was the source of that color, nor does it require knowledge of the device that was used to measure the color. Encoded input-compatible values *alone,* expressed in terms of the color encoding specification, completely and unambiguously define color.

For example, a triad of input-compatible encoded values, such as 83, 105, and 52, expressed in a particular data metric, would be sufficient to define a color. If some *additional* qualification is necessary in order for the color to be completely defined—such as "the values were measured from (a particular medium)" or "the values were measured by (a particular scanner)" or "the values are meant for (a particular output device)"—then the meaning of the values alone must be ambiguous. So a *negative* test for input compatibility can be defined: If there is any ambiguity or inconsistency in the encoded values, then input compatibility has *not* been achieved. This test will be used often in the upcoming discussions of color-encoding methods.

Creating input compatibility is not always easy. In particular, it can be difficult to establish a common basis for color encoding in systems where the inputs are of fundamentally different types, such as systems that support input from both positive and negative photographic films and systems that support input from both hardcopy and electronic sources. Nevertheless, achieving input compatibility is the key to successful color encoding, and the focus of the next chapters will be on achieving that compatibility.

Input Compatibility and Tags

It is often suggested that the features that we have associated with input compatibility can be achieved instead by the use of image file *tags*. Tags are image file headers containing additional information about the image data in the file. Such information is useful for specifying basic properties, such as image size and spatial resolution. Tags also can be used to provide information required to interpret the encoded color data. This type of identification is the basis for file format standards such as *TIFF* (Tagged Image File Format).

Although the use of tagged files certainly is a vast improvement over using image files in which there is no way of knowing what the numbers really mean, tagging alone is not a *substitute* for achieving input compatibility. The previously described system features cannot be achieved unless the fundamental differences among inputs are removed somewhere along the signal processing chain. For example, mixed image types, even if tagged, cannot be *directly* edited into seamless composites. Editing together portions of an image from a negative film with portions from a positive film certainly would not be seamless unless the image data first are translated into some common (input compatible) form.

The use of tags does, however, provide flexibility as to *when* and *where* input compatibility is created. For example, in Fig. 8.8a, input compatibility is achieved in the color encoding specification itself. In Fig. 8.8b, image files first are produced, in any of a variety of different color encoding specifications, and tagged appropriately. Input compatibility is not created until later, when the tagged image files are read and processed on a workstation.

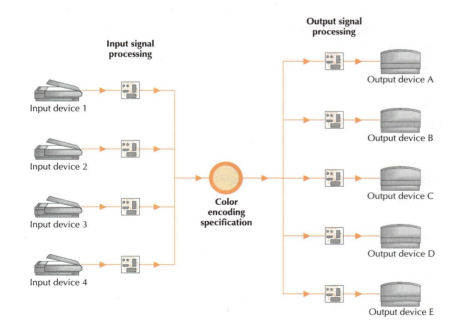

Figure 8.8a

To achieve the system features described in the text, input compatibility must be created somewhere along the signal-processing chain. One option is to create that compatibility directly in the color encoding specification.

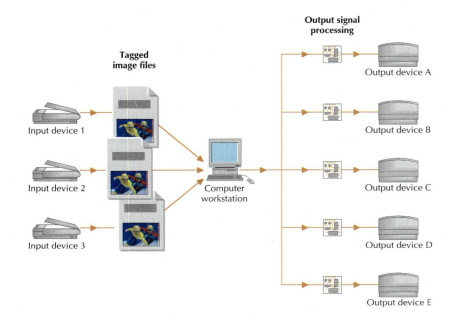

Both approaches are valid, and the decision as to which should be used for a given system will depend on the particular capabilities and requirements of that system. In most circumstances, however, we favor the approach in which input compatibility is created in the color encoding specification itself. Systems based on that approach still can use tags—all of the systems that we have designed have, in fact, used tags. But such systems are not dependent on tags for their basic operation. Tags instead are used to provide supplemental information that can enhance overall system performance. For example, a sophisticated user or application might perform some special image processing if auxiliary information about the origin and destination of an image are known.

One concern regarding an approach that is entirely dependent on the use of tags to define the meaning of encoded data is that the problems caused by different input types are not solved up front; they are passed to the user of the workstation. That may be perfectly acceptable if that user is knowledgeable and/or has access to applications that can deal appropriately with the tagged information, but that may not always be the case.

That concern is eliminated if any input compatibility problems are solved in the color encoding specification, before image files are created. When that is done, simpler applications and relatively unsophisticated users can more easily make use of the image files that are subsequently produced. An additional concern is that tags have a way of getting lost or corrupted as images are passed from system to system, edited, or merged with other images. Tagged information also may never have been filled in, or information may have been entered incorrectly.

In our opinion, then, whenever it is possible to do so, a system should be designed to work well with all image files, even if any supplemental information that might be supplied by tags is missing. In some systems, there really is no choice, because image files are meant to be played "as is" on an output device. Since under such circumstances there is no opportunity for image data to be processed on an intermediary workstation or other signal-processing device, input compatibility must be created in the color encoding itself.

Input Compatibility and Device-Independent Color

Another frequent suggestion is that input compatibility can be achieved simply by the use of a single "device-independent" color metric to encode data from all input sources. The most common proposal is to use a metric based on a CIE color space such as XYZ, CIELAB, or CIELUV. However, the use of such metrics *alone*—i.e., without regard to the encoding *method*—will *not* ensure input compatibility.

One way to explain the distinction between the use of a device-independent encoding metric and the achievement of true input compatibility is by analogy. Suppose that instead of the scanning and reproduction of images, the problem was the scanning and reprinting of pages of printed text. If such a system is limited to a single input and output language—if, for example, it is used for scanning and reprinting English words only—the encoding can be simple (Fig. 8.9).

Figure 8.9
A simple text-
scanning system,
which is restricted
to a single input/
output language.

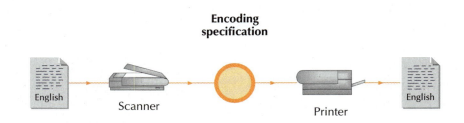

Because the text-scanning system shown in Fig. 8.9 is restricted to a single input/output language, encoded information only would have to represent the patterns of black and white on the scanned input page. Under these circumstances, even a conventional photocopier would be sufficient.

Now suppose that there was an additional requirement for the system also to scan text that is written in two other languages, say French and Spanish (Fig. 8.10). Again, the encoding can be simple, and a conventional photocopier will be sufficient, *if* the system is restricted to reprinting only English from input English texts, reprinting only French from input French texts, and reprinting only Spanish from input Spanish texts.

Figure 8.10
A multi-language
text-scanning sys-
tem. This system is
restricted in that
the output must
be in the same
language as the
input.

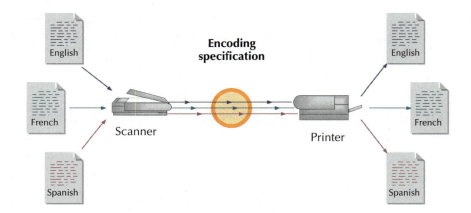

But what if the system was required to scan words in *any* of the input languages and print out these words in *any* of the output languages? And what if, in addition, the system was to be used to edit input text? In particular, what if it was to be used to cut and paste words scanned from different languages and then to produce composite pages of text in any of the output languages? Would an approach analogous to the use of a "device-independent" color metric work?

Let us try using a "language-independent" text metric to see what happens. The Roman letters A–Z can serve as such a metric because they can be used to represent text in any of the input languages. The scanned letters can be encoded in ASCII, which provides a convenient, efficient, standardized language-independent encoding metric (Fig. 8.11).

But that language-independent encoding would contribute *nothing* toward solving the basic problem. The reason is that the encoding alone would be *ambiguous* (the key word in our test of input compatibility). The same pattern of letters could have entirely different meanings, depending on what input language is assumed. For example, the meaning of the pattern of letters p-l-u-m-e is ambiguous (Fig. 8.12). That pattern means "pen" in French, but it means "large fluffy feather" in English!

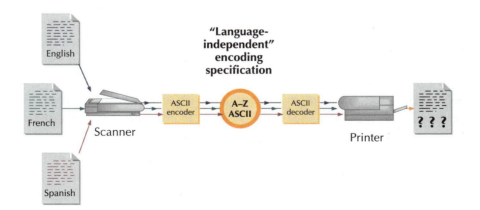

Figure 8.11

A text-scanning system that is based on a common "language-independent" *metric*. The system will *not* work.

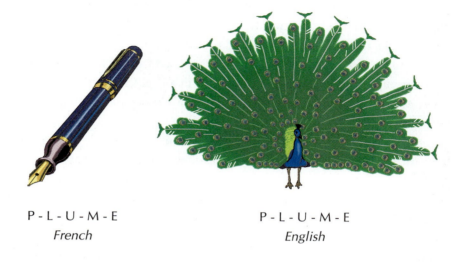

P - L - U - M - E
French

P - L - U - M - E
English

So despite the use of a language-independent text-encoding metric in this example, the *meaning* of a given pattern of letters remains *language dependent*. The language of origination would have to be identified, perhaps by a tag, along with the encoded letters in order to produce meaningful text output from the system.

The real problem, then, is that the letters alone are not sufficient to convey their meaning. It is important to understand that this is *not* a metric problem, i.e., it is not a problem with the A–Z characters or with ASCII. There is an *inherent* ambiguity, and therefore a basic incompatibility, in the inputs because they are in *different languages*. Since that ambiguity is not *caused* by a metric, it cannot be *solved* by the selection of a particular metric, whether that metric is language independent or not.

In order to achieve true input compatibility in this system, it is necessary to do more than convert all of the input words to a common *metric*. It is necessary to use an encoding *method* that *interprets the meaning* of all inputs and expresses that meaning in a *common language*.

Let us now try that approach to see what happens. It will not really matter what language is used as the common language (at least not yet), so let us use Latin. The system then would be as shown in Fig. 8.13.

The role of each input transform in the arrangement now is apparent: Each must *translate* from the particular input language to Latin. The role of each output transform also is apparent: each must *translate* from Latin to the particular output language. The output transforms are independent of the input language; it does not matter what language(s) the original input words were in, because once transformed to the encoding specification, *all* words are in Latin. The system can be used to cut and paste encoded words, again because they all are expressed in Latin. Editing can be done without knowing in which language the final document will be printed. The system can, in fact, produce output in any or all of the output languages from the same encoded text. New input and output languages easily can be added; each would require just one translation transform. All of this was accomplished by the creation of *compatibility* among the system inputs; it could *not* have been done by the use of a "language independent" metric alone.

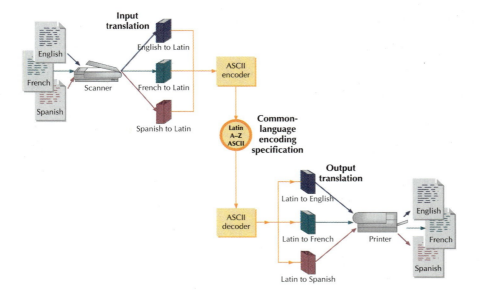

Figure 8.13

A text-scanning system based on a common encoding *language*. This system *will* work.

Creating Input Compatibility in Color-Imaging Systems

The language analogy essentially defines what is needed to establish input compatibility in a color-imaging system: *The meaning of the color information from each input source must be* interpreted *before encoding.*

That is not always simple to do. Consider the multiple-input system shown in Fig. 8.14. Color information provided by the digital still camera most likely was captured directly from live original scenes. Color information from the reflection and slide scanners comes from positive reproductions on two very different types of imaging media. And, to keep things interesting, the negative scanner provides information scanned from images that have recorded color "backwards."

Figure 8.14

A color-imaging system with four fundamentally different types of inputs.

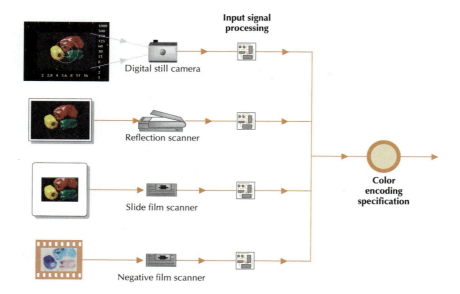

The system is dealing with inputs having *fundamentally* different colorimetric properties. These inputs are, in effect, speaking very different "languages." An appropriate color-encoding *method* must be used that will allow the *meaning* of the color information from each input to be interpreted and translated into a common color "language."

This translation, and the encoding method itself, must be based on some color property—a particular aspect of color—that all of the inputs have in common. It is that aspect of color that then must be measured and digitally encoded in order to represent color completely and unambiguously in the encoding specification. Measurement and encoding methods that might be considered include the following:

Densitometric encoding:

- Measurements made according to spectral responsivities that are not equivalent to a set of visual color-matching functions
- Encoding based on the densitometric measurements

Standard colorimetric encoding:

- Measurements made according to the spectral responses of the CIE Standard Colorimetric Observer
- Encoding based on standard colorimetric computations

Advanced colorimetric encoding:

- Measurements made according to the spectral responses of the CIE Standard Colorimetric Observer
- Encoding includes colorimetric adjustments for certain physical and perceptual factors

In the next chapters, each of these measurement and encoding methods will be examined. These examinations will show which methods will work, and which ones will not, in various types of practical imaging systems. The examinations also will show why it was necessary to invent a fundamentally different method of color encoding for the *Photo CD* System.

Summary of Key Issues

- The basic functions of digital color encoding in a color-imaging system are to link system inputs and outputs and to provide a digital representation of color for editing, storage, and interchange.

- Support of multiple input and output types can best be accomplished by first dividing the digital signal processing into two parts—input processing and output processing—and by then using an appropriate color encoding specification to link the inputs and outputs.

- A complete definition for a color encoding specification includes both a color-encoding method and a color-encoding data metric. Other attributes, such as image file format, also may be defined.

- A color-encoding method defines the actual meaning of the encoded data, while a color-encoding data metric defines the color space and numerical units in which encoded data are expressed.

- Input signal processing to the color encoding specification must be based on an encoding method that creates input compatibility among all input sources.

- Input compatibility means that data from all input sources are encoded on a common basis and are expressed, in terms of a color encoding specification, such that encoded values completely and unambiguously define color.

- To achieve input compatibility, it is necessary to define the color encoding specification in terms of an aspect of color that all the system inputs have in common.

- When the colorimetric properties of the input sources are fundamentally different, appropriate input signal processing must be used to create input compatibility. In such cases, input compatibility cannot be achieved simply by the use of a common data metric.

9

Densitometric Color Encoding

Densitometric color encoding is based on input-image color measurements made according to defined sets of spectral responsivities that are not equivalent to a set of visual color-matching functions. The responsivities can be those of a particular type of densitometric instrument, such as an ISO Status A or Status M densitometer (Fig. 9.1). The responsivities also can be those of an actual scanner or of some hypothetical reference scanner. Encoded colors can be expressed in terms of red, green, and blue densities, transmittances, reflectances, CMY or CMYK colorant amounts, or other values associated with the densitometric measurements.

Figure 9.1

Figure 9.1

Two sets of red, green, and blue responsivities that could be used for densitometric color encoding: ISO Status A (solid lines), and Status M (dotted lines).

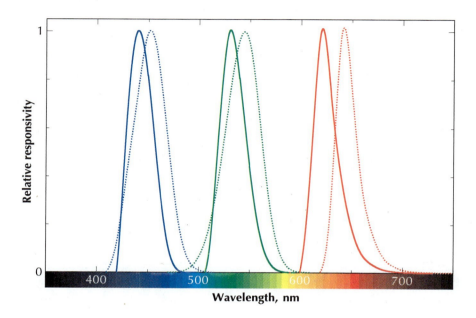

The principal advantage of this type of encoding is that, because it corresponds quite directly to physical measurements of input images, it often simplifies color signal processing. Consider, for example, the system shown in Fig. 9.2. Let us assume that the objective of the system is to produce output images that visually match scanned input images, and also that the output thermal-print medium has CMY image-forming dyes that are *identical* to those of the input medium.

The responsivities of the system's densitometric scanner can be designed such that each R, G, or B channel primarily "sees" just one image-forming dye of the input medium (Fig. 9.3). Each scanner color signal therefore will represent the amount of the corresponding C, M, or Y dye for each pixel in the scanned image. If the output is also designed such that each R, G, or B color signal primarily controls the amount of just one of the C, M, or Y image-forming dyes produced on the output medium, little or no color signal processing will be needed in the system.

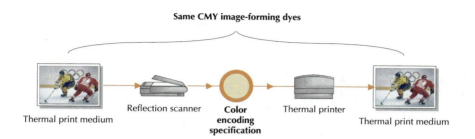

Figure 9.2

An imaging system using the same medium for input and output.

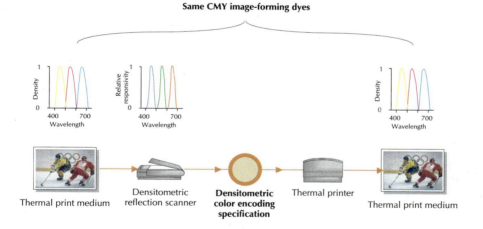

Figure 9.3

In this system, densitometric scanning and color encoding will minimize, and may even eliminate, the need for color signal processing.

The system shown in Fig. 9.3 simply will measure input dye amounts and produce those amounts on the output. The output image will be a one-to-one *physical* copy—what is known as a *duplicate*—of the input image. If the input and output images are viewed under identical conditions, they of course will *visually* match.

This example certainly is a special case. Nevertheless, it illustrates an important point: It is commonly assumed that output devices *must* be sent color data expressed in terms of human-observer-based colorimetry, such as CIE colorimetry, in order to produce a visual match to the input. But that is not true. Ultimately, output devices must generate color signals that will *result* in a visual match (or some other desired colorimetric result). But that does not necessarily mean that an output device must be *supplied* with CIE colorimetric values in order to do so. Nor does it mean that it is even useful to *measure* the CIE colorimetry of the input in all cases.

For example, in a system like that shown in Fig. 9.3, a *colorimetric scanner* having responsivities equivalent to those of the CIE Standard Observer could be used instead of a densitometric scanner (Fig. 9.4). The colorimetric scanner would provide direct measurements of CIE *XYZ* tristimulus values of the input image. But what would be done with those values? To produce an output image having those colorimetric values, it would be necessary to transform the *XYZ* values back to *RGB* values in order to produce the proper output signals. Unless there were some other purpose for the *XYZ* values (such as for image editing in a CIE color space), it would be simpler to scan with a densitometric scanner and avoid the need for an *XYZ*-to-*RGB* output transform.

Also, in a system based on densitometric scanning of a single medium, an input transform could be used to convert scanner *RGB* values to CIE *XYZ* tristimulus values (Fig. 9.5). But again, what would be done with those values? In order to produce an output print having that colorimetry, it again would be necessary to use an output transform. For the system shown, using an input transformation from scanner *RGB* values to *XYZ* values followed by an output transform from *XYZ* back to *RGB* values serves no purpose. Moreover, the transformations may result in reductions in signal-processing speed and accuracy.

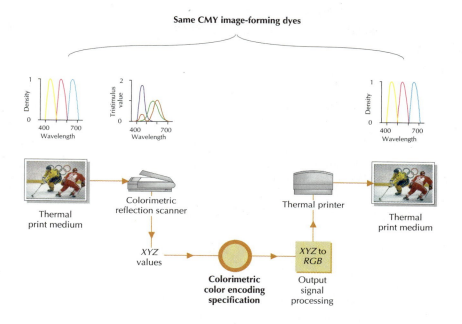

Figure 9.4

In this system, colorimetric scanning adds no real value, and its use requires additional color signal processing.

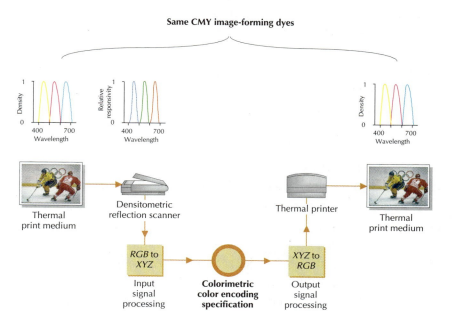

Figure 9.5

In this system, colorimetric encoding adds no real value, and its use requires additional color signal processing.

Now, relatively few systems use the same imaging medium for both input and output. Still, the scanned *RGB* input and required *RGB* output values of many practical systems often are remarkably similar. They are, at least, much more similar to each other than either is to any set of CIE colorimetric values. Numerous systems have failed because of the unnecessary use of color transformations of scanned *RGB* values to colorimetric and other types of color spaces, followed by complex transformations from those spaces to *RGB* output values. In virtually every case, the systems would have worked much better if simple *RGB*-input to *RGB*-output transformations had been used instead.

Densitometric Encoding and Input Compatibility

Densitometric color encoding generally can be used when an imaging system is restricted to having just one input medium and a single scanner. In such cases, there is no real issue of input compatibility because all scanned data inherently are input compatible. There are no fundamental disparities among the scanned images because all image data are produced from the same scanner measuring images on the same medium. The meaning of the scanned values themselves therefore is unambiguous.

What happens, however, if there is more than one scanner (but still just one input medium)? If all the scanners have identical densitometric characteristics, then the situation remains the same, and densitometric color encoding will be sufficient (Fig. 9.6). There will be no ambiguity, because an image measured on any of the scanners would yield the same scanned values.

But what if the scanners have *different* densitometric characteristics, or if the densitometric characteristics of a single scanner change over time? Because there still is only one input medium, densitometric measurements again can be used as the basis for color encoding. However, input compatibility will not result automatically from a direct encoding of these measurements. The meaning of measured values alone will be ambiguous; it will depend on which particular scanner is used (or on when the values are measured by a scanner having densitometric characteristics that change over time).

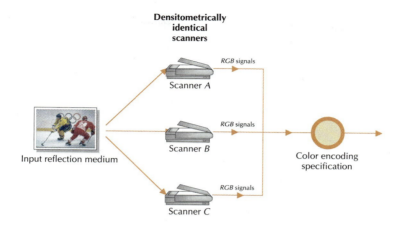

Figure 9.6
The use of multiple input scanners is not a complication if all scanners are identical.

One way of dealing with a multiple-scanner situation would be to equip each output device with an arsenal of output transforms—one for each input scanner. A simpler solution, however, would be to create input compatibility among the scanners themselves. The methodology for doing so also addresses the problem of scanners that change characteristics over time.

In order to create input compatibility among multiple (or variable) scanners, the signal processing of each scanner in the system must include an appropriate correction transform, based on a *calibration* of the particular device (Figs. 9.7a and 9.7b). The correction transforms primarily would compensate for differences in the spectral responsivities among the scanners. The transforms also would correct for other measurement differences due to the optical and electronic properties of the individual scanners. When each scanner is used with its own correction transform, each will produce identical values for the same input image. If scanner characteristics change over time, the calibration can be updated at appropriate intervals to compensate.

It will be shown later that in color-imaging systems with disparate types of input media, input scanner calibration *alone* is not sufficient to create input compatibility. However, all successful color-imaging systems incorporate some form of scanner calibration-based correction as *part* of their input signal processing. Such corrections, which essentially make all system scanners behave identically, will be assumed in all further examples.

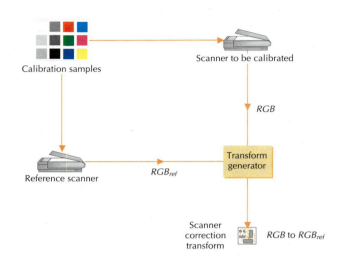

Figure 9.7a
Scanner correction. Calibration samples are read on both the reference scanner and the scanner to be calibrated. A correction transform is then computed. This transform relates scanned *RGB* values to corresponding *RGB*$_{ref}$ values for the reference scanner.

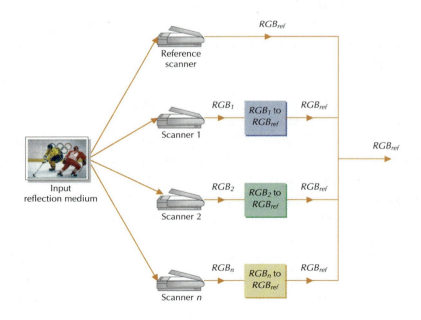

Figure 9.7b
The use of multiple scanners and correction transforms. With appropriate correction transforms in place, each scanner produces *RGB* values equal to those that would be produced by the reference scanner.

In one practical implementation of this calibrated densitometric approach, shown in Fig. 9.8, all of the input scanners at a major motion picture special-effects studio were calibrated to produce *RGB* values equal to those measured according to ISO Status M densitometric standards. This simple calibration was *all* that was required to achieve input compatibility in this multi-million-dollar system because a single input medium—a particular motion picture color negative film—always is used. Many color electronic prepress systems also successfully use color encoding that is based solely on calibrated densitometric measurements. Scanner calibration is all that is required to create input compatibility in these systems, again because a single input medium (generally a particular photographic transparency film) is used.

But what happens if the system must support more than one input medium? Will densitometric color encoding still work? That depends on the nature of the differences among the media, as will be shown in later chapters. However, in the next example, color encoding based on densitometric measurement not only works for the described multiple-input-medium system, it essentially is the *only* type of encoding method that will work.

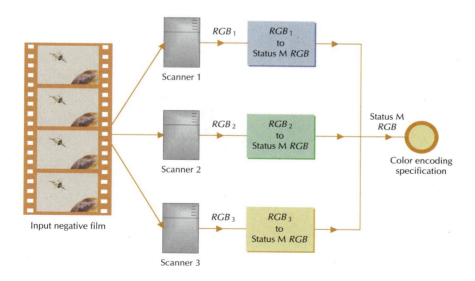

Figure 9.8
The use of densitometric color encoding in a motion picture special-effects studio.

A Multiple-Negative Film System

This next practical example is based on the *Cineon* Digital Film System (Fig. 9.9), which is used widely in the motion picture industry for special effects and other post-production work. The *Cineon* System is designed to scan multiple types of motion picture negative films for input to an electronic editing workstation. A film writer then is used to produce output on another type of motion picture negative film. The figure shows an example of three different negative films being scanned and edited together to form a single composite negative. Input compatibility is essential in this application in order to produce seamless-appearing composite images from portions of the three different input negative films.

Figure 9.9

The *Cineon* Digital Film System.

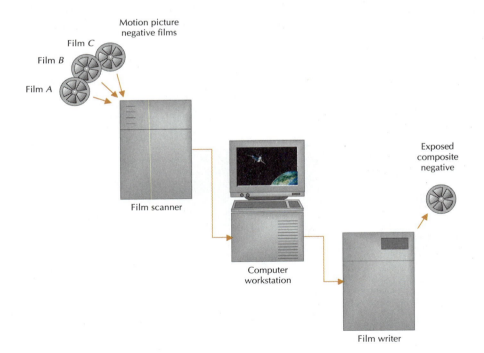

How can input compatibility be created on this system? It was stated earlier that input compatibility must be based on some aspect of color that all of the system inputs have in common. In order to identify what the particular input films of this system have in common, it is necessary to know something about how they are designed to be used. The key piece of information is that these negative films are all meant to be printed onto a specific motion picture print film, using a particular type of optical printer. The negatives accordingly are designed in terms of a particular type of densitometric measurement described earlier: *printing density*.

As discussed in Chapter 7, printing densities are the densities of the negative as measured according to a specified set of reference print material spectral sensitivities and a defined reference printer illuminant. The spectral characteristics of a particular reference print film and printer illuminant used for optically printing motion picture negatives are shown in Fig. 9.10.

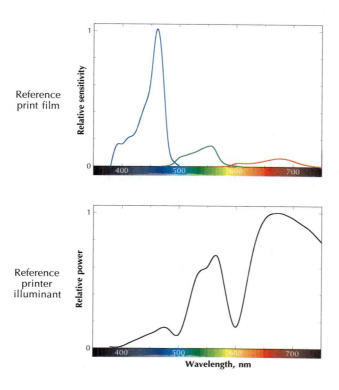

Figure 9.10

Spectral characteristics of a particular reference print film and printer illuminant used for motion picture negatives.

Recall that if two areas of a negative are "seen" as having the same *RGB* densities by the print material, the areas have—by definition—the same printing densities. If both areas have the same printing densities, they both will produce the same color when identically printed onto the reference print material. That will be true even if the areas having the same printing densities are on two different types of negative films having different sets of CMY image-forming dyes. Printing-density values defined according to a particular print medium and printer, then, are *unambiguous*. If the printing-density values for an area of a negative are known, no additional information as to the origin of those values is required. Color encoding based on printing densities therefore meets our criterion for input compatibility.

To encode scanned image data in terms of printing-density values, printing densities can be measured *directly* using a scanner having effective red, green, and blue spectral responsivities equivalent to the effective red, green, and blue spectral responsivities of the reference print material and printer. The effective spectral responsivities of a scanner (Fig. 9.11a) are the product of the spectral power distribution of the scanner light source and the red, green, and blue spectral sensitivities of the scanner sensor. Similarly, the effective spectral responsivities for a print medium (Fig. 9.11b) are the product

Figure 9.11a

The effective spectral responsivities of a scanner are the product of the spectral power distribution of the scanner light source and the red, green, and blue sensitivities of the sensor.

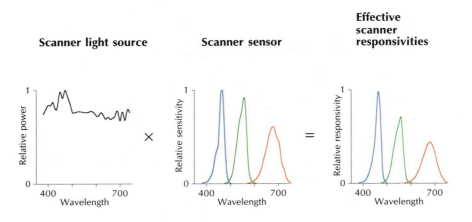

of the spectral power distribution of the printer light source and the inherent red, green, and blue spectral sensitivities of the print medium.

If the effective spectral responsivities of the scanner are *not* equivalent to the effective spectral responsivities of the reference print material and printer, another approach to printing-density encoding can be taken. An input signal-processing transform can be used to convert densitometric measurements from the scanner to printing-density values. In this case, however, the scanner would require a different input transform for each type of input film, i.e., for each film having a different set of image-forming dyes.

In the *Cineon* System, color encoding in terms of printing-density values not only results in seamless cutting and pasting, it also directly provides the information necessary to produce output negatives. These output negatives must be printing-density copies of the input negatives (unless deliberate editing has been done). The following example illustrates why.

In the original negative of a recently released motion picture, an overhead microphone occasionally was visible during a scene. Reshooting the scene would have been prohibitively expensive. So instead, the involved frames were scanned on a *Cineon* System, and the resulting image data were digitally "retouched" to remove the microphone. The output negative frames then were

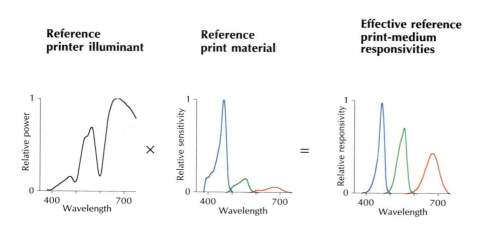

Reference printer illuminant

Reference print material

Effective reference print-medium responsivities

Figure 9.11b

The effective spectral responsivities for a print medium are the product of the spectral power distribution of the printer light source and the red, green, and blue spectral sensitivities of the print medium.

physically spliced in with the good frames of the original negative, and all the frames were optically printed onto the print film. None of this trickery was noticeable in the final print because, except for the retouched areas, the *printing densities* of the output negative perfectly matched those of the original negative. Any other type of matching would have produced unacceptable results, because images printed from the retouched frames would have been noticeably different from those printed from the original frames.

Discussion

In the examples that have been described, the use of a densitometric color-encoding method resulted in encoded values that are *consistent* and *unambiguous* in their meaning. Those features are the essence of input compatibility, and they are the key to successful color encoding.

In some of the examples, other encoding methods could have been used successfully. But densitometric color encoding often is preferred because transformations from scanner *RGB* values to densitometric values, and transformations from densitometric values to output device *RGB* values, generally are quite simple. That simplicity can translate to optimum signal-processing accuracy and speed.

Although considerations affecting processing speed are becoming less of an issue, they cannot yet be ignored completely. For example, the *Cineon* System recently was used in the production of *every frame* of a full-length animated motion picture. That involved the processing of billions of individual pixels. Obviously, in such systems, signal-processing efficiency still is an extremely important issue. Processing efficiency also is a concern on relatively modest desktop computer systems.

Although densitometric encoding was successful in the examples discussed in this chapter, the input sources of the described systems were limited to particular types. In the following chapters, it will be shown that other encoding methods are needed in order to produce input compatibility in more complex, multiple-input situations.

Summary of Key Issues

- Densitometric color encoding is based on color measurements made according to a defined set of spectral responsivities that are not equivalent to any set of visual color-matching functions.

- The principal advantage of densitometric color encoding is that it simplifies color signal processing, which can result in optimum signal-processing speed and accuracy.

- Densitometric color encoding can be used only when an imaging system is restricted to having one basic type of input medium.

- All successful color-imaging systems incorporate some form of correction for input scanner variations. Such correction is based on calibration and is included in the input signal processing.

- Many color electronic prepress and motion picture systems successfully use color encoding based solely on calibrated densitometry.

10
Colorimetric Color Encoding

Colorimetric encoding is based on measurements made according to the spectral responses of a human observer. One of the principal advantages of this method of color encoding is that it is based on well-established CIE recommendations for color measurement.

At first glance, colorimetric encoding would seem to offer the perfect method for encoding color; and in practice, colorimetric encoding sometimes can provide input compatibility where methods based on other forms of measurements cannot. In other cases, however, the use of standard colorimetric techniques alone will not work.

Since colorimetric encoding is the method most often promoted as the ideal "device-independent" solution to color encoding, it is very important to understand its capabilities—and its limitations. The examples given in this chapter should help.

A Case Where Colorimetric Encoding Works Well

Consider a system, such as the one shown in Fig. 10.1a, that supports input from an assortment of reflection media having different image-forming colorants—printing inks, photographic dyes, thermal-transfer dyes, etc.—with different spectral absorption characteristics. A color-encoding method based on red, green, and blue *densitometric* measurements alone, as was described in the previous chapter, will *not* provide a meaningful representation of color in this multiple reflection-media system.

Figure 10.1a

A multiple reflection-media system in which a densitometric scanner is used. Densitometric measurements alone will *not* provide a meaningful representation of color in this system.

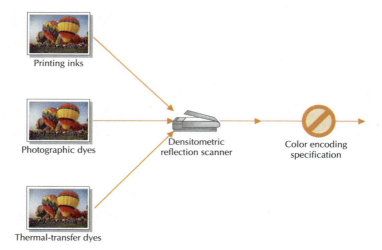

Printing inks

Photographic dyes

Thermal-transfer dyes

Densitometric reflection scanner

Color encoding specification

For example, Fig. 10.1b illustrates that a pair of colors on two different media can look identical, but they most likely will produce quite different *RGB* densitometric values. Conversely, a pair of colors on two different media might appear quite different from one another, but they might happen to produce the same *RGB* densitometric values. These inconsistencies will occur whenever the spectral absorption characteristics of the colorant sets used in the two media are different.

The meaning of measured *RGB* densitometric values alone, then, would be ambiguous in this system. The color associated with a given set of *RGB* values would depend on which particular medium was measured. Such ambiguity indicates that compatibility has not been established among the system inputs, and the system will fail unless something is done to establish that compatibility where it does not inherently exist.

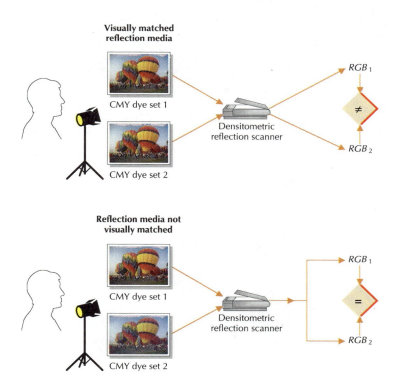

Figure 10.1b
Color encoding based on red, green, and blue densitometric measurements alone will fail in this system. Densitometric color values are ambiguous when media having different colorants are used.

It was stated earlier that in order to create input compatibility among disparate input media, it is necessary to identify a color-related property that all of the media have in common. There is such a property here in that all of the input media of this system were originally designed to be directly viewed by human observers. That fact suggests that the color encoding should be based on *colorimetry* rather than on densitometry, and indeed that is true. However, that colorimetry must be measured in a very specific way.

Input compatibility will be realized, by definition, if visually matched colors on the different input media produce identical encoded color values (Fig. 10.2). However, since the colorants differ from medium to medium, such visual matches will be metameric, not spectral. As discussed in Chapter 1, metameric matching is *viewing illuminant dependent*; pairs of colors on different media that match when viewed under one illuminant might not match when viewed under another. What this means is that color encoding based on standard CIE colorimetric measurements *can* achieve input compatibility among multiple reflection media, but *only* under the following two conditions:

1. A reference illuminant, i.e., the illuminant used for metameric matching, must be specified, and

2. Colorimetric values must be determined according to the spectral properties of that reference illuminant.

Figure 10.2

Input compatibility will be realized in this system if visually matched colors on the different input media produce identical encoded values.

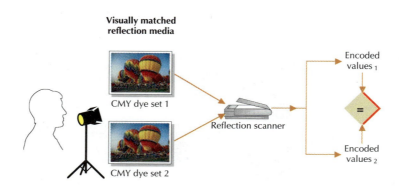

Visually matched reflection media

CMY dye set 1

CMY dye set 2

Reflection scanner

Encoded values 1

Encoded values 2

=

For example, suppose it is specified that two different input media will be encoded in terms of their being viewed under identical conditions in which a light source that simulates CIE Standard Illuminant D_{50} is used. If a pair of colors on the two media visually match under those conditions, their *colorimetric* values measured using that D_{50} source would be identical. Color encoding derived from those identical values would properly represent the fact that the colors matched, which indicates that the colorimetric encoding method has established input compatibility for the two media.

Colorimetric values of scanned input media can be determined in two fundamentally different ways. The first approach uses densitometric scanning (Fig. 10.3). Media-dependent transforms are then used to convert *RGB* densitometric values to CIE colorimetric values that have been determined using the reference illuminant. *It is important to note that a different transform is needed for each input medium having a different set of image-forming colorants.* Implementing this approach requires some means for identifying the input medium so that the proper conversion transform can be selected.

The second approach uses a *colorimetric scanner* to *directly* measure the colorimetry of the input media. Figure 10.4a shows one arrangement for a colorimetric scanner in which the spectral power distribution of the scanner light source is identical to that of the reference illuminant. In addition, the

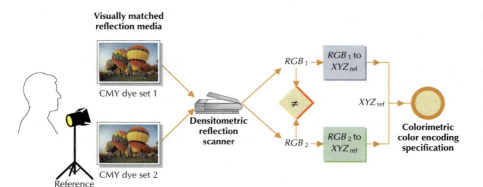

Figure 10.3
Media-dependent transforms are required when an RGB densitometric scanner is used for colorimetric color encoding.

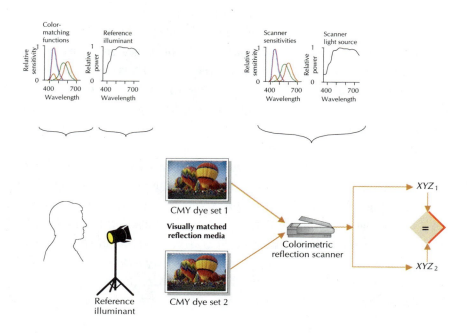

Figure 10.4a

Use of a colorimetric scanner for colorimetric color encoding. In this arrangement, the spectral power distribution of the scanner light source is identical to that of the reference illuminant. Measured values are input compatible, so no media-dependent input transforms are required.

spectral sensitivities of the scanner sensors are equivalent to the color-matching functions of the CIE Standard Colorimetric Observer (or to any other set of visual color-matching functions). The values directly measured by this scanner are input compatible, so no media-dependent transforms are required.

The colorimetric scanner in Fig. 10.4b is identical to that in Fig. 10.4a except that the spectral power distribution of its light source differs from that of the reference illuminant. Due to this light source difference, colorimetric values measured by this scanner are *not* input compatible *with respect to the reference illuminant specified for the metameric matching*. For example, the scanner values for a pair of colors on two different media might be identical, but those colors might not visually match under the reference illuminant. Conversely, a pair of colors on two different media that visually match under the reference illuminant might produce different scanner values. To eliminate these inconsistencies, media-dependent input transforms must be used to

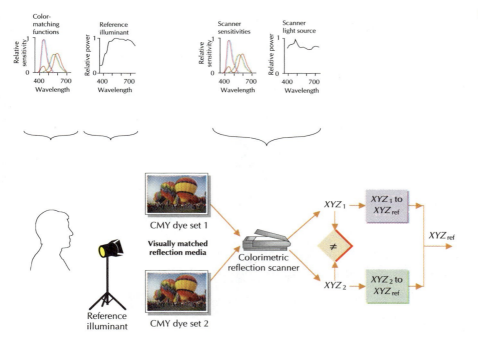

Figure 10.4b
Media-dependent
input transforms
are required in
this colorimetric
scanner because
the spectral power
distribution of its
light source differs
from that of the
illuminant speci-
fied for metameric
matching.

convert actual measured colorimetric values to those that would have been measured under the reference illuminant. The need for these transforms largely negates the principal advantage of colorimetric scanning over densitometric scanning.

The colorimetric scanner shown in Fig. 10.4c again uses a light source having a spectral power distribution different from that of the reference illuminant. In this case, however, the spectral sensitivities of the scanner sensors are *not* equivalent to a set of visual color-matching functions. Instead, the sensitivities are designed such that the *effective spectral responsivities* of the scanner, i.e., the products of the spectral power distribution of the scanner light source and the spectral sensitivities of the scanner sensors, are equivalent to the product of the spectral power distribution of the reference illuminant and a set of visual color-matching functions.

Figure 10.4c

In this colorimetric scanner, the effective spectral responsivities are equivalent to those of the scanner in Fig. 10.4a. Measured color values are input compatible, thus media-dependent transforms are not required.

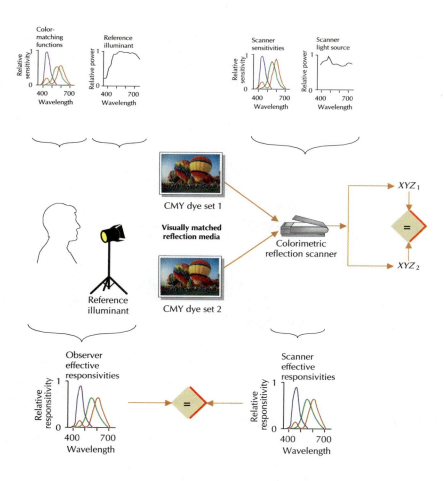

In the example shown in the figure (Fig. 10.4c), the spectral sensitivities of the sensors have been designed such that the effective spectral responsivities of the scanner are identical to those of the scanner described in Fig. 10.4a, despite the fact that a different scanner illuminant has been used. Except in some special circumstances, generally involving input media having fluorescent properties, the color values measured by the two scanners will be identical. Since those measured values are input compatible, no media-dependent input signal-processing transforms are required.

A Case Where Colorimetric Encoding Provides a Partial Solution

Colorimetric encoding can work well in systems that are limited to reflection media input, because reflection prints are viewed in environments containing white objects and other visual cues that strongly influence the general-brightness adaptive state and chromatic adaptive state of the observer. As a result, there typically is good correlation between color appearance and measured colorimetry. For example, a reflection image that appears too dark or too green in color balance also will measure that way. That is not the case for all media, however. In particular, it is not the case for projected images, such as photographic slides.

Figure 10.5a shows a system with input from two different photographic slide films. Since these films both are designed to be viewed directly by a human observer, it again might seem logical to encode the inputs according

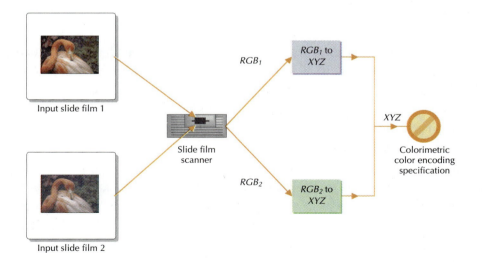

Input slide film 1

Input slide film 2

Slide film scanner

RGB_1

RGB_2

RGB_1 to XYZ

RGB_2 to XYZ

XYZ

Colorimetric color encoding specification

Figure 10.5a

A system using multiple types of photographic slide films. Standard colorimetric encoding will achieve input compatibility in this example, to a degree. But there is a complication that may not be obvious, as explained in the text.

to CIE colorimetric measurements. As in the previous example, this could be accomplished either by the use of a colorimetric scanner or by the use of an RGB densitometric scanner and appropriate media-specific transforms. These standard colorimetric approaches will achieve input compatibility, *to a degree*. But there is a complication that may not be obvious.

The problem is that when an image is viewed in an otherwise dark viewing environment, there can be a significant amount of visual adaptation by the observer to the image itself. As discussed in Chapter 6, this adaptation to the image occurs because other visual cues and references are absent. As a consequence, fairly significant shifts in image colorimetric characteristics may not be obvious to an observer.

This can be demonstrated by sequentially projecting a series of slides of the same subject matter in which the color balance is slightly more blue in each successive slide. If given a few seconds to adapt to each slide, most observers do not detect any differences in the projected images even though the colorimetry of the final slide indicates it is much bluer than the first. This demonstration, and a similar one described in Chapter 6 in which overall neutral density was increased, show that the relationship between *colorimetric measurement* and *color appearance* is not straightforward for photographic slides, motion picture prints, and other media viewed in conditions where there is significant adaptation to the image itself.

That is a problem when images on such media are used for input to a color-imaging system. The colorimetry of images can be expected to vary because of scene-illuminant differences, exposure errors, media manufacturing variability, chemical process variations, and a host of other factors. Although they might not be noticeable to an observer viewing projections of the images, those variations will be faithfully measured and encoded when standard colorimetric encoding methods are used.

Whether the resulting encoded differences will be visually noticeable in subsequent output images will depend on what output media and viewing environments are used. If the output is on another projected medium, the resulting image-to-image variations will be no more visually noticeable than those of the input images. If, however, the output is to a different type of

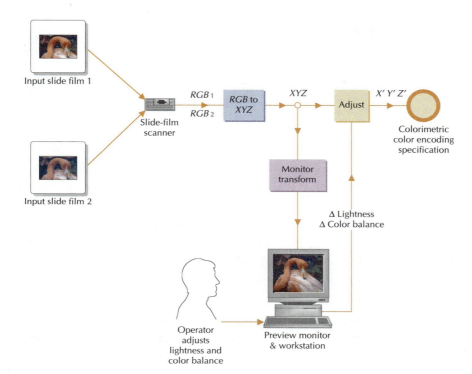

Figure 10.5b
Adjusting scanned
image data prior
to encoding.

medium, such as a reflection medium, visually undetected input-image colorimetric variations may be unacceptably noticeable in the output images. Image-to-image variations also might be very apparent, on *any* form of output, in a composite image made from portions of different input images or in a display in which multiple images are viewed simultaneously.

This is a tough problem to solve. What generally is done in practice is that scanned slide images are previewed on a monitor by a scanner operator (Fig. 10.5b). The operator can adjust data from each scanned image for lightness and color balance before the final encoding is done. This process requires considerable skill and patience. It will be shown later how the *Photo CD* System encoding process greatly facilitates the use of algorithms that can perform this operation automatically.

A Case Where Colorimetric Encoding Does Not Work

Figure 10.6 shows a system supporting *both* of the input types that have been discussed in this chapter—a photographic slide film and a reflection medium. Since both media are designed to be viewed directly by human observers, it again might seem that encoding according to CIE colorimetric measurements should work at least reasonably well. But standard colorimetric encoding actually would drastically fail to achieve input compatibility for this combination of input media. The reason is that these media are designed to produce images intended to be viewed in very different environments. Their colorimetric characteristics therefore are fundamentally different.

As described in Chapter 6, three types of colorimetric adjustments that are not required for reflection media are built into photographic slide films. First, the overall image density is increased in order to allow an extension of the

Figure 10.6

A system supporting both a photographic slide film and a reflection medium. The use of standard colorimetry alone will not work.

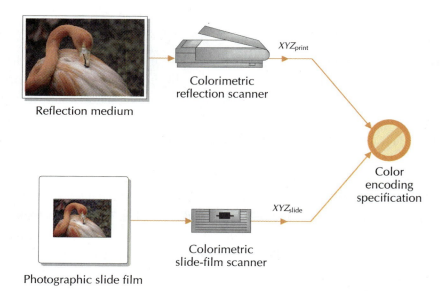

exposure dynamic range. This can be done on a slide film because the overall higher density goes unnoticed as a result of the observer's general-brightness adaptation to images viewed in a dark-projection environment. Second, the photographic gamma of the grayscale is increased to compensate for the reduced luminance contrast an observer will perceive due to the dark areas surrounding a projected image. And third, the color balance is shifted cyan-blue to compensate for the observer's incomplete chromatic adaptation to the reddish-yellow color of the projector illuminant.

Obviously, a measuring device, such as a colorimetric input scanner, is not subject to these perceptual effects, so its measurements will not necessarily correspond to actual color appearances. A colorimetric scanner would measure a photographic slide as being darker, higher in luminance contrast, and more cyan-blue in color balance than the projected slide actually appears. Those characteristics would be readily apparent in an output reflection image made according to the slide's measured colorimetry (Fig. 10.7).

In this dual-medium system, then, the meaning of a set of standard colorimetric values would be ambiguous. The color appearance associated with those values would be entirely different depending on whether the values were produced by scanning a slide film or by scanning a reflection medium. In this system, colorimetric encoding will *not* consistently yield a proper interpretation of the meaning of the input images. As a result, input compatibility will not be achieved, and the system will fail.

This outcome is not limited to isolated examples. A color-encoding method based on standard CIE colorimetric measurements *alone* will fail any time it is used for a mix of media that are designed to be viewed in different environments. But if colorimetric encoding fails, what else can be done?

There are two basic alternatives, each having its own advantages and disadvantages. One is to encode in terms of the reproduced color *appearance*, rather than the measured colorimetry, of the scanned image. This involves the use of advanced forms of colorimetry that appropriately account for perceptual factors. That approach will be described later, in Part IV, as part of the discussion of color management. A fundamentally different approach, which we devised for the *Photo CD* System, will be described in the next chapter.

Figure 10.7
A normal reflection print (upper image). A reflection print made according to colorimetry measured from a photographic slide will be too dark, too high in luminance contrast, and too cyan-blue in color balance (lower image).

Discussion

The rigor and elegance of CIE colorimetric methods can lead the unwary to believe that color can be readily encoded by straightforward application of standardized physical measurement and computational techniques. However, the examples in this chapter have shown that standard CIE colorimetric techniques alone are not always sufficient for meaningful color encoding. Lack of understanding of this point has been responsible for the failure of numerous color-imaging systems, color-management products, and color-encoding methods.

This should not be interpreted as a criticism of CIE colorimetry. The CIE system was designed for particular types of applications—primarily those involving the color matching of samples under identical viewing conditions—that have little to do with imaging. For more than 60 years, the system has been shown to work extremely well for such applications. What is being discussed here is the inappropriate usage of the CIE system.

One should be wary of systems that seem to "prove" the applicability of colorimetric color encoding. In most cases, such systems are limited to reflection input and output media. Since there generally is good correlation between standard colorimetry and color appearance for reflection media, these systems will work reasonably well. When other types of media are used, however, the systems fail. Some systems that work across media types (such as prepress systems that use photographic transparency film input and reflection print output) may seem to be using standard CIE colorimetry. If these systems are examined carefully, however, it will be found that input colorimetric values are significantly altered before being sent to the output device. Somewhere in the signal-processing path, colorimetric values measured from the transparency grayscale are transformed to those of a typical reflection print. Without the use of such colorimetric alterations, these "colorimetric" systems do not work.

Unfortunately, as such limitations have become more widely acknowledged, a certain backlash has resulted. It is now not unusual to hear it said, in effect, that CIE colorimetry does not work, so it should be abandoned. Abandoning CIE colorimetry would be at least as big an error as assuming that it is entirely sufficient for all color-encoding situations. As will be shown in upcoming chapters, colorimetry is still the basis for encoding methods that achieve true input compatibility in complex color-imaging systems.

Summary of Key Issues

- Colorimetric encoding is based on measurements made according to the spectral responses of a standard human observer.

- Colorimetric encoding works well only in situations where there is good correlation between colorimetry and color appearance for the system media.

- Colorimetric encoding requires that the conditions for input-media metamerism be specified.

- A true colorimetric scanner has effective spectral responsivities equivalent to the product of a set of visual color-matching functions and the spectral power distribution of the illuminant specified for input-media metamerism.

- An RGB densitometric scanner that uses a transform to generate colorimetric values is not a true colorimetric scanner. Media-specific input transforms are required in such scanners.

- Colorimetric encoding alone is insufficient for achieving input compatibility when there is inconsistent correlation between colorimetry and color appearance for the system media.

Photo CD
Color Encoding

In 1992, the *Kodak Photo CD* System (Fig. 11.1) was introduced by Eastman Kodak Company. This sophisticated color-imaging system produces digital images from photographic negatives, transparencies, reflection prints, and electronic cameras and stores them on compact discs. *Photo CD* Discs can be used to produce video images on television receivers and monitors using special disc players. Video images also can be displayed on computer systems using CD-ROM drives and appropriate software. Hardcopy images, such as 35-mm slides, larger-

Figure 11.1

The *Kodak Photo CD* System. The system supports a disparate array of input sources and output devices.

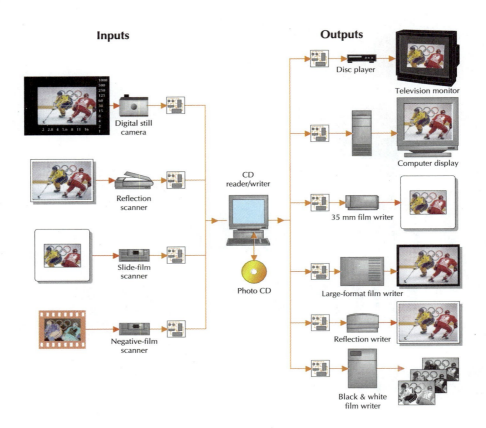

Figure 11.1

The *Kodak Photo CD* System. The system supports a disparate array of input sources and output devices.

format transparencies, reflection prints, and color separations for graphic arts applications, can be produced from *Photo CD* Discs on systems equipped with film writers, thermal printers, and other types of digital hardcopy output devices.

Our main assignment in the development of this system was to devise a method for digitally encoding color on *Photo CD* Discs. Because the *Photo CD* System was specified to include a disparate assortment of inputs and both hard-copy and softcopy outputs, the task turned out to be an interesting challenge. This chapter is a first-hand account of the development of the resulting color-encoding method. The development of the associated encoding data metric, *Kodak PhotoYCC* Color Interchange Space, will be described in Chapter 12.

Encoding Approaches

We began by considering existing methods for encoding color. Various encoding methods based on RGB densitometric or standard CIE colorimetric measurements alone were ruled out immediately, since neither approach would have worked for the disparate mix of input types specified for the *Photo CD* System.

We considered and also ruled out encoding schemes that would have been dependent on the use of image file identification tags. *Photo CD* Format image files do include tags, but the tagged information is supplemental. As was discussed earlier, a system that is *entirely* dependent on tags requires some form of intermediary signal processing, such as that provided by a workstation equipped with an appropriate color-management application. In the absence of that intermediary processing, every output device would be required to have a complete array of output transforms—one for every possible type of input. That requirement would have made *Photo CD* Disc players and similar devices too expensive. Moreover, the required amount of output signal processing would have prevented fast video displays of *Photo CD* Format images on most desktop computer systems.

We gave very serious consideration to using some type of appearance colorimetry to encode images in terms of their reproduced color appearance. As described earlier, appearance colorimetry begins with standard colorimetric methods, but it includes adjustments for various perceptual effects. In addition to its complexity, however, this method had two drawbacks.

First, for input compatibility, a color negative must be encoded not in terms of its own appearance, but in terms of the appearance of a print made from that negative. This can be accomplished by appropriate transformations of data scanned from the negative. The principal problem with that approach is that some information that was recorded by the negative is irretrievably lost in the encoding (Fig. 11.2).

This fact was particularly important for the *Photo CD* System. As the system was originally envisioned, negatives were to be the principal form of input. It would not have made much sense to design a system that compromised the quality of image data derived from its principal source of input.

Figure 11.2

Printing a photographic negative results in the loss of some recorded information. Encoding in terms of print color appearance can result in a similar loss of information from the negative.

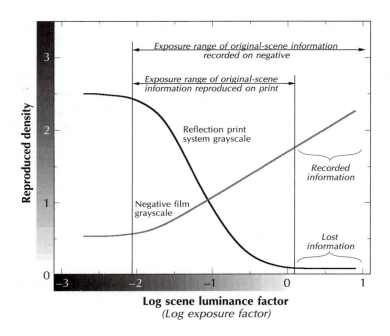

Moreover, the system design specifications included software tools that would allow shifts in color-balance and lightness to be applied to images *after* they have been encoded and recorded on disc. Such shifts, when applied to images from negatives, should result in new information being made visible. For example, if image data encoded directly from a negative are shifted to produce a lighter output image, details that could not otherwise be seen in dark shadow areas of that image should be revealed. If the encoded data are shifted to produce a darker output image, details that could not otherwise be seen in highlight areas should be revealed (Fig. 11.3a).

However, making similar shifts using data encoded in terms of the color appearance of a *print* made from a negative would not produce comparable results. For example, if such data are shifted to produce a darker output image, the highlight areas of that image simply would be darker. No additional highlight information would be revealed because it is not present in the encoded print data (Fig. 11.3b). In Part IV, color appearance encoding techniques that minimize the loss of information from color negative films will be described. But

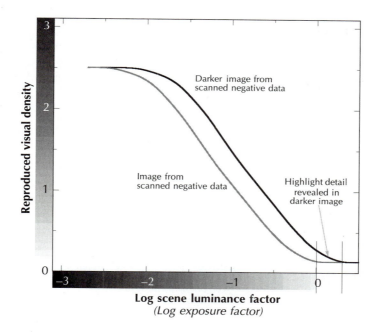

Figure 11.3a
Producing a darker image from data scanned from a photographic negative should reveal more information in highlight areas, as shown in the grayscale characteristic for the darker image. The greater slope of the grayscale in the marked region indicates that additional scene highlight information will be visible in the output image.

the complexity of the overall scheme would have made it impractical for the *Photo CD* System.

The second problem with encoding based on reproduced color appearance relates to a topic discussed earlier: Each type of input medium, and each individual medium within the different types, has its own distinctive "look" or "personality." For example, some media are considerably higher or lower than others in attributes such as grayscale contrast, luminance dynamic range, and overall color saturation. Although such differences might not always be apparent when images on different media are viewed separately, they become *very* noticeable when images are viewed simultaneously or merged to form composite images. This was a concern, because it was expected that *Photo CD* Discs would be used in applications, such as desktop publishing, to create composite images and to produce individual pages containing multiple images.

A related concern was that the differences among images from various input types would be noticeable when *Photo CD* Format images were viewed in succession. That was important, because it was felt that *Photo CD* Discs

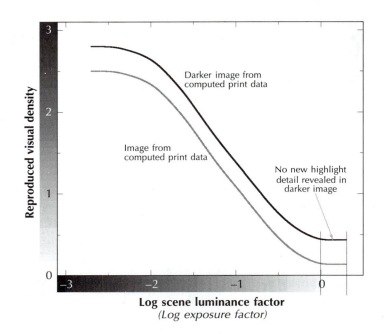

Figure 11.3b

A darker image produced from corresponding print data will not contain any additional information. The slope of the grayscale characteristic for the darker image is unchanged in the marked region, which indicates that no additional scene highlight information will be visible in the output image.

Darker image from computed print data

Image from computed print data

No new highlight detail revealed in darker image

Log scene luminance factor
(Log exposure factor)

frequently would be used to display sequences of images, as is done in 35 mm slide presentations. Tests proved that this concern was justified. It was found that if discs were created from a variety of input media, and the appearance of each input image was preserved, input media differences were very apparent when images where shown in sequence. The overall effect was quite unpleasant. Images seemed to "jump" whenever the original input medium changed from one type to another. As a result of those tests, producing *consistency* in the appearance of output images became an important objective. The complete list of objectives for the color-encoding method then was as follows:

- To support input of photographic negative, transparency, reflection and electronic camera images.
- To preserve the extensive range of original scene information recorded on both positive and negative photographic media.
- To provide for the production of consistent, high quality output images.

Since no existing color-encoding method met all of these objectives, we needed to develop a new one.

A New Approach for the *Photo CD* System

The basic approach that we took can best be explained by returning to the multi-language text-scanner analogy that first was discussed in Chapter 8 (shown again in Fig. 11.4). Recall that input compatibility was achieved in that system by the translation of words from each input language to a common encoding language. It is important to understand exactly *why* that approach worked.

The reason is that there is a basic *commonality* among all languages. Although different words are used in different languages, they represent objects, ideas, etc., that exist independently of those words. For example, consider the apple shown in Fig. 11.5. Regardless of what word or what language is used to *name* or "encode" that apple, it is still the same apple. In the figure, it is represented by the Latin word for apple, *mela*, but any language could have been used. The basis for input compatibility in the text-scanner system, then, is an inherent commonality that is independent of the languages involved.

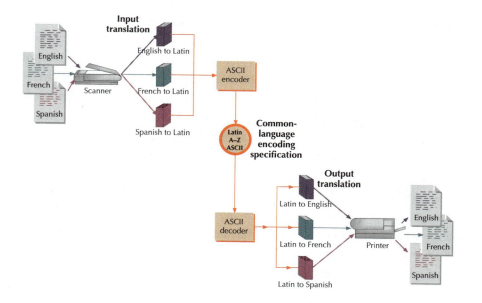

Figure 11.4

A multi-language text-scanning system.

Figure 11.5

Figure 11.5

The basis for input compatibility in this text-scanner system is an inherent commonality that is independent of the languages involved. "So that which we call an apple by any other name…"

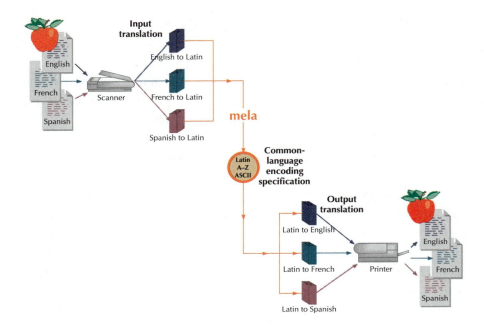

Figure 11.6 shows that in an analogous imaging situation, the same inherent commonality exists. If an apple were photographed using three different types of media and the resulting images were scanned, very different measured values would result. In effect, there would be three different "translations" of the same original object color. The signal values from the digital camera would represent a fourth "translation". But if it could be determined exactly *how* the apple's color has been "translated" to reproduced color values by each input, it would be possible to "translate" *backwards* from those values to recover the fact that the same apple color was indeed photographed by each medium.

This line of thinking suggested an entirely different approach to color encoding. Instead of encoding in terms of color *translations* represented by the *reproduced* colors of each input, it should be possible to encode in terms of *interpretations* of those translations. In other words, it should be possible to encode in terms of *original scene colors*.

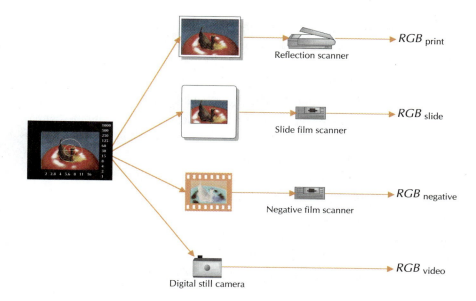

Figure 11.6
These four sets of
RGB color values
represent different
"translations" of
the apple's color.

It was clear that this new color-encoding approach, if feasible, would accomplish all the objectives of the system:

- The color-encoding would support input from *any* source, because any fundamental incompatibilities among the inputs would be removed by the process that "translates" back to original scene colors.

- Because it is not based on reproduced colors, the approach would allow the preservation of all original scene information recorded by the input device or medium.

- The approach would allow the production of consistent output images, because the encoding itself would be consistent. It would be free of the color reproduction differences that exist among the input sources.

In theory, the approach seemed ideal for the *Photo CD* System. But what about its practical implementation? Would it really be possible to interpret original-scene colors from reproduced "translations" of those colors?

Making the New Approach Work

In order to investigate the possibility of interpreting original-scene colors from reproductions, we first needed to take a detailed look at the translation process of those colors to reproduced color values, as measured by an input scanner. That process is illustrated, for an original color stimulus and its reproduction on a photographic transparency film, in Fig. 11.7.

As the figure shows, the stimulus is captured according to the film's red, green, and blue spectral sensitivities. The resulting exposure signals (recorded in the latent image) later are chemically processed, and an image is formed by the cyan, magenta, and yellow dyes of the film. The end result is a color area on the film, having a particular spectral transmittance. When that area is scanned, scanner RGB values R_s, G_s, and B_s are produced. These values depend on the spectral transmittance of the color area, the scanner illuminant, the red, green, and blue spectral responsivities of the scanner, and any electronic signal processing that might operate on the scanned signals.

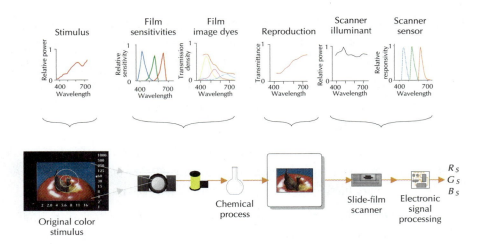

Figure 11.7

Translation of a color stimulus to scanner RGB values R_s, G_s, and B_s.

Because of the interlayer interactions and other complexities of modern photographic films, the relationship between the original color stimulus and scanner *RGB* values is not at all simple. Two approaches were used in the attempts to quantify that relationship.

The first involved mathematically modeling the color reproduction characteristics of the film and scanner, using models previously developed for designing and optimizing new photographic products. The second approach treated the input film and the scanner as a single "black box." The properties of this "black box" could be characterized, from experimental data, by photographing a variety of original color stimuli and scanning the resulting color patches produced on the film.

The strength of a characterization technique is that it can provide very accurate data, since it is based on actual measurements. However, the results apply only to the specific sample of film and the particular scanner used for the measurements. Models generally are not quite as accurate, but their results are free from the normal variabilities of film manufacturing, chemical processing, scanner calibration errors, and so on.

In the end, the best description of the relationship between original color stimuli and scanner values was obtained from a combination of the two approaches. The combined approach is based on characterization, but modeling is included to account for any differences between the actual film and chemical process and a nominal film and process. The nominal film and process are based on manufacturing specifications for the particular type of film being used. Compensations also are included for any differences between the actual scanner and a nominal scanner, where the nominal scanner also is based on manufacturing specifications.

Once the relationship between stimuli and scanner values was determined, the inverse of that relationship could be used to convert scanner values to original stimuli values. This required a method for representing the original color stimuli in terms of three data channels. For that purpose, and others that will be described later, we created a mathematical concept called the *Photo CD* Reference Image-Capturing Device.

Figure 11.8 shows this hypothetical Reference Image-Capturing Device and an individual color stimulus. When the device captures light from the color stimulus, it produces *RGB* exposure-factor values. More will be said in the next chapter about the specific characteristics of the reference device, but it is important to note here that its spectral responsivities correspond to a set of color-matching functions. The use of such responsivities is critical, because it means that *the RGB exposure-factor values of the Reference Image-Capturing Device are tristimulus values that correspond directly to CIE tristimulus values of original color stimuli.*

Figure 11.9 shows the application of the basic encoding approach to a single input film. A number of original color stimuli, with known spectral power distributions, are photographed. In most cases, the stimuli would consist of a light source of known spectral power distribution and color patches of known spectral reflectances. The exposed film is chemically processed and scanned. The scanned values are corrected for any deviations of the actual film, chemical process, and scanner from a nominal film, process, and scanner to form *RGB* values R_s, G_s, and B_s.

Figure 11.8

The *Photo CD* System Reference Image-Capturing Device and a color stimulus. The *RGB* exposure-factor values of the device are tristimulus values that correspond directly to CIE tristimulus values of original color stimuli.

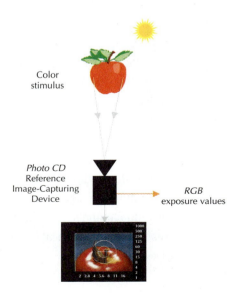

Color stimulus

Photo CD Reference Image-Capturing Device

RGB exposure values

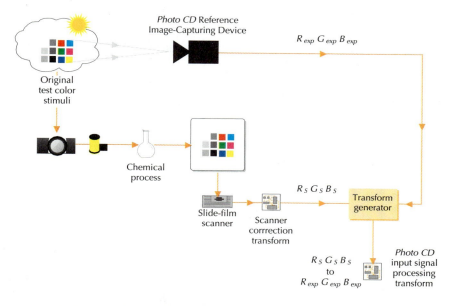

Figure 11.9
Building a *Photo CD* System input signal-processing transform. The transform relates scanner RGB values R_s, G_s, and B_s to Reference Image-Capturing Device exposure-factor values R_{exp}, G_{exp}, and B_{exp}.

Reference Image-Capturing Device exposure-factor values are then calculated for each original color stimulus, using the following equations:

$$R_{exp} = k_r \sum_{\lambda} S(\lambda)R(\lambda)\bar{r}(\lambda)$$

$$G_{exp} = k_g \sum_{\lambda} S(\lambda)R(\lambda)\bar{g}(\lambda) \qquad \{11.1\}$$

$$B_{exp} = k_b \sum_{\lambda} S(\lambda)R(\lambda)\bar{b}(\lambda)$$

where R_{exp}, G_{exp}, and B_{exp} are the Reference Image-Capturing Device red, green, and blue exposure-factor values; $S(\lambda)$ the spectral power distribution of the light source; $R(\lambda)$ is the spectral reflectance of a color patch; $\bar{r}(\lambda)$, $\bar{g}(\lambda)$, and $\bar{b}(\lambda)$ are the red, green, and blue spectral responsivities of the Reference Image-Capturing Device; and k_r, k_g, and k_b are normalizing factors determined such that R_{exp}, G_{exp}, and B_{exp} = 1.00 when the stimulus is a perfect white. Finally, a mathematical transform is built relating the scanner R_s, G_s, and B_s values to Reference Image-Capturing Device R_{exp}, G_{exp}, and B_{exp} values.

Figure 11.10, which shows the relationship of the Reference Image-Capturing Device to actual *Photo CD* System inputs, illustrates the overall *Photo CD* System color-encoding concept. Color-image signals from a Reference Image-Capturing Device (if one actually existed) would be encoded directly, without additional input signal processing. Signals from any real source of input, such as a scanned film or a digital still camera, are processed through input signal-processing transforms such that *the resulting encoded values equal those that would have been produced by the Reference Image-Capturing Device had it captured the same original color stimuli*.

Figure 11.10

Relationship of the Reference Image-Capturing Device to actual *Photo CD* System inputs. As a result of the input signal-processing transformations, encoded values from each input equal those that would have been produced by the Reference Image-Capturing Device had it captured the same original color stimuli. Note that no transform is required for the reference device itself.

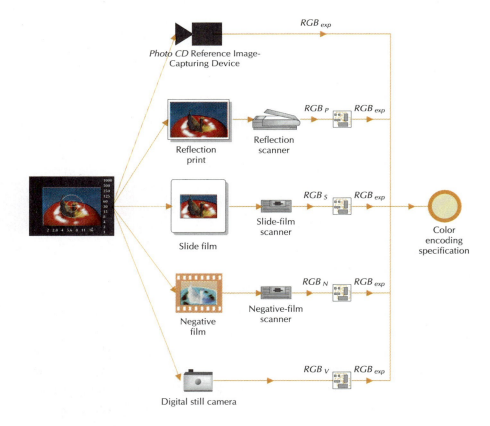

Practical Considerations

If the encoding approach worked perfectly, the encoded values for the stimuli of a given original scene would be the same, regardless of which device or medium actually was used to capture that scene. In *concept,* then, the method should create perfect compatibility among the inputs. In practice, however, there are complications that must be considered.

The first is that there is a limit to how closely the values scanned from a given input can be transformed into the values that would have been produced by the reference device. That limit is determined primarily by the spectral sensitivities of the input medium. The more closely the spectral sensitivities correspond to a set of color-matching functions, the more closely the encoded values theoretically can match those of the reference device.

Extensive tests showed that colorimetric accuracy was reasonably high for most input media when this theoretical limit was approached, despite the fact that the spectral sensitivities of all tested media differed from color-matching functions. Figure 11.11 shows the colorimetric errors associated with the spectral sensitivities of a representative photographic film. For certain color stimuli, such as those that might be produced by the blue flower and green fabric described in Chapter 1, the colorimetric errors can be somewhat larger. In virtually all cases, however, the errors are considerably smaller than those typically found in the *reproduced* colors of the tested media. Moreover, the test showed that input compatibility among all tested media was excellent when the theoretical limit was approached, even though the spectral sensitivities differed somewhat from medium to medium.

Achieving that degree of compatibility required careful control over the entire process. It also required calibration of the actual medium and equipment that was used and the application of computational techniques that generally would not be available in ordinary practice. Another consideration, then, was whether adequate input compatibility could be achieved under typical operating conditions.

Experiments showed that in order to create a high degree of input compatibility, two things were required. First, different input signal-processing transforms were needed for each input product. In the *Photo CD* System, these transforms are now called product-specific *film terms*. Most *Photo CD* Imaging Workstations (PIWs) used to write *Photo CD* Discs have more than 100 sets of film terms, representing virtually every negative and transparency film from all major manufacturers. The appropriate film terms are selected, at the start of the scanning process, based on an identification of the specific input film. That identification can be made manually by the operator, or it can be made automatically on workstations equipped with product identification-code readers. However, the use of product-specific film terms alone cannot account for other sources of variability that can occur *within* a given product. For a photographic film, these might include the following:

- Variations in manufacturing of the film
- Changes in the film after manufacturing, but prior to exposure
- Underexposure or overexposure of the film
- Exposure of the film under nonstandard illumination
- Changes in the unprocessed film and/or latent image after exposure
- Variations and/or deliberate alterations of film chemical processing
- Changes in the film's dye image after processing
- Variations in scanning

The second thing that was needed, then, was some method to compensate for such variations. For that reason, PIWs are equipped with an automatic lightness-adjustment and color-balance adjustment algorithm, called the *Scene Balance Algorithm* (SBA). This algorithm uses image data histograms, pattern recognition, and other analysis techniques to determine a set of red, green, and blue corrections that are applied as part of the input signal processing.

The *Photo CD* System encoding method is ideally suited for application of this algorithm. Because all inputs are encoded on a common basis, it is not necessary to have separate balance algorithms for each different type of input medium. Moreover, the encoding method allows balance corrections to be made in RGB exposure space, which is the space in which most input media variations occur. Under and overexposure errors, for example, are very common, and spectral power distribution differences among scene illuminants also result in

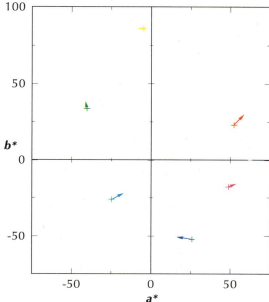

Figure 11.11
Comparison of
CIELAB *a*, *b**
values determined
from Reference
Image-Capturing
Device *RGB* val-
ues (+ marks) and
from a representa-
tive photographic
medium (arrow
heads). The differ-
ences are due to
the departures of
the spectral sensi-
tivities of the film
from a true set of
color-matching
functions.

relative red, green, and blue exposure variations. The *Photo CD* System encoding method makes it possible to compensate simply and accurately for these unwanted exposure variations. *Photo CD* Imaging Workstations also provide a video display of the scanned image. This video preview allows the scanner operator to make additional adjustments, if necessary, to the scanned image prior to final encoding. The *Photo CD* System encoding method is of benefit here, again because it allows corrections to be made directly and easily in RGB exposure space. In addition, since the method creates compatibility among the input sources, the same set of software tools can be used to adjust any scanned image, regardless of its origin.

Use of product-specific film terms, together with the SBA and manual adjustments, enhances the consistency of the scanning/encoding process, which in turn results in a very high degree of input compatibility. That raises an interesting question: How much input compatibility really is *needed*? For that matter, how much compatibility actually is *wanted*?

Degrees of Input Compatibility

Throughout Part III, the advantages of achieving input compatibility have been emphasized. But *complete* input compatibility may not always be necessary, and it may not always be desirable.

In the case of the *Photo CD* System, certainly the fundamental incompatibilities of image data from negatives, transparencies, reflection prints, and digital cameras have to be eliminated for the system to work at all. But the *Photo CD* System color-encoding method is capable of going farther. It can make all encoded images of the same original scene, recorded by any of the input media, virtually *identical*. But should that always be the objective?

By analogy, suppose one were making an audio CD from an old 78-rpm record, and the technical capability existed to process the sound from that record such that the audio CD sounded like a modern digital recording. Should that capability be used, or should the CD reproduce the sound that is characteristic of all 78-rpm records? Stated in more general terms, are there properties of the original recording medium itself that should be retained, or should the effects of all such properties be eliminated whenever possible?

There are no "right" or "wrong" answers to such questions, either for audio applications or for imaging applications. For some advertising and scientific work, it may be desirable to produce image files that are highly accurate colorimetric records of the original scenes, regardless of the actual media used to record those scenes. Similarly, it most often would be preferable for image files produced from transparencies taken of museum paintings to represent the colors of the paintings themselves rather than the colors reproduced on the transparencies. Applications in which cutting and pasting of images is done also will work best when images from all input sources are made as much alike as possible.

For other applications, however, an accurate digital record of the photographic reproduction itself might be more desirable. For example, a photographer may have produced an image having very high color saturation by deliberately using a film known to have that type of color reproduction. In that case, it would be preferable to encode the image in a way that retains this high saturation. There is, then, a range of possibilities to consider, from encoding in terms of original scene colors, thereby achieving complete input compatibility, but with no retention of the particular characteristics of the input media, to encoding in terms of input-media densitometry or colorimetry, thereby achieving complete retention of the particular characteristics of the media, but with no input compatibility.

These two possibilities represent extremes on a continuum of possible trade-offs between input compatibility and retention of specific input-medium characteristics (Fig. 11.12). Between these extremes, there are many useful points on the continuum. One of the important advantages of the color-encoding method used in the *Photo CD* System is that the point that is reached along the continuum can be readily adjusted.

The degree of input compatibility is controlled by the correspondence between the actual image being scanned and the signal-processing transform being used in the scanner. For example, using transforms specifically developed for every individual input image achieves virtually complete input compatibility. On the other hand, using less-specific signal processing results in somewhat less compatibility, but it retains more of the "personality" characteristics of the particular input medium.

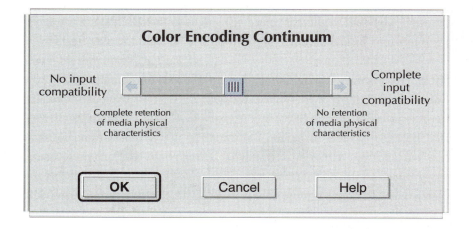

Figure 11.12
There are many useful positions between the two extremes of the color encoding continuum.

The *Photo CD* System currently provides this compatibility control in the form of two different types of input signal-processing transforms called *product-specific film terms* and *universal film terms.*

Each *product-specific* film-term transform is designed to be used only with the specific input medium for which it was developed. When appropriate product-specific film terms are used for all inputs, as shown in Fig. 11.13, product-to-product differences among the input media are minimized, and a point quite far to the right on the input-compatibility continuum is reached. Product-specific film terms, rather than universal terms, should be used when it is important to produce discs with a consistent image-to-image look from a mix of different input media. Use of product-specific film terms also results in more seamless compositing of images. Perhaps most importantly, it produces a more accurate extraction of original-scene colorimetry; thus, product-specific film terms should be used when the primary purpose is to encode such colorimetry.

Universal film-term transforms are developed for more general use; they can be used for all products of the same basic type (Fig. 11.14). For example, there is one universal film-term transform that can be used for most photographic slide films. A universal film-term transform is based on the characteristics of a reference film of the same basic type as that being scanned. When universal terms are used, *differences of each scanned film from the reference film* will be reflected in the color encoding.

For example, a photographic slide film with grayscale contrast above that of the reference slide film will produce encoded values representative of that higher contrast. Similarly, slide films with other particular characteristics—such as high or low color saturation, or a tendency to reproduce reds as somewhat orange or somewhat magenta—will produce *Photo CD* Format image files that reflect these characteristics. This option therefore represents a point somewhat more to the left on the continuum, i.e., it favors a greater retention of the characteristics of the particular input medium.

It may be helpful to think of the universal-film-term option this way: Although it is consistent with the basic definition of *Photo CD* System color encoding in that it encodes original scene colors, it results in encoded scene colors that are altered somewhat according to the particular color-reproduction

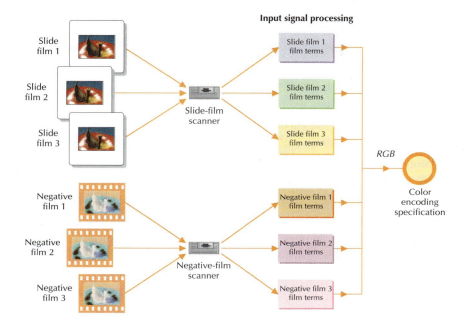

Figure 11.13
Use of product-specific film terms in the *Kodak Photo CD* System.

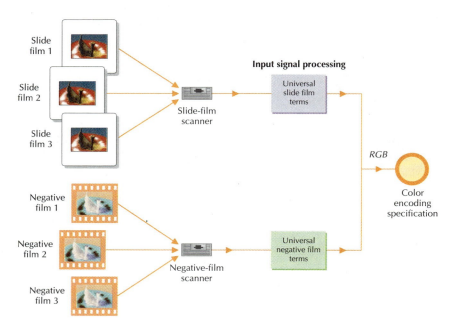

Figure 11.14
Use of universal film terms in the *Kodak Photo CD* System.

characteristics of each input film. It is as if the original scenes themselves had been different, having somewhat higher or lower contrast, higher or lower color saturation, more orange or more magenta reds, and so on. When thought about from that perspective, it can be seen why *Photo CD* Format image files created using the universal film terms are fundamentally compatible with image files created using product-specific film terms.

The *Photo CD* System encoding method also allows other encoding possibilities, as shown in Fig. 11.15, including the option to encode in terms of *reproduced* color appearance. This option will be discussed in more detail in Part IV, but the basic idea is that reproduced colors can be encoded by transforming them to a "virtual" scene space. This transformation makes these colors compatible with actual scene colors. The advantage of using an original-scene-based approach, even for reproduced colors, is that the approach makes it possible to retain *all* of the information recordable by present-day photographic media and anticipated to be recordable by future electronic image-capture devices.

Figure 11.15
The *Photo CD* System encoding method provides for alternative encoding possibilities. A basic level of input compatibility is achieved in all cases.

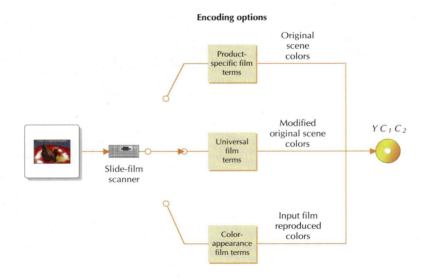

Discussion

Throughout this section, the importance of input compatibility has been emphasized. It was shown that input compatibility is achieved by representing input colors in such a way that encoded values have a single, unambiguous interpretation. In order to best meet the specific needs of the *Photo CD* System, that interpretation was chosen to be the colorimetry of the original scene, as measured by a reference image-capturing device.

In earlier chapters in this section, it was shown that color-encoding methods based on other interpretations can be appropriate for systems with more restricted sets of inputs. It was emphasized that the use of a single interpretation of color values within a system is fundamentally different from simply having a single data metric. Several examples and analogies were used to show that the use of a common data metric alone contributes nothing towards solving the basic problems caused by disparate input sources.

In fact, to this point no mention has been made of any particular color-encoding data metric. This was done deliberately in order to emphasize that the choice of a metric is unrelated to the achievement of input compatibility. Nevertheless, it often is conceptually and operationally convenient to identify a particular data metric for a given color-encoding method. Selecting the most appropriate data metric for a given method or system is the topic of the next chapter.

Summary of Key Issues

- Conventional color-encoding methods, such as those based on densitometry or on standard CIE colorimetry, cannot meet the objectives of the *Photo CD* System.

- The *Photo CD* System color-encoding method can create input compatibility among all types of input media and devices.

- A unique characteristic of *Photo CD* System color encoding is that the common color property on which its input compatibility is based can be independent of the color reproduction characteristics of the input sources.

- When optimum input compatibility is desired, *Photo CD* System color encoding is based on the colorimetry of the original scene that caused the image to form on the input imaging medium being scanned.

- The values that are used to encode the original-scene colorimetry are based on the *RGB* exposure-factor values that would have been produced by the Reference Image-Capturing Device, had it captured the same original scene.

- Reference Image-Capturing Device values are derived using signal-processing transformations of *RGB* values scanned from input media.

- Practical color encoding must give consideration to trade-offs between input compatibility and retention of the individual characteristics of input sources. The *Photo CD* System color-encoding method allows such considerations to be incorporated as part of the encoding process by the use of product-specific or universal film terms.

- When product-specific film terms are used, the *Photo CD* System color-encoding method minimizes product-to-product differences among input media.

- When universal film terms are used, the *Photo CD* System color-encoding method retains product-to-product differences among input media of the same basic type.

- The *Photo CD* System encoding method also allows encoding in terms of reproduced color appearance. For input compatibility, reproduced colors are transformed to a "virtual" scene space.

12
Color-Encoding
Data Metrics

To this point, the first principal attribute of a complete color encoding specification, the color-encoding *method,* has been discussed. The second principal attribute, the color-encoding *data metric,* defines the color space and numerical units in which the encoded color values are expressed. Although it seldom is necessary to restrict a particular encoding method to a single data metric, it often is convenient to do so. Most color-encoding methods do in fact have a particular data metric associated with them.

Many data metrics currently are in use, and attempts frequently are made to identify which of them is best. Almost every conceivable data metric seems to have its dedicated supporters and its equally dedicated detractors. Our opinion is that the particular requirements of a specific color-imaging system will dictate the most appropriate data metric *for that system*. In practice, systems vary widely in their principal uses, productivity requirements, quality requirements, and computational capabilities. Therefore, there is no single "best" data metric for all systems.

That does not mean, however, that the data metric for a given system can be chosen arbitrarily. Among other things, the data metric affects the efficiency of the color encoding and the requirements for signal processing. The data metric also will affect other factors, such as the visibility of quantization and compression artifacts. In virtually all applications, there are engineering considerations that will favor the use of one data metric over another. In this chapter, the most important of these considerations will be examined.

To do that, the process by which one data metric was developed to meet the specific color-encoding and engineering requirements of a particular system will be described. The data metric is *Kodak PhotoYCC* Color Interchange Space, which was developed specifically for the *Photo CD* System. This data metric was chosen for examination because it is completely defined and widely used. Also, since it is a metric that we developed, we can offer a first-hand account of the development process.

Photo CD System Requirements

In order to meet the overall objectives of the *Photo CD* System, as described in Chapter 11, the data metric for the system had to meet five criteria:

1. The metric had to be capable of encoding a wide gamut of colors and an extensive dynamic range of luminance information.
2. The metric had to provide for image compression incorporating spatial subsampling.
3. The metric had to encode images such that digital quantization effects would be visually undetectable.

4. The metric had to allow the system to produce photographic-quality hardcopy output images.

5. The metric had to allow the system to produce excellent quality video images on television monitors, home computers, and computer workstations, using minimal signal processing.

Each of these criteria significantly influenced the final specifications for the *PhotoYCC* Space data metric. The influence that each criterion had will now be described, starting with the video requirements.

1. Video Requirements

In order for *Photo CD* Discs to produce high-quality images on existing video systems, and to do so without requiring any special monitor adjustments, the output video signals produced by devices using those discs must conform closely to industry standards for other devices that produce output video signals.

It might seem logical, then, to encode image data on *Photo CD* Discs directly according to those standards. That would minimize the amount of required output signal processing, which should translate to the simplest, fastest, and least expensive generation of output video signals. However, there is a fundamental problem with that approach: It is inconsistent with the color-gamut requirements for the system.

2. Color Gamut Requirements

Figure 12.1a shows the chromaticity locations of a typical set of video primaries, as defined by the chromaticities of the light emitted by the red, green, and blue phosphors of a representative video display. To a first approximation, the gamut of colors that can be displayed using these primaries is indicated by the triangle formed by connecting the chromaticity coordinates of the three primaries. (This is only an approximation because the actual color gamut is three-dimensional, and the chromaticity limits of the gamut will differ at different luminance-factor levels.) The triangle also indicates the chromaticity boundaries of the color gamut that would result if an encoding data metric based strictly on existing video standards were used.

Figure 12.1a

CIE u', v' chromaticity diagram showing the chromaticity locations of a representative set of red, green, and blue video primaries.

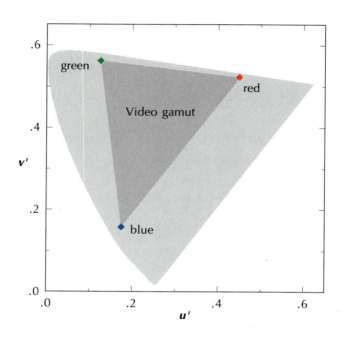

Figure 12.1b

Chromaticity boundaries for colors that can be produced using a variety of different photographic CMY image-forming dyes, compared to those for an encoding data metric strictly based on existing video standards.

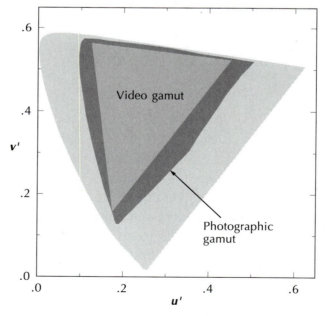

The chromaticity boundaries for colors that can be produced using a variety of different photographic CMY image-forming dyes, on both reflection and transmission supports, are shown in Fig. 12.1b. Note that many of the photographic colors are outside the displayable color gamut of the video system. Consequently, hardcopy output images of full photographic quality cannot be produced from digital images encoded in terms of a data metric that is restricted to a video display color gamut. This is illustrated below (Fig. 12.2). The image on the right represents the color of the original photograph. The image on the left represents a restriction to a video display color gamut.

Figure 12.2

The image on the right represents the color of the original photograph. The image on the left represents a restriction to a video color gamut. Note the resulting loss of color saturation in the cyan balloons.

Figure 12.3

Chromaticity
boundaries for a
collection of col-
ors representing
real-world surface
colors, compared
to those for photo-
graphic dyes and
those for an
encoding data
metric based
strictly on existing
video standards.

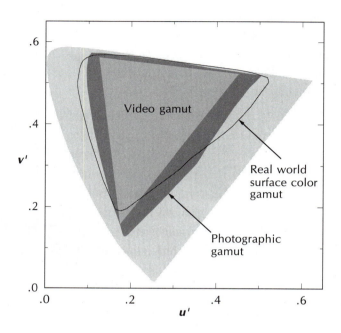

Figure 12.3 shows chromaticity boundaries for a collection of colors we have studied that represent real-world surface colors. This collection includes natural colors as well as manufactured colors produced by various pigments, dyes, and printing inks. Because many of these colors lie well outside the video display gamut, they also cannot be encoded accurately in—or be reproduced from—a data metric restricted to a video display color gamut.

So there was a conflict. If *Photo CD* Format images were color encoded using a data metric defined strictly according to existing video standards, the output signal processing required to produce video signals would be simple and fast. But, as has just been shown, the color gamut of that metric would not have included all photographic and real-world colors.

At this point, it seemed that the only option was to use a "device-independent" data metric based on *imaginary* primaries, such as CIE XYZ primaries. There would be a significant price to pay in signal processing speed and complexity; but because these primaries easily encompass all real-world

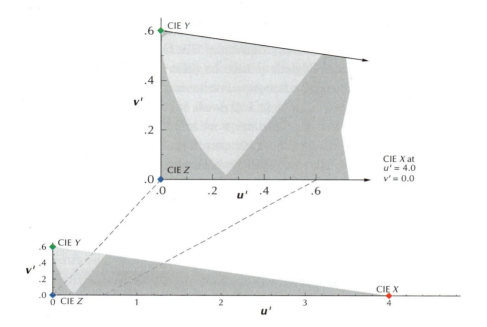

Figure 12.4
Chromaticity
boundaries of CIE
XYZ primaries.

colors (Fig. 12.4), at least the color-gamut restrictions of a metric based on real device primaries would be avoided. But there was a much better alternative.

The apparent conflict could be resolved by staying with a "device-dependent" metric based on video primaries *if the boundaries of that metric could be extended*. We did this by basing the data metric on the *RGB* tristimulus values of the *Photo CD* Reference Image-Capturing Device, which was described in Chapter 11, and by specifying the capture properties for this device such that it became a theoretically perfect video camera.

One "theoretically perfect" characteristic of the reference device is its set of red, green, and blue spectral responsivities (Fig. 12.5). We defined these responsivities to be equivalent to the color-matching functions for a set of red, green, and blue video primaries. In particular, we specified the video primaries to be those of CCIR Recommendation 709, *The HDTV Standard for the Studio and for International Programme Exchange*. This recommendation is now ITU-R BT.709, which often is referred to informally as Rec. 709.

Figure 12.5
The red, green, and blue spectral responsivities of the *Photo CD* Reference Image-Capturing Device.

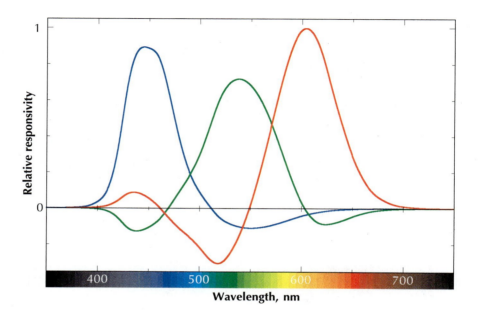

We chose to use these primaries because they are consistent with phosphors typically used in the CRTs of modern televisions and computer monitors. Note that since the red, green, and blue video primaries are real, the corresponding spectral responsivities are negative at certain wavelengths. But that was not a problem. There was no need to actually *build* this device; it was needed only as a mathematical reference for the data metric.

The advantage of using these particular responsivities is that *positive RGB* exposure-factor values of the Reference Image-Capturing Device are equivalent to signal values that would be produced by an *actual* video camera that conformed to Rec. 709 specifications. So very minimal signal processing is required to produce standard video signals from data encoded in terms of reference device *RGB* values. Unlike an actual video camera, however, the hypothetical Reference Image-Capturing Device also is capable of forming *negative* exposure-factor values. These values make it possible to represent colors *outside* the displayable color gamut of a video system (Fig. 12.6).

For example, the cyan color indicated by the ◆ mark in Fig. 12.6 (below) would be represented by exposure-factor values that are positive for both green and blue, but negative for red. The figure also indicates other areas where the chromaticities are such that one or more of the exposure-factor values would be negative.

To summarize the discussion so far: Because its color representation is based on a reference device whose spectral responsivities are derived from standard video primaries, the *PhotoYCC* Space data metric provides encoded values that can be transformed easily to values appropriate for video applications. Positive red, green, and blue exposure-factor values of the Reference Image-Capturing Device are equivalent to signal values that would be produced by a real video camera that conformed to Rec. 709 specifications. But at the same time, because both positive and negative red, green, and blue exposure-factor values are allowed for the theoretical reference device, the chromaticity boundaries of the encodable color gamut are not restricted to those defined by the Rec. 709 video primaries.

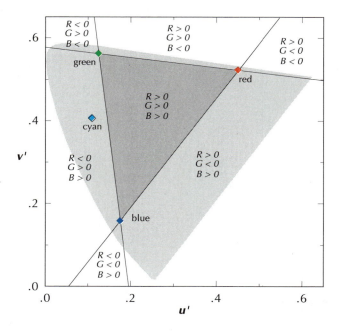

Figure 12.6

Colors outside the displayable color gamut of a video system can be represented by combinations of positive and negative *RGB* values. The indicated cyan color can be represented by values that are positive for green and for blue, but negative for red.

3. Luminance Dynamic Range Requirements

Another consideration for a data metric is the dynamic range of the luminance values that can be represented. Most original scenes contain information that covers a broad range of luminances. In many cases, a considerable amount of that information occurs at very high luminances, including luminances above that of a perfect white diffuse reflector in the principal subject area of a scene. As discussed in Chapter 6, sources of such information include specular highlights, certain types of diffuse highlights, scene areas that are more highly illuminated than the principal subject area, and fluorescent colors.

Because of the visual importance of this above-white information, most photographic materials are designed to record an extensive dynamic range of luminance information. For example, when normally exposed, photographic transparency films have the capability to record (and discriminate) luminance-factor values up to two times that produced by a perfect white in the principal subject area of an original scene (Fig. 12.7). Photographic negatives can record an even greater range of luminance-factor values.

Figure 12.7

Photographic transparency films can record luminance-factor values up to two times greater (+0.30 log) than that produced by a perfect white.

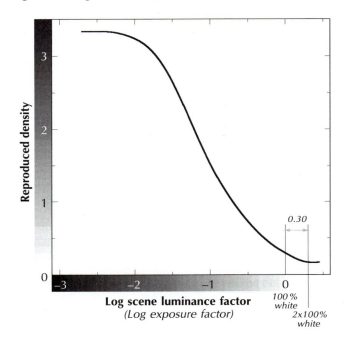

Log scene luminance factor
(Log exposure factor)

In order to produce photographic quality output images from scanned photographic input media, then, it is necessary to encode values corresponding to an extensive dynamic range of original-scene luminance information. Note in Fig. 12.8a, for example, the loss of highlight information in the lower image, produced from encoded values limited to the luminance-factor of a scene diffuse white, compared to the upper image, produced from the greater dynamic range of luminance-factor values recorded by the original photographic image.

Figure 12.8a

The upper image was produced using the full dynamic range of luminance-factor values recorded in the original photograph. The lower image was produced from encoded values limited to the luminance-factor of a scene diffuse white. Note the loss of highlight information, particularly in the clouds.

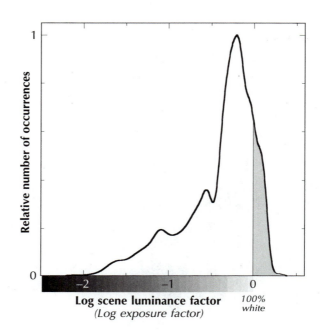

Figure 12.8b

Histogram showing the number of occurrences versus luminance-factor value of the original scene shown in Fig. 12.8a. The shaded region indicates scene information corresponding to luminance-factor values above those of perfect diffuse whites within the principal subject area.

The above histogram (Fig. 12.8b) shows the dynamic range of luminance-factor values of the original scene that was photographed for Fig. 12.8a. The histogram relates the number of occurrences (number of pixels) versus luminance-factor value of the original scene. The shaded area indicates scene information corresponding to luminance-factor values above those of perfect diffuse whites within the principal subject area.

Since the Reference Image-Capturing Device is hypothetical, we could continue to endow it with theoretical capabilities as needed. In this instance, we specified that the dynamic range of its *RGB* exposure-factor values, and therefore its luminance-factor dynamic range, would be unrestricted. When this capability is combined with the capability of forming both positive and negative exposure-factor values, the three-dimensional color gamut of the reference device—and therefore of the *color space* based on that device—also becomes unrestricted.

4. Digital Quantization Considerations

Because many *Photo CD* System applications use 24-bit color (8 bits per color channel), the potential visibility of digital quantization effects was a concern. If linear *RGB* exposure signals (or linear *YCC* signals derived later from those linear *RGB* signals) had been digitized, unacceptably visible digital quantization artifacts would have resulted. This is illustrated in Fig. 12.9, where the CIELAB a^*, b^* values for a set of original colors and the closest reproductions that can be made from digitized linear exposure signals representing the same original colors are compared.

The effect of digitizing linear exposure signals also is demonstrated in the left image of Fig. 12.10. *Note: For clarity and emphasis, the quantization effects have been greatly increased in Figs. 12.9 and 12.10 by digitizing to just 5 bits per color channel, rather than the normal 8 bits per channel.*

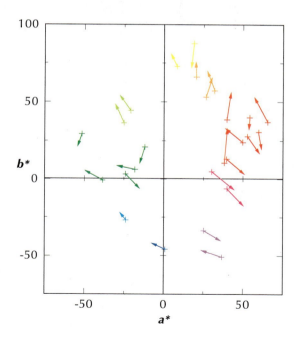

Figure 12.9
Color errors resulting from quantization of *linear* exposure signals (digitized to 5 bits per color channel). The + marks represent colors produced from unquantized signals; the arrow heads represent colors produced from quantized linear signals.

The image on the left was produced from quantized *linear* exposure signals (digitized to 5 bits per channel). The image on the right was produced from quantized *nonlinear* exposure signals (digitized to 5 bits per channel). Note the reduction in quantization artifacts in the critical skin-tone regions.

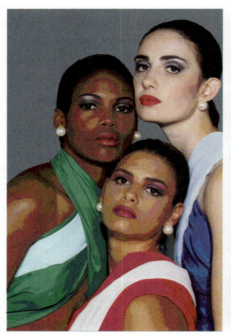 

To minimize color errors and to minimize the visibility of quantization artifacts, linear *RGB* exposure signals are transformed to nonlinear exposure signals, *R′G′B′*, before any digitization occurs. The transformation characteristic is shown in Fig. 12.11.

This nonlinear transformation is defined by the following equations. The first describes a basic power relationship between the linear and nonlinear signals. It is applied to linear values greater than or equal to 0.018.

For *R, G, B* ≥ 0.018:

$$R' = 1.099\,R^{0.45} - 0.099$$

$$G' = 1.099\,G^{0.45} - 0.099$$ $\{12.1a\}$

$$B' = 1.099\,B^{0.45} - 0.099$$

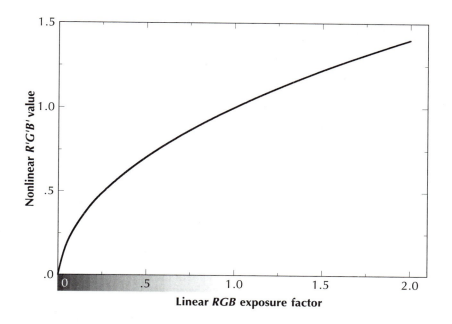

Figure 12.11
Nonlinear trans-
form for convert-
ing positive linear
exposure signals,
RGB, to positive
nonlinear signals,
R′ G′ B′.

The second equation describes a short linear portion of the transformation. It is applied to linear values less than 0.018.

For *R, G, B* < 0.018:

$$R' = 4.50\,R$$

$$G' = 4.50\,G \qquad\qquad \{12.1b\}$$

$$B' = 4.50\,B$$

This type of transformation ultimately results in a more perceptually uniform distribution of quantization errors, as shown in Fig. 12.12 and in the right image of Fig. 12.10. In particular, note the significant reduction in quantization artifacts in the skin-tone areas of the photographic image. (*Again, for clarity and emphasis, the quantization shown in these figures is for 5 bits per color channel, rather than the normal 8 bits per channel.*)

Figure 12.12

Color errors
resulting from
quantization of
nonlinear expo-
sure signals
(digitized to 5
bits per channel).
Note that the
errors are consid-
erably smaller
than those shown
in Fig. 12.9.

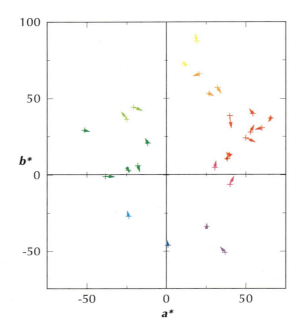

Although various other nonlinear transformations could have been used, we chose this particular set of equations for several reasons. First, when applied to positive *RGB* signal values, the transformation corresponds to the video camera *opto-electronic transfer characteristic* specified in Rec. 709. This characteristic defines the relationship between video camera exposures and camera output signal voltages. The use of this particular nonlinear transformation enhances the correspondence of *PhotoYCC* Space values to existing video standards, which further simplifies the signal processing required to produce video signals from *Photo CD* Discs.

These equations also produced quantization results that were among the best obtained from any of the nonlinear transformations tested. Moreover, these results were retained when images were edited *after* encoding. By comparison, the quantization produced by other nonlinear equations sometimes was quite good in the initial encoding, but problems occurred when image data subsequently were altered to produce modified output images. For example, when some nonlinear transformations were used, quantization effects became noticeable when lighter images were made from encoded values. With other transformations, the effects became noticeable when darker images were made. Images encoded according to the Rec. 709 equations held up well to these types of post-encoding adjustments. This was an important feature, because such adjustments would be an expected part of desktop publishing and other types of editing applications.

In addition to the published Rec. 709 equations, corresponding equations were needed for negative exposure signals in order to preserve the color gamut capabilities inherent in the color space. After performing a number of calculations and experiments, we determined that the best nonlinear transform for the negative values was simply a mirror image of the transform used for the positive numbers (Fig. 12.13). The resulting set of equations for transforming the complete range of positive and negative linear exposure signals, RGB, to nonlinear signals, $R'G'B'$, is shown below.

For $R, G, B \geq 0.018$:

$$R' = 1.099\,R^{0.45} - 0.099$$

$$G' = 1.099\,G^{0.45} - 0.099 \qquad \{12.2a\}$$

$$B' = 1.099\,B^{0.45} - 0.099$$

For $R, G, B \leq -0.018$:

$$R' = -1.099\,|R|^{0.45} + 0.099$$

$$G' = -1.099\,|G|^{0.45} + 0.099 \qquad \{12.2b\}$$

$$B' = -1.099\,|B|^{0.45} + 0.099$$

For $-0.018 < R, G, B < 0.018$:

$$R' = 4.50\,R$$

$$G' = 4.50\,G \qquad \{12.2c\}$$

$$B' = 4.50\,B$$

Figure 12.13
Complete nonlin-
ear transform for
converting posi-
tive and negative
linear exposure
signals, *RGB*, to
positive and nega-
tive nonlinear
signals, *R'G'B'*.

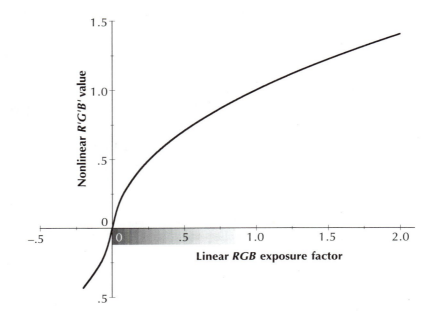

Figure 12.13
Complete nonlinear transform for converting positive and negative linear exposure signals, *RGB*, to positive and negative nonlinear signals, *R'G'B'*.

5. Image Compression

Before images are written to standard *Photo CD* Discs, they are decomposed into a sequence of image components in a hierarchy of resolutions, ranging from 192 pixels by 128 lines to 3072 pixels by 2048 lines. Higher resolution images, such as 6144 pixels by 4096 lines and greater, can be stored on *Photo CD* Discs intended for professional applications. In order to store a practical number of images on a disc (more than 100 images on a standard disc), images are stored in a compressed form.

The compression process includes a technique called *chroma subsampling.* In this technique, red, green, and blue signals are converted to an achromatic channel and two color-difference channels. Achromatic information is then stored at full resolution, while color-difference information is stored at a lower resolution. For example, most *Photo CD* Format image components are stored in terms of a full resolution achromatic channel and two color-difference channels that have been spatially subsampled by a factor of two in both the horizontal and vertical directions. Therefore, only one value from each of the color-difference channels is used for every four values from the achromatic channel. Because of the nature of the "signal processing" of the human visual system, images produced from full-spatial-resolution achromatic information together with lower-spatial-resolution color-difference information generally are perceived to have the visual quality of full-spatial-resolution color images.

To provide for this compression, the signal processing to the *Photo CD* System encoding data metric had to include a transformation of *RGB* signals to achromatic and color-difference signals. In theory, this transformation should be performed from *linear RGB* exposure signals (Fig. 12.14a). The result of that transformation would be an achromatic *luminance* channel, i.e., a channel corresponding to CIE *Y* values, and two color-difference *chrominance* channels, i.e., channels corresponding to CIE chromaticity values. However, we found that performing this transformation on linear exposure signals sometimes produced unacceptable subsampling artifacts.

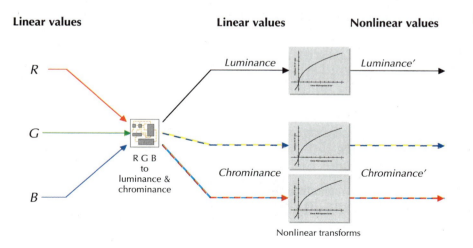

Linear values   **Linear values**   **Nonlinear values**

R

G

B

R G B
to
luminance &
chrominance

Luminance   *Luminance'*

Chrominance   *Chrominance'*

Nonlinear transforms

Figure 12.14a

This processing arrangement can form true luminance and chrominance channels, but it sometimes generates unacceptable artifacts in subsampled images.

A number of experiments were performed to examine this result, and computational models of the subsampling were developed. This work showed that the visibility of subsampling artifacts would be minimized if the achromatic and color-difference channels were derived from *nonlinear*, rather than linear, *RGB* signals (Fig. 12.14b). These experiments and computational models also allowed the optimum nonlinear function to be determined.

As it turned out, this optimum nonlinear function was very close to that of Fig. 12.13. Since that nonlinearity was needed anyway (to minimize quantization effects and to simplify the formation of output video signals), we simply placed the nonlinear transform *before* the derivation of the achromatic and color-difference signals, as in Fig. 12.14b. A similar approach has been used for many years in broadcast television.

One consequence of converting to achromatic and color-difference channels from nonlinear rather than linear signals is that true luminance and chrominance channels are not formed. The resulting channels therefore are more correctly referred to as *luma* and *chroma*.

Figure 12.14b

This processing arrangement produces images that generally are free of noticeable subsampling artifacts, although it does not form true luminance and chrominance signals. Its outputs are referred to as luma and chroma.

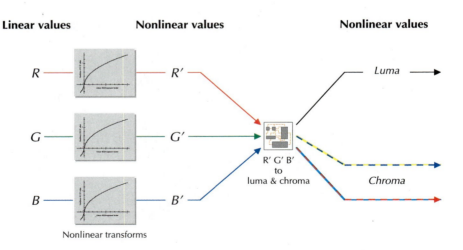

If one were to look at an image formed from either of the two chroma signals, with the luma signal held constant, it would be apparent that the luminance of the chroma image is not perfectly constant. Similarly, although a luma signal will always generate neutral signals (equal red, green, and blue), the luma levels for colors are affected to some extent by their chroma levels. None of this would matter if the red, green, and blue signals simply were converted to luma/chroma and then back to red, green, and blue. But when the chroma signals are subsampled, their luminance information also is affected. While a similar situation has had quite noticeable consequences in NTSC broadcast television, the effect on *Photo CD* Format images generally is undetectable. This result is not surprising, because the level of chroma subsampling in the *Photo CD* System is relatively small.

In the *PhotoYCC* Space data metric, the conversion of $R'G'B'$ nonlinear values to luma/chroma values is performed using the following equations:

$$Luma = 0.299R' + 0.587G' + 0.114B'$$

$$Chroma_1 = -0.299R' - 0.587G' + 0.886B' \qquad \{12.3\}$$

$$Chroma_2 = 0.701R' - 0.587G' - 0.114B'$$

The coefficients of these equations are derived from NTSC primaries, not from Rec. 709 primaries. This has relatively little effect on final images, however, because the inverse of each equation is included as part of the output signal processing. The NTSC equations were used because they are incorporated in most video-signal encoder and decoder circuits and in most video-based software. Their use helps to simplify the conversion of *PhotoYCC* Space values to standard output video signals.

Figure 12.15 shows the chromaticity locations for the *PhotoYCC* Space luma and chroma signals. Note that the chromaticity coordinates of the luma signal are those of D_{65}, which is the reference white for the data metric. This is a significant feature of the metric. What it means is that the extremely important neutrals of an image are represented solely by the luma signal, which is not spatially subsampled in the compression process.

Figure 12.15
Chromaticity
locations for the
PhotoYCC Space
luma and chroma
signals.

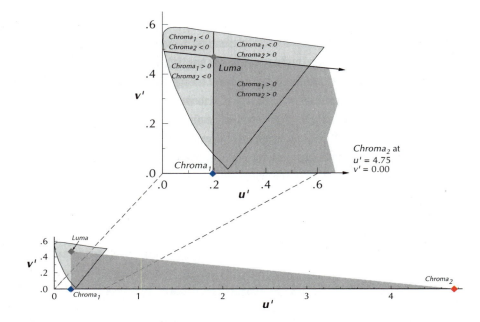

The final metric-related decision that we had to make involved the conversion of luma/chroma signals to digital code values. As stated earlier, the color gamut and luminance dynamic range of the *PhotoYCC* Color Space itself are unrestricted. But for digital encoding, upper and lower signal limits must be set when forming digitized luma and chroma values. Selecting such limits requires a compromise of dynamic range versus accuracy. For color gamut, it is important to include as much range as possible in each channel. But if the ranges are too great, errors due to digital quantization will become apparent.

After considerable calculation and experimentation, we specified the following equations for computing *PhotoYCC* Space Y, C_1, and C_2 digital code values (24-bit, 8 bits per channel) from luma/chroma values:

$$Y = (255/1.402)\, Luma$$

$$C_1 = 111.60\, Chroma_1 + 156 \qquad \{12.4\}$$

$$C_2 = 135.64\, Chroma_2 + 137$$

The values for the coefficients and constants of the C_1 and C_2 equations are such that virtually all surface colors, including those found in nature and those produced from manufactured colorants, can be encoded. The required color gamut was determined from a number of published studies and from additional research we had done. The gamut of these real-world colors is not symmetrical. That is why the C_1 and C_2 equations are not centered on a value of 128 and why different constants and coefficients are used in those equations.

The practical range of luminance-factor values that can be encoded according to Eqs. {12.4} extends from 0.0057 to 2.00, i.e., to twice the luminance factor of a perfect white. The total dynamic range therefore corresponds to an approximately 350:1 ratio of luminances, or a log luminance-factor range of about 2.5. This range is sufficient to retain the extensive dynamic range of scene luminances that can be recorded by most photographic media.

Implementation

The digital color encoding that has been described here is implemented in the *Photo CD* System in the following steps (Fig. 12.16):

1. A photographic image is scanned, and *RGB* transmission (or reflection) density values for each pixel are determined.

2. The *RGB* density values are corrected, according to individual scanner calibration transforms, to correspond to those densities that would have been measured by a mathematically defined reference scanner.

3. The corrected density values are processed through the selected film terms to determine the *RGB* exposure-factor values recorded by the photographic input image. This processing takes place in two steps. The first step removes cross-talk present in the *RGB* density values due to chemical signal processing in the film and to the unwanted absorptions of the film image-forming dyes, as measured by the scanner responsivities. The second step maps the resulting *RGB* density values to photographic *RGB* exposure-factor values.

4. The photographic *RGB* exposure-factor values are corrected for overall lightness and color balance, if desired, by the SBA and/or by the scanner operator.

5. The (corrected) photographic *RGB* exposure-factor values next are transformed to equivalent *RGB* tristimulus exposure-factor values for the Reference Image-Capturing Device.

6. The Reference Image-Capturing Device *RGB* tristimulus values are transformed to *R'G'B'* nonlinear values.

7. The *R'G'B'* values are transformed to luma and chroma values.

8. Finally, the luma and chroma values are transformed to *PhotoYCC* Space Y, C_1, and C_2 digital code values.

Figure 12.16

Digital color encoding in the *Photo CD* System.

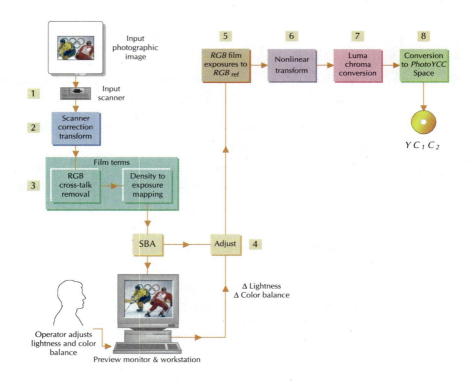

Discussion

This description has illustrated how the characteristics of a color-encoding data metric can be tailored to meet the specific requirements of the system on which it will be used. Certainly the *Photo CD* System data metric would have been very different if, for example, it was meant to minimize the signal processing required to make CMY or CMYK hardcopy images, rather than RGB video images. If image compression had not been required, the metric most likely would have used some form of RGB, rather than luma/chroma, color values. If a greater number of bits had been available, the metric might have been linear, rather than nonlinear, with exposure.

Although the *PhotoYCC* Space data metric was developed specifically for the *Photo CD* System, it has become widely used for general color interchange. That is because its principal features—large color gamut and luminance dynamic range, support for image compression, minimal quantization effects, and fast display to video—are important in a variety of computer-related applications. Later on, in Chapter 19, the use of this data metric for general color interchange will be discussed in greater detail.

Summary of Key Issues

- The data metric of a color encoding specification defines the color space and the numerical units in which encoded color values are expressed.

- The particular requirements of a specific color-imaging system will dictate the most appropriate data metric for that system.

- Because such requirements and system capabilities vary from system to system, there is no single "best" data metric for all color-imaging systems.

- The *PhotoYCC* Space data metric of the *Photo CD* System was designed to encode a gamut of colors and a range of luminances sufficient for photographic-quality output, to provide for image compression incorporating spatial subsampling, to minimize the effects of digital quantization, and to produce excellent quality video images using minimal signal processing.

- Although it is based on a set of real primaries, the color gamut and luminance dynamic range of the *PhotoYCC* Space data metric are restricted only by limitations imposed by the conversion to digital values.

13
Output Signal Processing

In the previous chapters, several different methods for encoding color images in terms of numerical values have been described. Once images are encoded according to such methods, they can be stored in digital form, edited, manipulated, and interchanged among systems. But the ultimate use of encoded color images is to produce hardcopy and softcopy output images.

Producing high-quality output images from digitally encoded color values involves consideration of many of the same factors that were discussed in regard to the input encoding process. There also are other considerations that are unique to output signal processing and output image formation. While a full discussion of all these considerations is beyond the scope of this book, there are certain aspects of the output process that should be discussed here because they directly relate to color encoding and because they will be referred to in later discussions on color management.

Generating Output Images

Generating output images requires the use of output signal processing, which converts encoded color values to output device digital code values. These code values control device drive signals, which in turn control the amounts of the color-forming elements that make up the output image.

For example, in the case of a CRT display, *RGB* device code values are processed through DACs to form red, green, and blue control voltage signals (Fig. 13.1). Each signal modulates the current of an electron beam aimed at the corresponding red, green, or blue phosphors, thereby determining the amount of red, green, or blue light produced by the CRT. Similarly, in a thermal printer, *RGB* device code values ultimately determine the amounts of cyan, magenta, and yellow dyes that are transferred to the support (Fig. 13.2).

Figure 13.1

Transformation of device RGB code values to CRT red, green, and blue light output.

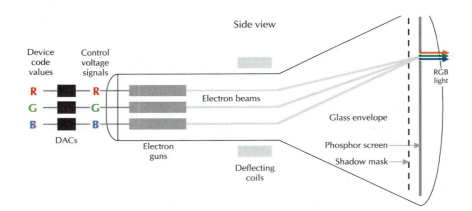

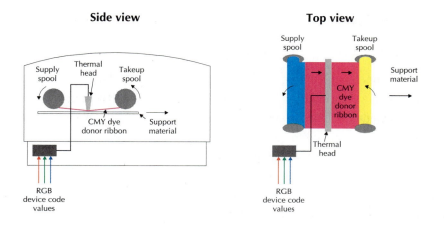

Side view

Supply spool

Thermal head

Takeup spool

CMY dye donor ribbon

Support material

RGB device code values

Top view

Supply spool

Takeup spool

Support material

CMY dye donor ribbon

Thermal head

RGB device code values

Figure 13.2
Transformation of device RGB code values to thermal print CMY dye amounts.

Output signal processing can be thought of as a series of individual transforms that perform three basic functions: colorimetric transformation, gamut adjustment, and output code value determination (Fig. 13.3). In some color-managed systems, these individual transforms can be concatenated (combined) into a single transform. However, that really is an implementation issue, as will be discussed in Chapter 20. The *effect* of applying a concatenated transform is fundamentally the same as sequentially applying each of the individual transformations discussed next in this chapter.

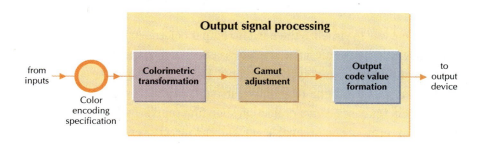

Output signal processing

from inputs

Color encoding specification

Colorimetric transformation

Gamut adjustment

Output code value formation

to output device

Figure 13.3
The three basic functions of output signal processing.

Colorimetric Transformation

The first function of output signal processing is to transform encoded values such that the colorimetry directly represented, or indirectly implied, by those values is modified appropriately for the given output. This type of output signal transformation is required, *regardless of the color-encoding method used,* on all systems that include multiple types of outputs. As discussed in Part II, the colorimetric properties of images on different types of media must be different in order for images to appear appropriately rendered on each medium. Thus, it is impossible to encode in terms of any *single* colorimetric specification that can be used directly for *all* types of output.

       The extent and nature of the colorimetric transformation for any given output will depend on the relationship between the method used to create the encoded values and the type of output that will be produced. For any given encoding method, it is possible that *one* particular type of output will not require a colorimetric transformation.

       For example, if the encoding method were based on the colorimetry of reflection images viewed under CIE D_{50} illumination, no colorimetric transformation would be required for output to a thermal printer that produces reflection prints for CIE D_{50} viewing. However, significant transformations of encoded colorimetric values would be required for output to a film writer that produces projection slides.

       One way to visualize the need for output colorimetric transformation is to consider the grayscale characteristics associated with different encoding methods and with different types of outputs. Figure 13.4 shows these characteristics for an original scene (the unity curve a), a reflection print (curve b), a video system (curve c), and a projection slide film (curve d). If the color encoding were in terms of the original scene and the output were to a video display, for example, the output colorimetric transformation would have to include a conversion of curve a values to corresponding curve c values. If this conversion were not included, the output video images would appear too low in luminance

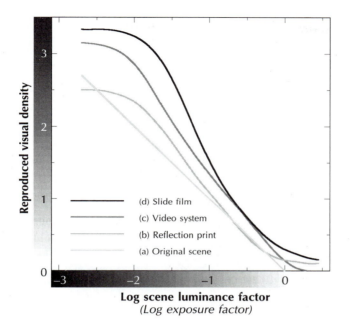

Figure 13.4
Grayscale characteristics for an original scene and three types of output.

contrast. If the color encoding were in terms of reflection images and the output were to a projection slide film, the output transformation would have to include a conversion of curve *b* values to corresponding curve *d* values. The actual output colorimetric transformations would, of course, involve more than just grayscale values, but the curves help to illustrate the concept.

It also might be helpful to consider output colorimetric transformations in terms of the text-scanning system discussed earlier (Fig. 13.5). Color output devices and media that produce images having different colorimetric properties are analogous to output devices that produce text in different languages. In the case of text, each output requires a translation transform from the encoding language to the particular output language. At best, the translation transform for *one* output can be eliminated if the encoding itself is in that output language. In the system shown in the figure, for example, no transform is required for output to Latin. But there is no single encoding language that can go directly, without translation, to *all* of the output languages.

Figure 13.5

Output from a multi-language text-scanning system. There is no single encoding language that can go directly, without translation, to *all* of the output languages.

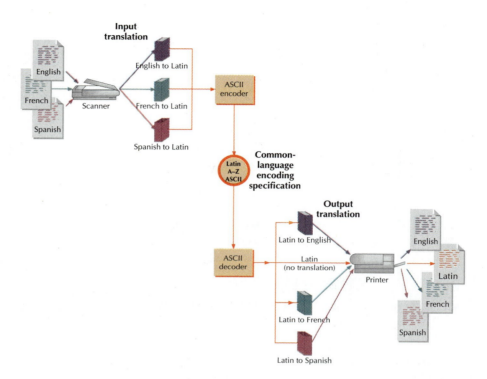

In some applications, the colorimetric transformation may include additional modifications of encoded colorimetric values. These modifications are used to deliberately *alter* the color appearance of the output images from that which otherwise would have been produced from the color-encoded values. Such alterations often are used for *simulation*, where one medium is used to emulate the appearance of another. For example, an image might be produced on a computer monitor in a way that simulates what that image would look like if it were produced on a particular type of hardcopy output.

Image editing applications sometimes are used to produce other types of deliberate alterations, such as hue shifts, chroma modifications, and lightness increases or decreases. These changes may be executed by including them in the colorimetric transformation of the output signal processing.

Gamut Adjustment

The second function of output signal processing deals with specified output colorimetric values that are not physically reproducible by the output medium and/or device. This function, sometimes called *gamut mapping,* replaces out-of-gamut colorimetric values with substitute values that can be attained. In-gamut values also may be adjusted slightly so that the substitute values can be accommodated. The criteria used in performing these adjustments and substitutions will vary according to the application for which the output is used.

For example, the mapping might be based on the shortest distance, in three-dimensional color space, from the out-of-gamut color values to the *gamut boundary* of the output (Fig. 13.6). Alternatively, the mapping might be based on a criterion that places a greater emphasis on maintaining a particular color aspect, such as hue, of the out-of-gamut colors. The most successful strategies allow alterations to occur in multiple color aspects. When applied appropriately, such strategies minimize the visibility of the mapping.

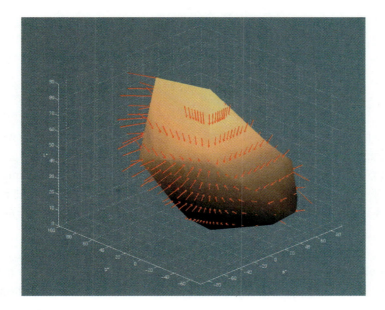

Figure 13.6
The vectors in this three-dimensional diagram illustrate the mapping of color values to a gamut boundary.

Color gamut adjustments are especially important when encoding methods and data metrics that allow the encoding of large color gamuts are used. The color gamut that can be encoded in terms of the *PhotoYCC* Space data metric, for example, is greater than that displayable by any existing output medium or device.

It is particularly critical to adjust the extensive luminance dynamic range of *PhotoYCC* Space image data to a range that is appropriate for a particular output. If this adjustment is not done correctly, important luminance information will be lost in the output signal processing, which in turn means that this information will not be visible in output images.

For example, some desktop imaging applications use the following equations for converting 8-bit-per-channel *PhotoYCC* Space values to 8-bit-per-channel $R'G'B'$ video code values:

$$Y_{video} = 1.3584\,Y$$

$$C_{1video} = 2.2179\,(C_1 - 156) \qquad\qquad \{13.1\}$$

$$C_{2\,video} = 1.8215\,(C_2 - 137)$$

$$R'_{video} = Y_{video} + C_{2\,video}$$

$$G'_{video} = Y_{video} - 0.194 C_{1video} - 0.509 C_{2\,video} \qquad\qquad \{13.2\}$$

$$B'_{video} = Y_{video} + C_{1video}$$

A scale factor of 1.3584 is used in Eqs. {13.1} so that a 90% reflectance white in an original scene (encoded in *PhotoYCC* Space values as $Y = 173$, $C_1 = 156$, $C_2 = 137$) produces $R'G'B'_{video}$ code values of 235, 235, 235, in accordance with current digital-video specifications. If such scaling is not done, displayed images appear too dark. But use of this scaling alone can result in a loss of information in displayed images.

Table 13.1 shows the *PhotoYCC* Space Y value and the $R'G'B'_{video}$ code values obtained using these equations for a grayscale (represented by a series of percent-scene-white luminance values). Note that luminance information

Percent Scene White	PhotoYCC Y Value	R'G'B'$_{VIDEO}$ Values	Modified R'G'B'$_{VIDEO}$ Values
1	8	11	11
2	16	22	22
5	34	46	46
10	53	72	72
15	67	91	91
20	79	107	107
30	98	134	134
40	114	155	156
50	128	174	175
60	141	192	192
70	152	206	204
80	163	221	213
90	173	235	222
100	182	247	228
107	188	255	232
120	199	270	238
140	215	292	245
160	229	311	250
180	243	330	253
200	255	346	255

Table 13.1

Luminance information above 107% scene white will produce R'G'B'$_{video}$ code values greater than 255. This can be prevented by appropriate nonlinear remapping (modified values).

above 107% scene white produces $R'G'B'_{video}$ code values greater than 255. If these values were used directly by an 8-bit-per-channel video display device, any information corresponding to those values would be lost because all values greater than 255 would be clipped at 255.

To prevent this, either the *PhotoYCC* Space values or the corresponding $R'G'B'_{video}$ code values should be transformed such that modified $R'G'B'_{video}$ code values that are within the range of the display code values are formed. The transformation must be nonlinear in order to avoid an unacceptable darkening of the image.

Figure 13.7
This lookup table
was used to
transform the
$R'G'B'_{video}$ code
values of Table
13.1 to modified
$R'G'B'_{video}$ code
values. Use of this
transformation
avoids a loss of
important high-
light information
in displayed
images.

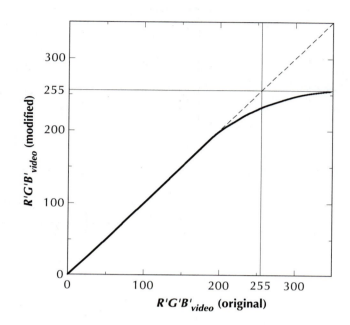

In many desktop imaging applications, this nonlinear transformation is implemented using one-dimensional lookup tables. For example, the modified $R'G'B'_{video}$ code values listed in Table 13.1 result from applying the lookup table shown above (Fig. 13.7) to the $R'G'B'_{video}$ code values from Eqs. {13.1} and {13.2}. Note that the full luminance dynamic range of the 8-bit-per-channel *PhotoYCC* Space encoding, which extends to 200% of scene white, produces modified $R'G'B'_{video}$ code values that are no greater than 255.

Output Code Value Determination

The third function of output signal processing is to generate output-device code values that will produce, on the particular output medium and/or device, output colors having the colorimetric values computed from the color encoding, the

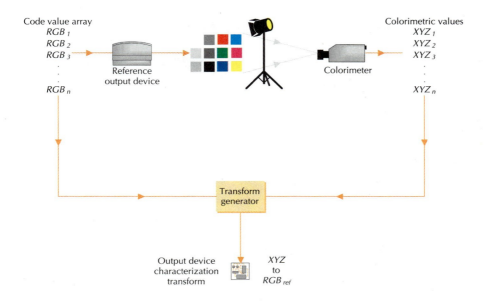

Code value array
RGB$_1$
RGB$_2$
RGB$_3$
.
.
RGB$_n$

Reference output device

Colorimeter

Colorimetric values
XYZ$_1$
XYZ$_2$
XYZ$_3$
.
.
XYZ$_n$

Transform generator

Output device characterization transform

XYZ to *RGB*$_{ref}$

Figure 13.8

Construction of a characterization transform for a hardcopy output device. An array of code values is used to generate a corresponding array of color patches from the output device. The color patches are illuminated, and their colorimetry is measured. A transform relating measured colorimetric values to device code values is then constructed.

colorimetric transformation, and the gamut-adjustment transformation. Derivation of a transformation required for this last function generally consists of two steps: output characterization and output calibration. These terms, which were briefly described earlier, sometimes are used as if they were interchangeable; however, their actual meanings are quite different.

Characterization is a procedure for defining the colorimetric characteristics of a reference device that is representative of the actual devices to be used. A colorimetric output-characterization transform can be developed from data obtained by measuring the colorimetric values of a large number of color patches, produced on the reference output device from an array of output-device code values (Fig. 13.8). A characterization transform also can be developed from a mathematical model of a reference output device. In either case, the characterization transform is used to relate desired output colorimetric values to the reference output device code values required to produce those colorimetric values.

Figure 13.9
Use of a single
characterization
transform and
multiple calibra-
tion transforms for
multiple outputs.

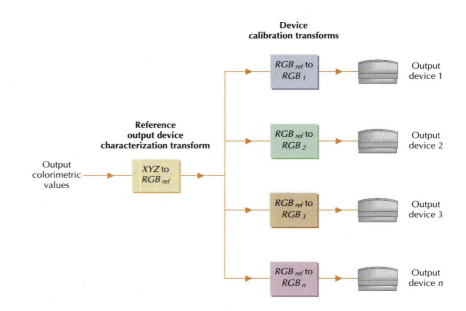

In some circumstances, the use of output characterization transforms alone is feasible. For example, it might be practical to build characterization transforms for each output device in a situation where there are relatively few devices, the devices are relatively stable, and the procedure for building the transforms is fast and economical. In most circumstances, however, it is more practical to build a single reference characterization transform for all devices of the same type and to then provide unique calibration transforms for each individual device (Fig. 13.9).

A *calibration* transform corrects for any deviation of a particular device from the reference device on which the characterization transform was based. This combined characterization/calibration approach has a number of advantages. In particular, because the bulk of the transformation is performed in the characterization transform, calibration transforms generally can be quite simple. In most cases, they can be derived using a relatively small set of test colors. For many three-color systems, calibration of the grayscale characteristic alone can be sufficient. This generally makes the calibration procedure very fast and inexpensive to perform.

Summary of Key Issues

- Output-signal-processing transforms are used to convert color values, encoded in terms of a color encoding specification, to output device code values. The nature of the conversion depends on the relationship between the encoding method and the characteristics of the output medium and/or device.

- Output-signal-processing transforms generally perform three basic functions: colorimetric transformation, gamut adjustment, and output-device code value determination.

- A colorimetric transformation is used to convert encoded colorimetric values to modified colorimetric values that are appropriate for the given output. Such transformations are always required, regardless of the method used for color encoding.

- Gamut-adjustment transforms are used to replace out-of-gamut colorimetric values with substitute values that are physically attainable by the output.

- Output-device code value determination is achieved by the use of appropriate characterization and calibration transforms.

- An output-characterization transform relates output colorimetric values to output-device code values for a reference device.

- An output-calibration transform compensates for deviations of a particular output device from a reference device.

14
Myths and Misconceptions

The great enemy of the truth is very often not the lie—deliberate, contrived and dishonest—but the myth—persistent, persuasive and unrealistic.

John F. Kennedy

In the preceding chapters, a number of misconceptions regarding color in general and color encoding in particular have been mentioned. These misconceptions are frequently repeated and widely circulated within the industry. Many have become so widespread that they now can be considered "modern myths."

While a few of these myths are relatively harmless, most have had very detrimental effects on the color-imaging industry. In particular, the persistent myths regarding "device-independent" color have seriously interfered with real progress in the areas of color management and color interchange.

It is important that these myths be examined and dispelled before we conclude this section and proceed to Part IV, where the pieces of the digital color-encoding puzzle will be sorted and assembled to form a total picture. For that to be done successfully, there must be no spurious pieces—no leftover myths—still lying around.

In this chapter, then, a number of the more persistent and persuasive-sounding myths related to color encoding will be examined. Some have been mentioned in earlier chapters, while others have not. We will attempt to dispel them all by contrasting each with reality (as we see it, of course!).

Myths of Device-Independent Color

Myths usually are created in an attempt to explain what seems otherwise inexplicable, and they often are used to provide support for ideas that people wish to believe. So it is not surprising that numerous myths have arisen regarding the concept of "device-independent" color. After all, color itself certainly seems quite inexplicable at times, and people strongly *want* to believe that color images can be interchanged freely among imaging systems if all images are encoded in a "device-independent" manner.

Unfortunately, the expression "device-independent color" most commonly means nothing more than the use of standard colorimetric methods and standard color spaces such as CIE XYZ, CIELAB, and CIELUV. As was shown earlier, this form of encoding works only in certain restricted cases; but perhaps because of these occasional successes, several popular myths persist:

Myth: CIE colorimetric values describe the appearance of color.

Reality: This may well be the most common of all color-encoding myths. As discussed earlier, CIE colorimetry was designed for quantifying the trichromatic characteristics of color stimuli. But standard CIE colorimetry alone does *not* specify the color appearance of those stimuli. Standard CIE colorimetry emulates the image-capture stage of human vision, but it does not emulate the mental signal processing and image formation stages that ultimately result in visual perceptions. A specification of color appearance requires the use of advanced forms of colorimetry that account for observer adaptation and other factors. Practical ways of doing that will be discussed in Part IV.

Myth: Device-independent color encoding allows the input of images from all types of media and devices.

Reality: The *successful* input of images from disparate sources ultimately requires creating input compatibility by color encoding in terms of a particular aspect of color that is common among all inputs. Encoding based on standard colorimetric values alone cannot create input compatibility among most types of media and devices.

Myth: Use of a standard, device-independent, CIE colorimetric color space is necessary to provide common image data for interchange among imaging systems.

Reality: Colorimetric *measurements* can provide a basis for color encoding in certain applications. But it is not always desirable—and it is never actually necessary—to express encoded values, derived from those measurements, in terms of standard colorimetric color spaces and numerical units.

In many applications, it is more practical to express colorimetric values in other terms, such as physically realizable device primaries (rather than CIE XYZ primaries), color-signal values for a reference output device (encoding based on a reference video monitor, for example), or tristimulus values for a reference input device (as in the *PhotoYCC* Space data metric).

Myth: CIE standard colorimetric values are device independent and thus specify actual output colorimetry, independent of which output medium or device is to be used.

Reality: As discussed in Chapter 13, encoded colorimetric values always must be modified appropriately for output to different devices, media, and viewing environments. The use of CIE standard colorimetric values alone does not and can not eliminate this requirement.

Myth: Only standard CIE representations (color spaces, data metrics, etc.) are device independent.

Reality: This myth stems from a common notion that, for device independence, the characteristics of a color representation must differ from those of *any* device or medium. For example, in one technical presentation, a speaker stated that *"PhotoYCC* Space is not device independent because it is referenced to a device. The fact that the reference device (the Reference Image-Capturing Device) is imaginary is not relevant. It is still a device." That is an interesting criterion for device independence, but using it raises questions about other color representations as well. For example, there are *real* XYZ devices (such as colorimeters). So the CIE XYZ color space must be even *more* "device dependent" than is *PhotoYCC* Space. We are being facetious, of course, in order to show that it does not make sense to evaluate the device independence of a color representation based solely on its relationship to a device (real or imaginary) or on its conformance to existing standard color spaces. To see why, let us return one last time to the text-scanner analogy.

In that system, Latin—a language that is "independent" of any of the actual languages being used for input or output—was used for encoding. But was it necessary to use an "independent" language? The answer is no. It was necessary to use a *single* language in order to provide input compatibility. But there was no real reason not to encode in one of the *actual* input or output languages. In fact, there might have been very good reasons to do so.

Suppose, for example, most of the output was to be in English. The system would work most efficiently if the encoding itself were in English, because no translation would be needed for English output. The fact that a "real" language is used is of no consequence, as long as that language has a large enough "gamut" to encode all words of interest. Similarly, there is nothing wrong with representing colors in terms of device-dependent values. Again, there are good reasons to do so, as long as all colors of interest can be expressed in terms of those values. We suggest this alternative definition for device independence, based on that criterion: *A data metric is device independent if the luminance dynamic range and color gamut of its color space are not restricted by an association with a device.*

Although this alternative definition certainly includes color representations used in standard colorimetry, it also includes other representations that may be more practical to implement in actual imaging applications. For example, color values expressed in color spaces based on reference input or output devices often can be used with minimal output signal processing on practical output devices. At the same time, such color spaces can be colorimetrically rigorous, and they can be used to represent an essentially unrestricted color gamut and luminance dynamic range *if appropriate encoding techniques are used.* For example, the gamut of a color space based on a reference video monitor can be unrestricted if negative *RGB* intensity values are allowed. By the definition just given, such color spaces are device independent; yet their values also are "device friendly."

Adaptation Myths

Visual adaptation effects are quite complex and difficult to quantify. Perhaps for that reason, a sizable number of myths related to adaptation phenomena have arisen. The following myths directly apply to color encoding.

Myth: Visual adaptation effects are so numerous, complex, and poorly understood that they cannot be accounted for in practical color-encoding methods.

Reality: Sometimes it does seem that there are endless types of visual adaptation phenomena, and it is true that their effects often are quite complex. But from our experience, we believe that there are just three important adaptation phenomena to be concerned with in most imaging applications: chromatic adaptation, general-brightness adaptation, and lateral-brightness adaptation. Although ongoing work continues to increase the understanding of these effects, the present level of knowledge is such that they can be accounted for reasonably well for most imaging purposes. In Part IV, a relatively simple, practical, appearance-based color-encoding method that accounts for these three perceptual effects will be described.

Myth: A chromatic-adaptation transform converts the colorimetry measured under one viewing illuminant to the colorimetry that will result (or would have resulted) under a different viewing illuminant.

Reality: A chromatic adaptation transformation, say from D_{50} to D_{65}, does *not* convert D_{50} tristimulus values to the tristimulus values that would have been formed if a D_{65} illuminant had been used instead of a D_{50} illuminant. What the transformation *does* do is determine the corresponding tristimulus values for a color stimulus that would produce, for a standard observer chromatically adapted to the chromaticity of D_{65}, a visual match to an original color stimulus viewed by a standard observer who is chromatically adapted to the chromaticity of D_{50}. It is important to note that only the chromaticities of the two adaptation conditions, not the illuminant spectral power distributions, are required for the determination of a chromatic adaptation transform.

It should be noted that in special circumstances, it *is* possible to determine, from colorimetric values, the colorimetry that would result under a different illuminant. However, this is *not* a chromatic adaptation transformation. In addition, the determination can be performed accurately only for colors made from three (or fewer) colorants of known spectral characteristics. For example, if the colorimetry (or densitometry) of a color photograph is measured, and if the spectral responsivities of the measuring device, the spectral power of the measuring illuminant, the spectral absorption characteristics of the CMY dyes, and the spectral absorption characteristics of the reflection support *all* are known, the spectral reflectance of each measured color can be calculated from the measured colorimetry or densitometry. This is possible because there is one, and only one, spectral reflectance that can be made from those CMY dyes on that support that will result in a particular triad of colorimetric or RGB values. Once the reflectance is determined, the colorimetry for that reflectance and *any* illuminant power distribution can be computed using ordinary colorimetric calculations. It is important to emphasize that this technique, which is used in some input scanners, works only because the original colorimetry is derived from a known set of three colorants. It also should be emphasized again that it is *not* a chromatic-adaptation transformation.

Myth: An observer adapts to the brightest color of an image, and that color is perceived as a perfect white.

Reality: This myth has been the cause of many color-interchange problems within the imaging industry. As discussed earlier, the amount of adaptation to an image will depend on the conditions in which that image is viewed. There can be a very significant amount of adaptation to projected and self-luminous images, especially when they are viewed in darkened environments.

However, what is perceived as a perfect white seldom, if ever, corresponds to the *brightest* color of the image. Experiments have shown that observer chromatic adaptation is controlled primarily by the chromaticity of colors judged to be scene neutrals of about 40% reflectance. A color that would be judged to be a perfect white would have that chromaticity, and it would have a perceived brightness equivalent to that of an ideal reproduction of a perfect white diffuse reflector in the original scene. The grayscale characteristics of all high-quality imaging media and systems are designed such that images contain areas that appear *brighter* than the reproduction of a perfect white. Such areas create the illusion of being "whiter than white." They are interpreted appropriately as specular highlights, highly illuminated diffuse objects, etc.; they are *not* perceived as white references—either in brightness or in chromaticity—for other colors.

This myth is even farther from reality for reflection images. The assumption underlying the myth is that observers adapt to the "white" defined by the reflection support, since the brightest areas that can be produced on a reflection image consist of the support alone. In reality, however, reflection images generally are judged as objects within a viewing environment. Under most viewing conditions, there is little or no adaptation to a reflection image itself because the viewing environment contains white objects and other visual cues that serve as references for the general-brightness adaptation and chromatic adaptation of the observer.

It might be useful to consider that if observers really did adapt to the brightest image color, media manufacturers would not bother spending as much time and money as they do trying to make reflection-print support materials as bright and as neutral as possible. In reality, customers *easily* can see differences among supports, even when those differences are so small that they are difficult to measure with the most sensitive instruments available. That would not be the case if observers did indeed adapt to the "white" of the support.

This myth will be discussed in greater detail in Chapter 17, where the problems associated with what is sometimes called "relative colorimetry," or, more appropriately, "media-relative colorimetry," are described.

Photo CD System and *Photo YCC* Space Data Metric Myths

The color-encoding method used to produce most *Photo CD* Discs is quite different from previous methods, and it often is misunderstood. As a consequence, many published explanations of that encoding have not been entirely accurate. In particular, most descriptions have not distinguished between the *Photo CD* System color-encoding method and the *PhotoYCC* Space data metric. This has led to a number of persistent myths that must be cleared up before we proceed to Part IV, where many of the principles of the *Photo CD* System color-encoding method will be incorporated in a comprehensive color-management system.

Myth: Colors encoded in terms of *PhotoYCC* Space values always represent original scene colors.

Reality: It is the color-encoding *method* presently used on *Photo CD* Imaging Workstations that results in the encoding of original scene colors. Other methods can be used to create *Photo CD* Discs in which *reproduced* colors are encoded in terms of *PhotoYCC* Space values. When this is done correctly, the resulting *Photo CD* Format images are completely compatible with standard *Photo CD* Format images. In fact, when appropriate procedures are used, the

PhotoYCC Space data metric can be used to encode colors from *any* source, regardless of whether that source represents original scene colors, reproduced colors, or any other types of colors. This will be discussed in greater detail in Part IV.

Myth: Use of product-specific film terms results in the encoding of original-scene colors, whereas use of universal film terms results in the encoding of colors as reproduced by the scanned film.

Reality: This myth began several years ago, spread rapidly, and is now widely believed. It has been repeated at numerous technical conferences and has appeared in several textbooks and other publications. But as described earlier, in Chapter 11, the use of *either* product-specific *or* universal *Photo CD* System film-term transforms results in the encoding of original scene colorimetry.

The real distinction is that using product-specific transforms for each input film will do this with greater accuracy. For a given input film, that accuracy is determined by the accuracy of the calibration procedures and by the correspondence of the film's spectral sensitivities to a set of visual color-matching functions. When a single universal transform is used for a group of related input films, the accuracy of the original-scene-colorimetry encoding is further influenced by the *differences* that exist among those films. Encoding colors on *Photo CD* Discs as actually *reproduced* on a scanned film requires an entirely different encoding method that will be discussed later.

Myth: Use of the *Photo CD* System Scene Balance Algorithm (SBA) results in the encoding of original-scene colors; turning it off results in an encoding of the reproduced colors of the scanned film.

Reality: The Scene Balance Algorithm is not a means for selecting between original and reproduced colors. The true function of the SBA, described in Chapter 11, is to determine overall lightness and color-balance corrections. The result of the algorithm is three numbers—red, green, and blue adjustments—that are applied to the scanned image data during the encoding process. The adjustments provided by the algorithm can be disabled, enabled fully, or enabled partially.

Myth: The luminance dynamic range of *PhotoYCC* Space values is 2.5; that is too small a range for encoding photographic slides, which have a density range of greater than 3.0.

Reality: There are two misconceptions here. First, luminance dynamic range and color gamut actually are unrestricted in the *PhotoYCC* Color Space. Limits are defined only when code values are computed based on the number of bits used in the encoding. It is only when the *PhotoYCC* Space encoding is limited to 24 bits (8 bits per channel) that the luminance dynamic range is restricted to about 2.5 (expressed in logarithmic units). A larger luminance dynamic range can be encoded in applications that support a greater bit depth.

The second, more basic misconception is that this 2.5 range can be compared directly to the density range of a medium. It cannot.

Figure 14.1

Relationship of *PhotoYCC* Space values to density values for a representative photographic slide film.

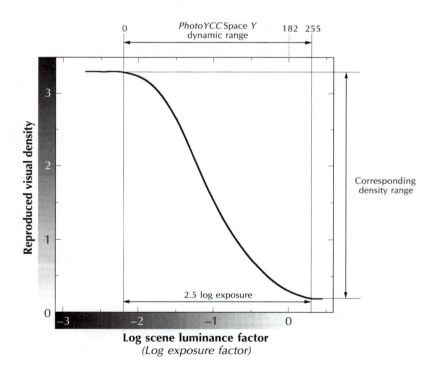

PhotoYCC Space values correspond most closely to exposure values *to* a medium, while density values correspond to what is produced *by* a medium. In other words, *PhotoYCC* Space values represent input values to a medium, while density values are a measure of the corresponding output. The ranges of these values are quite different. Figure 14.1 shows, for example, the relationship of *PhotoYCC* Space *Y* values to density values for a representative photographic slide film. Note that the 2.5 dynamic range of the *PhotoYCC* Space values covers the corresponding range of densities that can be produced by the slide film.

The figure illustrates the appropriate way to compare the luminance dynamic range of *PhotoYCC* Space to the density range for a medium. A direct comparison of *PhotoYCC* Space numerical values to output density values for a medium is an essentially meaningless "apples and oranges" comparison.

A Scanner Myth

Densitometric scanners, which were discussed in Chapter 9, and colorimetric scanners, discussed in Chapter 10, share many similarities. However, they have one fundamental distinction: While the physical spectral responsivities of a colorimetric scanner are based on a set of visual color-matching functions, those of a densitometric scanner are not. As a result of that difference, the functionality of the two types of scanners is quite different.

Myth: The functionality of a scanner that incorporates transforms to convert scanned *RGB* values to CIE colorimetric values is identical to that of a colorimetric scanner.

Reality: An RGB scanner will produce accurate CIE colorimetric values, based on a particular light source, *only* when used with a transform that is specifically designed for the particular medium being scanned. If a medium having a different set of colorants is scanned, the transformation likely will be inaccurate. A true colorimetric scanner can measure CIE colorimetric values, again based on a particular light source, for *any* medium. This will be true even for complex media, such as paintings, in which a large number of colorants have been used.

Color Reproduction Myths

Myth: The ideal grayscale reproduction should be one-to-one with the original scene.

Myth: The "S-shaped" grayscale characteristic of conventional photographic systems is unfortunate and results from chemical limitations. The grayscale characteristic should be a straight line.

Myth: Ideal color reproduction would exactly duplicate the colorimetry of the original scene.

Reality: These myths share a common theme: the relationship of reproduced colorimetry to original colorimetry. Each myth ignores physical and perceptual factors that must be taken into account in order to make reproductions that best approximate the appearances of original scenes.

When appropriate compensations for viewing flare, general-brightness adaptation, lateral-brightness adaptation, differences in scene and reproduction luminance levels, differences in scene and reproduction dynamic ranges, differences in scene and reproduction color gamuts, color memory effects, and color preferences all are factored in, the resulting optimum color-reproduction characteristics are quite similar to those of commercial photographic products. Optimum grayscale characteristics are highly nonlinear; they certainly do not have a simple one-to-one relationship to original scene luminance factors. Similarly, optimum color reproduction is not a simple one-to-one colorimetric match to the original scene.

One possible source of confusion on this issue is that original "scenes" can be live scenes, or they themselves can be reproductions. When an imaging system is used to produce a *copy* of an input that itself is a *reproduction,* that system *should* produce a one-to-one replication of the colorimetry of that input reproduction, as shown in Fig. 14.2. This assumes, of course, that the input reproduction and the output copy are to be viewed under identical conditions. In such cases, the departures from colorimetry required for realistic depictions of live scenes already have been incorporated in the input reproduction. Those departures need not, and should not, be made *again* in the replication process.

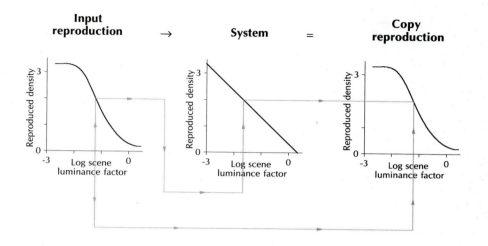

Figure 14.2

In the special case where an imaging system is used to produce a copy of an input image that itself is a reproduction, the system should produce a one-to-one replication of the colorimetry of the input image.

Myth: There are no whites "whiter" than a perfect white diffuse reflector.

Reality: This color-reproduction myth misses the distinction between objects and color stimuli. Most original scenes contain information at luminance levels well above that of a perfect 100% white diffuse reflecting object in the principal subject area of the scene. This information comes from stimuli produced by specular reflections, by certain types of diffuse reflections, by areas of a scene that are more highly illuminated than the principal subject area, and by certain types of fluorescent colors.

Because of the visual importance of this above-white information, high-quality imaging media and devices are designed to record and display that information. Therefore, digital color-encoding methods and data metrics used with such media and devices also must be designed so that this information can be retained and appropriately represented.

Figure 14.3

Reproduction of a perfect white on three types of media. Each medium can discriminate and represent input information recorded from above 100% scene white.

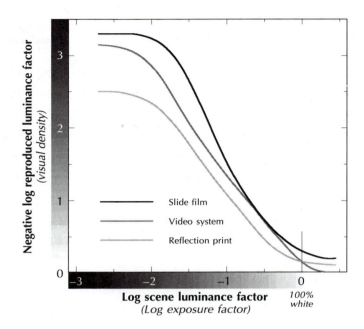

Myth: Output media and devices cannot produce greater than 100% white; therefore, there is no need to encode information above 100% white.

Reality: This related color-reproduction myth is a result of confusing inputs and outputs. Consider Fig. 14.3, which shows the overall system grayscale characteristics for three types of output: reflection print, photographic slide film, and video display. Note that even the reflection print medium, which has a minimum density of 0.10 (a reflectance of only about 80%), still can discriminate and represent *input* information recorded from above 100% scene white. The "S-shape" characteristic curve compresses the dynamic range of the input information, in both the shadow and highlight regions, such that it can be displayed appropriately. The other two media can discriminate and represent an even greater range of highlight information. Retaining such information is one of the goals for the remaining color-encoding method that will be developed in Part IV.

Discussion

Although reviewing these myths can be somewhat entertaining, the actual consequences of their existence are quite serious. They have caused many color-imaging systems and color-management products to fail, they have caused a great deal of confusion within the color-imaging industry, and they frequently have derailed discussions, which otherwise might have been meaningful and productive, on standards for color interchange.

Readers having remaining questions concerning any of the issues that have been discussed here are urged to review the relevant sections of this book. Some of the concepts that will be discussed in Part IV, although not technically difficult, are fairly subtle and sometimes can be difficult to grasp. Therefore, it is important for the reader to be free of any misconceptions before proceeding.

PART IV

A Unified Color-Management Environment

In the previous sections, the subjects of color measurement, imaging systems, color vision, the colorimetric characteristics of various types of color-imaging devices and media, color-encoding methods, color-encoding data metrics, and output signal processing have been discussed. Each of these topics is an important piece of a much larger picture.

In this final section, that picture will be completed. The individual pieces will be assembled in such a way that a plan is created for a unified color-management environment for the color-imaging industry.

If that plan is implemented, it will be possible for all imaging systems and applications—from the most basic to the most comprehensive—to function together within a single, global, color-managed environment.

Three things are required for the achievement of this objective:

- An overall paradigm that defines how the entire color-management environment will work.
- A color-encoding scheme that provides appropriate representation of color throughout the environment.
- An overall architecture that allows the environment to be implemented in a practical way.

In the next chapters, the various paradigms that define how color is managed in existing color-imaging systems will be described. It will be shown that although each offers essential (but different) features, no current paradigm is sufficiently comprehensive to support a truly global color-management environment. A new, *unified* paradigm then will be developed to meet that goal.

Most importantly, a color-encoding method capable of supporting the color-encoding requirements and color-interchange requirements defined by the unified paradigm will be described. This method, which is based on color appearance, was not discussed in Part III. That is because its usefulness is not fully realized outside the context of a comprehensive color-managed environment, such as that described in this section.

15
Color-Management Paradigms

Every successful color-imaging system employs one or more means for controlling and adjusting color information throughout the system. That is what is meant by *color management*. Color management may be incorporated in various forms: as software designed specifically for that purpose, as equipment calibration procedures, as operator adjustments, as chemical process control, etc., used either alone or in various combinations.

At the heart of every color-management approach is an implicitly or explicitly defined *paradigm*—an underlying conceptual model that ultimately determines how an imaging system using that color management will work. One of the problems facing the color-imaging industry today is that there are many different kinds of systems that all seem to work in very different ways. That would suggest there also must be many possible color-management paradigms; and if that is so, our goal of a unified, industry-wide, color-managed environment would seem quite hopeless.

We and a group of our colleagues spent some time thinking about this, and we eventually realized that although existing color-imaging systems might behave quite differently, they all can be described in terms of just *three* fundamental types of color-management paradigms. Each paradigm is perfectly valid, yet each produces very different color results. For convenience, and to avoid any names that unintentionally might imply a value judgment on our part, these paradigms will be referred to simply as Types *A, B,* and *C.*

The *ABC* Color-Management Paradigms

Color-imaging systems based on a Type *A* color-management paradigm (Fig. 15.1) are "input driven." Their color encoding represents the colors of the input images, and the colors produced by their outputs match (as much as possible) the input-image colors. Color copiers, for example, operate according to the Type *A* paradigm. This generally is the paradigm that first comes to people's minds when they think about color management. In fact, since the paradigm specifies that colors will match throughout an imaging system, the paradigm might seem to be the only one that is needed. But in many ways the basic concept of the paradigm is quite limited. That is why many commercial systems based on Type *B* and Type *C* paradigms also exist.

Systems based on a Type *B* color-management paradigm (Fig. 15.2) are "encoding driven." Their color encoding is based on a unifying color-encoding concept that tends to reduce or eliminate the colorimetric differences inherent

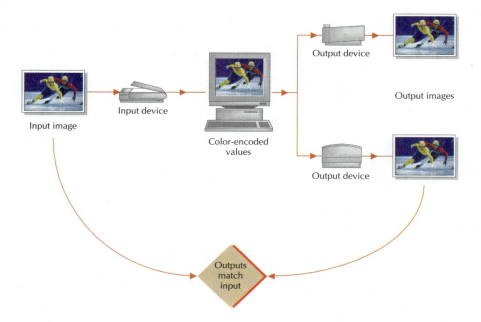

Figure 15.1
Color-imaging systems based on a Type *A* color-management paradigm are "input driven." Their color encoding represents the colors of the input images, and the colors produced by the outputs match the encoded input colors.

in the system inputs. For example, some electronic prepress systems encode color in terms of the colorimetric characteristics of a reference reflection-print medium. Colors scanned from actual reflection prints are encoded essentially in terms of their measured colorimetry. But colors scanned from photographic transparency films are *re-rendered,* i.e., their measured colorimetric values are *altered* such that they correspond more closely to those that typically would be measured from the reference reflection-print medium (Fig. 15.3). As in a Type *A* paradigm system, the colors produced by the outputs of a Type *B* paradigm system match the colors represented by the color encoding.

Systems based on a Type *C* color-management paradigm (Fig. 15.4) are "output driven." Like Type *B* systems, their color encoding is based on a unifying concept. However, their output colors do *not* necessarily match the colors represented by this encoding because certain *additional* re-rendering is performed, subsequent to encoding, as part of the output signal processing.

Figure 15.2
Color-imaging systems based on a Type *B* color-management paradigm are "encoding driven." Their color encoding is based on a unifying concept that reduces or eliminates the inherent colorimetric differences of the system inputs. Colors produced by the outputs match the encoded colors.

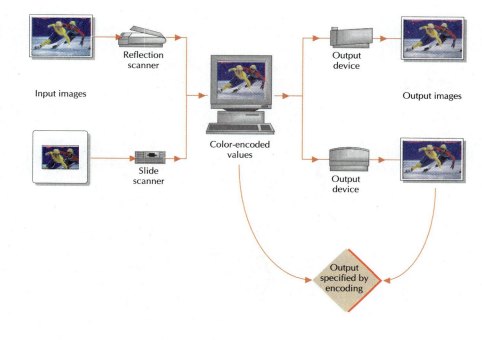

Figure 15.3
An example system, operating according to the Type *B* paradigm. In this electronic prepress system, colorimetric values measured from photographic transparency films are re-rendered to correspond more closely to those of reflection prints.

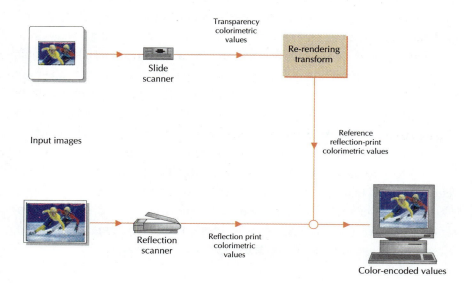

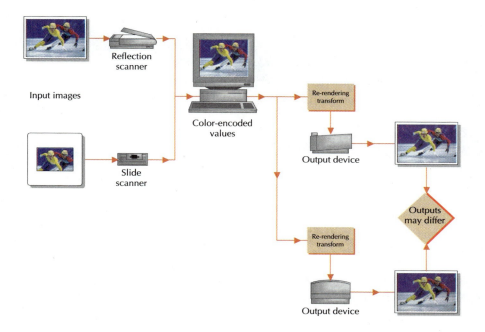

Input images

Reflection scanner

Slide scanner

Color-encoded values

Re-rendering transform

Output device

Re-rendering transform

Output device

Outputs may differ

Figure 15.4
Color-imaging systems based on a Type *C* color-management paradigm are "output driven." Images produced on different types of output devices and media will not necessarily match the encoding or each other because various output-specific re-renderings and color enhancements, which may take advantage of the particular capabilities of each output device and/or medium, are performed as part of the output signal processing.

The re-rendering performed in a Type *C* system might be done for *image simulation,* i.e., to make one output produce images that imitate the appearance of images normally produced by another type of output. Output re-rendering also might be done to *enhance* the output images by taking advantage of the particular capabilities of each output device or medium. For example, when an output medium having a large color gamut is used, the output signal processing might include some expansion of the gamut of the encoded colors in order to use the full capabilities of that particular medium.

This paradigm often is used in systems where the objective is for each output to produce the best images possible from the encoded data. As a consequence of the output-specific re-renderings and color enhancements that might be performed, images produced on different types of output devices and media will not necessarily match the encoding, nor will they necessarily match each other. This outcome is a principal feature of the paradigm; it is deliberate and should not be thought of as a shortcoming.

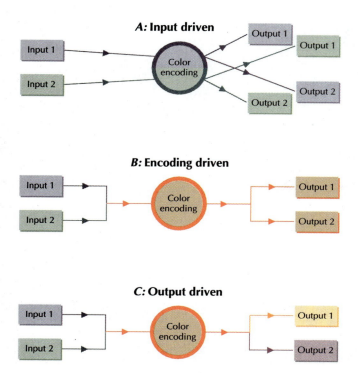

Figure 15.5 may help to clarify the distinctions among these paradigms. The figure illustrates the different behaviors of systems based on each of the three paradigms. Each system uses the same two types of input—a reflection print medium and a photographic slide film, for example—that differ in color appearance (symbolized by the different colors used in the figure). Each also uses the same two types of output, which also differ from one another.

In a Type *A* paradigm system, the different color appearances of the two inputs are retained and represented in the color encoding; and both outputs will match, as well as possible, whatever is encoded. So if a reflection print is scanned and encoded, the colors of *both* outputs will match those of that print. If a photographic slide is scanned and encoded, the colors of *both* outputs will match those of that slide. In either case, then, the outputs will match the inputs, and thus the outputs also will match each other (as much as possible).

In a Type *B* paradigm system, color appearance differences of the two inputs are reduced or eliminated by the color-encoding process. The colors of both outputs will match those represented by the color encoding. Therefore, the outputs also will match each other. However, they will match only one, or perhaps neither, of the inputs, depending on the nature of the unifying concept on which the color encoding is based. For example, if the unifying concept of the color-encoding process is based on the appearance of CMYK reflection prints, images produced on any output device/medium will have the characteristics of CMYK reflection-print images, regardless of the source of the input images and regardless of the characteristics of the actual output device/medium.

In a Type *C* paradigm system, color appearance differences of the two inputs again are reduced or eliminated by the color-encoding process. However, because output-specific re-renderings and/or color enhancements are performed subsequent to encoding, the outputs (deliberately) will not match the encoded colors, and therefore they may differ from one another.

Feature Comparisons

Table 15.1, shown below, lists the principal features associated with each of the color-management paradigms. These features are described, and the paradigms are compared, in the following pages.

Feature	Paradigm		
	A	*B*	*C*
Encoding represents input-image colors	√		
Encoding can represent original-scene colors		√	√
Can encode in terms of a reference device/medium		√	√
Output colors match encoded colors	√	√	
Seamless compositing of encoded images		√	√
Simpler color gamut mapping		√	√
Overall system optimization possible			√

Table 15.1

Comparison of the principal features of the Type *A*, Type *B,* and Type *C* color-management paradigms.

Encoding Represents Input-Image Colors

Only the Type *A* paradigm uses color encoding that represents the colors of the input image. There are many cases where that representation is the ultimate objective. For example, a photographer may want to create an archival digital record of his or her work. In such cases, the input photographic images would be considered to be *originals*, rather than reproductions, and the digital color encoding should faithfully represent the color appearance of those images.

Encoding Can Represent Original-Scene Colors

Systems based on either the Type *B* or Type *C* paradigm, but not on the Type *A* paradigm, can be used to encode in terms of original-scene colors rather than in terms of colors as reproduced by the input medium itself. One practical illustration of this important distinction between Type *A* and Types *B* and *C* paradigms occurs in telécine systems.

Telécine systems are used to scan motion picture films to produce video signals for taping and for television broadcast. Skilled operators, called colorists, make real-time signal-processing adjustments during this process in order to produce the best color. Colorists know, however, that the definition of "best" is subject to change, depending on who is making the decision.

For example, if the film being scanned is a theatrical motion picture, the director generally will insist that the television images look like those he or she created on the film. On the other hand, if the film is for a television commercial promoting a product with a trademark color, such as that of a famous soft drink, the director most likely will insist that the video images match the actual color of the product, regardless of whether or not that color was reproduced accurately on the film.

In the hands of a skilled colorist (motivated by a very vocal director) a telécine system effectively can be "switched" between a Type *A* paradigm and a Type *B* or Type *C* paradigm. There is a very important lesson here that will be revisited in Chapter 16.

Can Encode in Terms
of a Reference Device or Medium

Systems based on the Type B and Type C paradigms, but not the Type A paradigm, can be used to encode color in terms of the color characteristics of a reference input or output device or medium. For example, the color-encoding method used on *Photo CD* Imaging Workstations is based on a reference input (image-capturing) device. Some electronic prepress systems are based on the characteristics of a reference output, such as a particular CMYK reflection printer. Similarly, some desktop imaging applications are based on the characteristics of a reference display device—an RGB video monitor.

Output Colors Match
Encoded Colors

In the Type A and Type B paradigms, but not in the Type C paradigm, the system outputs match the color specified by the encoding (as closely as possible, given the limitations of the output color gamuts). This matching would be an important feature if, for example, a system were used to produce output color samples according to colorimetry specified in terms of the color encoding, or if it were used to produce output from a computer-generated image that was defined in terms of color-encoded values.

Seamless Compositing
of Encoded Images

The unique color characteristics of different media—the very characteristics that media manufacturers work to build into their products to differentiate them—are regarded mostly as a nuisance in applications where portions of images from different input media are merged to form composite images. When these color characteristics are retained, as they are in the Type A paradigm, the boundaries of the merged portions can be very apparent, depending on the disparity of the input media. In the Type B and Type C paradigms, color differences among the inputs are minimized, which results in more homogeneous-appearing composites.

Simpler Color Gamut Mapping

Gamut mapping is somewhat simpler in systems based on either the Type B or Type C paradigms than in systems based on the Type A paradigm. Mapping between two color gamuts—in this case, the gamut of the encoded colors and the gamut of the output colors—is more straightforward when both are well defined. Because the mapping is performed as part of the output signal processing of each individual output device/medium, the output color gamut can be explicitly defined. By comparison, in the Type A paradigm, the gamut of encoded colors will vary, depending on the color gamuts of the particular media that have been used for input. This makes it somewhat more difficult (but certainly not impossible) to develop a single, input-independent gamut-mapping transform for each output. Because the color-encoding methods used in Type B and Type C paradigm systems minimize color differences among the inputs, the potential color gamut of the encoded values is more consistent and therefore more easily defined.

Overall System Optimization

Only the Type C paradigm allows optimization of the color reproduction of an entire imaging system, from original scene to final output image. In a Type A paradigm system, the output image can be no better than the input image (by definition, it cannot be better if it matches). An imaging system based on the Type B paradigm can do better, in that a color-encoding method that extracts original-scene colorimetry from reproduced colors can be incorporated. But since, in the Type B paradigm, a further objective is for the outputs to match each other, the optimum use might not be made of capabilities unique to each particular output. In a Type C paradigm system, the objective instead could be for each output to produce the best possible rendition of an encoded image. If the output media are different—say a video display, a reflection print, and a photographic slide—the best renditions certainly will differ somewhat from medium to medium.

Discussion

These three paradigms appear to be sufficient for describing the basic functionality of all existing types of color-managed imaging systems. That is quite encouraging—or at least certainly more encouraging than if *dozens* of different paradigms were required. Yet to truly unite the color-imaging industry, and to achieve the goal of unrestricted color interchange among systems, it would seem necessary for *all* systems to operate from a *single* paradigm. But which of the three should it be? On what basis could a selection be made?

It cannot be made based on functionality. The color encoding and output results of systems based on each paradigm are different. Each paradigm has features that are essential to large numbers of users, and none of the three has all the features of the others. Nor can a selection be made based on technical merits. Successful color-imaging systems have been built based on each of the paradigms. Each is technically sound and practical to implement.

Numerous attempts have been made to negotiate a selection by industry-wide agreement. (Although we never heard the concept of an "underlying paradigm" expressed during these negotiations, in retrospect it is now apparent that various paradigms indeed were being proposed and discussed.) These attempts have failed because, we believe, all of the proposed paradigms have been too limited. The participants in such negotiations represent profit-making corporations. Understandably, they have been reluctant to give up system features that they know are important to their customers. As a result, the industry has continued to work with numerous alternative—and essentially incompatible—types of systems.

We, and a number of our colleagues, felt strongly that the color-imaging industry needed a *complete* solution to color management—one that would eliminate such incompatibilities. This required the development of an overall system architecture based on a single, comprehensive, unified color-management paradigm. That paradigm is the topic of Chapter 16.

Summary of Key Issues

- All successful color-imaging systems employ some form of color management for controlling and adjusting color information throughout the system.

- Any color-management approach is based, implicitly or explicitly, on an underlying paradigm that defines how color-imaging systems using that color management will behave.

- All existing color-imaging systems can be described in terms of three fundamental types of color-management paradigms.

- In the Type A paradigm, color encoding is based on the colors of the input image, and output colors match the input colors.

- In the Type B paradigm, color encoding is based on a unifying concept, such as a reference input or output. Output colors match the colors represented by that encoding.

- In the Type C paradigm, color encoding again is based on a unifying concept. However, the output colors generally differ from those represented by the encoding due to deliberate color enhancements and re-renderings performed subsequent to encoding.

- Each paradigm has features that are essential for various applications, and none has all the features of the other two.

- A complete solution to color management and color interchange requires a unified color-management paradigm.

16

A Unified Paradigm: Basic Properties

If the hope of unification should prove well founded,
how great and mighty and sublime....

Michael Faraday

At the time that we were wrestling with the problems resulting from the use of three different color-management paradigms within the color-imaging industry, we both happened to be reading a book entitled *Hyperspace*. In that book, theoretical physicist Michio Kaku describes a problem that scientists have puzzled over for more than 50 years: Why do the basic forces of the universe—gravity, electromagnetism, and the strong and weak nuclear forces—require markedly different mathematical descriptions?

Kaku explains that these apparent differences appear only because the basic paradigms used in their description are too limited. He shows that if all the basic forces are seen according to a larger *unified* paradigm—as vibrations in higher-dimensional spaces—their field equations suddenly unite in what he describes as an "elegant and astonishingly simple form."

Now, developing a color-management system is hardly the equivalent of trying to explain the workings of the entire universe (although there are times when we are not sure which would be easier). Nevertheless, there are parallels, and there are lessons that can be learned from the search for a unified field theory.

Perhaps the most important lesson is that, historically, when true understanding is reached, the results exhibit unity, simplicity, beauty, and elegance. For example, the eight Maxwell equations for electricity and magnetism are notoriously ugly, because time and space are treated separately. But when rewritten in relativistic form, where time is treated as a fourth dimension, the eight separate equations collapse to a single equation that is simple and elegant in form. Similarly, centuries ago, when the paradigm for the solar system placed the earth at the center, describing the motions of the planets required complex functions. When the system became better understood and could be envisioned in a larger paradigm, the motions were shown to be simple ellipses.

In a sense, the technology of color management seemed to be at the "pre-understanding" stage. The need to use three different paradigms to explain the color-imaging "universe" certainly indicated a lack of "unity and simplicity," and the methods required to transfer images and control color across systems were anything but "beautiful and elegant." But perhaps, we thought, if the *ABC* paradigms could be seen according to some larger paradigm, they also would be found to fit together in an "elegant and astonishingly simple form." Moreover, if a single paradigm uniting the *ABC* paradigms could be found, the first requirement for building a unified color-management environment for the industry would be met.

An Ideal Application

To determine the basic requirements of this unified paradigm, we and our colleagues began by imagining an "ideal application." We tried to envision a color-management application, such as a desktop publishing program, that was capable of making an imaging system perform in *all* the ways that users of any system, based on any of the three *ABC* paradigms, might want. We were not necessarily proposing that such an application be developed. The concept of an ideal application was used only to help focus on what color-managed systems should *do,* rather than on the technical details of how they might be designed and implemented. That would come later.

So what *should* color-managed systems do? That turned out to be a surprisingly difficult question to answer. For example, consider the system shown in Fig. 16.1. The figure shows an original object (a London bus) being photographed to produce a 35-mm slide. The slide is scanned to produce a digital image file on the computer workstation. That image file then is used to produce a video image on the workstation monitor, a reflection print from a thermal printer, and another 35-mm slide from a photographic slide-film writer.

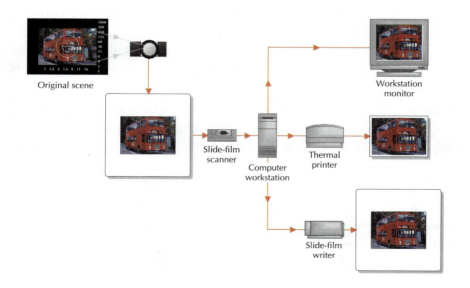

Original scene

Slide-film scanner

Computer workstation

Thermal printer

Workstation monitor

Slide-film writer

Figure 16.1
What should this color-managed system do?

If this system were color managed, what should its images look like? When a number of people were asked that question, many different answers were obtained. But perhaps that should have been expected. There are many possible answers because there are many reasons why color images are produced.

Let us look at how a single factor can generate a whole series of consequences. Assume that the slide film reproduces reds as somewhat orange, as some films tend to do. Now, should the system produce an output slide with an orange-red bus, or should it alter the input color values such that the output red matches the original red of the bus? If the latter is done, what should the video image look like? The input slide? The original bus? And what about the thermal print? Should it match the output slide? The input slide? The video?

As was discussed before, there are no right or wrong answers to these kinds of questions. The "right" answers will vary depending on the purpose for which a system is used. In fact, in most current systems, such questions are never even asked. The answers instead are "hard coded" by the system designers on the basis of certain assumptions they have made about the results system users will want.

Although a fixed, predetermined behavior may be fine for an individual system, an ideal application must provide much greater flexibility. It must allow the *user* to alter the *entire system behavior,* in much the same way that was described earlier in the example of the telécine system, in order to produce different output results.

As we considered the telécine system and a wide variety of other imaging systems, it became apparent that in order to provide functionality that is sufficiently flexible to cover *all* potential uses, an ideal application would have to ask the user three basic questions concerning input, output, and interchange.

The first question asks the user to define what interpretation will be given to an image that is about to be scanned or otherwise input to the system. For example, the image could be interpreted as an original, in which case the user would want to encode the image in terms of its own appearance under some specified set of viewing conditions. The image instead could be interpreted as a record of an original scene, in which case the user would want to encode the image in terms of the appearance of that scene. Or the image might be considered simply as a source of information from which various renderings can be made. For example, the image could be encoded as if it had been rendered on another medium and viewed under some defined set of conditions, or it might be re-rendered according to some set of criteria. These different input interpretations can be specified by responding to the following query:

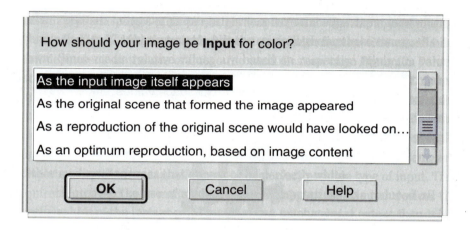

The next question asks the user to define an interpretation for an image that is to be output by the system. Although there are many possible variations, the responses would fall into the principal categories shown below.

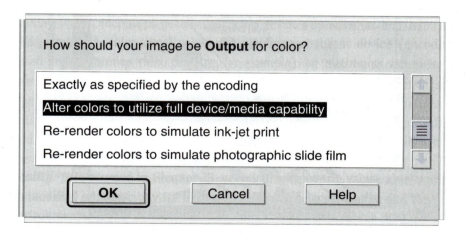

The final question asks the user to define how an encoded image will be transferred to another imaging system.

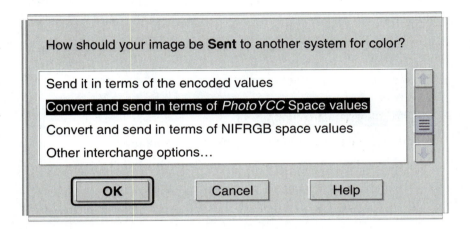

A color-imaging system controlled using an application that included these questions could be altered to duplicate the functionality of *any* of the *ABC* color-management paradigms.

For example, if one were to scan a photographic slide and answer *"As the input image itself appears (under a specified set of viewing conditions)"* for input and *"Exactly as specified by the input option"* for output to a reflection thermal printer, the system would produce a reflection print that matches, as much as possible, the appearance of the input slide. This is a Type *A* paradigm result, as shown in Fig. 16.2.

If one again were to scan a photographic slide, but instead answer *"As a reproduction of the original scene would have looked on (a particular reflection-print system)"* for input, and again answer *"Exactly as specified by the input option"* for output to a reflection thermal printer, the system would produce a thermal print that matches the appearance of a print that would have been produced by the specified reflection-print system. Because the encoding and output print represent a *re-rendering* of the input slide, rather than the appearance of the slide itself, this is a Type *B* paradigm result (Fig. 16.3).

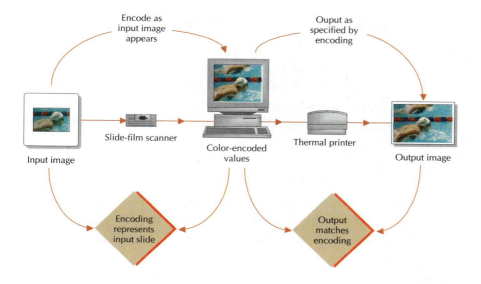

Figure 16.2

In this example, the ideal application produces a Type *A* paradigm result. The appearance of the output reflection print matches that of the input slide.

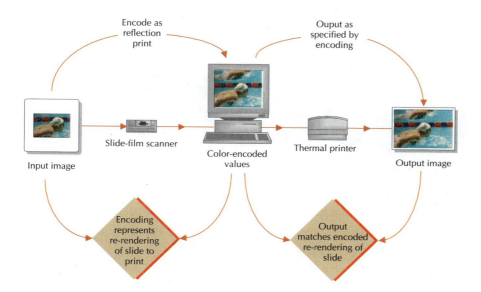

Figure 16.3

In this example, the ideal application produces a Type *B* paradigm result. The appearance of the output thermal print matches that of a print that would have been produced by the reflection-print system specified in the encoding option.

If one were to scan a reflection print and answer *"As the input image itself appears (under some specified set of viewing conditions)"* for input, and *"Alter the color specified by the input option; use the full capabilities of the output"* for output to a photographic slide-film writer, the system would produce a Type *C* paradigm result, as shown in Fig. 16.4. Because the color gamut of the output slide film is somewhat greater than that of the input reflection print medium, the gamut of the encoded colors would be expanded such that the gamut capabilities of the slide film are best utilized.

These examples demonstrate that a single system, controlled from a sufficiently flexible application, can be made to behave according to any of the *ABC* paradigms. The system can be directed such that the outputs match the input (the Type *A* paradigm). It can be directed such that the encoding is based on the properties of reference input or output, and the outputs match that encoding (the Type *B* paradigm). It also can be directed such that final outcome is determined by the specific characteristics of each output device/medium (the Type *C* paradigm).

Figure 16.4

In this example, the ideal application produces a Type *C* paradigm result. The colors represented by the encoding are enhanced for output to the slide film.

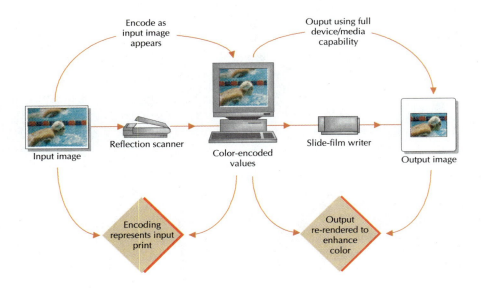

From an Ideal Application to a Unified Paradigm

The fact that the different behaviors of the *ABC* paradigms can be emulated using a single application supports the premise that all existing color-imaging systems are subsets of a larger, unified paradigm. Moreover, because that paradigm must be capable of *supporting* the ideal application, the features of that application essentially define the properties of the paradigm itself. Specifically, the unified paradigm must do the following:

- Support all types of input and output devices and media.
- Provide for multiple input interpretations, which must *not* be predetermined or limited by the paradigm itself.
- Provide for multiple output interpretations, which also must *not* be predetermined or limited by the paradigm.
- Allow input and output interpretation decisions to be made *independently* of one another; all possible input and output interpretation combinations must be allowed.

In addition, the paradigm must support the interchange of images among systems within a unified color-management environment. As was discussed earlier, different color data metrics may be most appropriate for the internal encoding of different systems. For that reason, the unified paradigm also must do the following:

- Support the use of various internal and interchange color-encoding data metrics.
- Allow the selection of interchange color-encoding data metrics to be made independently of input and output interpretation selections.

These basic properties of the paradigm are shown in diagrammatic form in Fig. 16.5.

Figure 16.5

A diagram of the unified paradigm.

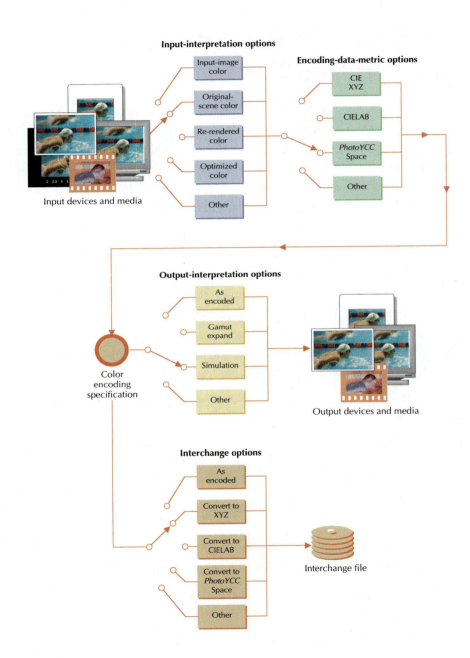

Discussion

The basic requirements of a unified paradigm can be listed and diagrammed readily enough, as has just been done. But can a practical color-management environment actually be *built* from a paradigm incorporating those requirements? After all, the unified paradigm supports all inputs and outputs, it allows the freedom to choose from an unlimited selection of input and output interpretations, it places no restrictions on the combinations of input and output interpretations that can be selected, and it supports all color-interchange data metrics. Is that really a meaningful color-management paradigm, or is it simply a prescription for anarchy?

It might, in fact, seem inevitable that a color-management environment based on such an unrestricted paradigm soon would break down into complete chaos. It also might seem that to prevent that from happening, some of the paradigm's flexibility should be restricted. However, restrictions would mean that certain types of system behaviors would be disallowed; *yet the need for those behaviors would not disappear.* A color-management environment based on a restricted paradigm only would serve to force certain users to bypass that environment in order to achieve the results they require. The inevitable outcome would be a continuation of the present types of incompatibilities that exist among systems.

In our opinion, no such restrictions are necessary. We believe that the full flexibility of the unified paradigm can be supported *if an appropriate color-encoding method is used*. That is the topic of the next chapter.

Summary of Key Issues

- The different behaviors of the *A, B,* and *C* color-management paradigms can be emulated by a single, unified paradigm.

- The unified color-management paradigm supports all types of input and output devices and media, it allows multiple input and output interpretations, and it supports multiple interchange data metrics.

- In the unified color-management paradigm, input and output interpretation decisions are independent of one another; all possible input/output interpretation combinations are allowed.

- In the unified color-management paradigm, the selection of encoding and interchange data metrics is independent of input and output interpretation decisions.

- The successful implementation of the unified color-management paradigm requires an appropriate method for representing color.

17

A Unified Paradigm: Color Encoding

The paradigm introduced in the previous chapter offers the promise of a unified color-management environment. However, the realization of that promise requires the use of a color-encoding method that is consistent with, and fully capable of supporting, the unified paradigm. The required properties of the color encoding best can be determined by relating the unified paradigm to practical systems and situations. In this chapter and Chapter 18, the paradigm will be applied to individual color-imaging systems, and an appropriate method for representing color on those systems will be developed. In Chapter 19, the principles of the paradigm will be used to develop a method for general color interchange within a comprehensive color-management environment.

Color-Encoding Requirements

Figure 17.1 illustrates the application of the unified paradigm to a color-imaging system having a single input and a single output. This system, operating on its own, is capable of performing all the functions of the "ideal application" that was used earlier to help define the properties of the paradigm. Although the basic signal-processing arrangement of this system is the same as that used in previous examples, the multiple input/output interpretation options of the paradigm have been added. Each option is implemented in the form of an individual signal-processing transform. In Fig. 17.2, the paradigm has been applied similarly to a more complex multiple input/output system.

For systems such as these to work successfully, the color-encoding method they use must, of course, achieve compatibility among all system inputs. However, the *definition* of what constitutes an "input" must be expanded.

Figure 17.1

Application of the unified paradigm to a single-input imaging system. The incorporation of multiple input/output interpretation options makes this system independently capable of performing all the functions defined by the paradigm.

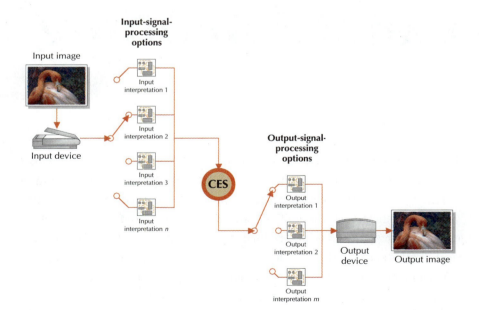

In the unified paradigm, an input no longer is just a particular medium; it is a particular *interpretation* of the color from a particular medium. *Each interpretation from each medium constitutes a unique input source.* What this means is that the color-encoding method of the unified paradigm must not only achieve input compatibility, it must do so *without imposing its own particular interpretation* on encoded colors. Its use must not restrict a system such that it behaves according to just one or two of the *ABC* paradigms.

None of the color-encoding methods described so far meets these requirements. Some fail because they cannot achieve compatibility among all input media, while others fail because they do not allow multiple interpretations of color. For example, in Part III it was shown that densitometric and standard colorimetric encoding methods do not achieve compatibility among disparate types of input media. Use of these methods therefore restricts the types of input media and devices that can be supported.

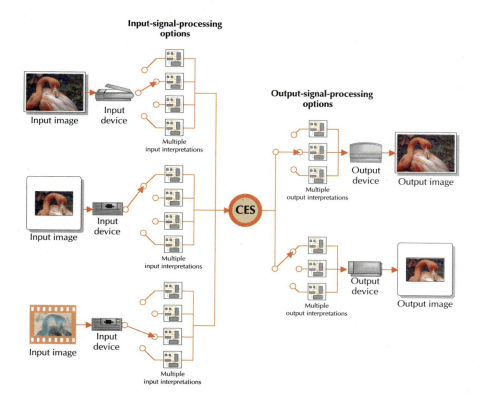

Figure 17.2

Application of the unified paradigm to a much more complex imaging system.

On the other hand, the original-scene encoding method used on most *Photo CD* Imaging Workstations, the rendered-print encoding method used on many graphic arts prepress systems, and other Type *B* or Type *C* paradigm encoding methods can achieve input compatibility among disparate forms of input media. However, they do so by imposing particular interpretations of input color. Those interpretations thus restrict the behaviors of systems on which the encoding methods are used.

How can this apparent dilemma be resolved? Throughout this book, each new color-encoding problem has been solved successfully by basing the solution on the principle of input compatibility. In each new situation, a specific aspect of color that all system inputs had in common was identified, and an appropriate color-encoding method was selected or developed based on that color aspect.

From a retrospective examination of those problems, it can be seen that their solutions have followed a definite pattern: As the types of inputs became more and more disparate, the common color aspect itself had to be more and more inclusive. In a sense, the logical conclusion of that process now has been reached. Since the unified paradigm must support multiple input types *and* multiple input color interpretations, *the only thing the inputs have in common is color itself.*

This means that in order to realize the promise of the unified paradigm, it will be necessary to answer a question that was raised at the start of this book: "How can *color* be represented in numerical form?"

Representing Color

Of the encoding methods that have been discussed so far, those based on CIE colorimetry come the closest to representing color (i.e., color *appearance*). But as has been shown, standard CIE colorimetry alone does not represent color appearance unambiguously. The same color stimulus defined by a set of CIE *XYZ* tristimulus or CIELAB *L*, a*, b** values can have any number of entirely different appearances, depending on the conditions under which the stimulus is viewed. That is a serious problem, because there are three different types of viewing environments involved in the color-imaging process (Fig. 17.3), and there are limitless possible sets of viewing conditions for each of those types.

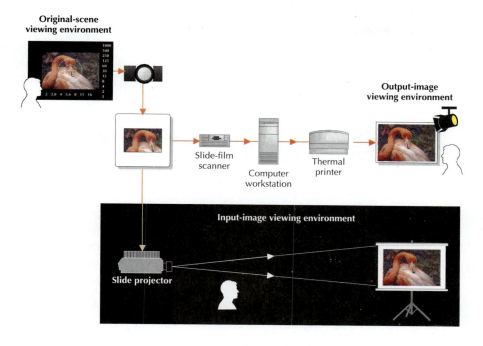

Figure 17.3

There are three basic types of viewing environments associated with the color-imaging process: original-scene, input-image, and output-image environments. The conditions of each can differ greatly.

On the input side of an imaging system, there are *original-scene environments,* i.e., the environments in which live original scenes are viewed and captured. Also, on the input side, there are *input-image environments,* where hardcopy and softcopy images that are to be input to a color-imaging system are viewed. Finally, there are *output-image environments,* where hardcopy and softcopy images produced by a color-imaging system eventually are viewed.

One way to deal with the complications caused by the different viewing conditions of these environments would be to impose a restriction that an *identical* set of conditions must be used for original-scene viewing and image capture, for input-image viewing, and for output-image viewing. In that case, a colorimetric specification alone would be sufficient to represent color. The color-encoding methods of some existing systems are, in fact, based on that type of restriction. For example, the manufacturer of a reflection copy system may specify that an output image produced by the system will be an accurate copy of an input image, but only if both images are viewed in a specified graphic-arts viewing booth.

Placing any such restrictions would be inappropriate here. A color-encoding method that is capable of providing all the features of the unified paradigm instead must do the following:

- Allow live scenes to be viewed and captured under any original-scene conditions.
- Allow input images to be viewed under any desired conditions and to be encoded in terms of their appearance under those particular input-image viewing conditions.
- Allow output images to be tailored specifically for display in any desired set of output-image viewing conditions.

Ironically, the real solution to this problem is not to *restrict* the conditions of the original-scene, input-image, or output-image viewing environments. Quite the contrary, the solution is to *add* yet another viewing environment with its own set of conditions.

Encoding Reference Viewing Conditions

The viewing conditions for this additional environment will be referred to as *encoding reference viewing conditions*. The following hypothetical examples (Figs. 17.4a and 17.4b) illustrate how the use of these reference conditions can help to represent color unambiguously.

Suppose one person (the sender) wanted to communicate a color to another person (the receiver), and suppose that they each had identical devices that could generate any color stimulus that was specified in terms of standard CIE colorimetric values. If the sender communicated a set of such values for a color, they could be input to the receiver's device. That device then would generate the color *stimulus* the sender intended. But it would not be certain whether the right *color* had been communicated, because the appearance of the stimulus would change depending on the conditions in which it was viewed.

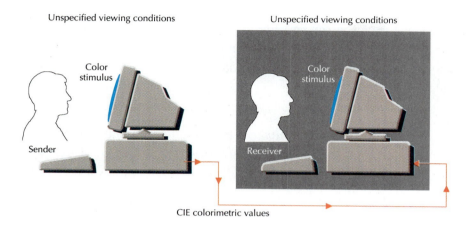

Figure 17.4a
Color representation and communication based on CIE colorimetric values alone is ambiguous.

That problem can be solved if the sender and receiver agree on a set of reference viewing conditions (Fig. 17.4b). The sender always would view the color-stimulus device under those conditions and would adjust the colorimetric values until the device generated a stimulus having the color that he or she wants to communicate. Those values would be sent to the stimulus generator of the receiver, and the receiver would view the resulting stimulus under an identical set of viewing conditions. The receiver then would see the *color* the sender intended to communicate (assuming, of course, that the sender and receiver have identical color vision).

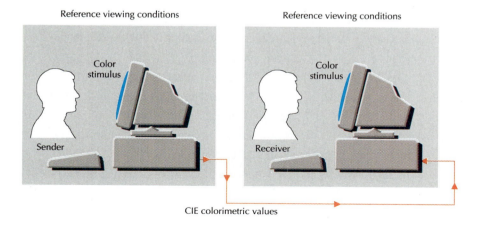

Figure 17.4b
Color representation and communication based on CIE colorimetric values and a set of reference viewing conditions is unambiguous.

A color-encoding method capable of supporting all the objectives for the unified paradigm can be based on this strategy for color communication. Encoded colors can be expressed in terms of colorimetric values, but the ambiguity that is inherent in a colorimetric specification alone is eliminated by the additional specification of a set of encoding reference viewing conditions. The concept of this encoding method can be stated as follows:

In the unified color-management paradigm, encoded values specify the colorimetry for a stimulus that, when viewed according to a defined set of reference conditions, would produce an intended color appearance.

This encoding method essentially provides a "recipe" for color representation. The combination of a colorimetric specification and a defined set of viewing conditions provides a complete formula for producing and displaying a color stimulus having the intended color appearance.

Colors encoded according to this method are *unambiguous,* because there is one and only one colorimetric specification that can produce a particular color appearance (to a standard observer) under the specified viewing conditions. At the same time, the method does not impose a particular interpretation on encoded colors. The "intended color appearance" can refer to an original-scene color, a color of a viewed input image, a user-created or user-edited color on a computer monitor, a color to be output for viewing, or any other type of color that a user wishes to represent.

It is important to emphasize that the use of a set of encoding reference conditions in no way restricts the behavior or flexibility of an individual system operating according to the unified paradigm. That is because the reference conditions do *not* specify the conditions that must be used for viewing and capturing original scenes, nor do they specify the input-image or output-image viewing conditions. Any light source spectral power distribution, any level of illumination, any amount of viewing flare, and any surround conditions can be used for the capture and display of actual system images.

In fact, no one need ever construct or use the reference conditions for actual viewing. The encoding reference viewing conditions apply *only to the color-encoding process itself.*

Color-Encoding Process

Figure 17.5 illustrates the overall concept of the color-encoding process. The color-encoding method is such that colors are represented in a color encoding specification (CES) in terms of their CIE colorimetric values, as measured in the absence of flare light. The CES includes a description of the encoding reference viewing conditions. Encoded values are expressed numerically in terms of the particular color-encoding data metric defined for the CES. As discussed earlier, the selection of a data metric for a given system is an engineering decision, so any of a number of different data metrics can be used.

As the figure shows, input signal-processing transforms are used to convert the colorimetry of color stimuli in actual original-scene and input-image viewing conditions to corresponding colorimetry for equivalent stimuli viewed in the encoding reference conditions. Similarly, output signal-processing transforms are used to convert encoded colorimetric values to corresponding values for equivalent stimuli to be viewed in the actual output-image viewing conditions. In special cases where the actual input or output viewing conditions are *identical* to the encoding reference viewing conditions, such conversions are not required. More typically, colorimetric transformations are needed in order to account for *differences* in the actual and encoding reference conditions.

The colorimetric transformations used in this appearance-based color encoding must account for any physical alterations the various viewing conditions might produce on an image. The transformations also must account for any alterations that the conditions might induce in an observer's perception of color. While accounting for physical factors (primarily differences in the amount and/or chromaticity of flare light) is quite straightforward, accounting for effects resulting from perceptual phenomena is somewhat more complex.

Over the years, there has been a great deal of theoretical and experimental work done to better understand such effects. One result of these efforts has been the development of several sophisticated color-appearance models. These models are extremely useful in many color-related applications, and their development has provided a number of important insights into the nature of human color vision.

Figure 17.5

The color-encoding strategy of the unified paradigm is designed to deal with the many different viewing conditions that can exist for original scenes, input images, and output images.

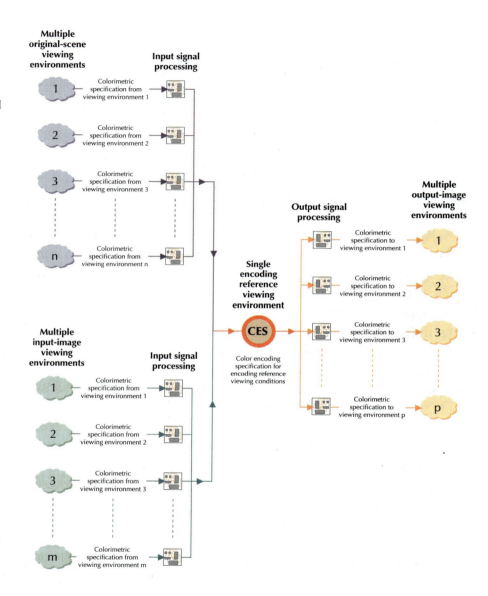

A complete discussion and comparison of these complex models is well beyond the scope of this book. Moreover, the paradigm and encoding method described here are not based on any particular color-appearance model; they are based on the *concept* of encoding in terms of color appearance. It is to be expected that the level of understanding of color appearance will continue to rise and that, as a consequence, color-appearance models will continue to become more sophisticated and more accurate. As that happens, those improvements should be incorporated in future implementations of systems based on the unified paradigm.

Our main goal here is to describe the *objectives* that must be achieved when applying color-appearance models to color encoding; it is not to recommend the use of any particular models or any specific appearance-modeling procedures. However, based on our experience in designing imaging media and systems, and from experience gained in developing a prototype implementation of the unified paradigm, we can provide some general guidelines for a straightforward, practical implementation of a color-appearance-based color-encoding method. These guidelines are as follows:

For simplicity, both in concept and in implementation, only the most important factors affecting the relationship between colorimetry and color appearance need be considered.

Although numerous perceptual phenomena have been identified, many of the effects they produce in typical image-viewing situations are small enough to safely ignore. Other effects, such as those induced by adjacent colors, need not be accounted for in most imaging applications. For example, if the presence of one color in an input image affects an observer's perception of an adjacent color, the same phenomenon should occur when an observer views an output reproduction of that image. So there is no real need to account for the perceptual effect in the color encoding. Strictly speaking, then, the encoding describes colors in terms of visually equivalent stimuli viewed in the context of the images in which they reside.

In the next subsection, *Colorimetric Transformations,* the perceptual factors that we believe to be most important will be specified, and methods of accounting for the effects of each factor will be described.

The magnitudes of all color-appearance factors should be consistent with the viewing of images.

Experimental work performed to study visual phenomena sometimes has involved the viewing of color patches and other types of simple color stimuli. Our experience is that quite different results are obtained when more complex stimuli, such as typical pictorial and graphics images, are viewed. In almost all cases, the magnitudes of the effects are reduced for complex stimuli. These reduced magnitudes should be used in the colorimetric transformations.

The magnitudes of all color-appearance factors should be consistent with the color-reproduction properties of actual imaging products.

In particular, it was shown earlier that the chromas of reproduced colors must be higher than those of outdoor scene colors in order to compensate for the relatively low absolute luminances of reproduced images. The chroma compensation required to actually *duplicate,* indoors, the colorfulness of outdoor scene colors would be quite large. However, in artwork and in commercial imaging products, the extent of such compensation is far smaller. Using a similarly reduced level of compensation for encoding color signals produced directly from live scenes—for signals from digital still cameras, for example— results in a consistency between the encoding of such signals and other color signals obtained from direct measurements of reproduced images. This strategy greatly enhances input compatibility, and it produces encoded colorimetric values that realistically can be achieved by actual output devices and media.

Whenever possible, the implementation of the transformations should be mathematically simple, and the transformations themselves must always be reversible.

Mathematical simplicity is a practical issue, especially on smaller systems having limited computational resources. Mathematical reversibility is particularly important in applications where the objective is to make duplicates of input images. In such cases, the input and output signal-processing transformations essentially must be mirror images of one another.

Colorimetric Transformations

In an implementation of an appearance-based color-encoding strategy consistent with these guidelines, colorimetric transformations must be incorporated to account for any differences of the original-scene, input-image, and output-image viewing conditions from the encoding reference viewing conditions. A typical arrangement of these transformations was shown previously (Fig. 17.5).

It is important to emphasize that the colorimetric transformations do *not* determine how the *appearance* of a color stimulus, specified in terms of its colorimetry, would *change* if it were moved from one set of viewing conditions to another. The transformations do just the opposite; they determine how the colorimetry of the stimulus *itself* must be modified such that its color appearance is *maintained* in each different set of viewing conditions.

Although other factors might also be considered, our experience is that excellent appearance-based color encoding can be achieved if the colorimetric transformations account for each of the following factors:

1. Viewing flare contribution to observed stimuli
2. Stimuli absolute luminances
3. Observer chromatic adaptation
4. Observer lateral-brightness adaptation
5. Observer general-brightness adaptation

In order to appropriately account for these factors, each set of original-scene, input-image, and output-image viewing conditions must be fully characterized in terms of viewing flare, observer state of chromatic adaptation, image absolute luminances, and image surround type. Appropriate colorimetric transformations then must be developed based on the relationships of those conditions to the encoding reference conditions. The components of the viewing-condition characterizations, and some example methods that can be used for determining the colorimetric transformations, will now be described.

1. Viewing Flare Transformations

The presence of viewing flare in an environment will physically alter the color stimuli—illuminated objects of live scenes, illuminated hardcopy images, or self-luminous softcopy images—viewed in that environment. In order to properly account for such alterations, the amount and chromaticity of the flare light in each set of viewing conditions must be defined. The amount of flare usually is specified relative to the amount of light from a stimulus that would be perceived as white in the viewing conditions.

If the flare differs for two sets of viewing conditions, an appropriate colorimetric transformation must be used to compensate for the effects of that difference. For example, if it is desired to encode the appearance of an input image as viewed in conditions in which the amount of viewing flare is greater than that specified for the encoding reference conditions, the colorimetric effects of that additional flare light must be included in the input colorimetric transformation. The effects of increased flare light on a system grayscale and on a small set of test colors are shown in Figs. 17.6a and 17.6b, respectively.

Figure 17.6a

Encoding the appearance of an input image as viewed in conditions having more viewing flare than that specified for the encoding reference conditions requires that the effects of the greater flare light be included as part of the input colorimetric transformation.

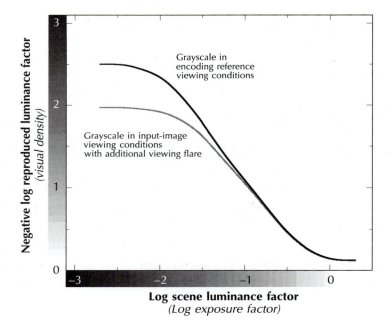

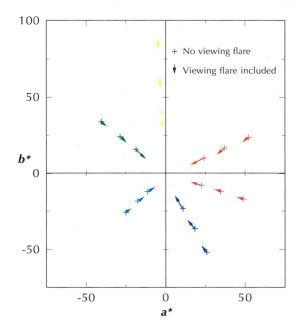

Figure 17.6b
The colorimetric effects of viewing flare. The effects can be computed by applying the principles of additive color mixing, as described in Eqs. {17.1}.

The colorimetric results of viewing flare shown in the figures can be computed using the principles of additive color mixing. The first step in this process is to determine the tristimulus values (X_{fl}, Y_{fl}, Z_{fl}) for the flare light, based on the specification of that light in terms of its chromaticity coordinates (x_{fl}, y_{fl}, z_{fl}) and its percentage (PF) relative to the white luminance (Y_{wt}) of the image. The tristimulus values of the flare light can be computed as follows:

$$Y_{fl} = \left(\frac{PF}{100}\right) Y_{wt}$$

$$X_{fl} = \left(\frac{x_{fl}}{y_{fl}}\right) Y_{fl} \qquad\qquad \{17.1a\}$$

$$Z_{fl} = \left(\frac{z_{fl}}{y_{fl}}\right) Y_{fl}$$

For each color stimulus, a modified stimulus is computed by adding the tristimulus values for the flare light to the tristimulus values for the color stimulus, as shown below:

$$X_f = X + X_{fl}$$

$$Y_f = Y + Y_{fl} \qquad \{17.1b\}$$

$$Z_f = Z + Z_{fl}$$

where X, Y, and Z are the tristimulus values for a stimulus with no flare light, and X_f, Y_f, and Z_f are the tristimulus values for a stimulus with flare light added. These and other viewing-flare calculations are described in greater detail in Appendix E.

2. Luminance-Level Transformations

As was discussed previously, the absolute luminances of stimuli will affect an observer's perception of luminance contrast and colorfulness. In order to account for such effects, the luminance levels of the stimuli being viewed must be defined. This can be done by specifying, for each set of viewing conditions, the luminance of a stimulus that would be perceived as white.

While the luminance levels of typical viewed input and output images certainly may differ, the effects of those differences often are small enough to ignore. However, the luminance levels of outdoor scenes generally are very different from those of most reproductions viewed indoors. The effects of those large differences *must* be accounted for in the colorimetric transformations.

One procedure for determining a luminance-level transformation is described in detail in Appendix G. The procedure is based on the concept of a reference rendering medium. The transformation relates original-scene colorimetric values and reproduced colorimetric values in a way that is realistic and consistent with the color-reproduction properties of practical imaging media. Figure 17.7a shows the effect of the colorimetric transformation on a system grayscale characteristic, and Fig. 17.7b shows the effect on a set of test colors.

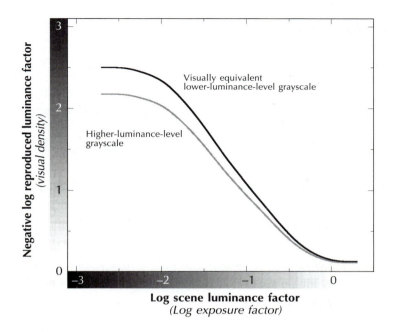

Figure 17.7a
The effect of a luminance-level transformation on a system grayscale characteristic. The transformation accounts for the fact that, for visual equivalence, higher luminance contrast is required at lower luminance levels.

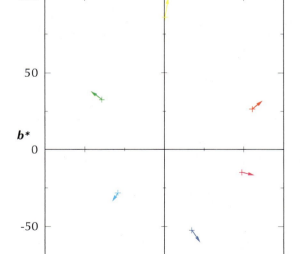

Figure 17.7b
The vector arrows illustrate the effects of a luminance-level transformation on a set of test colors. The transformation accounts for the fact that, for visual equivalence, higher chromas (the arrow heads) are required at lower levels of luminance.

3. Chromatic Adaptation Transformations

The perception of color stimuli is strongly affected by the observer's state of chromatic adaptation. That adaptive state therefore must be specified for each set of viewing conditions. The specification can be expressed in terms of an *adaptive white*.

An adaptive white defines the chromaticity of a color stimulus that an observer who is adapted to the viewing conditions would judge to be perfectly achromatic and to have a luminance factor of unity. It is very important to emphasize that it is only necessary to define an adaptive white in terms of its chromaticities; it is not necessary (nor is it useful) to define an adaptive white stimulus in terms of its spectral power distribution.

If the chromaticities of the adaptive whites are different in two sets of viewing conditions, the perceptual effects due to that difference must be accounted for by the use of an appropriate chromatic adaptation transformation. The transformation determines corresponding tristimulus values of a color stimulus that would produce, for a standard observer chromatically adapted to one set of viewing conditions, a visual match to another color stimulus viewed by a standard observer who is chromatically adapted to a different set of viewing conditions.

For example, Fig. 17.8 compares the colorimetric values for a set of stimuli that would produce, for an observer chromatically adapted to the chromaticity of D_{50}, a visual match to another set of stimuli viewed by an observer who is chromatically adapted to the chromaticity of D_{65}. The chromaticities for the visually equivalent stimuli of the figure were determined using the simple von Kries transformation below:

$$
\begin{Vmatrix} X_{D50} \\ Y_{D50} \\ Z_{D50} \end{Vmatrix} = \begin{Vmatrix} 1.0161 & 0.0553 & -0.0522 \\ 0.0060 & 0.9956 & -0.0012 \\ 0.0000 & 0.0000 & 0.7576 \end{Vmatrix} \begin{Vmatrix} X_{D65} \\ Y_{D65} \\ Z_{D65} \end{Vmatrix} \quad \{17.2\}
$$

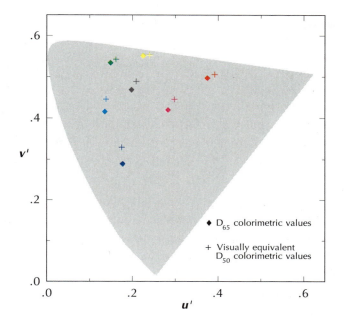

Figure 17.8
Comparison of the colorimetric values for a set of stimuli that would produce, for an observer chromatically adapted to the chromaticity of D_{50}, a visual match to the corresponding set of stimuli viewed by an observer who is chromatically adapted to the chromaticity of D_{65}.

More advanced methods, which account for incomplete adaptation and/or for nonlinearities in the adaptation process, also can be used. However, the methodology of all such methods basically is similar:

1. CIE *XYZ* tristimulus values for a color stimulus first are transformed into three cone-response tristimulus values.

2. The cone-response tristimulus values then are adjusted to account for observer chromatic adaptation effects.

3. The adjusted cone-response tristimulus values are transformed back to (modified) CIE *XYZ* tristimulus values.

In a von Kries transformation, the combined effect of these individual transformations is performed by a single matrix. A procedure for developing a von Kries transformation matrix is described in Appendix D.

4. Lateral-Brightness Adaptation Transformations

In certain viewing situations, an observer's perception of color stimuli will be influenced by lateral-brightness adaptation effects induced by the surround in which the stimuli are viewed. To account for such effects, each set of viewing conditions must be characterized in terms of *surround type*. The specification for surround type defines the characteristics of the visual field immediately surrounding the viewed stimuli. The surround can be specified in terms of chromaticity and luminance factor.

If the chromaticity of the surround is similar to that of the adaptive white, but the luminance factor of the surround differs from the average luminance factor of the viewed stimuli, the surround principally will influence an observer's perception of luminance contrast and overall brightness. This influence of the surround on perceived luminance contrast can be accounted for by using the procedure described in Appendix D.

As shown below, there are two basic steps to that procedure. First, the Y tristimulus value for each stimulus is modified according to an experimentally determined power factor, S, to form a visually equivalent tristimulus value, Y_S, for the different surround:

$$Y_S = Y^S \qquad \{17.3a\}$$

The X and Z tristimulus values for the stimulus then are scaled by the ratio of the Y_S tristimulus value to the unmodified tristimulus value, Y:

$$X_S = X\left(\frac{Y_S}{Y}\right)$$

$$\{17.3b\}$$

$$Z_S = Z\left(\frac{Y_S}{Y}\right)$$

This scaling produced by Eq. {17.3b} maintains the chromaticity values (x, y) for the stimulus. In certain other lateral-brightness adaptation transformation procedures, the chromaticity values are adjusted such that the chroma of the stimulus also is modified.

Applying a lateral-brightness adaptation transformation from darker-surround viewing conditions to lighter-surround viewing conditions results in a decrease in overall grayscale slope, as shown below in Fig. 17.9. The meaning of this transformation is that an image having a grayscale of lower slope would be required in lighter-surround viewing conditions in order to visually match the luminance contrast of an image viewed under darker-surround conditions. Conversely, a lateral-brightness adaptation transformation from lighter-surround conditions to darker-surround conditions produces the required increase in overall slope of the system grayscale.

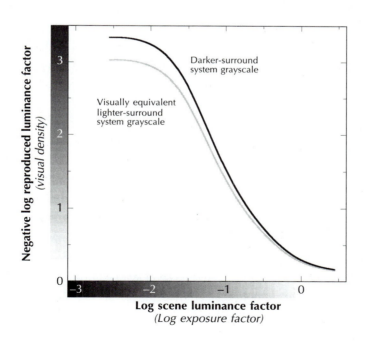

Figure 17.9
Results of applying a lateral-brightness adaptation, or "dark-surround," transformation to a grayscale characteristic curve.

5. General-Brightness Adaptation Transformations

The previous transformation accounted for the influence of surround conditions on perceived luminance contrast. Surround conditions also may influence the *brightness* of displayed stimuli. This effect, a form of general-brightness adaptation, is most likely to occur in darker-surround viewing conditions. The observer tends to adapt to the overall luminance level of the displayed stimuli themselves because there are few visual cues to otherwise influence brightness adaptation.

It is often suggested that general-brightness adaptation is automatically accounted for by the use of what has been called "relative colorimetry" or, more appropriately, "media-relative colorimetry," which will be described next. We do not agree with that position. Nevertheless, the use of such colorimetry is so widespread that it warrants extensive discussion here.

Moreover, this discussion will help to define the problems involved in dealing with imaging media that have been designed to be displayed under very different sets of viewing conditions. The discussion of media-relative colorimetry is followed by a description of a method that we believe more appropriately accounts for the effects of general-brightness adaptation.

5a. Media-Relative Colorimetry

Many colorimetric calculations yield values that are relative to those of a reference white. For example, in terms of CIELAB values, the reference white always will have an L^* value of 100.0, and it always will have a^* and b^* values of 0.0, regardless of the reference's absolute luminance or chromaticity. In most colorimetric calculations, the reference white is defined to be a *perfect* white. In "media-relative" colorimetry, however, something other than a perfect white—usually the support of the particular medium being measured—is used instead.

There are situations where the use of such colorimetry is appropriate. In certain graphic-arts applications, for example, media-relative colorimetry provides a convenient description of the colorimetry of the ink image, independent of the paper on which it is printed. That colorimetry can be useful when the intent is to produce the same ink image (rather than the same color appearance) on a number of different papers.

However, media-relative colorimetry also is sometimes used in an attempt to deal with the fundamental differences in the colorimetric properties of various types of images. These differences are very apparent in the grayscales of these media. For example, Fig. 17.10 shows the actual visual densities—which are equivalent to *standard* colorimetric values based on a perfect white reference—for four media:

a) A conventional photographic slide film, which has a minimum transmission visual density of about 0.15.

b) A high-quality video system, such as a home theater system, which has a minimum negative log luminance-factor value of 0.00, referenced to the stimulus produced from maximum video RGB control signals.

c) A conventional photographic reflection-print medium, which has a minimum visual density (or negative log luminance-factor value) of about 0.10.

d) A particular type instant-print film, which produces reflection images having a minimum reflection visual density of about 0.20.

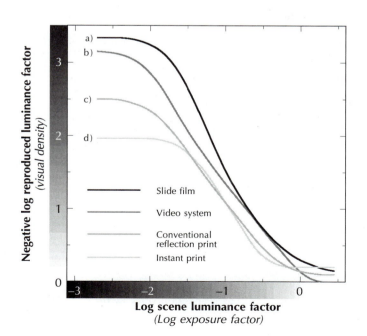

Figure 17.10

Grayscales for four media, measured in terms of standard densitometry (visual density) or standard colorimetry (negative log luminance factor) as a function of log scene luminance factor or log scene exposure factor.

In the computation of *media-relative* colorimetry of *reflection* images, the colorimetry of the paper support generally is used as the white reference. The underlying assumption is that observers adapt to the support because it is the brightest part of an image on that medium. However, as discussed earlier, that assumption is not correct. Reflection images are judged essentially as *objects* within the viewing environment. There is little or no adaptation to a reflection image itself because a typical reflection-image viewing environment contains white objects and other visual cues that strongly influence the adaptive state of the observer.

Our experience is that when the objective is to encode reflection images in terms of their color appearance, standard colorimetric values based on a *perfect* white reference should be used. In Fig. 17.11a, for example, the grayscales for the photographic and instant-print media of Fig. 17.10, measured relative to a perfect white diffuse reflector, show that the minimum visual densities of the media are different. That is consistent with how images on these media actually appear. In particular, the higher minimum visual density of the

Figure 17.11a

Grayscales for a conventional photographic reflection print and an instant print, measured in terms of *standard* densitometry or colorimetry. Output images made according to these values will have a correct brightness relationship.

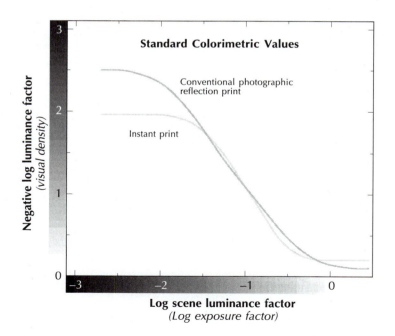

instant print is plainly visible under almost any reasonable set of viewing conditions. If standard colorimetric values of images on these two input media are encoded and output to the same device, the output images will have a correct brightness relationship. So if the output device is set up such that it produces images of proper brightness from one of the input media, the device also will produce images of proper brightness from the other input medium.

In Fig. 17.11b, the *media-relative* grayscales for these two media are shown. Since media-relative values are based on respective minimum values, each grayscale has a minimum media-relative reflection density value of *zero*. These grayscale values therefore imply that the minimum density areas of the media are visually identical to each other and that they are visually indistinguishable from a perfect white reflector. But that is *not* how they actually appear. The differences in their minimum density areas are very apparent, and neither medium has areas that appear to be perfectly white.

Moreover, the use of media-relative computations has reduced *all* the density values of the instant-print medium to a much greater extent than it has

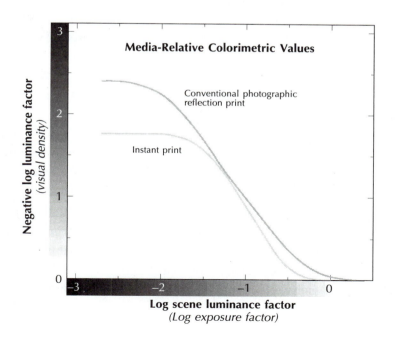

Figure 17.11b
Grayscales for a photographic reflection print and an instant print, measured in terms of *media-relative* densitometry or colorimetry. Output images made according to these values will *not* have a correct brightness relationship.

reduced those of the photographic medium. If the media-relative values were encoded and output to the same device, the resulting images would *not* properly represent the brightness relationships of the input images. Instead, output images from instant-print-film input would be much too light. If the output were adjusted to correct that problem, output images from photographic-print input then would be too dark. In the case of reflection images, then, the use of media-relative colorimetry only serves to *create* a problem in an attempt to "correct" a problem with standard colorimetry that, in reality, never existed.

The situation is somewhat different when media-relative colorimetry is used for color encoding other types of media. For example, in the computation of the media-relative colorimetry of transparency images, such as photographic slides, the minimum transmission visual density of the medium is used as the white reference. Again, the underlying assumption of relative colorimetry is that observers adapt to the brightest part of an image. As was discussed earlier, there *is* a significant amount of adaptation to projected images, especially when they are viewed in completely darkened environments. However, what is perceived as a perfect white seldom, if ever, corresponds to the *brightest* areas of these images. As discussed in Chapter 6, the grayscale characteristics of transparency media are designed such that the brightest areas appear to be *brighter* than a perfect white.

On the other hand, because some general-brightness adaptation does occur, the encoding of projected images cannot simply be based on a standard white reference. Doing so results in standard densities and standard colorimetric values that do *not* represent the perceived brightnesses of images. Figure 17.12a, for example, shows the grayscales for the photographic reflection print and slide media of Fig. 17.10, as measured by standard densitometric and colorimetric methods. The figure shows that, at any given exposure-factor value, the visual densities of the slide film are higher than those of the reflection print. This implies that projected slide images must be darker overall than reflection print images. But, of course, that is not how images on these media actually compare. Slide films have been manufactured and sold for more than 60 years. If it were true that they always produced images that were too dark, someone certainly would have noticed by now.

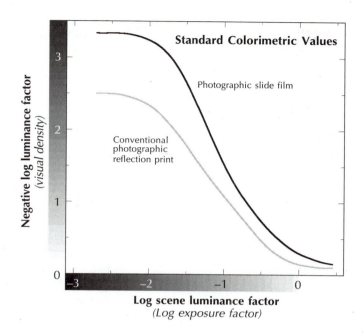

Figure 17.12a
Grayscales for a photographic reflection print and a slide film, measured in terms of *standard* densitometry or colorimetry. Output images made according to these values will *not* have a correct brightness relationship. Images produced from slide-film input would be darker than those from reflection-print input.

    In this particular example, the use of media-relative colorimetry (shown in Fig. 17.12b) will not greatly change the relationship described by standard colorimetry because the minimum visual densities of the two media happen to differ by only 0.05 density units. If values based on *either* standard *or* media-relative measurements were encoded and output to the same device, the resulting images would not have a correct brightness relationship. Images produced from slide-film input would be much darker than those produced from reflection-print input. In this situation, then, media-relative colorimetry was intended to fix a problem that indeed existed; but the use of that colorimetry actually had little effect.

    Figure 17.13a shows the grayscales for another pair of media, the photographic reflection print and the high-quality video display from Fig. 17.10. If images are made from this standard colorimetry, the images made from video-display values will be darker than those made from reflection-print values.

Figure 17.12b
Grayscales for a photographic reflection print and a slide film, measured in terms of *media-relative* densitometry or colorimetry. Output images made according to these values will *not* have a correct brightness relationship.

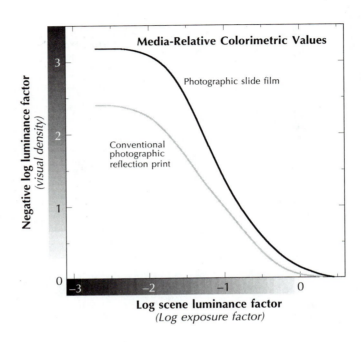

Figure 17.13a
Grayscales for a photographic reflection print and a high-quality video display, measured in terms of *standard* densitometry or colorimetry. Output images made according to these values will *not* have a correct brightness relationship.

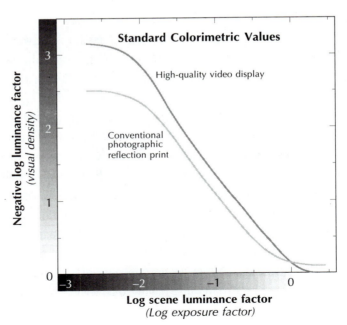

Figure 17.13b shows the media-relative grayscales for these media. These grayscales now imply that video images are even *darker* compared to reflection print images than was suggested by the standard colorimetric measurements. As a result, if an output device is set up such that good images are produced from reflection print input, images produced from media-relative video-display values will be much too dark. In this example, then, the use of media-relative colorimetry not only failed to correct a real problem associated with the use of standard colorimetry, it made that problem considerably *worse*.

Media-relative colorimetry has failed in each of these situations because it does not correlate well with actual color appearance. In particular, media-relative colorimetry does not properly describe the brightnesses of images viewed under different surround conditions. The meaning of colors encoded according to media-relative colorimetry therefore would be ambiguous; their brightnesses could not be determined from the encoded values alone. Since standard colorimetry also does not properly describe brightness under all viewing conditions, another type of color representation is required. One method for deriving this representation is described next.

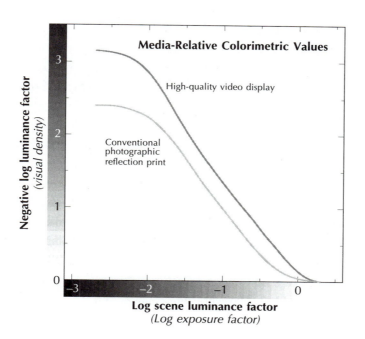

Figure 17.13b
Grayscales for a photographic reflection print and high-quality video display, both in terms of *"media-relative"* densitometry or colorimetry. Output images made according to these values will *not* have a correct brightness relationship.

5b. Brightness-adapted Colorimetry

Appearance color encoding of the media in Fig. 17.10, and all other types of media, requires proper accounting for the observer's general-brightness adaptation. One simple procedure for doing that is shown below. First, the CIE XYZ Y tristimulus value for each stimulus is adjusted by an experimentally determined scale factor, B, to form a brightness-adjusted tristimulus value, Y_b:

$$Y_b = BY \qquad \{17.4a\}$$

The X and Z tristimulus values for each stimulus then are scaled by the ratio of the Y_b tristimulus value to the unadjusted tristimulus value, Y:

$$X_b = X\left(\frac{Y_b}{Y}\right)$$

$$Z_b = Z\left(\frac{Y_b}{Y}\right) \qquad \{17.4b\}$$

This scaling maintains the chromaticity values for the stimulus. The effect of a general-brightness adaptation transformation is shown in Fig. 17.14. Note that the transformation results in an overall visual density shift of the grayscale. The photographic gamma (slope) of the curve is not affected.

In Fig. 17.15, the grayscales for the four media of Fig. 17.10 are shown in terms of visual density values that have been *adjusted for general-brightness adaptation* according to the procedure just described. The magnitudes of the brightness adjustments (values for scale factor B) were determined from visual judging experiments. In these experiments, images from various input media were encoded, the encoded values were output to a single device or medium, and the resulting output images were viewed simultaneously. The encoding included colorimetric transformations for viewing flare, chromatic adaptation, and lateral-brightness adaptation. The value of the brightness-adaptation scale factor was varied in the encoding of images from each input medium until the output images from all input media matched in brightness as closely as possible. The scale factor value for the two reflection media was 1.0; the values for the slide film and the video display were approximately 1.5 and 1.6, respectively.

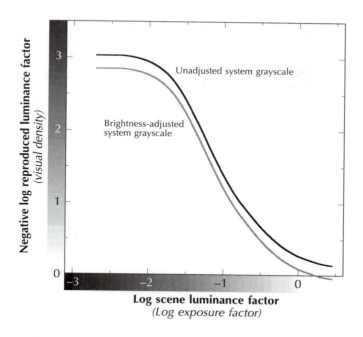

Figure 17.14
Effect of applying an appropriate general-brightness adaptation transformation to a system grayscale.

Due to the different luminance dynamic ranges and other color reproduction differences of the various input media, the output images never were made *identical* by these brightness adjustments. Nor should they have been. Although that result could have been obtained by *re-rendering* each input to achieve a single output color-reproduction position, that was *not* the intent. The intent was to produce a set of images that matched for overall brightness and that also matched the different color appearances of images on the various types of input media that were used.

As an analogy, consider a comparison of two loudspeakers—a small bookshelf speaker and large multi-speaker system. The two will not sound *identical* because of the greater frequency range that can be reproduced by the larger speaker system. However, they can be made to sound equally *loud* by making proper adjustments of the amplifiers. A point will be reached where no further improvements in the match can be made by loudness adjustments alone; it is at that point that the speakers can be compared most fairly.

Figure 17.15

Grayscales for four media, in terms of *brightness-adapted* densitometry or colorimetry. Output images made according to these values *will* have a correct brightness relationship.

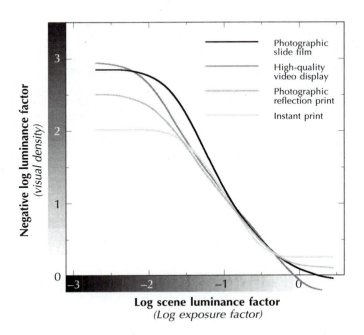

When output images from different input media are encoded in terms of their own color appearances and adjusted for overall brightness, a similar point is reached when the matching cannot be improved further by brightness adjustments alone. That point can be used to determine the scale factor for calculating brightness-adapted colorimetric values.

Note that two of the brightness-adapted grayscales in Fig. 17.15 have some visual densities *less than* zero. These negative visual densities correspond to luminance-factor values greater than 1.0, and to CIE Y tristimulus values and CIELAB L^* values greater than 100. That is as it should be. When high-quality images are viewed under appropriate conditions, they will *appear* to have areas that are brighter than a reference white. The encoding of such areas in terms of color-appearance *should* have luminance-factor values greater than that of a perfect white reference. This is an extremely important outcome that will have to be considered in the development of any appearance-based color encoding specifications.

Discussion

This chapter has described a method for representing color in a way that is consistent with the requirements of individual imaging systems that are based on the unified paradigm. The combination of a colorimetric specification and a set of encoding reference viewing conditions makes the color representation unambiguous. Because the representation is of color itself, it is not subject to any restrictions that might be imposed by a particular interpretation, context, medium, or device. The appearance of any given color, regardless of its origin or ultimate destination, can be represented.

It is very important to point out, however, that while an appearance-based color representation solves the basic problem of *specifying* color in a unified way, it does not provide a complete solution to the overall problem of *encoding* color in systems that are to be capable of performing all the functions described by the unified paradigm.

In order to support additional input-interpretation options, other color-encoding methods must be incorporated as part of the input signal processing. For example, the color-encoding method used on *Photo CD* Imaging Worksta-tions might first be used to transform color values measured from the slide to original-scene colorimetry. Appropriate colorimetric transforms then would be used to transform that colorimetry to color-appearance values for encoding. Other color-encoding methods, such as those based on re-rendering to refer-ence output devices or output media, also must be included in the overall design in order to provide other Type *B* and Type *C* paradigm colorimetric values. The re-rendered colorimetric values produced by these methods again would be transformed to color-appearance values for encoding.

An appearance-based color-encoding method, then, is not a *replace-ment* for the other color-encoding methods discussed in Part III. Instead, it is a means for achieving input compatibility in a way that can support the incorpo-ration of most other color-encoding methods. Examples of the use of alternative color-encoding methods in combination with a color-appearance-based color encoding specification are given in the next chapter.

Summary of Key Issues

- In the unified color-management paradigm, each alternative interpretation of color from each input medium constitutes a unique input source.

- The color encoding of the unified paradigm, which is based on color appearance, supports all input sources.

- Unambiguous, color-appearance-based encoding can be achieved by the use of colorimetric values together with a defined set of encoding reference viewing conditions.

- The specification of the encoding reference viewing conditions and other sets of viewing conditions must include descriptions of viewing flare, adaptive white, luminance level, and surround type.

- The specification for the encoding reference viewing conditions applies only to the color encoding itself; the conditions for original-scene, input-image, and output-image viewing are entirely independent of the encoding reference conditions.

- Input and output colorimetric transformations used for color-appearance encoding must account for viewing flare and for observer chromatic adaptation, lateral-brightness adaptation, and general-brightness adaptation.

- Color encoding based on media-relative colorimetry will not properly account for observer general-brightness adaptation. Output images produced from such encoding will not have the correct brightness relationships.

- Encoding the color appearance of images from high-quality imaging devices and media requires the representation of luminance-factor values greater than those corresponding to the reproductions of perfect whites.

- Color encoding based on color appearance does not, in and of itself, provide all the features of the unified color-management paradigm. Other encoding methods must be used in combination with appearance-based encoding in order to provide alternative interpretations of input colors.

18

A Unified Paradigm: A Prototype System

In order to evaluate the concept of appearance-based color encoding in an actual color-imaging system, we and a group of our colleagues designed and assembled a prototype system based on the unified paradigm. A diagram of that system is given in Fig. 18.1.

The prototype system includes all major types of inputs, outputs, and options and is designed to be independently capable of providing all the functions of the unified paradigm. As was discussed in the previous chapter, not every system operating in the unified environment must have that capability; however, the comprehensive scope of the prototype system allowed both the paradigm and the proposed color-encoding method to be evaluated fully.

Figure 18.1

A prototype imaging system based upon the unified color-management paradigm. This prototype system can provide all the functions of the paradigm.

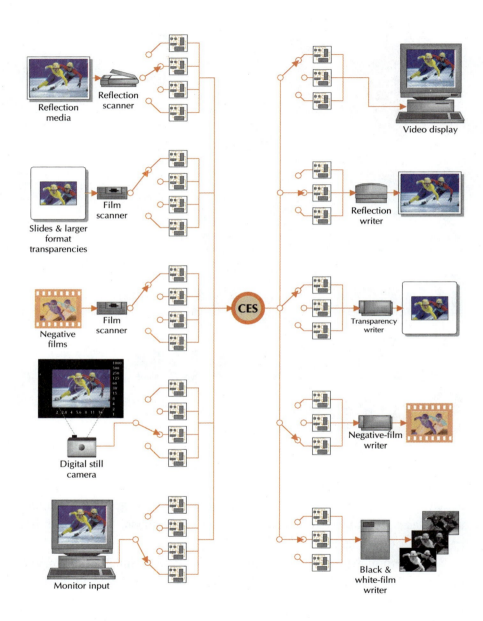

Encoding Reference Viewing Conditions

The first task in setting up the system was to define a set of reference viewing conditions for the color encoding. In theory, encoding reference viewing conditions can be chosen essentially arbitrarily. It makes more sense, however, to choose conditions that are representative of those likely to be used for actual input and/or output images. Doing so minimizes the magnitudes of the colorimetric transformations required to account for appearance factors.

The encoding reference viewing conditions for the prototype system were chosen to be consistent with those typical of indoor viewing of reflection prints. In most respects, the conditions also are consistent with the viewing of back-illuminated transparencies and some types of video displays. The viewing conditions are defined in terms of the four characteristics that we consider to be most important:

- *Viewing Flare:* Viewing flare luminance is specified as equal to 1.0% that of a white in the viewed image.
- *Surround Type:* The surround is defined as *average* or *normal,* i.e., the area surrounding the image being viewed has a luminance factor of about 0.20 and is equal in chromaticity to the observer adaptive white.
- *Luminance Level:* The luminance of a white in the viewed image is specified to be between 60 and 160 candelas per square meter (cd/m^2).
- *Adaptive White:* The chromaticity coordinates of the observer adaptive white are specified to be those of CIE Standard Illuminant D$_{50}$.

The relationship of these factors to the color encoding of the prototype system, and how the encoding was used to implement the unified paradigm, can best be explained by a series of examples. The examples have been chosen to demonstrate particular aspects of the unified paradigm and the color-encoding method. The color-appearance transformations described in these examples, although quite simple, have provided results that are satisfactory for most applications. Other, generally more complex transformations could be used in cases where more demanding requirements must be met.

Example 1

In this first example, illustrated in Fig. 18.2a, the image to be input to the system is a reflection print. The selected input-encoding option is to represent the color appearance of that print. The print is illuminated by a light source approximately simulating CIE Standard Illuminant D_{50}, and it is viewed under the following conditions:

- *Viewing Flare:* Viewing flare luminance, due to front surface reflection from the print, is about 1.0% that of a white in the print.
- *Surround Type:* The print is surrounded by a neutral gray area of approximately 20% reflectance. The surround type therefore can be considered average.
- *Luminance Level:* The luminance of a white in the print is about 150 candelas per square meter.
- *Adaptive White:* The observer is chromatically adapted to the chromaticity of the simulated D_{50} light source ($x = 0.3457, y = 0.3585$).

These actual input-image viewing conditions match the encoding reference viewing conditions; therefore, the reflection print can be encoded directly in terms of its standard CIE colorimetric values. These values would be based on the simulated D_{50} source. They could be measured using a colorimetric scanner or a densitometric scanner, as described in Chapter 10.

Figure 18.2b illustrates one procedure for developing and applying an input-signal-processing transform based on this example. First, CIE colorimetric values are determined for an array of test colors on the reflection medium. These values can be computed from the spectral reflectances of the test colors and the spectral power distribution of the simulated D_{50} source, or they can be measured directly using a colorimeter and the light source. The colorimetric values then are converted to the particular data metric of the color encoding specification. The same test colors also are scanned to produce scanner code values. An appropriate application then is run to generate a mathematical transform relating scanner code values to color-encoding values. The resulting transformation, which may be in the form of one-dimensional lookup tables, matrices, polynomial equations, and/or three-dimensional lookup tables, then is applied in the input signal processing of the imaging system.

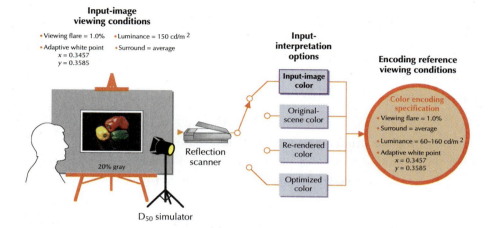

**Input-image
viewing conditions**

- Viewing flare = 1.0%
- Adaptive white point
  $x = 0.3457$
  $y = 0.3585$
- Luminance = 150 cd/m^2
- Surround = average

20% gray

Reflection
scanner

D$_{50}$ simulator

**Input-
interpretation
options**

Input-image
color

Original-
scene color

Re-rendered
color

Optimized
color

**Encoding reference
viewing conditions**

Color encoding
specification
- Viewing flare = 1.0%
- Surround = average
- Luminance = 60–160 cd/m^2
- Adaptive white point
  $x = 0.3457$
  $y = 0.3585$

Figure 18.2a
Input from a
reflection image,
as described in
Example 1.

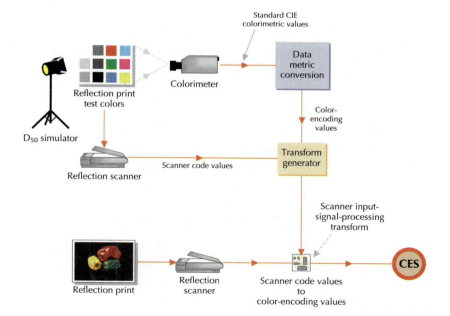

Standard CIE
colorimetric values

Reflection print
test colors

Colorimeter

Data
metric
conversion

D$_{50}$ simulator

Reflection scanner

Scanner code values

Color-
encoding
values

Transform
generator

Reflection print

Reflection
scanner

Scanner input-
signal-processing
transform

Scanner code values
to
color-encoding values

CES

Figure 18.2b
Derivation of a
scanner input-
signal-processing
transform based
on Example 1.
No colorimetric
transformations of
the input image's
standard colori-
metric values are
required because
the actual input-
image viewing
conditions match
the encoding
reference viewing
conditions.

Example 2

The input in this example again is a reflection print (Fig. 18.3a). The input-encoding option is to represent the appearance of that print when illuminated by a light source approximately simulating CIE Standard Illuminant D_{65}. The print is viewed under the following conditions:

- *Viewing Flare:* Viewing flare luminance, due to front surface reflection from the print, is about 1.0% that of a white in the print.
- *Surround Type:* The print is surrounded by a neutral gray area of approximately 20% reflectance. The surround type therefore can be considered average.
- *Luminance Level:* The luminance of a white in the print is about 150 candelas per square meter (cd/m^2).
- *Adaptive White:* The observer is chromatically adapted to the chromaticity of the simulated D_{65} light source ($x = 0.3127, y = 0.3290$).

In this example, the actual input-image viewing conditions match the encoding reference viewing conditions except that the observer is chromatically adapted to the chromaticity of D_{65}, rather than to the chromaticity of D_{50}.

The reflection image can be encoded by first determining its standard CIE colorimetric values. These values would be determined using the spectral power distribution of the simulated D_{65} source. However, to be consistent with the reference viewing conditions defined for the color encoding, those colorimetric values must be transformed to visually equivalent colorimetric values for an observer who is chromatically adapted to the chromaticity of D_{50}. This can be done using any of a number of different chromatic adaptation transformation procedures, such as the von Kries procedure described earlier.

One result of the chromatic adaptation transformation is that an area of the image that appeared neutral (i.e., the area had a chromaticity equal to that of D_{65}) in the actual input-image viewing conditions would be encoded as a neutral for an observer adapted to the encoding reference viewing conditions (i.e., the area would have a chromaticity equal to that of D_{50}).

A scanner input-signal-processing transform for this example can be derived and applied using the procedures illustrated in Fig. 18.3b.

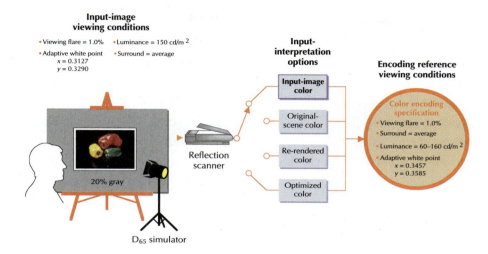

Figure 18.3a
Input from a reflection image, as described in Example 2.

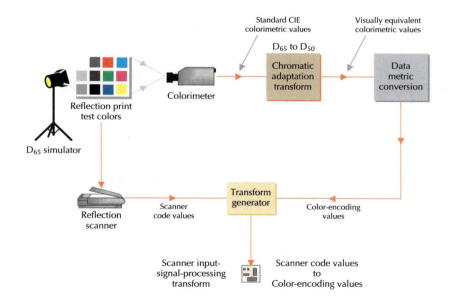

Figure 18.3b
Derivation of a scanner input-signal-processing transform based on Example 2. The transform includes a transformation of measured D_{65} values to visually equivalent D_{50} values.

The conditions of the next two examples admittedly are somewhat unusual, but they are not entirely unrealistic. They are similar to conditions used in art museums to display paintings, drawings, and photographs. The two examples have been included to illustrate the important (but somewhat elusive) distinction between the *actual input-image illuminant,* which directly contributes to the colorimetry of the input image, and the *observer adaptive white,* which describes the chromatic adaptation state of the observer who is viewing that image. As the examples show, the observer may not be chromatically adapted to the image illuminant.

Example 3

In the first of these examples (Fig. 18.4a), the input is a reflection print that is illuminated by a small spotlight having a spectral power distribution that approximately simulates CIE Standard Illuminant D_{65}. The print is in a well-lighted room that is illuminated by a light source approximately simulating CIE Standard Illuminant D_{50}. The input-encoding option is to represent the color appearance of that print. The viewing conditions are as follows:

- *Viewing Flare:* Viewing flare luminance, due to front surface reflection from the print, is about 1.0% that of a white in the print.
- *Surround Type:* The print is surrounded by a neutral gray area of approximately 20% reflectance. The surround area is illuminated by room light, but no room light falls on the print itself.
- *Luminance Level:* The luminance of a white in the print is about 150 candelas per square meter.
- *Adaptive White:* The observer is chromatically adapted to the chromaticity of the *room* illuminant (the simulated D_{50} light source).

As was discussed earlier, the observer adaptive white describes the chromatic adaptation state of the observer; it does *not* describe a reference viewing illuminant. Therefore, *the actual input-image viewing conditions still correspond to those of the encoding reference viewing conditions, despite the fact that the image itself is illuminated by a D_{65} light source.* The only difference from Example 1 is that the *colorimetry* of the print would be determined

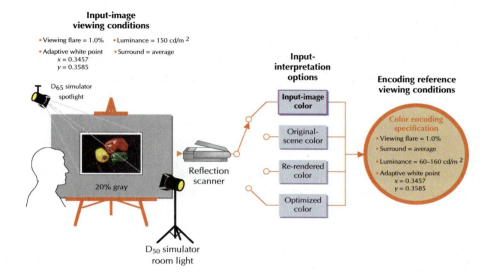

Figure 18.4a
Input from a reflection print, as described in Example 3. Although the print is illuminated by a D$_{65}$ spotlight, the observer is chromatically adapted to the chromaticity of the D$_{50}$ room light source.

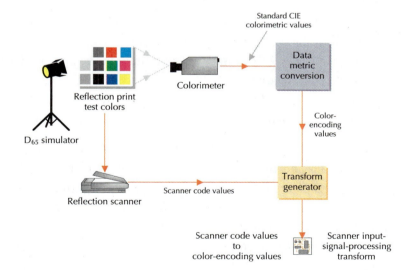

Figure 18.4b
Derivation of a scanner input-signal-processing transform based on Example 3. No transformations of the colorimetric values of the input image are required because the actual input-image viewing conditions match the encoding reference viewing conditions.

using the spectral power distribution of the D_{65} spotlight. That colorimetry, and therefore the color encoding, would reflect the fact that the print would appear somewhat bluish because it is illuminated by a D_{65} source and the observer is chromatically adapted to the (yellower) chromaticity of D_{50}. A scanner input-signal-processing transform for this example can be derived and applied using the procedure illustrated in Fig. 18.4b.

Example 4

In this example (Fig. 18.5a), the input is a reflection print that is illuminated by a small spotlight having a spectral power distribution that approximates CIE Standard Illuminant D_{50}. The print is in a well-lighted room that is illuminated by a light source approximately simulating CIE Standard Illuminant D_{65}. The input-encoding option is to represent the actual color appearance of the print. The viewing conditions are as follows:

- *Viewing Flare:* Viewing flare luminance, due to front surface reflection from the print, is about 1.0% that of a white in the print.
- *Surround Type:* The print is surrounded by a neutral gray area of approximately 20% reflectance. The surround area is illuminated by room light, but no room light falls on the print itself.
- *Luminance Level:* The luminance of a white in the print is about 150 candelas per square meter.
- *Adaptive White:* The observer is chromatically adapted to the chromaticity of the room illuminant (the simulated D_{65} light source).

These viewing conditions *no longer correspond to the reference viewing conditions,* despite the fact that the print is illuminated by a D_{50} light source. The colorimetry of the input image should be determined using the spectral power of that D_{50} source. However, those colorimetric values then must be transformed, using a chromatic adaptation transformation from D_{65} to D_{50}, because the observer is adapted to the chromaticity of D_{65}. That transformation will reflect the fact that the print would look somewhat yellowish because it is illuminated by a D_{50} source and the observer is chromatically adapted to the chromaticity of D_{65}. An input signal-processing transform for this example can be derived and applied using the procedure illustrated in Fig. 18.5b.

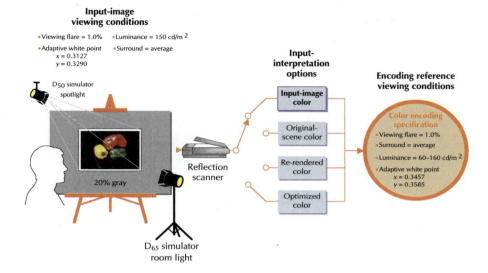

Figure 18.5a
Input from a
reflection image,
as described in
Example 4.

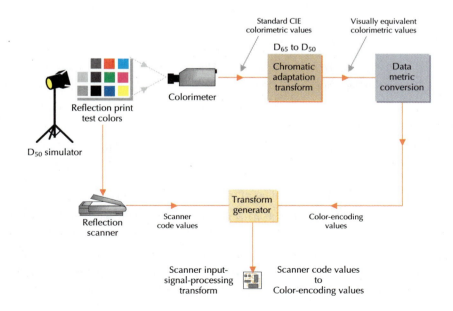

Figure 18.5b
Derivation of a
scanner input-
signal-processing
transform based
on Example 4.
A chromatic adap-
tation transforma-
tion is required
here because the
observer is chro-
matically adapted
to the D_{65} room
light.

Note that in both Example 3 and Example 4 it was stated that the observer is chromatically adapted to the chromaticity of the room illuminant. Depending on the specific conditions, the observer instead might be chromatically adapted to the chromaticity of the spotlight or to other chromaticities somewhere between those of the two illumination sources. Part of the "art" of color-appearance encoding is determining the chromaticity of the observer adaptive white. As described earlier, the criterion is that a stimulus having that chromaticity would appear perfectly achromatic to the observer.

Example 5

This example (Figs. 18.6a and 18.6b) illustrates that the *difference* in the amount of flare in the input-image viewing conditions from that in the reference conditions must be accounted for in the encoding process. The input is a reflection print, illuminated by a light source simulating CIE Standard Illuminant D_{50}. The encoding option is to represent the print's appearance when viewed under the following conditions:

- *Viewing Flare:* Viewing flare luminance, due to front surface reflection from the print, is about 2.5% that of a white in the print.
- *Surround Type:* The print is surrounded by a neutral gray area of approximately 20% reflectance. The surround type therefore can be considered average.
- *Luminance Level:* The luminance of a white in the print is about 150 candelas per square meter.
- *Adaptive White:* The observer is chromatically adapted to the chromaticity of the simulated D_{50} light source ($x = 0.3457, y = 0.3585$).

These conditions correspond to those of the encoding reference viewing conditions except that there is 2.5%, rather than 1%, viewing flare. The effect of the additional 1.5% viewing flare must be accounted for in the encoding. This can be done using the transformation method described in Appendix E. The transformed colorimetric values will reflect the fact that in the actual input-image viewing conditions, the print will be lower in luminance contrast (shown in Fig. 18.6c) and color saturation (Fig. 18.6d) than it would be if viewed in the encoding reference viewing conditions.

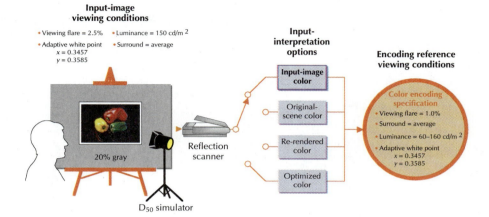

Figure 18.6a
Input from a reflection image, as described in Example 5.

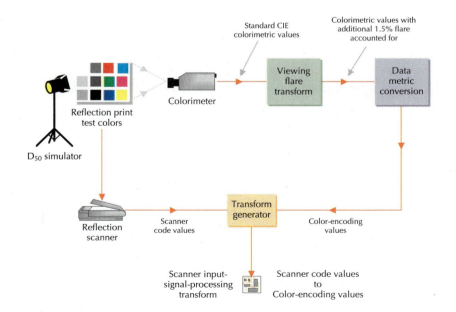

Figure 18.6b
Derivation of a scanner input-signal-processing transform based on Example 5. The effect of the additional viewing flare must be accounted for in the input transform.

Figure 18.6c

Comparison of reflection-image grayscales in viewing conditions of 1% and 2.5% viewing flare, as described in Example 5.

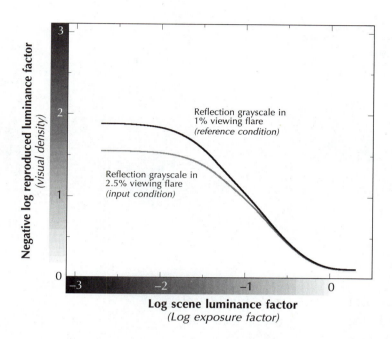

Figure 18.6d

Comparison of CIELAB *a**, *b** values, reflection-print colors in viewing conditions of 1% and 2.5% viewing flare, as described in Example 5.

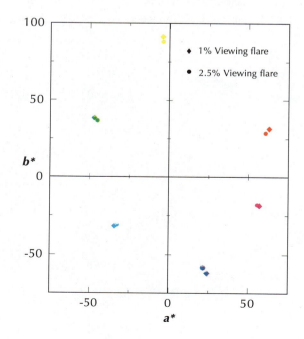

Example 6

In this example, the input is a photographic negative. A direct encoding of the color appearance of that negative would make little sense (unless, for some reason, the user really wants backwards orange images). Appearance encoding of negative images requires some form of *rendering* of the scanned data.

An input-signal-processing transform for doing that can be constructed by first printing test negatives onto a suitable print medium, such as a photographic paper (Fig. 18.7a). The colorimetry of the resulting reflection prints then can be measured and encoded using the same procedures described in the earlier examples of reflection-print input. In this particular example, the specified viewing conditions for the rendered image are those of the encoding reference conditions, so no additional colorimetric transformations are required. In cases where the specified viewing conditions for the rendered image differ from those of the encoding reference conditions, appropriate colorimetric transformations must be included in the input signal processing.

In the prototype system, data scanned from images on negative films are "computationally printed" by using mathematical models of various print media. For example, if the output medium is a conventional photographic paper, the printing densities of the negative would first be computed, based on the effective spectral responsivities of that paper. The printing densities then would be used with a model of the paper to compute print colorimetric values.

This method is considerably more convenient than methods involving actual printing, especially when it is desired to produce transforms for a number of different input negative films as printed onto a variety of different print media. Moreover, the modeled print media used in these transformations need not be real. For example, because of their extended exposure and density dynamic ranges, the two hypothetical print media shown in Fig. 18.7c each can render more information from a negative than can the actual photographic paper shown in the same figure. Use of such hypothetical media helps to minimize the loss of information that occurs when images scanned from negatives are encoded in terms of color appearance (Fig. 18.7d).

Input-signal-processing transforms based on this example can be constructed, either from actual or computed prints, using the procedure illustrated in Fig. 18.7b.

Figure 18.7a

Input from a photographic negative, as described in Example 6. Data from a negative image must be rendered to a positive image for color-appearance encoding.

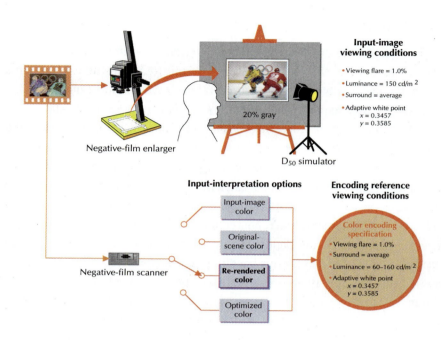

Input-image viewing conditions
- Viewing flare = 1.0%
- Luminance = 150 cd/m^2
- Surround = average
- Adaptive white point
  $x = 0.3457$
  $y = 0.3585$

20% gray

Negative-film enlarger

D$_{50}$ simulator

Input-interpretation options

Input-image color

Original-scene color

Re-rendered color

Optimized color

Negative-film scanner

Encoding reference viewing conditions

Color encoding specification
- Viewing flare = 1.0%
- Surround = average
- Luminance = 60–160 cd/m^2
- Adaptive white point
  $x = 0.3457$
  $y = 0.3585$

Figure 18.7b

Derivation of a scanner input-signal-processing transform based on Example 6. Data scanned from negative images are rendered for color-appearance encoding.

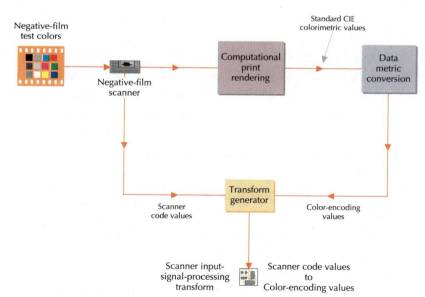

Negative-film test colors

Negative-film scanner

Computational print rendering

Standard CIE colorimetric values

Data metric conversion

Scanner code values

Transform generator

Color-encoding values

Scanner input-signal-processing transform

Scanner code values to Color-encoding values

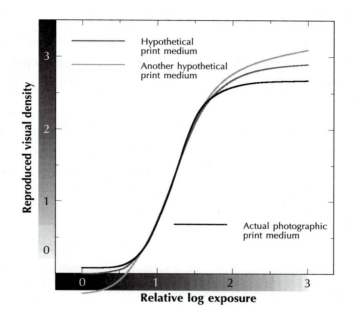

Figure 18.7c
Grayscales for
an actual photo-
graphic reflection-
print medium and
two hypothetical
reflection-print
media.

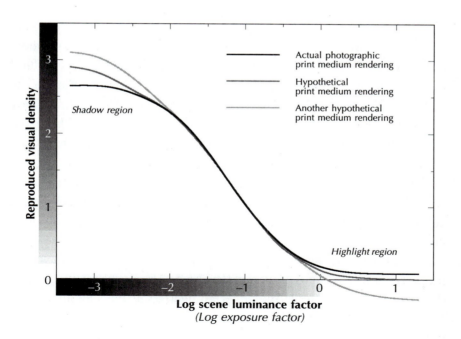

Figure 18.7d
Rendering based
on hypothetical
print media helps
minimize the loss
of information that
occurs when neg-
ative films are en-
coded in terms of
color appearance.
The renderings on
the hypothetical
media retain sig-
nificantly greater
information in the
highlight and
shadow areas.

Example 7

The input for this example is a photographic slide (Fig. 18.8a). The input-encoding option is to represent the appearance of the slide as projected in a darkened room, using a tungsten-halogen lamp. The slide is viewed under the following conditions:

- *Viewing Flare:* Viewing flare, due to stray projector light, equals about 1.0% of the luminance of a white in the slide.
- *Surround Type:* The areas surrounding the projected image are not illuminated. The surround type therefore can be considered dark.
- *Luminance Level:* The luminance of a white in the projected image is 125 candelas per square meter.
- *Adaptive White:* The observer is chromatically adapted to the chromaticities of the projected neutrals of the slide film. The average chromaticity coordinates for the neutrals of this particular combination of film and light source are $x = 0.3611, y = 0.3809$.

In order to encode the appearance of the projected slide in terms of corresponding colorimetric values for the encoding reference viewing conditions, it is necessary to account for the effects of the dark-surround viewing environment. First, the reduction in perceived luminance contrast, due to observer lateral-brightness adaptation, must be considered. The encoded grayscale data must reflect the fact that a lower luminance contrast image would be required in the reference conditions in order to match the appearance of the projected slide in the dark-surround conditions. The increase in brightness (lower apparent overall density, due to observer general-brightness adaptation) that occurs in the the dark-surround viewing conditions also must be considered. Methodologies for determining the required colorimetric adjustments were discussed earlier, and they are described in greater detail in Appendix D.

In this example, it also is necessary to apply a chromatic adaptation transform to account for the fact that the observer is chromatically adapted to the average chromaticity of the projected neutrals of the slide film. Figure 18.8b illustrates the procedure for constructing an input-signal-processing transform appropriate for this example.

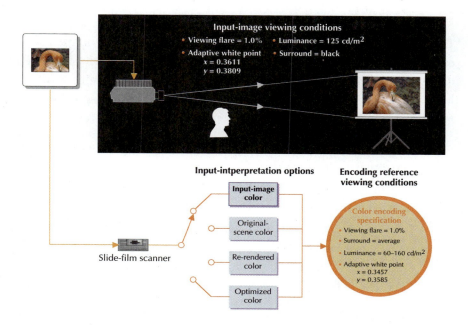

Figure 18.8a
Input from a dark-projected slide, as described in Example 7.

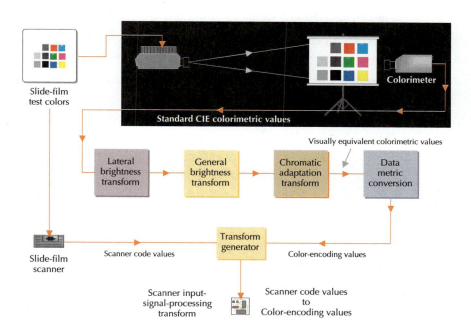

Figure 18.8b
Derivation of a scanner input-signal-processing transform based on Example 7. The transform must account for the perceptual effects that result from the dark surround viewing conditions. A chromatic adaptation transform is also required.

Example 8

The input in this example is a photographic slide taken of an original scene on a cloudy bright day (Fig. 18.9a). The spectral power distribution of the daylight illumination corresponds to that of CIE Standard Illuminant D_{55}. The input-encoding option is to encode in terms of original-scene colors. The original-scene viewing conditions are as follows:

- *Viewing Flare:* There is no viewing flare in the original scene. This will be discussed in the example.
- *Surround Type:* The surround type is normal. This also will be discussed in the example.
- *Luminance Level:* The luminance of a white in the original scene is about 6,000 candelas per square meter.
- *Adaptive White:* The observer is chromatically adapted to the chromaticity of the D_{55} illumination ($x = 0.3324, y = 0.3474$).

Figure 18.9b illustrates a procedure for constructing an input-signal-processing transform based on this example. The transform relates scanner code values to *original-scene colorimetric values* that have been transformed to corresponding values for the encoding reference viewing conditions. Because the viewing conditions of the original scene differ significantly from the encoding reference conditions, several factors must be taken into account in this transformation.

First, it is necessary to incorporate a chromatic adaptation transform to account for the fact that the observer is chromatically adapted to the chromaticity of D_{55}. Next, colorimetric adjustments must be made to compensate for the reductions in perceived luminance contrast and colorfulness that result from the much lower luminance levels of stimuli in the encoding reference viewing conditions. Finally, compensation for the full 1% viewing flare of the encoding reference viewing conditions also must be provided. This compensation is required because the original scene is considered to have no viewing flare. Any stray light present in the scene would appear as part of the scene itself. No adjustment is required for image surround. In an original scene, objects typically are surrounded by other objects, so the surround conditions can be considered to be average.

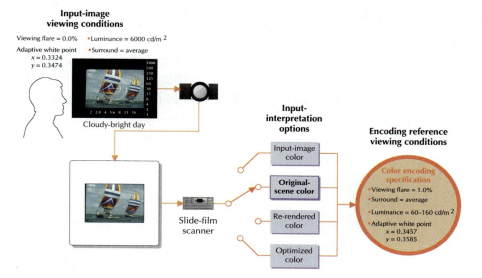

Figure 18.9a
Color encoding of
a photographic
slide film in terms
of original-scene
colors, described
in Example 8.

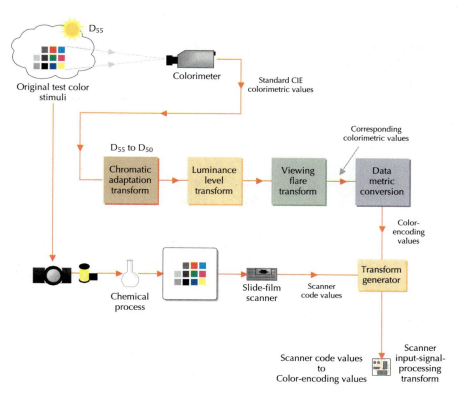

Figure 18.9b
Derivation of a
scanner input-
signal-processing
transform based on
Example 8. Scene
colorimetric values
are transformed to
corresponding
colorimetric values
for the encoding
reference viewing
conditions.

There are various ways that the required colorimetric adjustments of these transformations can be determined. In the prototype system, methods that are consistent with the properties of actual imaging products are used. The use of these methods ensures input compatibility among images transformed from original-scene colorimetry to corresponding colorimetry, images computationally rendered from photographic negatives and from digital cameras, and reproduced images encoded in terms of their own appearance. Procedures for applying viewing flare, luminance contrast, and colorfulness compensations are described in Appendix G.

Example 9

The input in this example is a photographic slide (Fig. 18.10a). The input-encoding option is to re-render the information scanned from the slide such that encoded values represent an image produced by a reference reflection-print system and viewed in the encoding reference viewing conditions.

Figure 18.10b illustrates a procedure for constructing an input-signal-processing transform for this example. Test colors are imaged using both the reference reflection-print system and the slide film. The colorimetry of the resulting reflection image then is determined and encoded in terms of the color encoding specification, using the techniques previously described for reflection images. The slide film is scanned, and a transform is derived relating scanner code values to encoded values for the corresponding colors of the reference reflection-print system.

Other re-rendering methods also can be used in this transformation. For example, the measured CIE XYZ Y tristimulus values for the slide film can be mapped to those of a reflection-print medium. The mapping can be determined based on the respective grayscale characteristics of the media. New X and Z tristimulus values then can be computed such that the x and y chromaticity values for the slide film are unchanged. This type of transformation, which is commonly used in prepress systems, retains somewhat more of the look of the slide film while producing a grayscale that is appropriate for reflection images. Additional colorimetric transformations may be required, depending on the viewing conditions specified for the re-rendered images.

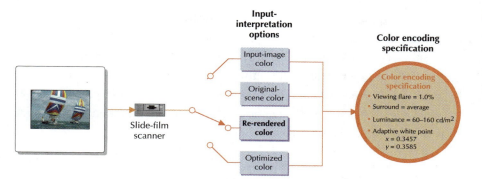

Figure 18.10a
Input from a photographic slide, as described in Example 9.

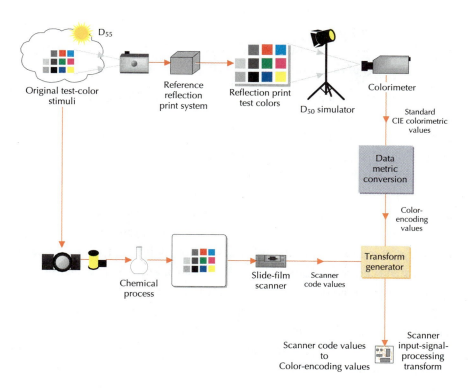

Figure 18.10b
Derivation of a scanner input-signal-processing transform, based on Example 9. The transform re-renders the colors of the slide film to the colors that would have been produced by a reference reflection print system.

Example 10

The input in this example (Fig. 18.11a) is an image that has been created on a computer monitor. When used in this manner, a monitor is functioning as an *input* device rather than as an output display device. In this example, the selected input-encoding option is to represent the appearance of the image as it appears on the monitor. The monitor display and the conditions under which it is viewed are as follows:

- *Viewing Flare:* Viewing flare luminance, due to reflections from the faceplate of the monitor, is about 1.0% that of a white in the image.
- *Surround Type:* The non-image area on the monitor is a uniform gray having the same chromaticity as the monitor white. The luminance of that gray area is about 18 cd/m^2. This value is about 20% that of an image white. The surround type therefore can be considered average.
- *Luminance Level:* The luminance of a white in the image is about 90 candelas per square meter.
- *Adaptive White:* The observer is chromatically adapted to the chromaticity of the monitor white: $x = 0.2832, y = 0.2971$.

The actual input-image viewing conditions of this example match the encoding reference conditions quite closely. The only important exception is that the observer is chromatically adapted to the chromaticity of the monitor white, which is different from the D_{50} reference adaptive white.

The monitor image can be encoded by first determining its standard CIE colorimetric values. This can be done by direct measurement or, more practically, by the use of a mathematical model relating image *RGB* code values to colorimetric values for the resulting stimuli produced on the monitor. Because a monitor is an additive-color device, it is easily modeled, and the colorimetric values can be determined quite accurately. For color encoding, the measured or computed monitor colorimetric values must be transformed to visually equivalent colorimetric values for an observer chromatically adapted to the encoding reference adaptive white chromaticity ($x = 0.3457, y = 0.3585$).

Figure 18.11b illustrates the general procedure for constructing an input-signal-processing transform for this example.

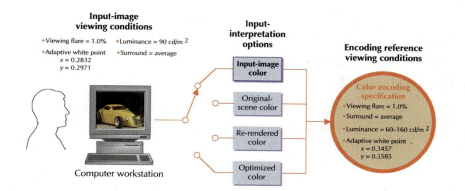

Figure 18.11a
Input from a computer monitor, as described in Example 10.

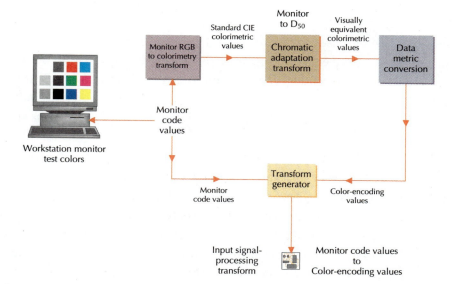

Figure 18.11b
Derivation of an input-signal-processing transform, based on Example 10. The transform must include a chromatic adaptation transformation from monitor chromaticities to visually equivalent D_{50} chromaticities.

Example 11

In this example (Fig. 18.12a), the input is from a digital still camera that has recorded the colorimetry of an original scene. The scene was illuminated by D_{55} daylight. The viewing conditions for the scene are as follows:

- *Viewing Flare:* There is no viewing flare in an original scene. As was previously discussed, any flare present in a live scene is considered part of the scene itself.
- *Surround Type:* The surround type is normal. As previously discussed, scene objects typically are surrounded by other similar objects.
- *Luminance Level:* The luminance of a white in the original scene is about 6,000 candelas per square meter.
- *Adaptive White:* The observer is chromatically adapted to the chromaticity of the scene's D_{55} illumination ($x = 0.3324, y = 0.3474$).

The viewing conditions of the original scene differ significantly from the encoding reference viewing conditions, so several factors must be taken into account, as shown in Fig. 18.12b. A chromatic adaptation transform must be used, because the observer is chromatically adapted to the chromaticity of D_{55}. Colorimetric adjustments must be made to compensate for the reductions in perceived luminance contrast and colorfulness that result from the much lower stimuli luminance levels in the encoding reference viewing conditions. Compensation for the 1% viewing flare of the encoding reference viewing conditions also must be provided.

In the prototype system, methods that are consistent with the properties of actual imaging products are used in the transformation of original-scene colorimetric values to equivalent colorimetric values for the conditions of the encoding reference viewing environment. Use of these methods ensures that an appropriate degree of input compatibility is created for these images. This allows them to be used together with images that have been computationally rendered from digital cameras or photographic negatives and with reproduced images that have been encoded in terms of their own color appearance. The procedures used for the transformation of original-scene colorimetry to equivalent reference-environment colorimetry are described in Appendix G.

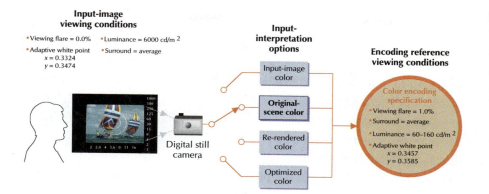

Figure 18.12a
Input from a digital camera, as described in Example 11.

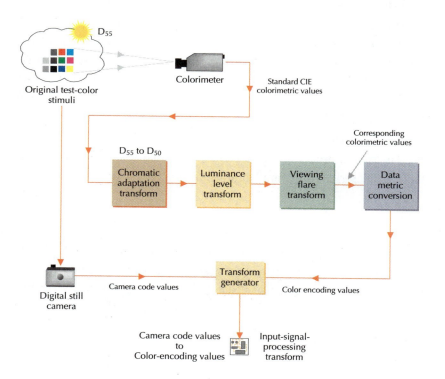

Figure 18.12b
Derivation of an input-signal-processing transform, based on Example 11. The transform compensates for the effects of the lower luminance levels and greater flare of the encoding reference viewing conditions. A chromatic adaptation transformation (from D_{55} to D_{50}) also is required.

Output Transformations

In the prototype system, output signal processing is performed according to the three basic functions previously described in Chapter 13 and shown again here in Fig. 18.13. Encoded values first are transformed by appropriate colorimetric transformations to visually equivalent colorimetric values for the actual output-image viewing environment. The methods used in deriving these transforms are the same as those used in the derivation of input colorimetric transforms. The directions of the transformations, of course, are opposite. Input transformations convert colorimetry from actual input-image viewing conditions to the encoding reference conditions, while output transformations convert colorimetry from the encoding reference conditions to the actual output-image viewing conditions that will be used.

The transformed colorimetric values define an output color stimulus that, when viewed in the actual output-image viewing conditions, will match the appearance of the encoded stimulus if it were viewed in the encoding reference viewing conditions. Because some of the resulting output color stimulus values may be outside the color gamut and/or luminance dynamic range of the output device or medium, some form of gamut adjustment (mapping) must be included in the output signal processing. The gamut-adjusted values then are transformed to output device code values, using the characterization and calibration methods described previously (Chapter 13). The final example of this chapter, Example 12, illustrates the overall approach.

Figure 18.13
The three basic functions of output signal processing.

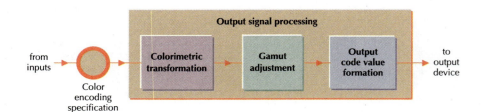

Example 12

In this example (Fig. 18.14a), the output is to a reflection printer. The output-image option is to produce a displayed print that matches the color appearance described by the encoding. A source simulating CIE Standard Illuminant D_{55} will be used to illuminate the output print, which will be viewed in the following conditions:

- *Viewing Flare:* Viewing flare luminance, due to front surface reflection from the print, will be about 2.0% that of a white in the print.
- *Surround Type:* The print will be surrounded by a neutral gray area of approximately 20% reflectance.
- *Luminance Level:* The luminance of a white in the print will be about 150 candelas per square meter.
- *Adaptive White:* The observer will be chromatically adapted to the chromaticity of the D_{55} source ($x = 0.3324, y = 0.3474$).

Because the observer will be chromatically adapted to the chromaticity of the D_{55} light source, encoded colorimetric values first must be transformed from encoding reference D_{50} colorimetric values to equivalent D_{55} colorimetric values. This can be done using the same type of chromatic-adaptation procedure, such as a von Kries transformation, that was used for input encoding. Using the same method for input and output is operationally convenient, and it also results in an important overall symmetry of the system. So, for example, if the adaptive whites of both the input-image and output-image viewing environments are the same, and all other factors are equal, the output colorimetric values will accurately match the input colorimetric values.

The effect of the *additional* 1% viewing flare in the actual output-image viewing conditions, compared to that in the encoding reference viewing conditions, also must be accounted for in the output signal processing. The transformed colorimetric values must be higher in luminance contrast to help compensate for the additional flare (Fig. 18.14c). The transformed values also must be higher in chroma in order to provide compensation for the loss in color saturation produced by the additional viewing flare of the actual output-image viewing conditions (Fig. 18.14d). An output-signal-processing transform for this example can be derived using the procedure illustrated in Fig. 18.14b.

Figure 18.14a

Output to a reflection printer, as described in Example 12.

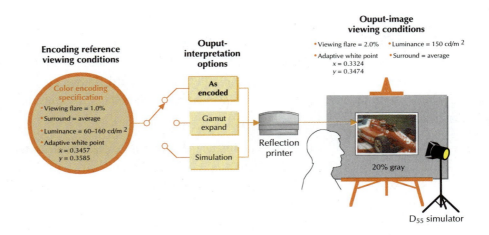

Figure 18.14b

Derivation of an output-signal-processing transform based on Example 12. The colorimetric transform must include a chromatic adaptation transformation of encoded D_{50} values to visually equivalent D_{55} values and a compensation for the additional viewing flare of the output-image viewing environment.

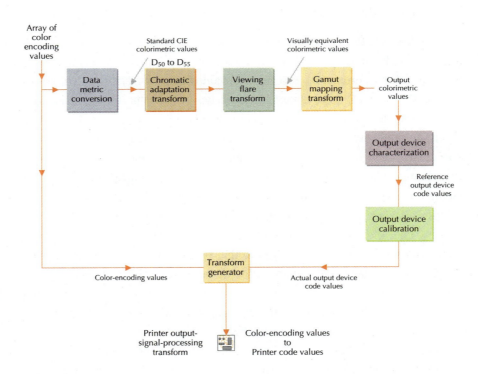

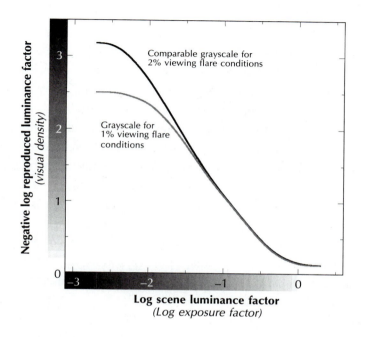

Figure 18.14c
Comparison of reflection-image grayscales that will produce comparable color appearance when viewed in environments having 1% and 2% viewing flare, respectively.

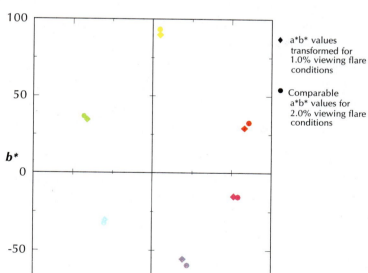

Figure 18.14d
Comparison of reflection-image CIELAB *a**, *b** values that will have comparable color appearance when viewed in environments having 1% and 2% viewing flare, respectively.

Discussion

The greatest challenge in the development of the prototype system came from its complex input/output requirements. The system had to support a highly disparate collection of input devices and media. Moreover, as was discussed earlier, the definition of an input source in the unified paradigm is not limited to the input medium or device; it also includes a user-selected interpretation of input color and a user-specified set of input-image viewing conditions. Thus the number of possible input sources essentially is unlimited. Similarly, in the unified paradigm, the definition of an output includes not only an output device or medium but also a user-selected output interpretation of the encoded color and a user-specified set of output-image viewing conditions.

The prototype system demonstrated that, despite this complexity, the use of appearance-based color-encoding allows color from any system input to be communicated unambiguously, and without a restricted interpretation, to any system output. As a result of this flexibility, this single system can be made to function successfully according to *any* of the *ABC* paradigms.

The prototype system has shown that all aspects of the unified color-management paradigm can be implemented in a practical, but *independent*, color-imaging system. In the next chapter, this discussion of the unified color-management paradigm will continue with a description of how colors can be interchanged successfully among *multiple* systems.

Summary of Key Issues

- A comprehensive prototype color-imaging system has demonstrated the basic technical feasibility of the unified color-management paradigm.

- Appearance-based color encoding is implemented in the system by the use of a colorimetric specification and a defined set of encoding reference viewing conditions.

- Actual and encoding reference viewing conditions are specified in terms of viewing flare, luminance level, surround type, and observer adaptive white.

- In cases where the actual input-image viewing conditions match the encoding reference conditions, input images are encoded directly in terms of standard CIE colorimetric values.

- In cases where the actual input-image viewing conditions differ from the encoding reference conditions, standard colorimetric values of input images are appropriately transformed for encoding.

- In cases where the actual output-image viewing conditions match the encoding reference conditions, colorimetric transformations are not required in the output signal processing. However, gamut mapping and output device characterization transformations are still necessary.

- In cases where the actual output-image viewing conditions differ from the encoding reference conditions, appropriate colorimetric transformations are included in the output signal processing.

19

A Unified Paradigm: Color Interchange

In Chapters 17 and 18, the principles of the unified paradigm were applied to various types of individual color-imaging systems. In this chapter, those same principles will be applied to our ultimate goal—a comprehensive, unified color-management environment. It will be shown that the unifying factor of the environment is the unambiguous and unrestricted communication of color among all systems operating within that environment.

Figure 19.1

A unified color-management environment. Some systems operating within this environment are providing all the functions of the unified paradigm. Others are operating according to various system-specific restrictions.

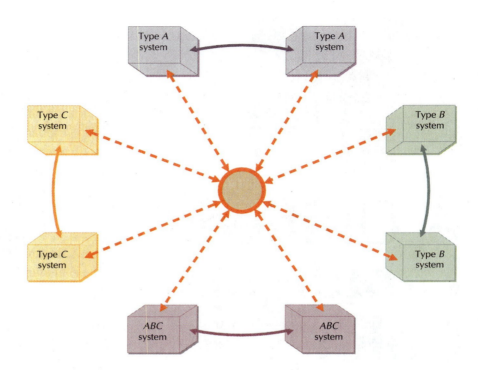

Figure 19.1 illustrates a unified color-management environment in which various types of systems are operating. Some systems (the *ABC* systems) are independently providing all functions of the unified paradigm. Others are operating according to a single Type *A, B,* or *C* paradigm. That is as it should be. There are valid reasons—simplicity, for one—to limit the functionality of particular systems, and a truly unified environment must include such systems.

Similarly, different color-encoding methods and color-encoding data metrics might be used internally on various systems operating within the overall environment. As was discussed earlier, there are important engineering reasons for using different color-encoding methods and data metrics on different types of imaging systems. A color-management environment that excluded systems based solely on their use of particular encoding methods and/or data metrics would not truly be unified.

Figure 19.1 also shows various forms of system-specific color interchange (indicated by the different colored solid arrows) being used between pairs of related systems. For example, two identical imaging systems might be directly interchanging color information encoded in terms of system-specific densitometric or colorimetric values. They might also be using some specific type of device-dependent color-interchange method. Those forms of interchange are unambiguous when they are used between pairs of systems that are based on the same color encoding specification. A unified color-management environment must allow these direct, system-specific forms of color interchange because they generally are fast and efficient. In some cases, they may provide the only practical form of interchange for large amounts of color data between systems of the same type.

However, the ultimate success of a unified color-management environment also requires a *general* form of color interchange (indicated by dashed arrows in the figure) that can be used for communicating color among different, as well as like, types of imaging systems operating within the environment. As with all successful color communication, this communication must be unambiguous. The receiving system should not need to seek additional information in order to interpret an interchanged color. General color interchange also must be unrestricted. The method on which it is based must not impose limitations on luminance dynamic range, color gamut, or color interpretation.

These criteria are identical to those determined earlier as being essential for the *internal* input-to-output communication of color for individual color-imaging systems that are independently capable of providing all the functions of the unified paradigm. Because the criteria are the same, the same appearance-based solution that was used for internal color encoding on those systems can be used for general color communication among systems.

This solution can be expressed in terms of what will be referred to as a *color interchange specification* (CIS). A fully defined CIS must include:

- A complete colorimetric specification of the color to be communicated.
- A fully defined data metric in which to express that colorimetry.
- A specified set of interchange reference viewing conditions.

A color-imaging system can participate in this general color interchange if (and *only* if) its internal color encoding is defined *completely*. The color encoding specification for a system's internal encoding, like a color interchange specification, must include complete descriptions of its colorimetry, data metric, and associated viewing conditions. This degree of specificity is required in order for meaningful conversions to be made from a given system's internal encoding to the interchange specification for outgoing color communication, and from the interchange specification to a system's internal encoding for incoming color communication (Fig. 19.2).

Providing a complete definition of the internal color encoding of a system requires an examination of how that system is used in practice. That can be an interesting exercise. In many cases, it will be found that a system has operated well only because certain rules were adhered to, even though those rules may never have been specified formally. For unambiguous color communication to and from other systems, such rules must be defined explicitly.

For example, one system that we have used for many years consists of a negative-film scanner and several photographic paper writers. In that system, colors are encoded and communicated to the output writers in terms of Status A reflection density values (Fig. 19.3).

Figure 19.2

Use of a color interchange specification (CIS) for color communication between two imaging systems.

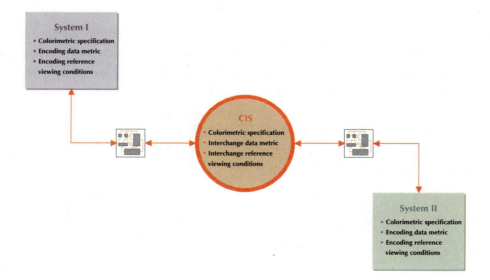

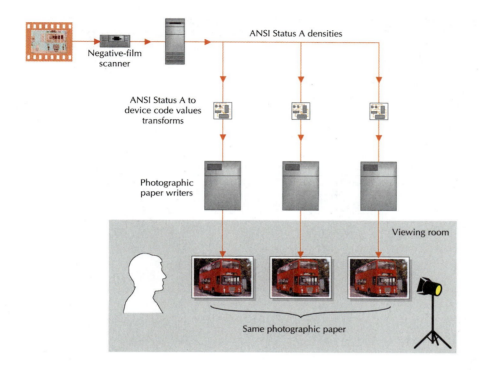

Figure 19.3
An example of system-specific color communication. This type of communication can work successfully, but only if certain rules are adhered to.

That method of color interchange has worked quite well, but only because two unwritten rules always are followed: one, the same photographic paper always is used on each of the output writers; and two, the resulting output prints always are examined in the same viewing room.

For communication with other types of imaging systems in our prototype color-management environment, these rules had to be defined explicitly so that encoded Status A density values could be translated unambiguously to a specification of color appearance. That color-appearance specification then could be expressed in terms of color-interchange values defined according to the CIS of the prototype system.

The definition of the Status A color interchange specification and the definition of the CIS are compared in Table 19.1. Once these definitions were completed, a translation between the two color representations could be developed. That process is discussed next.

Table 19.1

Comparison of a densitometric color interchange specification to the CIS for the prototype unified environment.

	Example System	Prototype CIS
Colorimetry	ISO Status A	1931 CIE
Data metric	Status A density $*$ 100	24-bit CIELAB
Viewing Conditions:		
Viewing flare	1.0%	1.0%
Surround type	Average	Average
Luminance level	150 cd/m²	60 – 160 cd/m²
Adaptive white	$x = 0.3303, y = 0.3395$	$x = 0.3457, y = 0.3585$

Figure 19.4

A transform to convert Status A density values to CIE colorimetric values can be derived from colorimetric measurements of test colors generated from encoded Status A values.

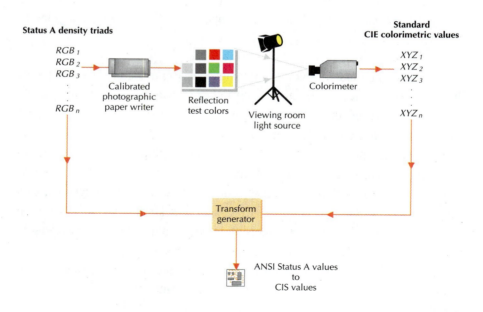

The first step in this translation process was to convert the encoded Status A density values to standard CIE colorimetric values. The conversion was performed using a model of the illuminated photographic paper. The model included the spectral characteristics of the paper's CMY image-forming dyes, the optical characteristics of the paper medium, and the measured spectral power distribution of the viewing-room illuminant. The conversion also could have been derived empirically, using the method illustrated in Fig. 19.4.

The chromaticity coordinates of the viewing-room illuminant then were computed, and those values ($x = 0.3303, y = 0.3395$) were used to determine an appropriate chromatic adaptation transformation (from the viewing-illuminant adaptive white to the D_{50} adaptive white of the CIS).

No other colorimetric transformations were required because the other conditions conformed to the interchange specifications: The room illumination was such that the luminance of a white in a viewed image typically was about 150 cd/m²; the viewing flare luminance was approximately 1% that of a white in a print; and the prints always were viewed on a neutral gray surface of about 20% reflectance, which is consistent with an average-surround condition.

Many commercial systems have operated successfully under similar sets of tacit rules. For example, graphic arts images frequently are interchanged in terms of CMYK values. That interchange has worked reasonably well because what it really has meant is "CMYK values, for a particular assumed set of inks, printed onto an assumed substrate, for images to be viewed under a particular assumed set of conditions." As long as everyone involved in the interchange process follows the same rules, this specialized form of color interchange can be sufficient. For general color interchange, however, CMYK values would have to be translated to colorimetric values, and the image-viewing conditions would have to be defined explicitly so that appropriate color-appearance transforms can be derived.

Similarly, digital images often are interchanged in terms of *RGB* video code values. That also can work without additional transformations if everyone involved uses similar monitors and viewing conditions. But again, for general color interchange, the *RGB* values must be translated to colorimetric values. This can be done by specifying the characteristics of a reference monitor. In addition, a set of monitor-viewing conditions must be defined explicitly.

Interchange Transforms

An interchange transform can be developed for any color-encoding method and data metric that can be *completely* specified in terms of the factors listed in Table 19.1. The transform must account for any differences in the methods used in making colorimetric measurements, for any differences in the data metrics, and for any differences in the viewing conditions associated with the color-encoding method and the color interchange specification involved.

The CIS of our prototype color-management environment is identical to the color encoding specification of our prototype color-imaging system, so no transformation is needed between the two. In most cases, however, transformations will be required. For example, Table 19.2 compares the specifications for *Kodak PhotoYCC* Color Interchange Space to the prototype CIS. Details of the methodology used to form an interchange transformation between the two are given in Appendix G. The basic steps involved in the transformation are shown in Fig. 19.5. For transformation of *PhotoYCC* Space values to CIS values, the steps are as follows:

- Data metric conversion from *PhotoYCC* Space Y, C_1, and C_2 digital code values to *PhotoYCC* Space CIE XYZ tristimulus values

- Adjustment of the XYZ values to compensate for the greater level of viewing flare in the CIS reference viewing conditions

- Further adjustment of the XYZ values to compensate for the lower luminances present in the CIS reference viewing conditions

- Further adjustment of the XYZ values to account for the change in adaptive white chromaticity from that of D_{65} to that of D_{50}

- Metric conversion of the adjusted XYZ values to CIELAB L^*, a^*, and b^* values

- Scaling of the CIELAB L^*, a^*, and b^* values to form digital code values, CV_1, CV_2, and CV_3, as defined by the data metric of the prototype CIS.

	PhotoYCC Space	Prototype CIS
Colorimetry	1931 CIE flareless measurement	1931 CIE flareless measurement
Data metric	*PhotoYCC* Space $Y = (255/1.402)\, Luma$ $C_1 = 111.60\, Chroma_1 + 156$ $C_2 = 135.64\, Chroma_2 + 137$	CIELAB $CV_1 = 2.10\, L^*$ $CV_2 = a^* + 128$ $CV_3 = b^* + 128$
Viewing Conditions:		
Viewing flare	None	1.0%
Surround type	Average	Average
Luminance level	>1,600 cd/m²	60 – 160 cd/m²
Adaptive white	$x = 0.3127, y = 0.3290$	$x = 0.3457, y = 0.3585$

Table 19.2
Comparison of *PhotoYCC* Space and the CIS of the prototype system.

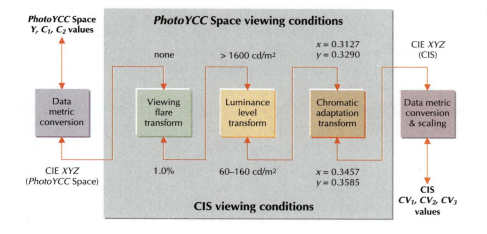

Figure 19.5
Transformation between *PhotoYCC* Space and the CIS of the prototype system.

Discussion

Interchange transforms based on a completely defined, appearance-based color interchange specification do not alter the color appearance represented by the values being transformed. This property is essential for the successful implementation of the unified paradigm. It allows individual systems to use various encoding methods and data metrics most appropriate for their needs, yet it also allows all systems to communicate unambiguously with one another.

The concept of an appearance-based color interchange specification can be used to describe more accurately the critical distinction drawn earlier between a color-encoding *method* and a color-encoding *data metric*. For example, in the discussion of the *Photo CD* System, it was shown why the encoding method generally used on *Photo CD* Imaging Workstations produces *PhotoYCC* Space color values that represent original-scene colorimetry. In the context of a color interchange specification, *PhotoYCC* Space values can be defined more generally as representing *the appearance of colors with respect to a particular set of reference viewing conditions*. Those conditions correspond to conditions typical of outdoor scenes. But the *PhotoYCC* Space data metric itself is completely independent of the source or interpretation of the encoded color.

Kodak PhotoYCC Color Interchange Space therefore can be used to represent *any* color—an outdoor scene color, a reproduced color or a colored object viewed indoors, a color created on a monitor, or color in any other context, as long as that color can be completely defined in terms of its colorimetry, data metric, and associated viewing conditions. When appropriate transformations to the *PhotoYCC* Space data metric are applied, that representation is not altered; yet the resulting values are fundamentally compatible with all other *PhotoYCC* Space values. The reason for this is that, regardless of their source, colors will be encoded in the common context of the *PhotoYCC* Space reference viewing conditions. The use of *Kodak PhotoYCC* Color Interchange Space as a color interchange standard is discussed in greater detail in Appendix G.

With the solution described in this chapter to the problem of general color interchange, nearly everything required for a unified color-management environment is in place. The last piece of the puzzle—a practical architecture for implementation—is the topic of our final chapter.

Summary of Key Issues

- A unified color-management environment must be capable of supporting restricted (as well as unrestricted) color-imaging systems operating within that environment.

- A unified color-management environment must support the internal use of various color-encoding methods and data metrics on systems operating within that environment.

- A unified color-management environment must support the use of various system-specific forms of color interchange among like systems.

- A unified color-management environment also requires a general method for interchanging color among all types of imaging systems operating within the environment.

- General color interchange must be unambiguous and unrestricted; the interchange method itself must not impose limitations on luminance dynamic range, color gamut, or color interpretation.

- In the unified color-management environment, general color interchange among systems is based on a color interchange specification (CIS). The CIS includes a complete colorimetric specification, a fully defined data metric, and a specified set of interchange reference viewing conditions.

- For participation in general color interchange, the internal color encoding of a given system also must be completely defined in terms of its colorimetric specification, data metric, and associated viewing conditions.

- When appropriate techniques are used, interchange transformations retain the color appearance represented by the values to be transformed.

20

A Unified Paradigm: Overall System Architecture

The widespread implementation of the unified color-management paradigm that has been described would be significantly accelerated if the color-imaging industry were to adopt common color-interchange standards and, wherever practical, a common overall color-management architecture. Doing so would greatly facilitate the interchange of digital images among various applications (image-processing, desktop publishing, etc.) and among different computer platforms and operating systems.

A number of individual companies, and industry groups such as the International Color Consortium (ICC), have worked to develop such standards and architectures. Although these efforts are being made by a diverse mix of hardware, software, and media providers, virtually all participants share one common goal: to increase the overall usage of images by promoting interoperability among color-imaging systems.

In this chapter, a number of alternative implementations of the unified paradigm will be discussed in a context based upon one of several possible overall system architectures that could be used to help achieve that goal. Although the described architecture and implementations do not correspond exactly to those presently available, their basic concepts are consistent with many ideas currently being discussed within the color-imaging industry. The terminology used in their description also is consistent with that currently in use.

General Architecture and Components

The architecture that will be described in this chapter incorporates two basic components. The first type, called a *profile,* contains a digital signal-processing transform (or a collection of transforms) plus additional information concerning the transform(s), the device, and the data itself. Input, or *source,* profiles and output, or *destination,* profiles provide the information necessary to convert device color values to-and-from values expressed in a color space that is referred to as a *profile connection space* (PCS). In any practical implementation, detailed format standards for these profiles must be developed so that profiles from different providers can be used interchangeably. The second basic component, a *color-management module* (CMM), is a digital-signal-processing "engine" for performing the actual processing of image data through profiles. A CMM also may perform other computational tasks, as will be described shortly.

Figure 20.1 shows a simple arrangement for connecting a single input device to a single output device, using a source profile, a destination profile, and a CMM. Figure 20.2 shows a more complex multiple input/output arrangement.

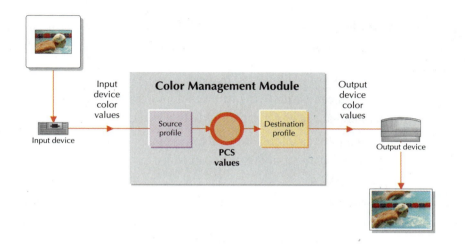

Figure 20.1
Connection of a single input device to a single output device, using a source profile, a destination profile, and a CMM.

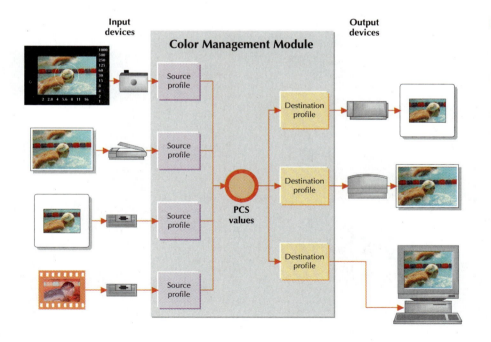

Figure 20.2
A more complex imaging system, having multiple source profiles, multiple destination profiles, and a CMM.

In an overall color-management environment that is based on the use of profiles and CMMs, color-image data can be interchanged unambiguously among imaging systems in three different ways, as illustrated in Fig. 20.3. These three alternatives are as follows:

- Image data can be processed through appropriate source profiles and then interchanged directly in terms of PCS values.

- Image data can be interchanged in terms of input-device values, and an appropriate source profile can be imbedded in the image file for later use by a CMM.

- Image data can be interchanged in terms of device values, but without an imbedded source profile. The image file header then would include an identification tag that can be used by a CMM to select a particular source profile from a stored array of profiles. This third alternative would, of course, require some accepted method for administering the registration of profiles and profile identifiers.

Figure 20.3

Digital images can be interchanged among systems in three different ways.

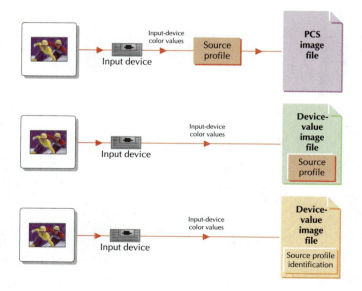

Overall Architecture

One basic concept for an overall architecture is shown below (Fig. 20.4). At the top of the architecture are user applications. These applications are linked to graphics libraries and imaging libraries through an application programming interface (API). The API in turn is linked to a color-management framework. Connected to this framework are individual profiles, which conform to profile format standards, and CMMs. In most cases, a default CMM would be provided by a computer operating system. The architecture also allows for other (perhaps more advanced) CMMs to be provided by other parties. This architectural arrangement provides considerable flexibility, and it allows for future expansion of the overall structure.

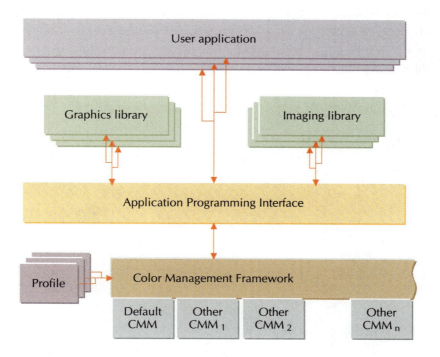

Figure 20.4
One possible overall system architecture for a color-managed environment.

Figure 20.5a
A CMM might
process an image
by first computing
image values
through a source
profile to PCS
values, and by
then computing
those PCS values
through a destina-
tion profile to
output values.

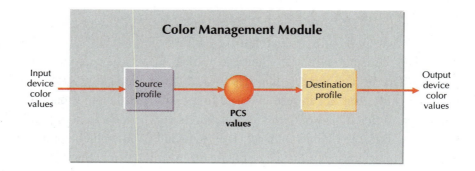

There are two ways that a CMM operating in this architecture might process an image. It might do so by first processing input device color values through a source profile to form PCS values and then processing those values through a destination profile to form output device color values (Fig. 20.5a). A CMM instead might first generate a concatenated composite profile from the separate source and destination profiles and then process input device color values through the composite profile (Fig. 20.5b). The two techniques will yield similar results, although the latter generally is more efficient. It also avoids quantization errors that can occur when PCS values are digitized.

Figure 20.5b
A CMM instead
might generate a
composite profile
from the separate
source and desti-
nation profiles
and then process
image values
through this
composite profile.

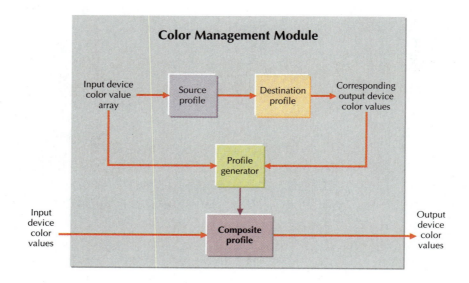

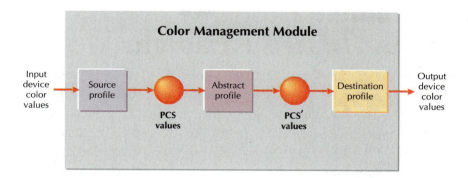

Figure 20.6a
Use of an abstract profile.

The overall architecture also allows the use of other types of profiles, called *abstract* profiles. Abstract profiles can be used to perform operations such as data-metric conversions. They also can be used to implement transformations specified from a user application. For example, an imaging application might create an abstract profile as a means for producing an overall color-balance adjustment to an image. The image then would be processed through the source, abstract, and destination profiles to generate color-balanced output-device values (Fig. 20.6a). Alternatively, a composite profile generated by a concatenation of the three separate profiles could be used (Fig. 20.6b).

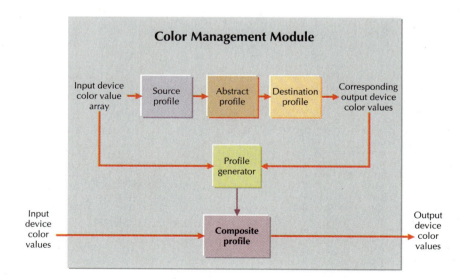

Implementations of the Unified Paradigm

There are several approaches that can be considered for implementing the unified color-management paradigm in an environment based on the described architecture. The first, illustrated in Fig. 20.7, conforms most closely with the general approach used in previous chapters. The source and destination profiles perform all of the input/output transformations (viewing-flare compensations, adaptation adjustments, gamut mappings, etc.) that have been discussed. Other transformations, specified according to various user-selected input options, also are implemented in the profiles. That is why *multiple* source profiles are shown for each input—each profile in the stack represents a different user-specified interpretation of input color. The different destination profiles for a given output device similarly represent various user-selected output options, such as alternative re-rendering or gamut-mapping strategies.

Figure 20.7
In this implementation, the PCS functions as a color encoding specification within a given system, and as a color interchange specification for the overall environment. Since any difficult color transformations are contained in the profiles, the CMM can be basic.

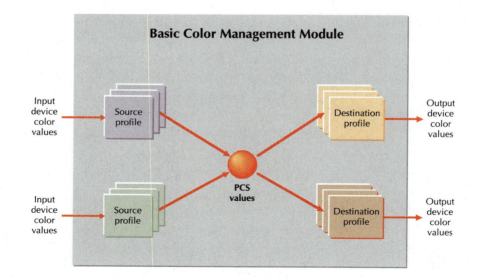

In this implementation, the PCS essentially functions as a color encoding specification (CES) within any given system. The PCS also functions as a color interchange specification (CIS) for the overall environment. In Fig. 20.7, for example, the PCS serves as a CES to connect each system input to its own output, and it serves as a CIS to connect any input of one system to any output of another. The principal feature of this implementation is that a CMM can be very simple; its only function is to provide a direct connection between source and destination profiles. No additional image data identification tags are required, because the source profiles themselves serve to create compatibility among all the input sources.

A second approach, shown in Fig. 20.8, uses simpler source/destination profiles. In this implementation, the profiles might represent transformations to and from standard CIE colorimetric values. This approach requires the use of image file tags or some other means of providing information concerning the type of device, medium, viewing environment, and so on. In addition, it requires a somewhat more advanced CMM that can use that information, together with

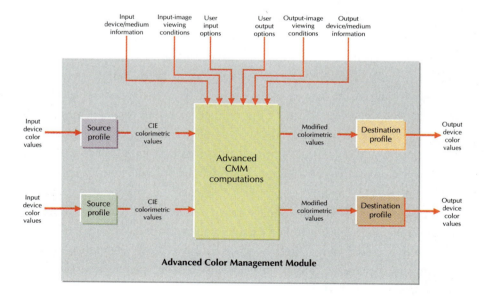

Figure 20.8

In this implementation, the profiles are simpler, and the more difficult transformations are handled by a more advanced CMM.

the information provided by the user's responses to the input and output options of the unified paradigm, to determine the required signal-processing transformations. For example, suppose the input medium is identified as being a photographic slide film, the output is to be an inkjet reflection printer, and the user option is to match the output to the input. The CMM computations would have to include appropriate colorimetric transformations to account for the different viewing conditions associated with the input and output media. The CMM computations also could provide appropriate output color gamut mapping, although that might instead be included in the destination profiles.

Figure 20.9 shows a third approach. In this implementation, simpler source and destination profiles again are used. But instead of the appearance transformations and other difficult transformations being handled entirely by a CMM, they are handled either by the application alone or by some combination of the application and a CMM. This approach, like the second approach, requires image identification tags or some other means for providing information to the application concerning factors such as input/output device types, media, viewing conditions, and color-interpretation options. In the particular implementation shown in Fig. 20.9, that information is used to first construct an abstract profile, which then is used by a basic CMM.

Each of these approaches has important advantages, and each warrants further consideration. However, we believe other approaches that *combine* the best features of the three described approaches also should be considered. We suggest that particular consideration be given to combined approaches in which the color encoding of the PCS is defined such that excellent results can be obtained using *basic* CMMs and user applications. These basic CMMs and applications would only need to provide direct connection of source, abstract, and destination profiles. In addition, however, our proposed approaches would incorporate a tagged image file format. The tagged information would be used by more advanced CMMs and applications that optionally can go beyond the direct connection of profiles. For example, an advanced CMM or application might derive a destination profile incorporating a highly customized gamut-mapping transformation, based on knowledge of the specific input medium, output medium, and user preferences. Again, however, the PCS would be defined such that advanced CMMs and/or applications are not mandatory.

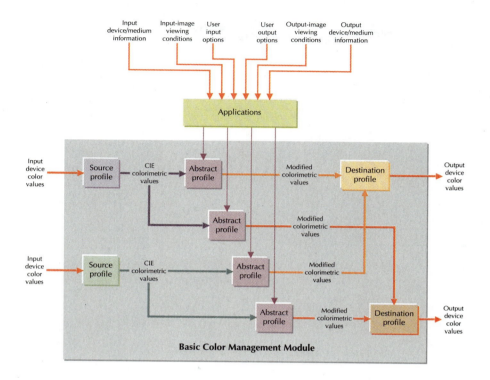

Figure 20.9

In this implementation, a basic CMM can be used because the more difficult color transformations are handled by the application.

One possible combined approach is shown in Fig. 20.10a (and also in Figs. 20.10b and 20.10c). The basic approach is most like that of the first implementation, which was shown earlier in Fig. 20.7, in that the PCS is acting as an appearance-based color encoding specification and color interchange specification. Note, however, that the source and destination profiles have been *split* into two parts.

Source profiles convert input device values to standard colorimetric or densitometric values, and destination profiles convert from standard colorimetric or standard densitometric values to output device values. Additional profiles, containing the more complex color-appearance transformations, then are used to convert between standard colorimetric or densitometric values and PCS values. Figure 20.10b shows a similar arrangement and the optional use of tagged information by an advanced CMM. That CMM derives customized source and/or destination profiles based on the information provided in the tags.

Figure 20.10a

In this split-profile implementation, source and destination profiles convert between standard colorimetric or densitometric values and device values. Additional profiles are used to convert between those standard values and PCS values.

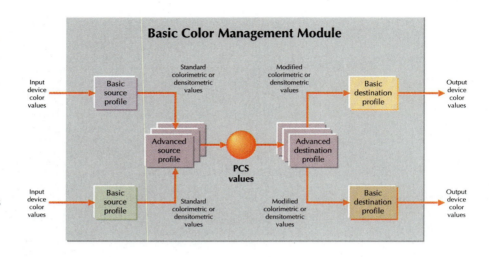

Figure 20.10b

Use of tagged information by an advanced CMM in a split-profile implementation. The advanced CMM derives customized source and/or destination profiles based on the information provided in the tags.

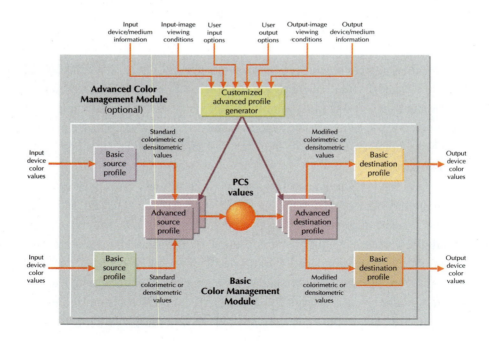

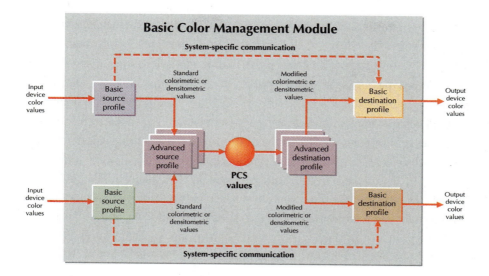

Figure 20.10c
In a split-profile implementation, system-specific color values can be communicated directly (indicated by dashed lines) among related devices. In some implementations, such communication offers faster signal-processing speed and greater accuracy.

One advantage of a split-profile approach is that it allows direct communication of system-specific color values among related devices, as shown in Fig. 20.10c. For example, two related devices might communicate in terms of printing-density values, monitor RGB values, or other system-specific values. In some implementations, this direct communication can offer greater signal-processing speed and accuracy.

Perhaps the most important advantage of the split-profile approach is that it greatly simplifies the task of equipment manufacturers and suppliers who wish to provide profiles for their devices. For example, a scanner or digital-camera manufacturer only would need to provide a relatively simple source profile for transforming input device values to standard colorimetric or densitometric values, rather than a more complex profile that also included color-appearance transformations. Similarly, the manufacturer of an output device only would need to provide a relatively simple destination profile for transforming standard colorimetric or densitometric values to output device code values. Profiles containing the more complex transformations then could be supplied by others, such as color-management software developers.

In practice, it also might be useful to further divide the source and destination profiles into separate *characterization* and *calibration* profiles, as illustrated in Fig. 20.11a. This arrangement is particularly advantageous in imaging systems having multiple input and/or multiple output devices of the same basic type. As explained in Chapter 13, the advantage is that a single (and generally more complex) characterization profile can be used for a number of related devices. Each individual device then only would need a relatively simple calibration profile. Figure 20.11b illustrates this use of multiple calibration profiles, with related characterization profiles, in a split-profile implementation.

In some situations, it would be more advantageous for the calibration profiles to reside in the input/output devices (Fig. 20.11c). For example, in a system that uses many output devices of the same basic type, output image files could be produced by the CMM without requiring knowledge of the specific output device that will be used. Image data then could be sent to any of the output devices because, in a calibrated state, each device matches the characteristics of the reference device for which the characterization profile was derived.

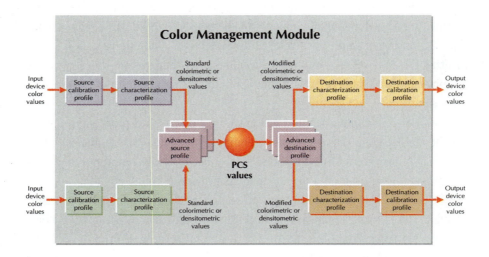

Figure 20.11a
In this split-profile implementation, the source and destination profiles are further divided into characterization and calibration components.

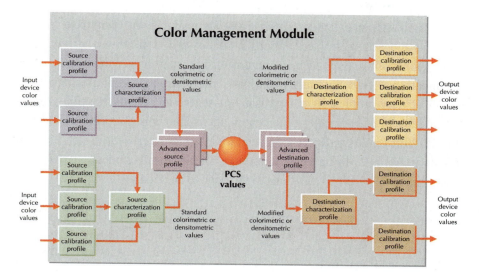

Figure 20.11b
Use of multiple calibration profiles, with related characterization profiles.

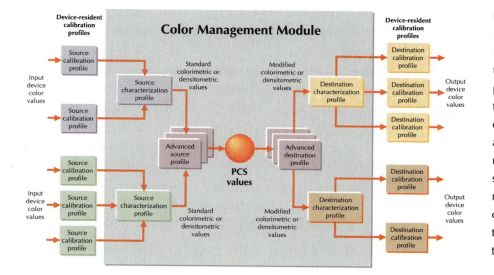

Figure 20.11c
In this split-profile implementation, the calibration profiles reside in the input/output devices. This arrangement is recommended for systems having many input and/or output devices of the same basic type.

Another advantage, shared by all of these split-profile implementations, is that updates can be implemented easily. For example, the technology for performing appearance transformations no doubt will continue to be improved. With split profiles, implementing improvements could be accomplished simply by updating a relatively small number of colorimetry-to-PCS profiles and PCS-to-colorimetry profiles. By comparison, *all* source and *all* destination profiles would have to be replaced in the combined-profile approach previously shown in Fig. 20.7. Similarly, in the advanced-CMM approach shown in Fig. 20.8, all CMMs would have to be updated; and in the advanced-application approach shown in Fig. 20.9, all applications would have to be updated.

Current Implementations

At the time of this writing, many of the ideas that have been discussed here are being put into practice. In particular, the concept of profile connection spaces and color interchange spaces based on colorimetric values and an associated set of reference viewing conditions has been well received.

There are, however, two aspects of some current implementations and specifications that we believe will hinder the completely successful adoption of the unified paradigm. The first is that some system PCSs use media-relative colorimetry. As described earlier, the use of media-relative colorimetry does not produce a proper brightness adjustment of image data. As a result, the interpretation of PCS values alone becomes ambiguous. Although it is possible to get around this problem, doing so *requires* the use of tagged information to define the various media white references used for encoding. Unfortunately, the basic CMMs currently installed in many computer operating systems cannot make use of that tagged information. We believe that the overall color-management environment would be more robust if the ambiguity caused by the use of different media-specific white references was eliminated. This could be done by using color-appearance encoding that is based on brightness-adapted colorimetric values, as described in Chapter 17.

The second problem is that some current specifications define the maximum CIELAB L^* value encodable in the PCS to be 100. This L^* restriction limits encodable luminance dynamic range values such that the full dynamic ranges of current high-quality imaging devices and media are not preserved. In our opinion, specifications being developed today should fully support the capabilities of current media and devices. Moreover, the demands of new imaging devices and media having capabilities greater than those of current products should be anticipated and accommodated in the specifications.

Discussion

A number of different approaches that can be used to implement the unified paradigm have been described in this chapter. It is important to emphasize that regardless of the approach used, the color transformations that are required to produce a given output image from a given input image do not fundamentally change with these different approaches. The approaches differ principally in whether the transformations are performed entirely by profiles alone, by color-management modules alone, by applications alone, or by various combinations of the three. The approaches also may differ in where the transforms reside.

It also is important to emphasize that while different approaches can be used, any successful implementation of the unified paradigm must be based on a meaningful representation of color throughout the color-management environment. As was shown earlier, when the environment is defined to be truly global and completely unrestricted, that representation must unambiguously describe color itself.

Summary of Key Issues

- Implementation of a unified color-management environment would be facilitated by an industry-wide adoption of interchange standards and a common overall architecture.

- Basic architectures similar to those currently being developed within the industry can be used to implement the unified paradigm.

- Although various implementations can be used, the color transformations that are required to produce a given output image from a given input image do not fundamentally change.

- Successful implementation of the paradigm must be based on a meaningful representation of color throughout the color-management environment. When the environment is defined to be global and unrestricted, that representation must unambiguously describe color itself.

Final Thoughts and Conclusions

At the time of this writing, there is not yet an agreed-upon method for interchanging color images among different types of imaging systems. However, there has been a great deal of progress in that direction. Also encouraging is the fact that many of the technical problems discussed in this book are becoming more generally acknowledged and understood.

In particular, there is growing acceptance of the two principal issues that were addressed: first, that digital color encoding involves much more than standard colorimetry; and second, that there is more to successful color interchange than the use of standard file formats and data metrics. There also is a much greater understanding of the need for appearance-based colorimetry, and the need to provide various input-encoding and output-rendering options is gradually becoming more recognized.

Unfortunately, many problems remain. There still are misconceptions regarding the roles of color encoding specifications and color interchange specifications in color communication. There is confusion regarding the concept of encoding reference viewing conditions and the distinction between encoding reference conditions and actual input/output conditions. There also is confusion regarding specific concepts related to reference viewing conditions, such as the distinction between a reference illuminant and a reference adaptive white, the difference between media-relative colorimetry and brightness-adapted colorimetry, and the function of chromatic adaptation transforms. We sincerely hope that our book has helped to clarify these issues.

Of some concern to us is that encoding based on color appearance will be misunderstood as being sufficient to provide a complete solution to color encoding, just as encoding based on standard colorimetry has often been misunderstood to do so. As discussed in the text, appearance-based color encoding provides a means for integrating other color-encoding methods, but it is not a substitute for those methods. Encoding methods that can extract original-scene colorimetry from reproduced images, that can render images from negatives and digital still cameras, and that can re-render reproduced images in various ways are required in order to provide the complete array of input-interpretation options defined by the unified paradigm. Again, we hope that our book has helped to explain such issues.

Despite these concerns, we are optimistic that our ultimate goal of a unified color-management environment for the color-imaging industry someday will be reached. We envision a global environment encompassing a complete hierarchy of imaging systems and applications, from the simplest to the most sophisticated, all operating according to a single underlying paradigm. In this environment, the unifying force will be the unrestricted and unambiguous representation of color.

When this goal is realized, the full potential of digital color imaging will be achievable; and when that happens, imaging applications that we can only imagine today will be accepted as commonplace.

Appendix A:
Colorimetry

References made throughout this book to *standard colorimetry,* or to *standard colorimetric values,* refer to colorimetric values determined according to CIE (Commission Internationale de l'Éclairage) recommended practices. All standard colorimetric values shown have been determined using the color-matching functions for the CIE 1931 Standard Colorimetric Observer (Fig. A1), whose color-matching characteristics are representative of those of the human population having normal color vision. The CIE 1931 Standard Colorimetric Observer is often referred to as the *2° Observer*, because test fields subtending a viewing angle of 2° were used in the judging experiments from which the color-matching functions were derived.

Figure A1

Color-matching functions for the CIE 1931 Standard Colorimetric Observer.

.

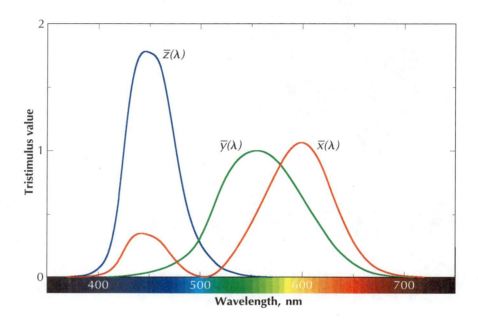

The CIE also has defined the 1964 Supplementary Standard Colorimetric Observer (Fig. A2), often referred to as the *10° Observer*. The color-matching functions of the 10° Observer are used for colorimetric measurements and calculations related to relatively large areas of color. The color-matching functions of the 2° Observer are used for most colorimetric measurements and calculations related to pictorial and graphics imaging, where individual areas of color generally subtend relatively small viewing angles.

The 2° Observer color-matching functions are used in the calculation of CIE tristimulus values X, Y, and Z, which quantify the trichromatic characteristics of color stimuli. The X, Y, and Z tristimulus values for a given object (characterized by its spectral reflectance or transmittance) that is illuminated by a light source (characterized by its spectral power distribution) can be calculated for the 2° Observer (characterized by the appropriate set of CIE color-matching functions) by summing the products of these distributions over the visible wavelength (λ) range (usually from 380 to 780 nm, at 5-nm intervals). The calculation of X, Y, and Z values is shown in Eqs. {A1}, and the basic procedure is diagrammed in Fig. A3.

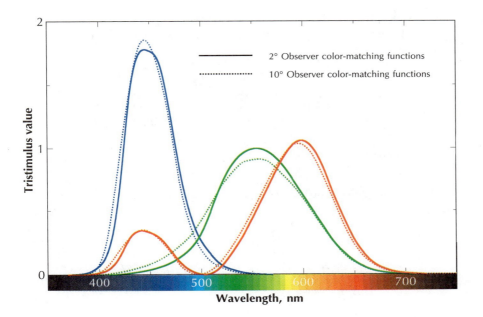

Figure A2
Color-matching
functions defined
for the CIE 1964
Supplementary
Standard Colori-
metric Observer
(10°) and the CIE
1931 Standard
Colorimetric
Observer (2°).

$$X = k \sum_{\lambda=380}^{780} S(\lambda)R(\lambda)\bar{x}(\lambda)$$

$$Y = k \sum_{\lambda=380}^{780} S(\lambda)R(\lambda)\bar{y}(\lambda) \qquad \{A1\}$$

$$Z = k \sum_{\lambda=380}^{780} S(\lambda)R(\lambda)\bar{z}(\lambda)$$

where X, Y, and Z are the CIE tristimulus values; $S(\lambda)$ is the spectral power distribution of the light source; $R(\lambda)$ is the spectral reflectance or transmittance of the object; $\bar{x}(\lambda)$, $\bar{y}(\lambda)$, and $\bar{z}(\lambda)$ are the color-matching functions of the 2° Observer; and k is a normalizing factor. By convention, k generally is determined such that $Y = 100$ when the object is a *perfect white*. A perfect white is an ideal, nonfluorescent, isotropic diffuser with a reflectance (or transmittance) equal to unity throughout the visible spectrum.

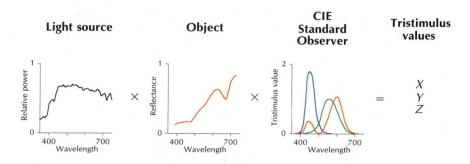

Chromaticity coordinates x, y, and z are derived from the tristimulus values as follows:

$$x = \frac{X}{X + Y + Z}$$

$$y = \frac{Y}{X + Y + Z} \qquad \{A2\}$$

$$z = \frac{Z}{X + Y + Z}$$

The CIE also has recommended the use of other coordinate systems, derived from *XYZ*, in which visual differences among colors are more uniformly represented. These systems include the CIE 1976 u', v' uniform-chromaticity-scale diagram and the CIE 1976 $L^*a^*b^*$ (CIELAB) color space.

In this book, u', v' diagrams (Fig. A4) are used for describing the chromaticities of color primaries, the chromaticity boundaries of color gamuts, and the results of applying chromatic adaptation transformations. The chromaticity values u' and v' are computed from *XYZ* values as follows:

$$u' = \frac{4X}{X + 15Y + 3Z}$$

$$\qquad \{A3\}$$

$$v' = \frac{9Y}{X + 15Y + 3Z}$$

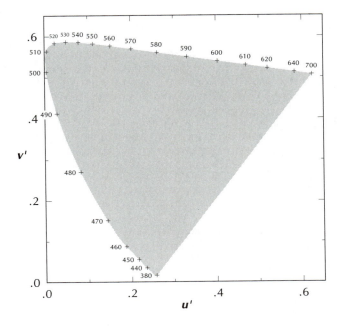

Figure A4
CIE u', v' chromaticity diagram.

Also in this book, CIELAB values are used for making comparisons of colorimetric color reproductions and for describing device and media color gamuts in three dimensions. CIELAB L^*, a^*, and b^* values are computed from the tristimulus values X, Y, and Z of a stimulus, and the tristimulus values X_n, Y_n, and Z_n of the associated reference white, as follows:

$$L^* = 116 \left(\frac{Y}{Y_n}\right)^{(1/3)} - 16 \qquad\qquad \text{for } \frac{Y}{Y_n} > 0.008856$$

$$L^* = 903.3 \left(\frac{Y}{Y_n}\right) \qquad\qquad \text{for } \frac{Y}{Y_n} \leq 0.008856$$

and

$$a^* = 500\left[f\left(\frac{X}{X_n}\right) - f\left(\frac{Y}{Y_n}\right)\right]$$

$$b^* = 200\left[f\left(\frac{Y}{Y_n}\right) - f\left(\frac{Z}{Z_n}\right)\right] \qquad\qquad \{A4\}$$

where

$$f\left(\frac{X}{X_n}\right) = \left(\frac{X}{X_n}\right)^{(1/3)} \qquad \text{for } \frac{X}{X_n} > 0.008856$$

$$f\left(\frac{X}{X_n}\right) = 7.787\left(\frac{X}{X_n}\right) + \left(\frac{16}{116}\right) \qquad \text{for } \frac{X}{X_n} \leq 0.008856$$

$$f\left(\frac{Y}{Y_n}\right) = \left(\frac{Y}{Y_n}\right)^{(1/3)} \qquad \text{for } \frac{Y}{Y_n} > 0.008856$$

$$f\left(\frac{Y}{Y_n}\right) = 7.787\left(\frac{Y}{Y_n}\right) + \left(\frac{16}{116}\right) \qquad \text{for } \frac{Y}{Y_n} \leq 0.008856$$

$$f\left(\frac{Z}{Z_n}\right) = \left(\frac{Z}{Z_n}\right)^{(1/3)} \qquad \text{for } \frac{Z}{Z_n} > 0.008856$$

$$f\left(\frac{Z}{Z_n}\right) = 7.787\left(\frac{Z}{Z_n}\right) + \left(\frac{16}{116}\right) \qquad \text{for } \frac{Z}{Z_n} \leq 0.008856$$

Throughout the book, colorimetric comparisons of original and repro-duced color stimuli are illustrated in terms of vector arrows on CIELAB a^*, b^* diagrams, such as that shown in Fig. A5. In that diagram, the a^*, b^* coordinates of the original color stimuli are represented by the + marks at the tails of the vector arrows. The heads of the arrows represent the coordinates of the corresponding reproduced color stimuli. The lengths of the connecting vectors indicate the magnitudes of the *chromatic* (hue and chroma) differences between the original stimuli and their reproductions. Note, however, that these vectors alone do not completely describe the *colorimetric* differences of the stimuli. Differences in L^* are part of the total colorimetric difference, and L^* differences are not shown on a CIELAB a^*, b^* diagram.

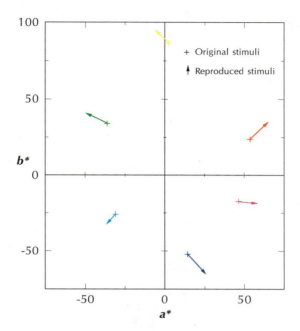

+ Original stimuli

▲ Reproduced stimuli

Figure A5
In CIELAB *a**, *b**
diagrams such as
this, the length of
a vector arrow
connecting two
stimuli indicates
their chromatic
difference.

Appendix B: Densitometry

Throughout this book, the word *density* refers specifically to optical density. Optical density measurements and density-measuring devices (densitometers) are important in color imaging for several reasons: Most forms of color encoding are based directly or indirectly on density readings, most input and output devices are calibrated using density measurements, and most reflection and transmission scanners essentially are densitometers.

Figure B1 illustrates the basic concept of optical density measurement. A densitometer consists of a light source, a means for inserting a sample to be measured, a photodetector, an amplifier, and some type of analog or digital density-value indicator. Density readings are made by measuring the amount of light with and without the sample in place.

For transmissive samples, the transmission density is determined from the transmittance factor of the sample. The transmittance factor, T, is the ratio of the amount of light transmitted, I_t, measured with the sample in place, to the amount of incident light, I_i, measured without the sample (Fig. B2). The transmission density, D_t, of the sample is the negative logarithm of its transmittance factor.

$$T = \frac{I_t}{I_i} \qquad\qquad\qquad \{B1a\}$$

$$D_t = \log_{10}\left(\frac{1}{T}\right) \ \text{ or } -\log_{10}(T) \qquad\qquad \{B1b\}$$

Figure B1

Components of a basic optical densitometer.

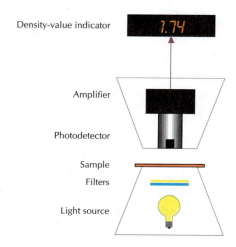

Density-value indicator

Amplifier

Photodetector

Sample

Filters

Light source

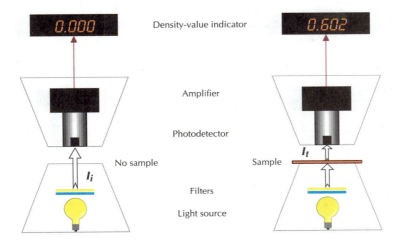

Figure B2
Measurement of transmission density.

The following examples may help to illustrate the basic relationships of sample transmission characteristics, measured transmittance factor, and computed transmission density:

- If a sample were a perfect transmitter, the amount of incident and transmitted light would be equal, the measured transmittance factor would be 1.00, and the computed transmission density of the sample would be zero.

- If a sample were perfectly opaque, the amount of transmitted light would be zero, the measured transmittance factor would be zero, and the computed transmission density would be infinite.

- If a sample transmitted one-quarter of the incident light, the measured transmittance factor would be 0.25, and the computed transmission density would be $-\log_{10}(0.25)$ or 0.602.

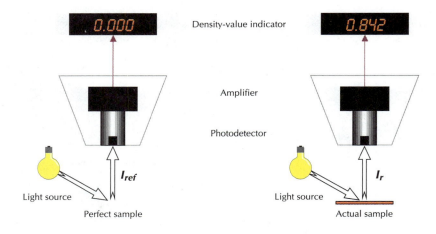

Figure B3
Measurement of reflection density.

Reflection samples are measured similarly (Fig. B3). The ratio of the amount of light reflected by a sample, I_r, relative to that reflected by a perfect diffuse reflector, I_{ref}, is the reflectance factor, R. Reflection density, D_r, is the negative logarithm of the reflectance factor.

$$R = \frac{I_r}{I_{ref}} \qquad\qquad \{B2a\}$$

$$D_r = \log_{10}\left(\frac{1}{R}\right) \ \text{ or } -\log_{10}(R) \qquad\qquad \{B2b\}$$

The concept of density is quite straightforward for samples that are spectrally nonselective, i.e., samples that transmit (or reflect) light equally at all wavelengths of interest (Fig. B4). Since the transmittance or reflectance—and therefore the density—of such samples is the same at every wavelength, it will not matter which wavelengths are used in their measurement.

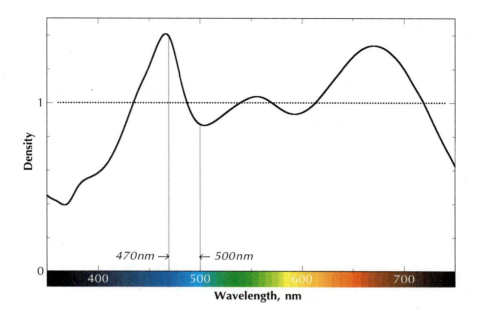

Figure B4
This spectrally selective sample (solid line) has a density of 1.39 at 470 nm, but a density of only 0.87 at 500 nm. A spectrally non-selective sample, such as the one shown by the dotted line, has equal densities at all wavelengths of interest.

In imaging applications, however, samples generally are made up of dyes, inks, or pigments that are spectrally selective, like the selective sample also shown in Fig. B4. When the density of a sample varies with wavelength, it no longer can be said that the sample has a particular density unless the spectral characteristics of the measurement also are specified. For example, the spectrally selective sample in Fig. B4 has a density of 1.39 if measured at 470 nm, but it has a density of only 0.87 if measured at 500 nm.

For color measurements, red, green, and blue densities generally are measured. But again, the spectral characteristics of those measurements must be specified. For example, in Fig. B5, the sample has RGB densities of 1.10, 0.97, and 1.10 respectively when measured using a densitometer having the spectral responsivities shown. In Fig. B6, the same sample has RGB densities of 1.24, 1.00, and 1.16 respectively when measured using a densitometer having somewhat different spectral responsivities.

Figure B5

A spectrally selective sample and a set of red, green, and blue spectral responsivities. The sample (A) has *RGB* density values of 1.10, 0.97, and 1.11 when measured by a densitometer having the RGB responsivities shown in B.

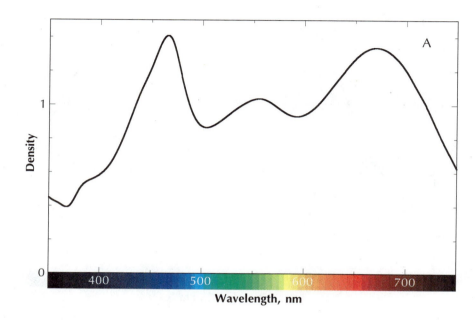

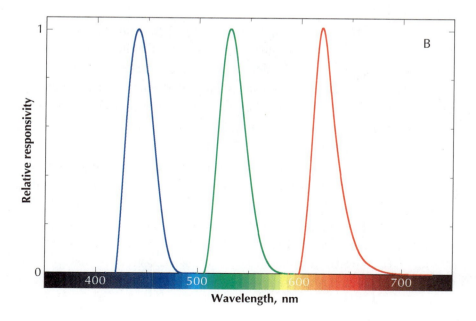

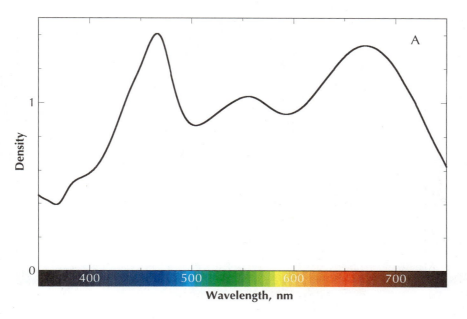

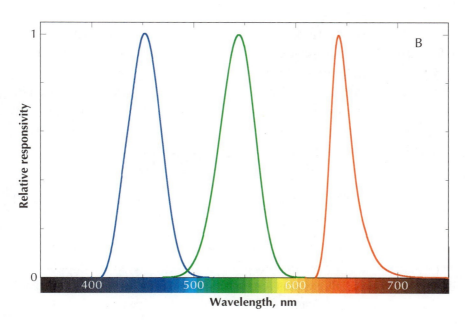

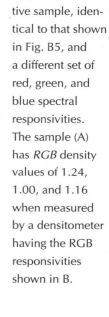

Figure B6
A spectrally selective sample, identical to that shown in Fig. B5, and a different set of red, green, and blue spectral responsivities. The sample (A) has *RGB* density values of 1.24, 1.00, and 1.16 when measured by a densitometer having the RGB responsivities shown in B.

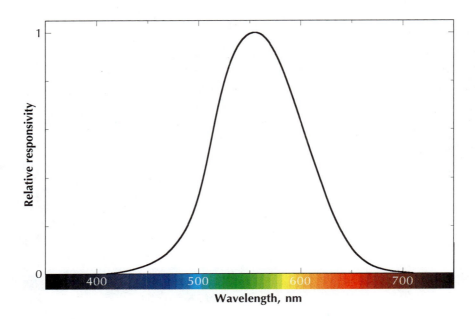

In this book, several different types of density measurements, based on different spectral responsivities, are used: *visual* densities; ISO *Status A* and *Status M* densities; *scanner* densities; and *printing* densities.

Visual densities, which are used throughout the book to express grayscale characteristics, are measured according to a responsivity equivalent to the CIE XYZ $\bar{y}(\lambda)$ function (Fig. B7). This measurement yields the CIE XYZ Y tristimulus value, and visual density is computed from that value as follows:

$$\text{Visual density} = -\log_{10}\left(\frac{Y}{100}\right) \qquad \{B3\}$$

Status A densities are measured using the red, green, and blue responsivities specified by the International Standards Organization (ISO) for Status A densitometers (Fig. B8). Status A densitometers are used in measuring photographic reflection prints and slides and other types of imaging media that are

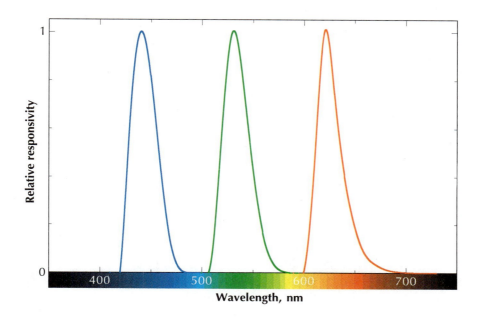

designed to be viewed directly. Note, however, that these responsivities are spectrally narrow. They were *not* designed to correspond to visual sensitivities; they were determined such that each channel primarily measures just one image-forming dye. The blue channel primarily measures the relative amount of yellow dye. Similarly, the green channel primarily measures the relative amount of magenta dye, and the red channel primarily measures the relative amount of cyan dye. This type of measurement is useful for monitoring media manufacturing operations and subsequent image-forming processes.

   Status M densities are measured using the red, green, and blue responsivities specified by the ISO for Status M densitometers (Fig. B9). Status M densitometers are used in measuring photographic negative media. Like those of Status A densitometers, the responsivities of Status M densitometers are spectrally narrow so that each channel primarily measures just one image-forming dye. Status M measurements are useful for monitoring negative film manufacturing operations and subsequent chemical processing.

Figure B9
Spectral respon-
sivities for an
ISO Status M
densitometer.

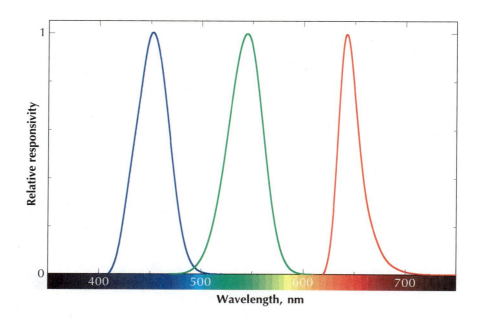

Scanner densities are densities measured by an input scanner having a particular set of *effective spectral responsivities, ESR*(λ). The effective responsivities are the product of the spectral sensitivity of the sensor and the spectral characteristics of any components in the optical chain that contribute to the overall spectral responses. These components include the scanner light source, lenses, mirrors, and filters. For example, the effective responsivity for one of the color channels of a scanner would be:

$$ESR(\lambda) = S(\lambda)M(\lambda)L(\lambda)F(\lambda)Ssens(\lambda) \qquad \{B4\}$$

where $ESR(\lambda)$ is the effective responsivity of the channel, $S(\lambda)$ is the spectral power distribution of the scanner light source, $M(\lambda)$ is the spectral reflectance of a mirror, $L(\lambda)$ is the spectral transmittance of a lens, $F(\lambda)$ is the spectral transmittance of a filter (or a series of filters) in the optical path of the particular color channel, and $Ssens(\lambda)$ is the spectral sensitivity of the sensor.

Printing densities are the densities that would be measured by a real or computational densitometric device having effective spectral responsivities equivalent to those of a particular photographic print medium and a specified printer. These effective responsivities are the product of the spectral sensitivity of the print medium and the spectral characteristics of any components in the printer that contribute to the overall spectral responses, such as the printer light source, lenses, mirrors, and filters. For example, the effective red spectral responsivity would be:

$$ESR_{Red}(\lambda) = S(\lambda)M(\lambda)L(\lambda)F(\lambda)Sens_{Red}(\lambda) \qquad \{B5\}$$

where $ESR_{Red}(\lambda)$ is the red-channel effective responsivity, $S(\lambda)$ is the spectral power distribution of the printer light source, $M(\lambda)$ is the spectral reflectance of a mirror in the printer optics, $L(\lambda)$ is the spectral transmittance of the printer lens, $F(\lambda)$ is the spectral transmittance of a filter (or a series of filters) in the optical path of the particular color channel, and $Sens_{Red}(\lambda)$ is the red spectral sensitivity of the print medium.

The red transmittance factor T_{Red}, for a sample having the spectral transmittance $T(\lambda)$, measured according to the red-channel effective spectral responsivity $ESR_{Red}(\lambda)$, can be calculated as follows:

$$T_{Red} = k_R \sum_{\lambda} T(\lambda)ESR_{Red}(\lambda) \qquad \{B6\}$$

where k_R is a normalizing factor, determined such that $T_{Red} = 1.00$ when the sample is a perfect transmitter. The red printing density, PD_{Red}, of the sample then can be calculated as follows:

$$PD_{Red} = -\log_{10}(T_{Red}) \qquad \{B7\}$$

Green and blue effective responsivities, transmittance factors, and printing density values can be calculated similarly.

Appendix C: Photographic Media

Three principal types of conventional photographic media are referred to throughout this book: photographic *negative films,* such as those widely used in still and motion picture cameras; photographic *print media,* such as photographic papers and print films respectively used for making reflection and transmission prints from photographic negative films; and photographic *transparency films,* such as projection slide films and larger-format sheet films generally used with back illumination.

Photographic Negative Films and Print Media

Figure C1 shows a simplified cross-section of a photographic negative film. The film has a blue-light-sensitive layer, a green-light-sensitive layer, and a red-light-sensitive layer coated on a transparent support. Because the green-light and red-light-sensitive layers are also inherently sensitive to blue light, a yellow filter layer is coated above these layers to prevent blue light from reaching them. This layer is made colorless during subsequent chemical processing of the film.

The light sensitivity of each layer is due to the silver halide grains that are dispersed within the layer. The grains of each layer are chemically treated during the manufacturing process in order to produce the appropriate spectral sensitivity for the particular layer. The resulting red, green, and blue spectral sensitivities for a typical photographic negative film are shown in Fig. C2. Also dispersed in each layer is an appropriate *coupler*. The function of the coupler will be explained shortly.

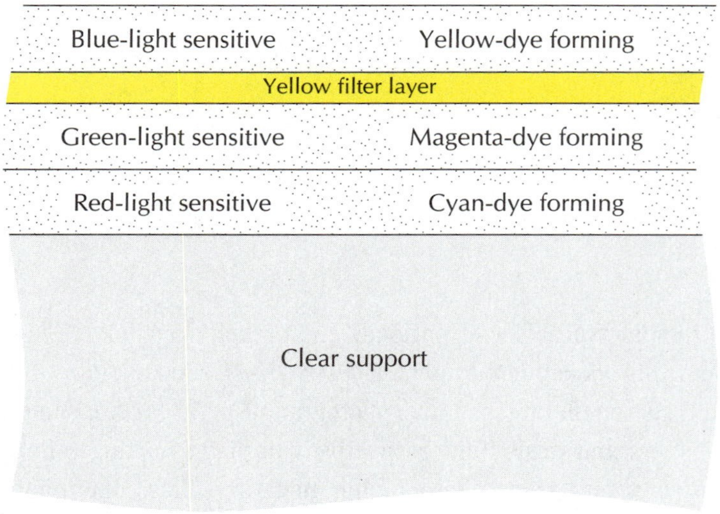

Figure C1
Simplified cross-section of a color negative film (prior to chemical processing).

Blue-light sensitive	Yellow-dye forming
Yellow filter layer	
Green-light sensitive	Magenta-dye forming
Red-light sensitive	Cyan-dye forming

Clear support

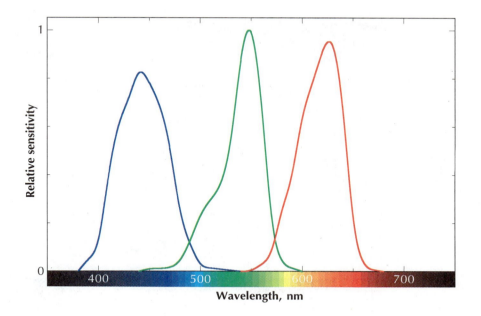

Figure C2
Spectral sensitivities for a typical photographic negative film.

When an exposed photographic negative film is chemically processed, yellow, magenta, and cyan image dyes are formed in the blue-light, green-light, and red-light-sensitive layers, respectively. The nature of the chemical processing is such that a *negative* image results, i.e., the *maximum* amount of dye forms at the *maximum* exposure; the *minimum* amount of dye forms at the *minimum* exposure. Also during chemical processing, the yellow filter layer is made colorless.

Figure C3 (a) shows a series of color stimuli that are to be photographed by a photographic negative film. Figure C3 (b) shows how each layer of the film is affected by exposure to the stimuli. The red stimulus exposes primarily the red-light-sensitive (bottom) layer, leaving the other layers essentially unexposed. Similarly, the green stimulus exposes primarily the green-light-sensitive (middle) layer, and the blue stimulus exposes primarily the blue-light-sensitive (top) layer. The other stimuli represent mixtures of additive primaries, and thus they will expose more than one layer of the negative.

Figure C3
Effect of various color stimuli on a photographic negative film, and the results of printing that film onto a photographic print medium.

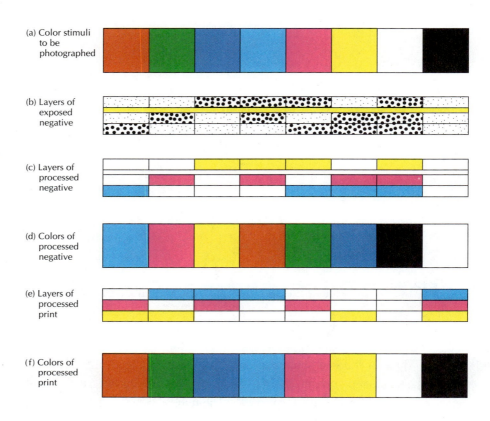

(a) Color stimuli to be photographed

(b) Layers of exposed negative

(c) Layers of processed negative

(d) Colors of processed negative

(e) Layers of processed print

(f) Colors of processed print

The cyan (green plus blue) stimulus exposes primarily the green-light-sensitive and blue-light-sensitive layers, leaving the red-light-sensitive layer essentially unexposed. Similarly, the magenta (red plus blue) stimulus exposes primarily the red-light-sensitive and blue-light-sensitive layers, leaving the green-light-sensitive layer essentially unexposed, and the yellow (red plus green) stimulus exposes primarily the red-light-sensitive and the green-light-sensitive layers, leaving the blue-light-sensitive layer essentially unexposed. The white (red plus green plus blue) stimulus exposes all three layers, and a black stimulus leaves all layers essentially unexposed.

Figure C3 (c) shows the effect of subsequent chemical processing of the negative film. Note that a negative image, having colors complementary to those of the stimuli, has been formed. Where there was red exposure, there is cyan dye; where there was green exposure, there is magenta dye; and where there was blue exposure, there is yellow dye. Figure C3 (d) shows the resulting colors on the negative film.

Figure C3 (e) shows the result of exposing the negative film onto an appropriate photographic print medium and subsequently processing that print medium. Photographic print media intended for this purpose are also *negative working,* i.e., the amount of image dye they form increases with increased exposure of the medium. The result of exposing one negative medium onto another negative medium is a positive image, as shown in Fig. C3 (f). Print media having a paper support are used to make reflection-print images, and media having a clear support are used to make images for projection or back illumination.

Image dye formation in photographic negative media results from two basic chemical reactions. First, a negative black-and-white silver image is formed when exposed silver halide grains are chemically developed. The unexposed grains do not develop. In this development reaction, exposed silver halide (AgX_{exp}) is reduced by the developing agent to form metallic silver (Ag^0), a halide ion (X^-) is produced, and the developing agent itself is oxidized:

$$AgX_{exp} + \text{Developer} \rightarrow Ag^0 + X^- + \text{Oxidized developer} \qquad \{C1\}$$

Special developing agents are used such that the resulting oxidized developer is "half" of a dye molecule. The other "half" of the dye molecule is the coupler mentioned earlier. Different couplers are incorporated in the red-light, green-light, and blue-light-sensitive layers such that cyan, magenta, and yellow dyes image are produced, respectively. These image dyes are formed by the reactions of oxidized developer with the respective couplers:

$$\text{Oxidized developer} + \text{Cyan-dye-forming coupler} \rightarrow \text{Cyan dye}$$

$$\text{Oxidized developer} + \text{Magenta-dye-forming coupler} \rightarrow \text{Magenta dye} \qquad \{C2\}$$

$$\text{Oxidized developer} + \text{Yellow-dye-forming coupler} \rightarrow \text{Yellow dye}$$

In addition to their primary role of forming image dyes within each layer of a film, reactions {C1} and {C2} provide several opportunities to create desirable interactions among the layers. As explained in Part II, interactions among the color channels are required in virtually all color-imaging systems in order to achieve an appropriate level of overall color saturation and to produce other desirable colorimetric results. In photographic negative films and other silver-halide based photographic media, chemical interactions called *inter-layer effects* are used to produce these necessary color interactions. Various chemical techniques are used such that silver and/or image-dye formation in one film layer influences the amount of image dye that is formed in one or both of the other two layers.

Figure C4 illustrates the basic nature of an interlayer effect. The figure shows cross-sections of two photographic negative films. Both films have been exposed to green light that logarithmically increases in intensity from left to right. As a result of this exposure, the amount of magenta dye that forms in the green-light-sensitive layer of the processed film also will increase from left to right. In addition, both films have been exposed to red light of uniform intensity from left to right. The film on the left has no chemical interlayer interactions, so the amount of cyan dye that forms in the red-light-sensitive layer is uniform from left to right (like the light that exposed it). The film on the right shows a chemical interlayer interaction. Chemical by-products generated during the silver-formation reaction {C1} and/or by the dye-formation reaction {C2} travel to the red-light-sensitive layer and inhibit the formation of silver and/or image dye in that layer. The amount of cyan dye that forms in the red-light-sensitive layer therefore is reduced in proportion to the amount of magenta dye that forms above it.

The chemical interlayer interaction shown in the figure can be created by a number of different mechanisms. For example, the red-light-sensitive layer can be made responsive to the amount of halide ion created by silver development reaction {C1} in the green-light-sensitive layer. Also, a special coupler can be used in the green-light-sensitive layer so that a development inhibitor is released during the dye formation reaction {C2}.

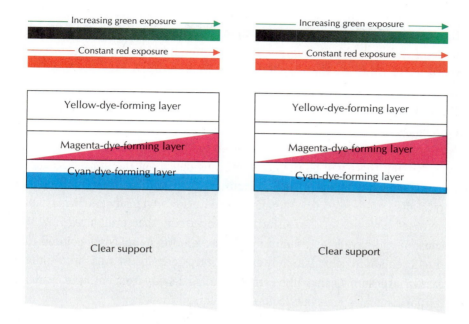

Figure C4

Film cross-sections for two photographic negative films. The film on the left does not exhibit a chemical interlayer effect; the amount of cyan dye that forms in the red-light-sensitive layer is independent of the amount of magenta dye that forms above it. The film on the right does exhibit a chemical interlayer effect; the amount of cyan dye that forms is reduced in proportion to the amount of magenta dye that forms above it.

Why Photographic Negative Films Are Orange

The overall orange cast of virtually all color photographic negative films results from another type of color-correction mechanism that primarily is used to compensate for the cross-talk that occurs in the transfer of color information from the negative to a print material. This cross-talk was discussed in some detail in Chapter 7. The compensating mechanism derives from the image-dye-formation reaction {C2} discussed previously.

As that reaction progresses, coupler is used as image dye is formed. So if the coupler itself has some color to it, *that* color will go away as image dye is formed. This provides a means to compensate for certain unwanted spectral absorptions, as "seen" by the print material, of the image dye that is formed.

For example, suppose that in addition to having red printing density, the cyan dye that forms also has unwanted green printing density (Fig. C5). The more of this cyan dye that forms, the more unwanted green printing density there will be (Fig. C6). However, if the cyan-dye-forming coupler *itself* has green printing density (in other words, if the coupler is magenta colored, as shown in Fig. C7), *that* green printing density will go *away* as the coupler is used to form cyan image dye.

As Fig. C8 shows, where there is *no* red-light exposure, there will be no cyan dye, but there will be the green printing density of the unused magenta-colored coupler. Where there is *full* exposure, there will be a maximum amount of cyan dye, so there will be a maximum red printing density and a maximum amount of unwanted green printing density from that cyan dye. However, because it will have been used to form the cyan dye, no magenta-colored coupler will remain to contribute any green printing density. In areas where there is *partial* exposure, there will be green printing density from both the cyan dye and from any unused magenta-colored coupler.

If the appropriate amount of a coupler having the appropriate spectral absorption characteristics is used, the green printing density will stay *constant* as a function of red-light exposure (Fig. C9). The entire image therefore will have an overall magenta cast, but that cast can be compensated for by the use of more green light when the negative is printed. Because the colored coupler effectively will have corrected for the unwanted green absorption of the negative's cyan dye, a final print will look the same as a print made from a negative having a cyan dye with no unwanted green-light absorption.

In practice, colored couplers are incorporated in the cyan and magenta dye-forming layers of virtually all color negative films. The colored coupler in the cyan layer is magenta-yellow; it corrects for the cyan image-forming dye's unwanted green and blue density. The colored coupler in the magenta layer is yellow; it corrects for the magenta image-forming dye's unwanted blue density. It is the presence of these magenta-yellow and yellow colored couplers that gives negative films their characteristic overall orange cast.

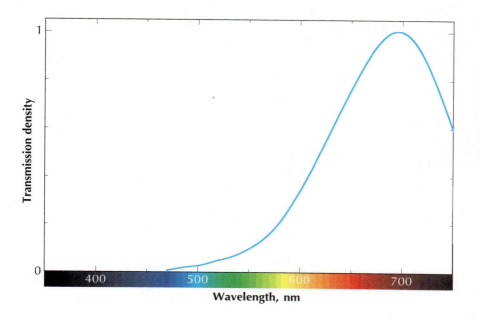

Figure C5
Spectral characteristics of a cyan dye having unwanted green printing density, as measured according to the spectral responsivities shown below.

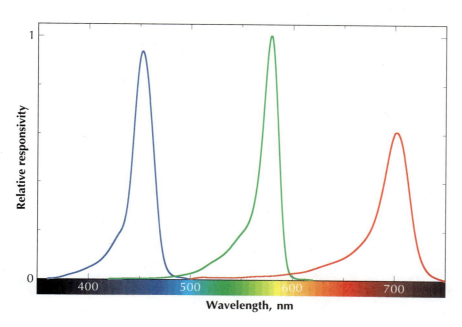

Figure C6

As the amount of cyan dye in a negative increases, the red printing density will increase. The green printing density also will increase with the amount of cyan dye due to the unwanted absorption of green light by that cyan dye.

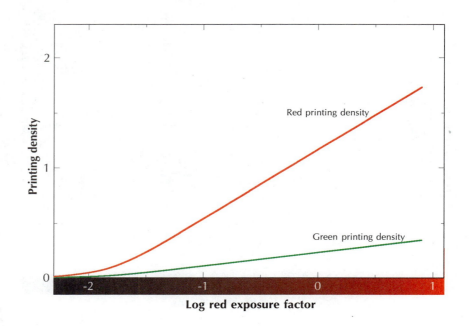

Figure C7

Spectral transmission density of a cyan-dye-forming colored coupler. The coupler itself is magenta, so it absorbs green light. Its use compensates for the unwanted green-light absorption of the cyan dye.

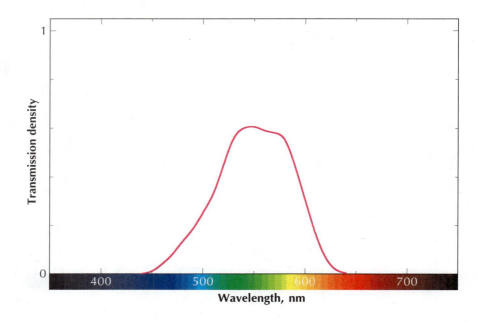

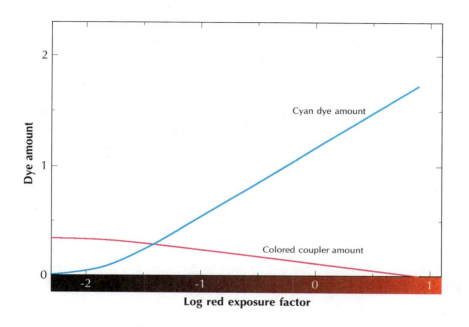

Figure C8
At minimum red exposure, there is minimum cyan dye and maximum colored coupler. At maximum red exposure, there is maximum cyan dye and minimum colored coupler. At intermediary exposures, cyan dye and unused colored coupler both are present.

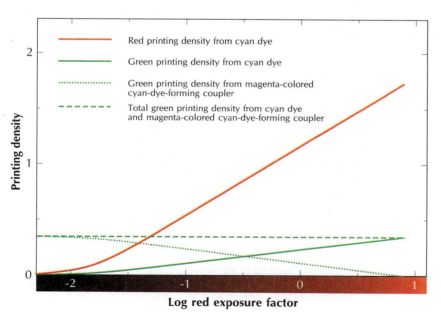

Figure C9
When a magenta-colored cyan-dye forming coupler is used in a color negative film, the green printing density of that film becomes independent of the amount of cyan dye that is formed. The resulting overall magenta cast is accounted for in printing.

Photographic Transparency Films

Figure C10 shows a simplified cross-section of a photographic transparency film. Like a photographic negative film, a photographic transparency film has a blue-light-sensitive layer, a green-light-sensitive layer, and a red-light-sensitive layer coated on a clear support. Because the green-light and red-light-sensitive layers also are inherently sensitive to blue light, a yellow filter layer must be coated above these layers to prevent blue light from reaching them. The red, green, and blue spectral sensitivities for a representative photographic transparency film are shown in Fig. C11.

When an exposed photographic transparency film is chemically processed, yellow, magenta, and cyan image dyes are formed in the blue-light, green-light, and red-light-sensitive layers, respectively. The nature of the chemical processing is such that a *positive* image results, i.e., the *maximum* amount of dye forms at the *minimum* exposure; the *minimum* amount of dye forms at the *maximum* exposure. Also during chemical processing, the yellow filter layer is made colorless.

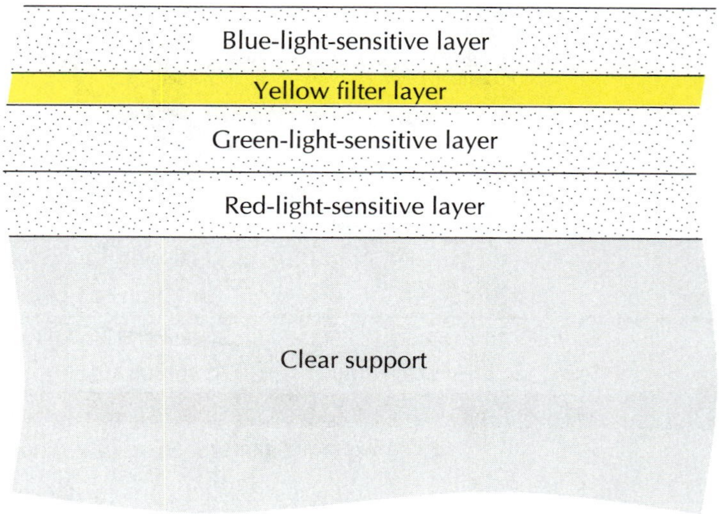

Figure C10

Simplified cross-section of a color photographic transparency film (prior to chemical processing).

Blue-light-sensitive layer

Yellow filter layer

Green-light-sensitive layer

Red-light-sensitive layer

Clear support

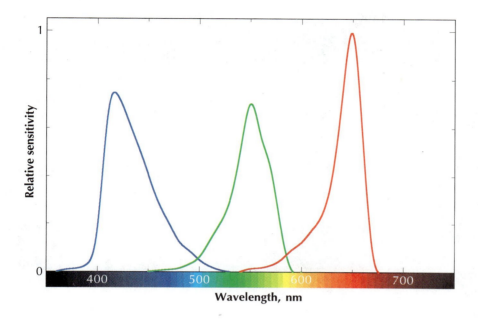

Figure C11
Spectral sensitivities for a typical photographic transparency film.

Figure C12 (a) shows a series of color stimuli that are to be photographed by a photographic transparency film. Figure C12 (b) shows how each layer of the film is affected by exposure to the stimuli. Figure C12 (c) shows the effect of subsequent chemical processing of the transparency film. In this processing, a negative silver image first is formed from the exposed silver halide. That image then is removed chemically, and a dye image is produced from the remaining (unexposed) silver halide. The result is a positive image having colors corresponding to those of the photographed stimuli, as shown in Fig. C12 (d). For example, where there was red exposure, there is magenta and yellow dye (a red image); where there was green exposure, there is cyan and yellow dye (a green image); and where there was blue exposure, there is cyan and magenta dye (a blue image).

Because photographic transparency films usually are intended to be viewed directly, the couplers incorporated in these films must be colorless. Desirable interlayer interactions therefore must be created using chemical mechanisms, which generally are based on the silver-development reaction {C1}.

Figure C12

Effect of various color stimuli on a photographic transparency film.

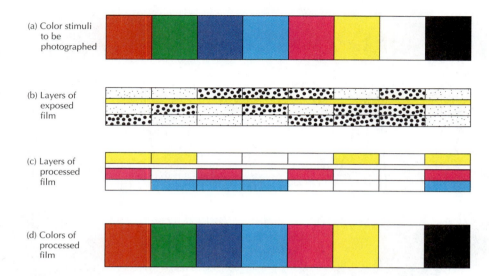

(a) Color stimuli to be photographed

(b) Layers of exposed film

(c) Layers of processed film

(d) Colors of processed film

Appendix D:
Adaptation

The term *adaptation* refers to various processes by which the visual mechanism adjusts to the conditions under which the eyes are exposed to radiant energy. The relationship between the physical characteristics of a given color stimulus and the perception of its color is strongly influenced by effects produced by a number of different forms of adaptation.

In this book, three types of visual adaptation of particular importance in color-imaging applications are considered: general-brightness adaptation, lateral-brightness adaptation, and chromatic adaptation.

General-Brightness Adaptation

General-brightness adaptation refers to the adjustments of the visual mechanism in response to the average luminance of the stimuli to which the eyes are exposed. General-brightness adaptation must be considered in the encoding of images displayed in viewing conditions in which the observer fully or partially adapts to the displayed image itself. Such adaptation will occur when images are viewed under conditions that eliminate or minimize other visual cues that might influence the adaptive state of the observer.

The following describes one procedure that can be used to transform the colorimetry of an image to *brightness-adapted* colorimetry. The procedure accounts for general-brightness adaptation effects.

First, the *XYZ* tristimulus values for each image pixel are determined, using standard colorimetric methods. Each *Y* tristimulus value then is adjusted by an experimentally determined scale factor, *B,* to form an adjusted tristimulus value, Y_b:

$$Y_b = BY \qquad\qquad \text{\{D1\}}$$

The value for the scale factor, *B,* will vary depending on the conditions of the viewing environment. For a reflection image, viewed in a normal environment, the factor is 1.0. For a transmission image, projected in a darkened environment, the factor will be greater than 1.0. This means that the projected image appears brighter than would be indicated by its unadjusted colorimetric values.

The *X* and *Z* tristimulus values of each pixel then are scaled by the ratio of the Y_b tristimulus value to the unadjusted tristimulus value, *Y.* This equal scaling of the tristimulus values maintains the chromaticity of the pixel:

$$X_b = X\left(\frac{Y_b}{Y}\right) = BX \qquad\qquad \text{\{D2a\}}$$

$$Z_b = Z\left(\frac{Y_b}{Y}\right) = BZ \qquad\qquad \text{\{D2b\}}$$

The effect of a general-brightness adaptation transformation from a dark-projection environment to a normal environment is shown in the measured and adjusted grayscales of Fig. D1. The adjusted grayscale produced by the transformation does *not* describe what images on the measured film would look like if viewed in the normal environment. The adjusted grayscale instead defines the film grayscale that *would be required* in the normal environment to produce images that match the brightness of images produced when the measured film is projected in a darkened environment.

Note that the general-brightness transformation results in a downward shift in overall visual density; the photographic gamma (slope) of the curve is not affected by the transformation. However, the dark-surround viewing conditions leading to the shift in observer general-brightness adaptation also may induce *lateral*-brightness adaptation effects. These effects do require compensating photographic gamma adjustments, as discussed next.

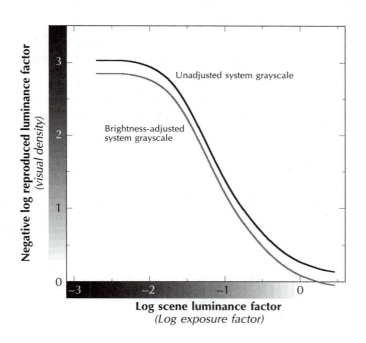

Figure D1
The effect of a general-brightness adaptation transformation. The transformation determines the grayscale required to produce images in an average environment that match the relative brightnesses of images projected in a darkened environment.

Lateral-Brightness Adaptation

Lateral-brightness adaptation refers to changes in the sensitivities of areas of the retina as a function of light being received by adjacent receptors. One manifestation of lateral-brightness adaptation is that the perceived luminance contrast of an image is lowered if the areas immediately surrounding the image are relatively dark. This effect, sometimes called the *dark-surround effect,* occurs when an image, such as a photographic slide or motion picture, is projected in a darkened environment, and the viewing arrangement is such that the surround fills a substantial portion of the observer's field of view. A significant, but somewhat smaller, effect occurs in some displays of video images where the displayed image is viewed in a room that is dimly illuminated, but not completely dark. Again, the viewing arrangement must be such that the surround fills a substantial portion of the observer's field of view.

The following procedure is one method that can be used to transform the measured colorimetry of an image to *surround-adjusted* colorimetry. The procedure accounts for lateral-brightness adaptation effects.

First, the *XYZ* tristimulus values for each image pixel are determined, using standard colorimetric methods. Each *Y* tristimulus value then is modified by an experimentally determined power factor, *S,* to form a visually equivalent tristimulus value, Y_S, for the different surround:

$$Y_S = Y^S \qquad\qquad \text{\{D3\}}$$

The *X* and *Z* tristimulus values for the stimulus then are scaled by the ratio of the Y_S tristimulus value to the unmodified tristimulus value, *Y*:

$$X_S = X\left(\frac{Y_S}{Y}\right)$$
$$Z_S = Z\left(\frac{Y_S}{Y}\right) \qquad\qquad \text{\{D4\}}$$

This scaling maintains the chromaticity values (x, y) for the stimulus. In certain other lateral-brightness adaptation procedures, the chromaticity values are adjusted such that the chroma of the stimulus also is modified.

Applying a lateral-brightness adaptation transformation from darker-surround conditions to lighter-surround conditions ($S < 1.0$) results in a lowering in overall grayscale photographic gamma, as shown in Fig. D2. The meaning of this transformation is that an image having a grayscale of lower photographic gamma would be required in lighter-surround conditions in order to match the luminance contrast of an image viewed in darker-surround conditions.

The value for the power factor, S, will vary depending on the particular conditions of the viewing environment. The magnitude of the dark-surround effect depends on the luminance of the surround relative to the average luminance of the viewed image and on the proportions of the visual fields filled by the image and by the surround.

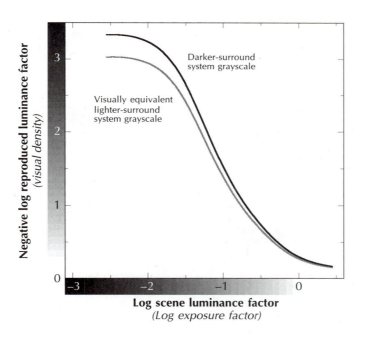

Figure D2
Results of applying a lateral-brightness (or dark-surround) transformation. The transformation accounts for the fact that an image having a grayscale of lower slope would be required in lighter-surround conditions in order to match the luminance contrast of an image viewed in darker-surround conditions.

It should be noted that because viewing conditions that induce lateral-brightness adaptation effects likely will also induce shifts in general-brightness adaptation, the magnitudes for the power-factor value, *S,* and the scale-factor value, *B,* will be related. In practice, both values are best determined from visual judging experiments. Such experiments should be performed using the actual viewing conditions involved. Figure D3 below shows the effect of applying both brightness-adaptation transformations.

Figure D3

Effects of applying lateral-brightness adaptation and general-brightness adaptation transformations to the grayscale visual density values of a photographic slide film.

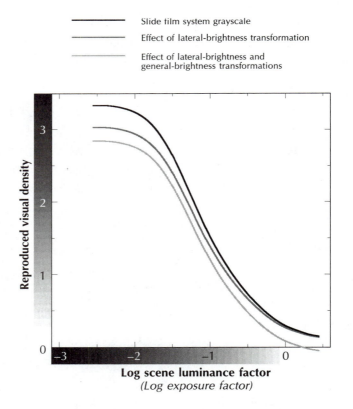

— Slide film system grayscale
— Effect of lateral-brightness transformation
— Effect of lateral-brightness and general-brightness transformations

Observer Chromatic Adaptation

Chromatic adaptation refers to the adjustments of the visual mechanism in response to the average chromaticity of the stimuli to which the eyes are exposed. Changes in the chromatic adaptation state of an observer must be accounted for in color encoding by the use of appropriate chromatic adaptation transformations. A chromatic adaptation transformation determines visually equivalent tristimulus values of a color stimulus that would produce, for a standard observer at one state of chromatic adaptation, a visual match to another color stimulus viewed by a standard observer at a different state of chromatic adaptation.

Although different types of chromatic adaptation transformations are available, their basic methodology generally is similar. First, XYZ tristimulus values, corresponding to a first state of adaptation, are transformed into three cone-response values, ρ, γ, and β. Next, the cone-response values are adjusted to account for the change in the observer's state of chromatic adaptation from the first state to a second state. Finally, the adjusted cone-response values are transformed to produce visually equivalent XYZ tristimulus values for the second state of chromatic adaptation.

In this book, von Kries transformations, in which cone-response values are adjusted by linear scaling, are used for all chromatic adaptation transformations. The following discussion and example illustrate the basic procedure.

In this example, a von Kries transformation from adaptive white chromaticity coordinate values $x = 0.3127$, $y = 0.3290$ (D_{65}) to the adaptive white chromaticity coordinate values $x = 0.3457$, $y = 0.3585$ (D_{50}) will be derived.

First, the XYZ values for both adaptive white chromaticities must be determined. By convention, the Y value for a perfect white is set equal to 100. The values for X and Z can be calculated from the x, y chromaticity coordinates, using the following relationships:

$$x + y + z = 1$$

$$\therefore z = 1 - x - y$$

$$X = x\left(\frac{Y}{y}\right) = x\left(\frac{100}{y}\right) \tag{D5}$$

$$Z = z\left(\frac{Y}{y}\right) = z\left(\frac{100}{y}\right)$$

For adaptive white chromaticity coordinates of $x = 0.3127, y = 0.3290$ (D_{65}):

$$z = 1 - 0.3127 - 0.3290 = 0.3583$$

$$X_{D_{65}} = 0.3127\left(\frac{100}{0.3290}\right) = 95.05$$

$$Y_{D_{65}} = 100.00$$

$$Z_{D_{65}} = 0.3583\left(\frac{100}{0.3290}\right) = 108.91$$

For adaptive white chromaticity coordinates of $x = 0.3457, y = 0.3585$ (D_{50}):

$$z = 1 - 0.3457 - 0.3585 = 0.2958$$

$$X_{D_{50}} = 0.3457\left(\frac{100}{0.3585}\right) = 96.43$$

$$Y_{D_{50}} = 100.00$$

$$Z_{D_{50}} = 0.2958\left(\frac{100}{0.3585}\right) = 82.51$$

Next, the ρ, γ, and β cone-response values are determined from the XYZ values. The following von Kries matrix can be used for these computations:

$$\begin{matrix} \rho = \\ \gamma = \\ \beta = \end{matrix} \begin{bmatrix} 0.40024 & 0.70760 & -0.08081 \\ -0.22630 & 0.16532 & 0.04570 \\ 0 & 0 & 0.91822 \end{bmatrix} \begin{bmatrix} X \\ Y \\ Z \end{bmatrix} \tag{D6}$$

For D_{65}:

$$\rho_{D_{65}} = \quad 0.40024\,(95.05) + 0.70760\,(100.) - 0.08081\,(108.91) = 100.00$$

$$\gamma_{D_{65}} = \; -0.22630\,(95.05) + 1.16532\,(100.) + 0.04570\,(108.91) = 100.00$$

$$\beta_{D_{65}} = \qquad\qquad\qquad\qquad\qquad 0.91822\,(108.91) = 100.00$$

For D_{50}:

$$\rho_{D_{50}} = \quad 0.40024\,(96.43) + 0.70760\,(100.) - 0.08081\,(82.51) = 102.69$$

$$\gamma_{D_{50}} = \; -0.22630\,(96.43) + 1.16532\,(100.) + 0.04570\,(82.51) = \;\;98.48$$

$$\beta_{D_{50}} = \qquad\qquad\qquad\qquad\qquad 0.91822\,(82.51) = \;\;75.76$$

Visually equivalent tristimulus values, $XYZ_{D_{50}}$, for a color stimulus that would produce, for a standard observer chromatically adapted to the chromaticity of D_{50}, a visual match to another color stimulus, having tristimulus values $XYZ_{D_{65}}$, viewed by a standard observer who is chromatically adapted to the chromaticity of D_{65}, can be determined from the von Kries matrix {D6}, the ratios $\rho_{D_{50}}/\rho_{D_{65}}$, $\gamma_{D_{50}}/\gamma_{D_{65}}$, $\beta_{D_{50}}/\beta_{D_{65}}$, and the inverse von Kries matrix as follows:

$$\begin{bmatrix} X_{D_{50}} \\ Y_{D_{50}} \\ Z_{D_{50}} \end{bmatrix} = \begin{bmatrix} \text{D6} \end{bmatrix}^{-1} \begin{bmatrix} \rho_{D_{50}}/\rho_{D_{65}} & 0 & 0 \\ 0 & \gamma_{D_{50}}/\gamma_{D_{65}} & 0 \\ 0 & 0 & \beta_{D_{50}}/\beta_{D_{65}} \end{bmatrix} \begin{bmatrix} \text{D6} \end{bmatrix} \begin{bmatrix} X_{D_{65}} \\ Y_{D_{65}} \\ Z_{D_{65}} \end{bmatrix} \quad \{\text{D7a}\}$$

These mathematical operations can be combined to form a single chromatic adaptation transformation matrix:

$$\begin{bmatrix} X_{D_{50}} \\ Y_{D_{50}} \\ Z_{D_{50}} \end{bmatrix} = \begin{bmatrix} 1.0161 & 0.0553 & -0.0522 \\ 0.0060 & 0.9956 & -0.0012 \\ 0.0000 & 0.0000 & 0.7576 \end{bmatrix} \begin{bmatrix} X_{D_{65}} \\ Y_{D_{65}} \\ Z_{D_{65}} \end{bmatrix} \quad \{\text{D7b}\}$$

Appendix E:
Viewing Flare

When an image is viewed, the observer ideally should see only the light from the image itself. But in most actual viewing conditions, the observer also will see *flare light,* i.e., stray light containing no image information. For example, when viewing a video image displayed on a monitor, the observer may see flare light reflected from the glass faceplate of that monitor. The light causing the flare might come from ordinary light sources in the viewing environment (overhead lamps, window light, etc.). It also might come from the video display itself—if, for example, a workstation user is wearing a white shirt that reflects monitor light back to the CRT faceplate.

In reflection-image viewing, flare occurs as light is reflected directly from the front surface of the medium, without passing through the colorants that make up the image. The amount of flare will vary, depending on the surface texture of the medium, viewing angle, and other factors. In projection-image viewing, viewing flare can be caused by stray projector light. Flare light also can come from projected light that first reflects from the projection screen to the various surfaces in the room and then reflects back to the screen. The amount of flare will depend on the type of screen, the characteristics of the room, the viewing angle, and other factors.

Effect of Viewing Flare on Image Grayscale

Viewing flare adds light, essentially uniformly, to the entire image being viewed. Flare light will significantly brighten darker areas of an image, but it will have a less apparent effect on brighter areas of the image. As a result, the luminance contrast of the image will be reduced.

The effect of flare light on the grayscale of an imaging medium can be computed from a measurement of the grayscale in the absence of viewing flare and a measurement of the relative amount of flare light (Fig. E1). For example, if the flare light in a reflection-print viewing environment is equal to 1%, referenced to the amount of light reflected from the print's reproduction of a perfect white, the computations can be performed as follows:

1. The density corresponding to the reproduction of a perfect white, $density_{white}$, is determined. For the example of Fig. E1, the $density_{white}$ is 0.12.

2. The $density_{white}$ value is converted to a linear reflectance value:

$$reflectance_{white} = 10^{-density_{white}} \qquad \{E1\}$$

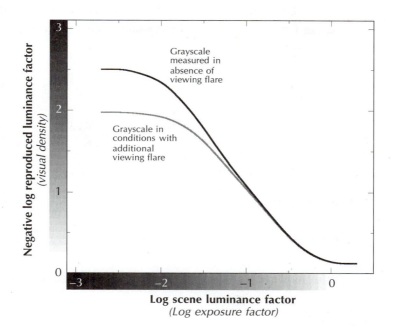

Figure E1
Effect of viewing
flare on a system
grayscale charac-
teristic.

In this example, where the *density*_{white} value is 0.12:

$$reflectance_{white} = 10^{-0.12} = 0.7586$$

3. The amount of flare light, *flare,* relative to the amount of light from the reproduced white, is determined from the percent flare, *PF,* and the *reflectance*_{white}:

$$flare = \left(\frac{PF}{100}\right) reflectance_{white} \qquad \{E2\}$$

In this example, where the percent flare is 1.0%:

$$flare = \left(\frac{1.0}{100}\right) 0.7586 = 0.007586$$

4. For each point on the grayscale characteristic, which is measured in the absence of flare light, flareless density values are converted to flareless reflectance values:

$$reflectance_{no\,flare} = 10^{-density_{no\,flare}} \qquad \{E3\}$$

For instance, at a point where the $density_{no\,flare}$ is 2.00,

$$reflectance_{no\,flare} = 10^{-2.00} = 0.0100$$

5. Flare then is added to each flareless reflectance value of the curve:

$$reflectance_{flare} = reflectance_{no\,flare} + flare \qquad \{E4\}$$

In this example, at a point where the density (flareless) is 2.00,

$$reflectance_{flare} = 0.0100 + 0.007586 = 0.017586$$

6. The computed reflectance (with flare) values are converted to density (with flare) values:

$$density_{flare} = -\log_{10}(reflectance_{flare}) \qquad \{E5\}$$

In this example, at a point where the density (no flare) is 2.00,

$$density_{flare} = -\log_{10}(0.017586) = 1.7548$$

At a point where the density (no flare) is 1.00,

$$density_{flare} = 0.9682$$

The 1% flare grayscale shown in Fig. E1 was computed by applying this procedure to all values of the flareless grayscale.

Colorimetric Effects

The colorimetric effects of viewing flare can be computed using the principles of additive color mixing. The tristimulus values for a stimulus (with flare) can be determined by adding appropriate amounts of the tristimulus values for the flare light itself to the tristimulus values for the stimulus (without flare). As shown in Fig. E2, the addition of flare light moves colors toward the color of flare light itself.

The first step in the computation is to determine the tristimulus values, X_{fl}, Y_{fl}, and Z_{fl}, for the flare light, based on the specification of that light in terms of its chromaticity coordinates x_{fl}, y_{fl}, and z_{fl}, and its percentage, PF, of the image white luminance, Y_{wt}:

$$Y_{fl} = \left(\frac{PF}{100}\right) Y_{wt}$$

$$X_{fl} = x_{fl} \left(\frac{Y_{fl}}{y_{fl}}\right) \qquad \{E6\}$$

$$Z_{fl} = z_{fl} \left(\frac{Y_{fl}}{y_{fl}}\right)$$

For each color stimulus, a modified stimulus then can be computed by adding the tristimulus values for the flare light to the tristimulus values for the color stimulus, as shown below:

$$X_f = X + X_{fl}$$

$$Y_f = Y + Y_{fl} \qquad \{E7\}$$

$$Z_f = Z + Z_{fl}$$

where X, Y, and Z are the tristimulus values for a stimulus with no flare light, and X_{fl}, Y_{fl}, and Z_{fl} are the tristimulus values for a stimulus with flare light added. The effect of this stimulus modification is shown in Fig. E2.

Figure E2

Effect of viewing flare on colors. The addition of flare light moves colors toward the color of the flare light itself. Colors will be lower in chroma, as can be seen here. They also will be lighter and therefore less saturated.

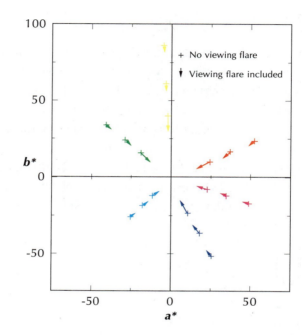

Appendix F:
PhotoYCC Color Space

Although it was designed and developed specifically for the *Kodak Photo CD* System, *Kodak PhotoYCC* Color Interchange Space is now widely used for the general interchange of color images. Its principal features—large color gamut and luminance dynamic range, support for image compression, minimal quantization effects—are all important in high-quality imaging applications. Its fast display to video also is important for many color-imaging systems.

When colors are encoded in terms of *PhotoYCC* Space values by the color-encoding method used on most *Photo CD* Imaging Workstations, encoded color values essentially represent original-scene colorimetry. However, it is important to distinguish between this encoding method and its associated data metric. Because it is a fully defined color encoding specification, which includes specified encoding reference viewing conditions, the *Kodak PhotoYCC* Color Interchange Space data metric can be used to represent reproduced colors as well as other types of colors, regardless of their origin.

For color stimuli that are meant to be viewed in actual conditions that correspond to the encoding reference conditions, *PhotoYCC* Space values are computed by a series of simple mathematical operations from standard CIE colorimetric values. For color stimuli that are meant to be viewed in actual viewing conditions that differ from those of the encoding reference, it is necessary to include appropriate colorimetric transformations to determine equivalent CIE colorimetric values for the encoding reference conditions.

The colorimetric transformations must account for differences in the amount of viewing flare in the actual and encoding reference viewing conditions, as well as for alterations in observer perception that would be induced by other differences in those conditions. The equivalent standard CIE colorimetric values resulting from these transformations then are encoded in terms of *Kodak PhotoYCC* Color Interchange Space values.

The specified conditions of the *PhotoYCC* Space encoding reference viewing environment, listed in Table F1, correspond to those of typical outdoor scenes. These conditions are as follows:

- *Viewing flare* is specified as *none*; any flare light in an original-scene environment is part of the scene itself.
- The *surround type* is defined as *average*; scene objects typically are surrounded by other, similarly illuminated scene objects.
- The *luminance level* is representative of typical daylight-illuminated objects. Note that the luminance is at least an order of magnitude higher than that typical of indoor conditions.
- The chromaticity coordinates of the observer *adaptive white* are those of CIE Standard Illuminant D_{65}.

	PhotoYCC **Color Space**
Colorimetry	1931 CIE flareless measurement
Data metric	*PhotoYCC* Space $Y = (255/1.402)$ Luma $C_1 = 111.60$ *Chroma$_1$* $+ 156$ $C_2 = 135.64$ *Chroma$_2$* $+ 137$
Viewing Conditions:	
Viewing flare	None
Surround type	Average
Luminance level	$>1{,}600$ cd/m²
Adaptive white	$x = 0.3127$, $y = 0.3290$

Table F1

PhotoYCC Space color encoding specification and color encoding reference viewing conditions.

An adaptive white is defined here, and throughout this book, as a color stimulus that an adapted observer would judge to be perfectly achromatic and to have a luminance factor of unity. Although the chromaticity of the adaptive white most often will be that of the scene illuminant, it may be quite different in certain cases. For example, it may differ if the observer is only partially adapted to the illuminant. The adaptive white therefore defines only the chromatic adaptive state of the observer; it does *not* define the chromaticity, or the spectral power distribution, of the scene illuminant. The following examples provide additional details on this point and on *PhotoYCC* Space color encoding.

Example 1—This example describes the *PhotoYCC* Space encoding of a daylight-illuminated scene, recorded using the *Photo CD* Reference Image-Capturing Device, when the adaptive white corresponds to D_{65} chromaticity.

The red, green, and blue spectral responsivities of the Reference Image Capturing Device, shown in Fig. F1, are equivalent to the color-matching functions for the reference primaries defined in Recommendation ITU-R BT.709. The CIE chromaticities for these red, green, and blue reference primaries, and for CIE Standard Illuminant D_{65}, are given in Table F2.

Figure F1

Responsivities of the *Photo CD* Reference Image-Capturing Device.

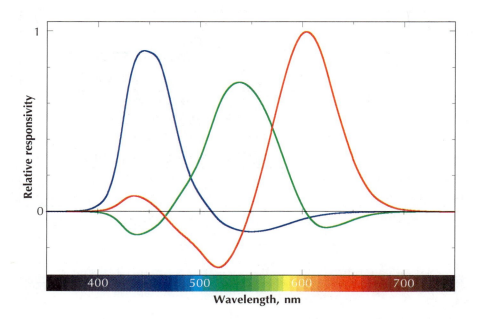

Photo CD Reference Image-Capturing Device RGB_{709} tristimulus values for the stimuli of a scene can be calculated using the spectral responsivities of the Reference Image-Capturing Device:

$$R_{709} = k_r \sum_\lambda S(\lambda)R(\lambda)\bar{r}(\lambda)$$

$$G_{709} = k_g \sum_\lambda S(\lambda)R(\lambda)\bar{g}(\lambda) \quad \{F1\}$$

$$B_{709} = k_b \sum_\lambda S(\lambda)R(\lambda)\bar{b}(\lambda)$$

where R_{709}, G_{709}, and B_{709} are the Reference Image-Capturing Device red, green, and blue tristimulus (exposure) values; $S(\lambda)$ is the spectral power distribution of a light source; $R(\lambda)$ is the spectral reflectance or transmittance of an object; $\bar{r}(\lambda)$, $\bar{g}(\lambda)$, and $\bar{b}(\lambda)$ are the red, green, and blue spectral responsivities of the Reference Image-Capturing Device; and k_r, k_g, and k_b are normalizing factors

	Red	Green	Blue	D$_{65}$
x	0.6400	0.3000	0.1500	0.3127
y	0.3300	0.6000	0.0600	0.3290
z	0.0300	0.1000	0.7900	0.3583
u′	0.4507	0.1250	0.1754	0.1978
v′	0.5229	0.5625	0.1579	0.4683

Table F2

Chromaticities of ITU-R BT.709 Reference Primaries and CIE Standard Illuminant D$_{65}$.

determined such that R_{709}, G_{709}, and $B_{709} = 1.00$ when the stimulus is a perfect white diffuser. By definition, all measurements made by the Reference Image-Capturing Device are flareless, so it is not necessary to adjust the calculated RGB_{709} tristimulus values for instrument flare.

Since the red, green, and blue spectral responsivities of the Reference Image-Capturing Device are linear combinations of the $\bar{x}(\lambda)$, $\bar{y}(\lambda)$, and $\bar{z}(\lambda)$ color-matching functions for the CIE 1931 Standard Colorimetric Observer, its RGB_{709} tristimulus values also can be calculated directly from CIE XYZ tristimulus values, using the following relationship:

$$
\begin{bmatrix} R_{709} \\ G_{709} \\ B_{709} \end{bmatrix} = \begin{bmatrix} 3.2410 & -1.5374 & -0.4986 \\ -0.9692 & 1.8760 & 0.0416 \\ 0.0556 & -0.2040 & 1.0570 \end{bmatrix} \begin{bmatrix} \dfrac{X_{scene}}{100} \\ \dfrac{Y_{scene}}{100} \\ \dfrac{Z_{scene}}{100} \end{bmatrix} \qquad \{F2\}
$$

where

$$
X_{scene} = k \sum_{\lambda=380}^{780} S(\lambda)R(\lambda)\bar{x}(\lambda)
$$

$$
Y_{scene} = k \sum_{\lambda=380}^{780} S(\lambda)R(\lambda)\bar{y}(\lambda) \qquad \{F3\}
$$

$$
Z_{scene} = k \sum_{\lambda=380}^{780} S(\lambda)R(\lambda)\bar{z}(\lambda)
$$

The value for the normalizing factor, k, in Eqs. {F3} is determined such that $Y_{scene} = 100$ when the stimulus is a perfect white diffuser. In the *PhotoYCC* Space encoding process, RGB_{709} tristimulus values less than zero and RGB_{709} tristimulus values greater than 1.00 are retained.

Reference Image-Capturing Device RGB_{709} tristimulus values next are transformed to nonlinear values, $R'G'B'_{709}$, as follows:

For $R_{709}, G_{709}, B_{709} \geq 0.018$:

$$R'_{709} = 1.099 R_{709}^{0.45} - 0.099$$

$$G'_{709} = 1.099 G_{709}^{0.45} - 0.099 \qquad \text{\{F4a\}}$$

$$B'_{709} = 1.099 B_{709}^{0.45} - 0.099$$

For $R_{709}, G_{709}, B_{709} \leq -0.018$:

$$R'_{709} = -1.099 |R_{709}|^{0.45} + 0.099$$

$$G'_{709} = -1.099 |G_{709}|^{0.45} + 0.099 \qquad \text{\{F4b\}}$$

$$B'_{709} = -1.099 |B_{709}|^{0.45} + 0.099$$

For $-0.018 < R_{709}, G_{709}, B_{709} < 0.018$:

$$R'_{709} = 4.50 R_{709}$$

$$G'_{709} = 4.50 G_{709} \qquad \text{\{F4c\}}$$

$$B'_{709} = 4.50 B_{709}$$

The $R'G'B'_{709}$ values then are transformed to luma and chroma values as follows:

$$
\begin{aligned}
Luma &= 0.299\,R'_{709} + 0.587\,G'_{709} + 0.114\,B'_{709} \\
Chroma_1 &= -0.299\,R'_{709} - 0.587\,G'_{709} + 0.886\,B'_{709} \\
Chroma_2 &= 0.701\,R'_{709} - 0.587\,G'_{709} - 0.114\,B'_{709}
\end{aligned}
\tag{F5}
$$

Finally, luma/chroma values are converted to digital code values Y, C_1, and C_2. For 24-bit (8 bits per channel) encoding, *PhotoYCC* Space values are the nearest integers to the values determined from the following equations:

$$
\begin{aligned}
Y &= \left(\frac{255}{1.402}\right) Luma \\
C_1 &= 111.40\ Chroma_1 + 156 \\
C_2 &= 135.64\ Chroma_2 + 137
\end{aligned}
\tag{F6}
$$

Example 2—This example describes the encoding of a daylight-illuminated scene, captured using a Reference Image-Capturing Device, or any other device having CIE color-matching-function spectral responsivities, when the observer adaptive white corresponds to a chromaticity *other than* that of D_{65}.

CIE *XYZ* tristimulus values for the illuminated objects of the scene are first computed, using standard colorimetric procedures. Because the observer adaptive white is other than that specified for the reference viewing environment, an appropriate chromatic-adaptation transformation (such as a von Kries transformation, as described in Appendix D) must be applied to form visually equivalent tristimulus values for the *PhotoYCC* Space reference viewing environment (D_{65} adaptive white chromaticity).

A chromatic-adaptation transformation matrix can be determined from the chromaticity of the actual adaptive white and the specified chromaticity of the *PhotoYCC* Space encoding reference adaptive white.

For example, if the actual adaptive white chromaticity coordinates correspond to those of D_{50}, the transformation matrix would be:

$$
\begin{bmatrix} X_{scene(D_{65})} \\ Y_{scene(D_{65})} \\ Z_{scene(D_{65})} \end{bmatrix} = \begin{bmatrix} 0.9845 & -0.0547 & 0.0678 \\ -0.0060 & 1.0048 & 0.0012 \\ 0.0000 & 0.0000 & 1.3200 \end{bmatrix} \begin{bmatrix} X_{scene(D_{50})} \\ Y_{scene(D_{50})} \\ Z_{scene(D_{50})} \end{bmatrix} \quad \{F7\}
$$

The $XYZ_{scene(D_{65})}$ tristimulus values next are transformed to Reference Image Capture Device RGB_{709} tristimulus values, using Eq. {F2}, and then are transformed to *PhotoYCC* Space digital code values using Eqs. {F4a} to {F6}.

Example 3—This example again describes the encoding of a daylight-illuminated original scene, but using an actual image-capturing device (such as a digital still camera) having red, green, and blue spectral responsivities that are *not* equivalent to any set of CIE color-matching functions.

Original-scene RGB_{device} tristimulus values, which have been measured by the actual image-capturing device, first must be corrected to compensate for any optical deficiencies, such as lens flare and spatial nonuniformities, of the device itself. The corrected RGB_{device} tristimulus values then are transformed to Reference Image-Capturing Device RGB_{709} tristimulus values. This can be accomplished by a matrix transformation:

$$
\begin{bmatrix} R_{709} \\ G_{709} \\ B_{709} \end{bmatrix} = [M] \begin{bmatrix} R_{device} \\ G_{device} \\ B_{device} \end{bmatrix} \quad \{F8\}
$$

However, because the device has spectral responsivities that are not equivalent to a set of color-matching functions, this transformation cannot be perfect for all possible original-scene stimuli. Therefore, appropriate statistical procedures must be used in the derivation of the transformation matrix. For example, the matrix may be derived such that the resulting colorimetric errors from a captured set of particularly important test colors are minimized. The remaining transformations, from the approximated RGB_{709} tristimulus values to *PhotoYCC* Space values, are the same as in Example 1, Eqs. {F4a} through {F6}.

Example 4—It sometimes is desirable to encode colors from reproduced images (such as reflection prints, transparencies, artwork, CRT displays, etc.) in terms of *PhotoYCC* Space values. One procedure for doing this is to first encode the reproduced colors in terms of the color encoding specification (CES), or the identical color interchange specification (CIS), of the prototype system described in Part IV. Numerous examples of this encoding are given in Chapter 18. The CES/CIS values then can be transformed to *PhotoYCC* Space values using the procedures described in Appendix G.

Appendix G: Transformations for Color Interchange

Transformations for color interchange can be developed for any pair of systems having fully defined color encoding specifications. For *system-specific* interchange, various restricted interchange methods and data metrics can be used. For *general* color interchange, the communication of color information must be unrestricted, i.e., the interchange method itself must not impose limitations on luminance dynamic range, color gamut, or color interpretation.

Figure G1

The interchange
transformations
described in this
appendix.

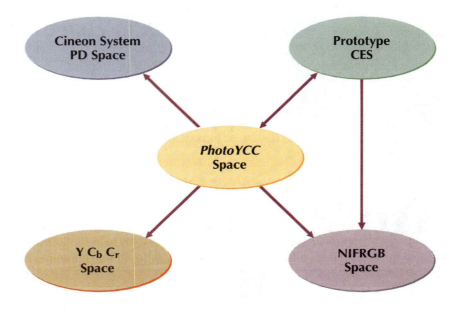

In this appendix, several example transformations based on both restricted and unrestricted color interchange will be developed. Most of the examples will link *Kodak PhotoYCC* Color Interchange Space to other color encoding specifications (Fig. G1). This particular interchange space was selected for most of the transformation examples because of its widespread usage and because its properties support both general and system-specific color interchange. Another important transformation, from the color encoding specification developed for the prototype color-management system described in Chapter 18 to a monitor-based color encoding specification called NIFRGB, also will be described. Figure G2 illustrates the colorimetric relationships of original scenes, the various color encoding specifications, and reproduced images. The characteristics of the individual color encoding specifications are as follows:

PhotoYCC **Space:** *Kodak PhotoYCC* Color Interchange Space, used in the *Photo CD* System, is based on color appearance defined in terms of colorimetry and a specified set of encoding reference viewing conditions. The conditions are consistent with those of outdoor scenes. Encoded colorimetric

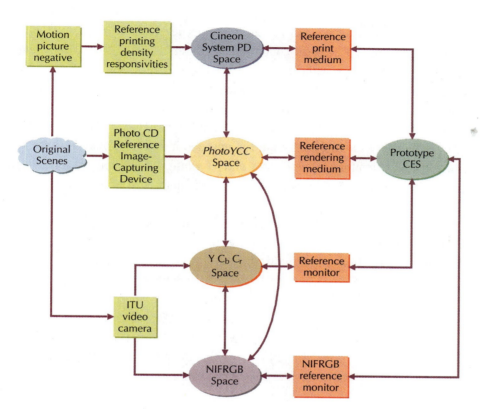

Figure G2

Relationships of the described color encoding specifications to original scenes and reproduced images.

values are expressed according to the properties of a specified Reference Image-Capturing Device. This hypothetical device produces color values representative of the colorimetry of original scenes. The device is based on a set of reference primaries and an opto-electronic transfer characteristic defined in Recommendations ITU-R BT.709 and ITU-R BT.601. However, unlike the video cameras described by those recommendations, the Reference Image-Capturing Device has an extended luminance dynamic range, and its color gamut is not restricted to that defined by positive intensities of its reference RGB primaries.

Prototype CES: The CES (color encoding specification) developed for the prototype color-management system, which was described in Part IV, is based on color appearance defined in terms of colorimetry and a specified set of encoding reference viewing conditions consistent with those typically used for indoor viewing of reflection images. The prototype CES is consistent with the Profile Connection Space (PCS) used in profiles developed by Eastman Kodak Company for use in systems conforming to International Color Consortium (ICC) Profile Format specifications.

YC_bC_r Space: YC_bC_r values are used in many software applications. Like *PhotoYCC* Space values, these values are based on the properties of a reference video camera defined according to Recommendations ITU-R BT.709 and ITU-R BT.601. However, the upper limit of the encoded luminance dynamic range is limited to the luminance factor of a perfect white. In addition, the encoded color gamut is restricted to that defined by positive intensities of the reference RGB primaries.

***Cineon* System PD Space:** The color encoding of the *Cineon Digital Film System* is based on printing-density measurements from scanned motion-picture negative films. Printing density values are measured according to a specified set of reference spectral responsivities defined by the spectral sensitivities of a reference print medium and the spectral properties of a reference printer.

NIFRGB Space: NIFRGB values are used in the *FlashPix*™ Format. The *FlashPix* Format is defined in a specification and a test suite, developed and published by Eastman Kodak Company in collaboration with Hewlett-Packard Company, Live Picture Inc., and Microsoft Corporation. Only products that meet the specification and pass the test suite may use the *FlashPix* file format name. NIFRGB values are defined according to the properties of a reference monitor viewed in a specified set of encoding reference viewing conditions. The upper limit of the encodable luminance dynamic range is restricted to the luminance factor of the maximum white stimulus that can be produced on that monitor. The encodable color gamut is restricted to that defined by positive intensities of the reference monitor primaries. For that reason, in addition to supporting the use of NIFRGB values, the *FlashPix* Format also supports the use of *PhotoYCC* Space values.

All of these color encoding specifications can be linked, as indicated by the arrows of Figs. G1 and G2. In some cases, however, information will be lost in the transformation of one encoding to another. Details of several of the more important transformations follow.

A Method for Transforming *PhotoYCC* Space Values to Prototype CES Values

Kodak PhotoYCC Color Interchange Space, and the color encoding specification (CES) developed for the prototype color-management system described previously in Part IV, both can support general color interchange. Each uses a CES that is fully defined in terms of colorimetry, data metric, and associated viewing conditions. Each provides an unambiguous specification of color, and each can represent any given color, regardless of its origin. The properties of the two specifications are compared in Table G1.

When appropriate procedures such as those described here are used, color interchange of *PhotoYCC* Space values to and from prototype CES values is unrestricted. The interchange transformation determines code values, in terms of the respective data metrics, that represent equivalent color stimuli in the respective viewing conditions. The determination of this equivalence includes consideration of the properties of actual imaging media and devices.

	PhotoYCC Color Space	Prototype CES
Colorimetry	1931 CIE flareless measurement	1931 CIE flareless measurement
Data metric	*PhotoYCC* Space $Y = (255/1.402)$ Luma $C_1 = 111.60$ *Chroma$_1$* $+ 156$ $C_2 = 135.64$ *Chroma$_2$* $+ 137$	CIELAB $CV_1 = 2.10\ L^*$ $CV_2 = a^* + 128$ $CV_3 = b^* + 128$
Viewing Conditions:		
Viewing flare	None	1.0%
Surround type	Average	Average
Luminance level	$>1{,}600$ cd/m²	$60 - 160$ cd/m²
Adaptive white	$x = 0.3127, y = 0.3290$	$x = 0.3457, y = 0.3585$

Table G1

Comparison of *PhotoYCC* Space specifications and the color encoding specification of the prototype color management system.

The encoding reference viewing conditions of *Kodak PhotoYCC* Color Interchange Space are typical of outdoor environments, whereas the encoding reference viewing conditions of the prototype CES are typical of indoor environments. A transform between the two must account for these different viewing conditions. In addition, the transform must account for any differences in the methods used in making colorimetric measurements and for any differences in the data metrics of the two color encoding specifications. These factors are compared and discussed below.

Colorimetric measurements: Both color encoding specifications are derived from flareless (or flare-corrected) colorimetric measurements based on the CIE 1931 Standard Colorimetric Observer. Therefore, no adjustments for measurement differences are required in the color interchange transformation.

Viewing flare: The transformation must include compensations for the physical reductions in both luminance contrast and color saturation associated with the higher level of viewing flare of the encoding reference viewing environment specified for the prototype CES.

Surround type: Both reference viewing environments assume a normal (or average) image surround; therefore, no adjustments for observer lateral-brightness adaptation or general-brightness adaptation are required in the color interchange transformation.

Luminance level: Compensations must be included for the perceived reductions in luminance contrast and colorfulness associated with the lower luminance levels of the prototype CES reference viewing environment.

Adaptive white: Colorimetric adjustments must be included to account for the differences in the respective adaptive-white chromaticity coordinates specified for the *PhotoYCC* Space and prototype CES encoding reference viewing environments.

Reference primaries: Colorimetric adjustments must be included to account for the differences in the reference primaries of the *PhotoYCC* Space and prototype CES data metrics.

Numerical units: The color interchange transformation must include appropriate mathematical conversions to account for numerical differences between the *PhotoYCC* Space and prototype CES data metrics.

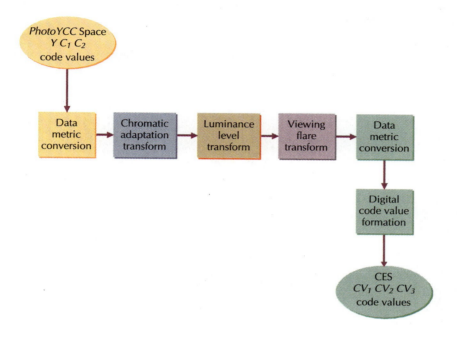

Figure G3

Transformation from *PhotoYCC* Space to the color encoding specification (CES) of the prototype color management system described in Part IV.

The steps involved in the transformation of *PhotoYCC* Space values to prototype CES values are shown above in Fig. G3 and include the following:

- A data-metric conversion from *PhotoYCC* Space Y, C_1, C_2 digital code values to CIE XYZ tristimulus values.
- Adjustment of the XYZ values to account for the change in adaptive white chromaticity coordinates from those of D_{65} to those of D_{50}.
- Further adjustment of the XYZ values to compensate for the lower luminance levels of the prototype CES reference viewing conditions.
- Further adjustment of the XYZ values to compensate for the greater level of viewing flare in the prototype CES reference viewing conditions
- A metric conversion of the adjusted XYZ values to CIELAB L^*, a^*, b^* values.
- Scaling of the CIELAB L^*, a^*, b^* values to form digital code values, CV_1, CV_2, and CV_3, as defined by the data metric of the prototype CES.

Figure G4

Use of a reference rendering medium in the transformation of *PhotoYCC* Space values to prototype CES values.

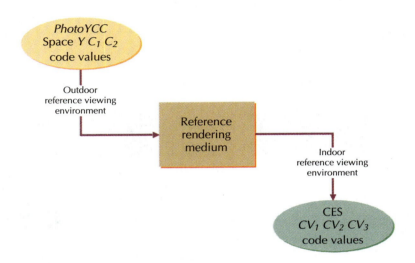

The following transformation from *PhotoYCC* Space values to prototype CES values represents one method that can be used to account for the differences in the reference viewing environments and numerical encoding methods of the two color encoding specifications. This transformation method includes the use of a reference rendering medium, as shown above (Fig. G4).

The reference medium provides a means for converting values encoded with respect to a reference environment normally associated with the viewing of outdoor scenes, to values encoded with respect to a reference environment normally associated with the viewing of reproduced images, in a way that is consistent with the properties of actual imaging media and devices. Inclusion of the reference rendering medium in the transformation ensures that image data transformed by this procedure will be compatible with image data of reproduced images that have been encoded directly in terms of prototype CES values.

The reference rendering medium for this transformation is defined to be a hypothetical additive color device having the following characteristics:

- The capability of producing, in the reference viewing environment, a white of $L^* \approx 121$ (an optical density of approximately -0.22) at the chromaticity of CIE Standard Illuminant D_{50}.

	Red	Green	Blue	D$_{50}$
x	0.8730	0.1750	0.0850	0.3457
y	0.1440	0.9270	0.0001	0.3585
z	−0.0170	−0.1020	0.9149	0.2958
u′	1.1710	0.0508	0.1201	0.2092
v′	0.4346	0.6057	0.0003	0.4881

Table G2
CIE x, y, z and u′, v′ chromaticity coordinates for the RGB primaries of the Prototype CES Reference Rendering Medium and for CIE Standard Illuminant D$_{50}$.

- The capability of producing, in the absence of viewing flare, a black of $L^* \approx 0$ (an optical density of approximately 4.0) at the chromaticity of CIE Standard Illuminant D$_{50}$.

- No cross-talk among its color channels, i.e., red output is affected only by red input, green output only by green input, and blue output only by blue input.

- Red, green, and blue primaries defined by the CIE chromaticity values given above in Table G2.

- An equal *RGB* rendering characteristic, as shown in Fig. G5. Sample input/output values for this characteristic are listed in Table G3.

In the first step of the transformation, luma and chroma values are computed from *PhotoYCC* Space Y, C_1, and C_2 digital values. For 24-bit (8 bits per channel) encoding, luma and chroma values are computed according to the following equations:

$$Luma = \left(\frac{1.402}{255}\right) Y$$

$$Chroma_1 = \frac{(C_1 - 156)}{111.40}$$

$$Chroma_2 = \frac{(C_2 - 137)}{135.64}$$

{G1}

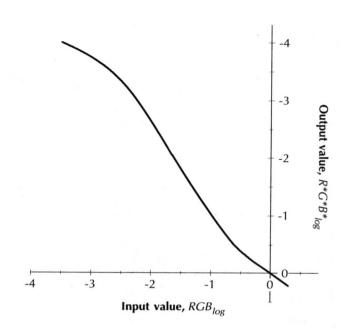

The resulting *Luma*, *Chroma$_1$*, and *Chroma$_2$* values are converted to nonlinear values, $R'G'B'_{709}$, using the following matrix transformation:

$$\begin{bmatrix} R'_{709} \\ G'_{709} \\ B'_{709} \end{bmatrix} = \begin{bmatrix} 1 & 0 & 1 \\ 1 & -0.194 & -0.509 \\ 1 & 1 & 0 \end{bmatrix} \begin{bmatrix} Luma \\ Chroma_1 \\ Chroma_2 \end{bmatrix} \qquad \{G2\}$$

The resulting $R'G'B'_{709}$ nonlinear values next are converted to linear values, RGB_{709}. This conversion to a linear space is necessary because the *RGB* values will subsequently be transformed to CIE *XYZ* values. That transformation will allow the application of a chromatic adaptation transform to the *XYZ* values to account for the change in adaptive white chromaticity coordinates from those of D_{65} to those of D_{50}.

RGB_{log} Input value	$R*G*B*_{log}$ Output value
≤ -3.50	-4.00
-3.45	-3.98
-3.30	-3.91
-3.15	-3.83
-3.00	-3.74
-2.85	-3.64
-2.70	-3.52
-2.55	-3.38
-2.40	-3.21
-2.25	-3.01
-2.10	-2.79
-1.95	-2.55
-1.80	-2.30
-1.65	-2.05
-1.50	-1.80
-1.35	-1.56
-1.20	-1.33
-1.05	-1.10
-0.90	-0.88
-0.75	-0.68
-0.60	-0.49
-0.45	-0.33
-0.30	-0.21
-0.15	-0.09
0.00	0.00
0.15	0.11
≥ 0.30	0.22

Table G3
Equal *RGB* characteristic for the Prototype CES Reference Rendering Medium, as shown in Fig. G5.

The $R'G'B'_{709}$ nonlinear values are converted to linear values, RGB_{709}, using the equations shown below.

For $R'G'B'_{709} \geq 0.081$:

$$R_{709} = \left(\frac{R'_{709} + 0.099}{1.099} \right)^{1/0.45}$$

$$G_{709} = \left(\frac{G'_{709} + 0.099}{1.099} \right)^{1/0.45} \qquad \{G3a\}$$

$$B_{709} = \left(\frac{B'_{709} + 0.099}{1.099} \right)^{1/0.45}$$

For $R'G'B'_{709} \leq -0.081$:

$$R_{709} = -\left(\frac{R'_{709} - 0.099}{-1.099} \right)^{1/0.45}$$

$$G_{709} = -\left(\frac{G'_{709} - 0.099}{-1.099} \right)^{1/0.45} \qquad \{G3b\}$$

$$B_{709} = -\left(\frac{B'_{709} - 0.099}{-1.099} \right)^{1/0.45}$$

For $-0.081 < R'G'B'_{709} < 0.081$:

$$R_{709} = \frac{R'_{709}}{4.5}$$

$$G_{709} = \frac{G'_{709}}{4.5} \qquad \{G3c\}$$

$$B_{709} = \frac{B'_{709}}{4.5}$$

The resulting RGB_{709} linear values are converted to CIE $XYZ_{D_{65}}$ values using the following matrix transformation:

$$\begin{bmatrix} X_{D_{65}} \\ Y_{D_{65}} \\ Z_{D_{65}} \end{bmatrix} = \begin{bmatrix} 41.24 & 35.76 & 18.05 \\ 21.26 & 71.52 & 07.22 \\ 01.93 & 11.92 & 95.05 \end{bmatrix} \begin{bmatrix} R_{709} \\ G_{709} \\ B_{709} \end{bmatrix} \qquad \{G4\}$$

The resulting CIE XYZ_{D65} values then are transformed to account for the different adaptive whites of the two color specifications. The following von Kries chromatic-adaptation matrix is used for this purpose:

$$\begin{bmatrix} X_{D_{50}} \\ Y_{D_{50}} \\ Z_{D_{50}} \end{bmatrix} = \begin{bmatrix} 1.0161 & 0.0553 & -0.0522 \\ 0.0060 & 0.9956 & -0.0012 \\ 0.0000 & 0.0000 & 0.7576 \end{bmatrix} \begin{bmatrix} X_{D_{65}} \\ Y_{D_{65}} \\ Z_{D_{65}} \end{bmatrix} \qquad \{G5\}$$

Transformation to the prototype CES must include compensation for both the physical and the perceptual reductions in luminance contrast and color saturation that result from the higher viewing flare and lower luminance levels of the prototype CES reference viewing conditions. This is accomplished using the previously described reference rendering medium.

In this procedure, which will be detailed on the following pages, $XYZ_{D_{50}}$ values are converted to corresponding values expressed in terms of the red, green, and blue primaries of the reference rendering medium. A nonlinear mapping corresponding to the equal RGB grayscale of the reference rendering medium then is applied, and the mapped values are converted to D_{50} tristimulus values, XYZ_{CES}. In addition to providing the required luminance contrast and color saturation compensations, these operations also have the desirable effect of mapping color values into the gamut of the reference rendering medium. This results in transformed color values that are consistent with the properties of practical imaging media.

In the first step of this procedure, the CIE $XYZ_{D_{50}}$ values from Eq. {G5} are converted to RGB tristimulus values for the red, green, and blue primaries of the reference medium, as defined in Table G2, using the following matrix transformation:

$$\begin{bmatrix} R \\ G \\ B \end{bmatrix} = \begin{bmatrix} 1.4521 & -0.2890 & -0.1349 \\ -0.1929 & 1.1713 & 0.0178 \\ 0.0015 & 0.1173 & 1.0682 \end{bmatrix} \begin{bmatrix} \dfrac{X_{D_{50}}}{100} \\ \dfrac{Y_{D_{50}}}{100} \\ \dfrac{Z_{D_{50}}}{100} \end{bmatrix} \qquad \{G6\}$$

The logarithms of the RGB tristimulus values then are calculated:

$$\begin{aligned} R_{log} &= \log_{10} R \\ G_{log} &= \log_{10} G \\ B_{log} &= \log_{10} B \end{aligned} \qquad \{G7\}$$

The resulting RGB_{log} values are transformed to $R^*G^*B^*_{log}$ values using the lookup table listed in Table G3 and shown in Fig. G5. The resulting $R^*G^*B^*_{log}$ values are converted to linear values,

$$\begin{aligned} R^* &= 10^{R^*_{log}} \\ G^* &= 10^{G^*_{log}} \\ B^* &= 10^{B^*_{log}} \end{aligned} \qquad \{G8\}$$

and transformed to XYZ_{CES} tristimulus values using the following matrix transformation:

$$\begin{bmatrix} X_{CES} \\ Y_{CES} \\ Z_{CES} \end{bmatrix} = \begin{bmatrix} 71.07 & 16.66 & 8.70 \\ 11.72 & 88.27 & 0.01 \\ -1.38 & -9.71 & 93.61 \end{bmatrix} \begin{bmatrix} R^* \\ G^* \\ B^* \end{bmatrix} \qquad \{G9\}$$

The resulting XYZ_{CES} tristimulus values then are converted to CIELAB values, $L^*a^*b^*_{CES}$, using the equations previously described in Appendix A and given again below. In these calculations, the tristimulus values for the reference white are those of CIE D$_{50}$ ($Xn_{CES} = 96.42, Yn_{CES} = 100.00, Zn_{CES} = 82.49$).

$$L^*_{CES} = 116 \left(\frac{Y_{CES}}{Yn_{CES}}\right)^{(1/3)} - 16 \qquad \text{for } \frac{Y_{CES}}{Yn_{CES}} > 0.008856$$

$$L^*_{CES} = 903.3 \left(\frac{Y_{CES}}{Yn_{CES}}\right) \qquad \text{for } \frac{Y_{CES}}{Yn_{CES}} \leq 0.008856$$

and

$$a^*_{CES} = 500 \left[f\left(\frac{X_{CES}}{Xn_{CES}}\right) - f\left(\frac{Y_{CES}}{Yn_{CES}}\right) \right]$$

$$b^*_{CES} = 200 \left[f\left(\frac{Y_{CES}}{Yn_{CES}}\right) - f\left(\frac{Z_{CES}}{Zn_{CES}}\right) \right]$$

$$\{G10\}$$

where

$$f\left(\frac{X_{CES}}{Xn_{CES}}\right) = \left(\frac{X_{CES}}{Xn_{CES}}\right)^{(1/3)} \qquad \text{for } \frac{X_{CES}}{Xn_{CES}} > 0.008856$$

$$f\left(\frac{X_{CES}}{Xn_{CES}}\right) = 7.787 \left(\frac{X_{CES}}{Xn_{CES}}\right) + \left(\frac{16}{116}\right) \qquad \text{for } \frac{X_{CES}}{Xn_{CES}} \leq 0.008856$$

$$f\left(\frac{Y_{CES}}{Yn_{CES}}\right) = \left(\frac{Y_{CES}}{Yn_{CES}}\right)^{(1/3)} \qquad \text{for } \frac{Y_{CES}}{Yn_{CES}} > 0.008856$$

$$f\left(\frac{Y_{CES}}{Yn_{CES}}\right) = 7.787 \left(\frac{Y_{CES}}{Yn_{CES}}\right) + \left(\frac{16}{116}\right) \qquad \text{for } \frac{Y_{CES}}{Yn_{CES}} \leq 0.008856$$

$$f\left(\frac{Z_{CES}}{Zn_{CES}}\right) = \left(\frac{Z_{CES}}{Zn_{CES}}\right)^{(1/3)} \qquad \text{for } \frac{Z_{CES}}{Zn_{CES}} > 0.008856$$

$$f\left(\frac{Z_{CES}}{Zn_{CES}}\right) = 7.787 \left(\frac{Z_{CES}}{Zn_{CES}}\right) + \left(\frac{16}{116}\right) \qquad \text{for } \frac{Z_{CES}}{Zn_{CES}} \leq 0.008856$$

Finally, the resulting $L^*a^*b^*_{CES}$ values are converted to digital code values, CV_1, CV_2, and CV_3, according to the 24-bit (8 bits per channel) data metric defined for the prototype CES. The CES digital code values are the nearest integers to the values determined from the following equations:

$$CV_1 = 2.10\, L^*_{CES} \qquad\qquad \text{\{G11a\}}$$

$$CV_2 = a^*_{CES} + 128 \qquad\qquad \text{\{G11b\}}$$

$$CV_3 = b^*_{CES} + 128 \qquad\qquad \text{\{G11c\}}$$

For implementation purposes, any sequence of consecutive matrix operations in the preceding transformation can be combined into a single matrix. Likewise, any sequence of consecutive one-dimensional functions can be combined into a single one-dimensional lookup table. The entire transformation also can be implemented in the form of a three-dimensional lookup table.

It should be noted that the use of the rendering characteristic shown in Fig. G5 results in L^*_{CES} values greater than 100. Such values are necessary in order to optimally encode the appearance of original scenes and to accurately encode the color appearance of high-quality reproductions, as viewed under optimal conditions. Currently, however, many color encoding specifications do not provide for L^* values greater than 100.

Such values can be avoided by the use of a rendering characteristic such as that shown in Fig. G6. However, use of such characteristics results in some compression of highlight detail, which may be undesirable when images are to be displayed on high-quality output devices and media. The scale factor of Eq. {G11a} should be modified to be consistent with any changes in the rendering characteristic. For example, if the rendering characteristic is modified such that L^* values are limited to 100, the scale factor should be changed from a value of 2.10 to a value of 2.55.

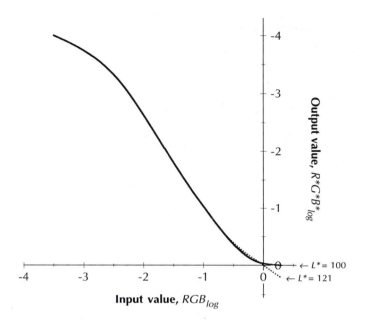

Modified equal *RGB* characteristic for a CES Reference Rendering Medium with an L^* limit of 100, (the solid line) compared to a preferred characteristic having an L^* limit of approximately 121 (the dotted line).

(In figure) Output value, $R^*G^*B^*_{log}$

Input value, RGB_{log}

$\leftarrow L^* = 100$
$\leftarrow L^* = 121$

A Method for Transforming Prototype CES Values to *PhotoYCC* Space Values

The transformation of prototype CES values to corresponding *PhotoYCC* Color Interchange Space values is, of course, the reverse of that just shown. The first step in this transformation is a conversion of CES 8-bit code values to CIELAB $L^*a^*b^*_{CES}$ values:

$$L^*_{CES} = \frac{CV_1}{2.10}$$

$$a^*_{CES} = CV_2 - 128$$

$$b^*_{CES} = CV_3 - 128$$

{G12}

The resulting CIELAB $L^*a^*b^*_{CES}$ values then are converted to CIE XYZ_{CES} values. In the following calculations, the tristimulus values for the reference white are those of CIE Standard Illuminant D_{50}: $Xn_{CES}= 96.42$, $Yn_{CES} = 100.00$, and $Zn_{CES} = 82.49$.

$$Y_{CES} = Yn_{CES} \left(\frac{L^*_{CES} + 16}{116} \right)^3 \qquad \text{for } L^* > 8$$

$$\{G13\}$$

$$Y_{CES} = Yn_{CES} \left(\frac{L^*_{CES}}{903.3} \right) \qquad \text{for } L^* \leq 8$$

$$f\left(\frac{Y_{CES}}{Yn_{CES}} \right) = \left(\frac{Y_{CES}}{Yn_{CES}} \right)^{(1/3)} \qquad \text{for } \frac{Y_{CES}}{Yn_{CES}} > 0.008856$$

$$f\left(\frac{Y_{CES}}{Yn_{CES}} \right) = 7.787 \left(\frac{Y_{CES}}{Yn_{CES}} \right) + \left(\frac{16}{116} \right) \qquad \text{for } \frac{Y_{CES}}{Yn_{CES}} \leq 0.008856$$

$$f\left(\frac{X_{CES}}{Xn_{CES}} \right) = \left(\frac{a^*_{CES}}{500} \right) + \left(\frac{Y_{CES}}{Yn_{CES}} \right)$$

$$f\left(\frac{Z_{CES}}{Zn_{CES}} \right) = f\left(\frac{X_{CES}}{Xn_{CES}} \right) - \left(\frac{b^*_{CES}}{200} \right)$$

$$X_{CES} = Xn_{CES} f\left(\frac{Y_{CES}}{Yn_{CES}} \right)^3 \qquad \text{for } f\left(\frac{X_{CES}}{Xn_{CES}} \right) > 0.008856^{1/3}$$

$$X_{CES} = \frac{Xn_{CES} \left[f\left(\frac{X_{CES}}{Xn_{CES}} \right) - \left(\frac{16}{116} \right) \right]}{7.787} \qquad \text{for } f\left(\frac{X_{CES}}{Xn_{CES}} \right) \leq 0.008856^{1/3}$$

$$Z_{CES} = Zn_{CES} f\left(\frac{Z_{CES}}{Zn_{CES}} \right)^3 \qquad \text{for } f\left(\frac{Z_{CES}}{Zn_{CES}} \right) > 0.008856^{1/3}$$

$$Z_{CES} = \frac{Zn_{CES} \left[f\left(\frac{Z_{CES}}{Zn_{CES}} \right) - \left(\frac{16}{116} \right) \right]}{7.787} \qquad \text{for } f\left(\frac{Z_{CES}}{Zn_{CES}} \right) \leq 0.008856^{1/3}$$

The next step in the transformation is to convert the resulting XYZ_{CES} tristimulus values to $R^*G^*B^*$ tristimulus values for the specified red, green, and blue primaries of the CES reference medium, which were defined in Table G2. This conversion is accomplished using the following matrix transformation:

$$
\begin{bmatrix} R^* \\ G^* \\ B^* \end{bmatrix} = \begin{bmatrix} 1.4521 & -0.2890 & -0.1349 \\ -0.1929 & 1.1713 & 0.0178 \\ 0.0015 & 0.1173 & 1.0682 \end{bmatrix} \begin{bmatrix} \dfrac{X_{CES}}{100} \\ \dfrac{Y_{CES}}{100} \\ \dfrac{Z_{CES}}{100} \end{bmatrix}
\qquad \{G14\}
$$

The logarithms of the $R^*G^*B^*$ tristimulus values then are calculated:

$$
R^*_{log} = \log_{10} R^*
$$
$$
G^*_{log} = \log_{10} G^* \qquad \{G15\}
$$
$$
B^*_{log} = \log_{10} B^*
$$

The resulting $R^*G^*B^*_{log}$ values then are transformed to RGB_{log} values by going "backwards" through the reference rendering characteristic listed in Table G3 and shown in Fig. G5. The resulting RGB_{log} values then are converted to linear values, RGB:

$$
R = 10^{R_{log}}
$$
$$
G = 10^{G_{log}} \qquad \{G16\}
$$
$$
B = 10^{B_{log}}
$$

The resulting RGB values next are transformed to $XYZ_{D_{50}}$ tristimulus values using the following matrix:

$$\begin{bmatrix} X_{D_{50}} \\ Y_{D_{50}} \\ Z_{D_{50}} \end{bmatrix} = \begin{bmatrix} 71.07 & 16.66 & 8.70 \\ 11.72 & 88.27 & 0.01 \\ -1.38 & -9.71 & 93.61 \end{bmatrix} \begin{bmatrix} R \\ G \\ B \end{bmatrix} \qquad \{G17\}$$

The $XYZ_{D_{50}}$ tristimulus values are transformed to $XYZ_{D_{65}}$ tristimulus values using the following von Kries chromatic adaptation matrix transformation:

$$\begin{bmatrix} X_{D_{65}} \\ Y_{D_{65}} \\ Z_{D_{65}} \end{bmatrix} = \begin{bmatrix} 0.9845 & -0.0547 & 0.0678 \\ -0.0060 & 1.0048 & 0.0012 \\ 0.0000 & 0.0000 & 1.3200 \end{bmatrix} \begin{bmatrix} X_{D_{50}} \\ Y_{D_{50}} \\ Z_{D_{50}} \end{bmatrix} \qquad \{G18\}$$

and then transformed to Reference Image Capture Device RGB_{709} tristimulus values:

$$\begin{bmatrix} R_{709} \\ G_{709} \\ B_{709} \end{bmatrix} = \begin{bmatrix} 3.2410 & -1.5374 & -0.4986 \\ -0.9692 & 1.8760 & 0.0416 \\ 0.0556 & -0.2040 & 1.0570 \end{bmatrix} \begin{bmatrix} \dfrac{X_{D_{65}}}{100} \\ \dfrac{Y_{D_{65}}}{100} \\ \dfrac{Z_{D_{65}}}{100} \end{bmatrix} \qquad \{G19\}$$

Reference Image-Capturing Device RGB_{709} tristimulus values next are transformed to nonlinear values, $R'G'B'_{709}$, as follows:

For $RGB_{709} \geq 0.018$:

$$R'_{709} = 1.099\, R_{709}{}^{0.45} - 0.099$$

$$G'_{709} = 1.099\, G_{709}{}^{0.45} - 0.099 \qquad \{G20a\}$$

$$B'_{709} = 1.099\, B_{709}{}^{0.45} - 0.099$$

For $RGB_{709} \leq -0.018$:

$$R'_{709} = -1.099 |R_{709}|^{0.45} + 0.099$$
$$G'_{709} = -1.099 |G_{709}|^{0.45} + 0.099 \qquad \{G20b\}$$
$$B'_{709} = -1.099 |B_{709}|^{0.45} + 0.099$$

For $-0.018 < RGB_{709} < 0.018$:

$$R'_{709} = 4.50 \, R_{709}$$
$$G'_{709} = 4.50 \, G_{709} \qquad \{G20c\}$$
$$B'_{709} = 4.50 \, B_{709}$$

The $R'G'B'_{709}$ nonlinear values are transformed to luma and chroma values as follows:

$$\begin{bmatrix} Luma \\ Chroma_1 \\ Chroma_2 \end{bmatrix} = \begin{bmatrix} 0.299 & 0.587 & 0.114 \\ -0.299 & -0.587 & 0.886 \\ 0.701 & -0.587 & -0.114 \end{bmatrix} \begin{bmatrix} R'_{709} \\ G'_{709} \\ B'_{709} \end{bmatrix} \qquad \{G21\}$$

Finally, luma and chroma values are converted to digital code values. For 24-bit (8 bits per channel) encoding, *PhotoYCC* Space values are formed according to the following equations:

$$Y = \left(\frac{255}{1.402} \right) Luma$$
$$C_1 = 111.40 \, Chroma_1 + 156 \qquad \{G22\}$$
$$C_2 = 135.64 \, Chroma_2 + 137$$

A Method for Transforming *PhotoYCC* Space Values to YC$_b$C$_r$ Values

Kodak PhotoYCC Color Interchange Space values can be transformed readily to YC$_b$C$_r$ digital code values, which are used in many software applications. One commonly used definition for YC$_b$C$_r$ is as follows:

$$Y_{CbCr} = 255\, E'_Y$$

$$C_b = 255\, E'_{Cb} + 128$$

$$C_r = 255\, E'_{Cr} + 128$$

{G23}

where E'_Y, E'_{Cb}, and E'_{Cr} are defined according to Recommendation ITU-R BT.601 (Rec. 601), and YC$_b$C$_r$ digital code values are the nearest integers to the values computed from the preceding equations.

In Rec. 601, E'_Y, E'_{Cb}, and E'_{Cr} are derived from nonlinear exposure signals, E'_r, E'_g, and E'_b, as shown below, using the primaries and nonlinear equations of Recommendation ITU-R BT.709 (Rec. 709).

$$E'_Y = 0.299E'_r + 0.587E'_g + 0.114E'_b$$

$$E'_{Cb} = 0.564\,(E'_b - E'_Y)$$

$$E'_{Cr} = 0.713\,(E'_r - E'_Y)$$

{G24}

Kodak PhotoYCC Color Interchange Space also is based on Rec. 709 primaries and nonlinear equations. Therefore E'_Y, E'_{Cb}, and E'_{Cr} have the same basic definitions as *PhotoYCC* Space Y, C_1, and C_2 values, although the scalings used in the respective data metrics are different, as shown below:

From Eqs. {G23} and {G24}:

$$Y_{CbCr} = 255\, E'_Y$$

$$C_b = 143.820\,(E'_b - E'_Y) + 128$$

$$C_r = 181.815\,(E'_r - E'_Y) + 128$$

{G25}

The comparable *PhotoYCC* Space equations are:

$$Y_{YCC} = \left(\frac{255}{1.402}\right) E'_Y$$

$$C_1 = 111.400\,(E'_b - E'_Y) + 156 \tag{G26}$$

$$C_2 = 135.640\,(E'_r - E'_Y) + 137$$

Therefore, *Kodak PhotoYCC* Color Interchange Space values can be transformed to YC_bC_r values as follows:

$$Y_{CbCr} = 1.402\,Y_{YCC}$$

$$C_b = 1.291\,C_1 - 73.400 \tag{G27}$$

$$C_r = 1.340\,C_2 - 55.638$$

It should be noted that in this transformation, *PhotoYCC* Space highlight information above 100% scene white will be clipped at code value 255. More satisfactory results generally are obtained by first performing an appropriate modification of the *PhotoYCC* Space values. One method for doing this is to first convert *PhotoYCC* Space Y, C_1, and C_2 values to $R'G'B'_{709}$ nonlinear values using Eqs. {G1} and {G2}. The resulting $R'G'B'_{709}$ values then can be remapped, using a lookup table such as that shown in Fig. G7, so that the remapped values do not exceed 1.00. These remapped values then can be converted back to modified *PhotoYCC* Space Y, C_1, and C_2 values using Eqs. {G21} and {G22}, and to YC_bC_r values using Eqs. {G27}.

YC_bC_r values can be transformed to *PhotoYCC* Space values using the inverse of the procedure that has been described here. However, the result of attempting to expand the YC_bC_r encoded highlight information may not be satisfactory. It also should be noted that the color gamut of YC_bC_r is significantly smaller than that of *Kodak PhotoYCC* Color Interchange Space. Therefore, the color quality of an image transformed to *PhotoYCC* Space values from YC_bC_r values may not match that of an image encoded directly in terms of *PhotoYCC* Space values.

Figure G7

Figure G7
Graphical representation of a lookup table for remapping *PhotoYCC* Space $R'G'B'_{709}$ values. This remapping prevents clipping of highlight information in the transformation to YC_bC_r values.

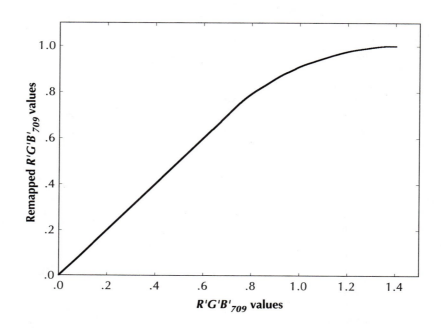

A Method for Transforming *PhotoYCC* Space Values to *Cineon* System Values

Cineon System code values correspond to printing densities for motion picture negative films. The printing densities are determined for a reference print medium and printer (Chapter 7). The basic steps involved in the transformation of *PhotoYCC* Space Y, C_1, C_2 values to *Cineon* System code values are shown in Fig. G8. These include the following operations:

- A data metric conversion from *PhotoYCC* Space Y, C_1, and C_2 values to Reference Image-Capturing Device R, G, and B tristimulus values.
- A transformation of those R, G, and B tristimulus values to corresponding R, G, and B exposure values for a representative motion picture negative film.

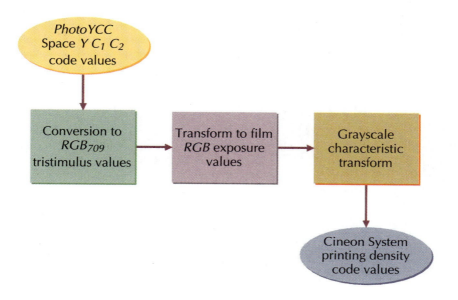

Figure G8

Transformation of *PhotoYCC* Space Y, C_1, and C_2 code values to *Cineon* System printing density code values.

- Mapping the resulting R, G, and B film exposure values through the grayscale characteristic of a representative motion-picture negative film to produce printing-density code values.

In the first step of the transformation, luma and chroma values are computed from *PhotoYCC* Space Y, C_1, and C_2 digital values. Luma and chroma values are computed from 24-bit (8 bits per channel) encoded *PhotoYCC* Space values according to the following equations:

$$Luma = \left(\frac{1.402}{255}\right) Y$$

$$Chroma_1 = \frac{(C_1 - 156)}{111.40}$$

$$Chroma_2 = \frac{(C_2 - 137)}{135.64}$$

{G28}

The resulting *Luma*, *Chroma*₁, and *Chroma*₂ values are converted to nonlinear values, $R'G'B'_{709}$, using the following matrix transformation:

$$\begin{bmatrix} R'_{709} \\ G'_{709} \\ B'_{709} \end{bmatrix} = \begin{bmatrix} 1 & 0 & 1 \\ 1 & -0.194 & -0.509 \\ 1 & 1 & 0 \end{bmatrix} \begin{bmatrix} Luma \\ Chroma_1 \\ Chroma_2 \end{bmatrix} \qquad \{G29\}$$

The $R'G'B'_{709}$ nonlinear values are converted to linear tristimulus values, RGB_{709}, as shown below.

For $R'G'B'_{709} \geq 0.081$:

$$R_{709} = \left(\frac{R'_{709} + 0.099}{1.099} \right)^{1/0.45}$$

$$G_{709} = \left(\frac{G'_{709} + 0.099}{1.099} \right)^{1/0.45} \qquad \{G30a\}$$

$$B_{709} = \left(\frac{B'_{709} + 0.099}{1.099} \right)^{1/0.45}$$

For $R'G'B'_{709} \leq -0.081$:

$$R_{709} = -\left(\frac{R'_{709} - 0.099}{-1.099} \right)^{1/0.45}$$

$$G_{709} = -\left(\frac{G'_{709} - 0.099}{-1.099} \right)^{1/0.45} \qquad \{G30b\}$$

$$B_{709} = -\left(\frac{B'_{709} - 0.099}{-1.099} \right)^{1/0.45}$$

For $-0.081 < R'G'B'_{709} < 0.081$:

$$R_{709} = \frac{R'_{709}}{4.5}$$

$$G_{709} = \frac{G'_{709}}{4.5} \qquad \{G30c\}$$

$$B_{709} = \frac{B'_{709}}{4.5}$$

The resulting RGB_{709} tristimulus values next are converted to corresponding RGB_{film} exposure values. The matrix used in this conversion was determined such that, for a particular set of test colors, the differences between colorimetric values computed using the spectral sensitivities for a representative motion picture negative film and values converted from the RGB_{709} tristimulus values are minimized.

$$\begin{bmatrix} R_{film} \\ G_{film} \\ B_{film} \end{bmatrix} = \begin{bmatrix} 0.8370 & 0.0800 & 0.0830 \\ 0.0023 & 0.9414 & 0.0563 \\ -0.0005 & 0.1046 & 0.8959 \end{bmatrix} \begin{bmatrix} R_{709} \\ G_{709} \\ B_{709} \end{bmatrix} \qquad \{G31\}$$

The logarithms of the RGB_{film} exposure values then are calculated:

$$R_{log} = \log_{10} R_{film}$$

$$G_{log} = \log_{10} G_{film} \qquad \{G32\}$$

$$B_{log} = \log_{10} B_{film}$$

The resulting RGB_{log} values are scaled and shifted as follows to form RGB values consistent with the input values of Table G4:

$$R = 1000\, R_{log} + 2500$$

$$G = 1000\, G_{log} + 2500 \qquad \{G33\}$$

$$B = 1000\, B_{log} + 2500$$

The resulting RGB values are transformed to *Cineon* System printing density code values (10 bits per channel) using the lookup table defined in Table G4. This table is based on the relationship of printing density to relative log exposure factor for a representative motion picture film (Fig. G9).

Table G4

Cineon System code values (10 bits per channel) versus *R*, *G*, or *B* input value from Eq. {G33}.

Input: R, G, or B value	Output: Cineon System code value	Input: R, G, or B value	Output: Cineon System code value
≤0	95	2100	560
100	95	2200	590
200	95	2300	623
300	97	2400	655
400	100	2500	685
500	104	2600	715
600	115	2700	745
700	137	2800	775
800	165	2900	805
900	195	3000	835
1000	225	3100	860
1100	255	3200	880
1200	285	3300	897
1300	318	3400	910
1400	350	3500	920
1500	380	3600	925
1600	410	3700	928
1700	440	3800	930
1800	470	3900	933
1900	500	≥4000	935
2000	530		

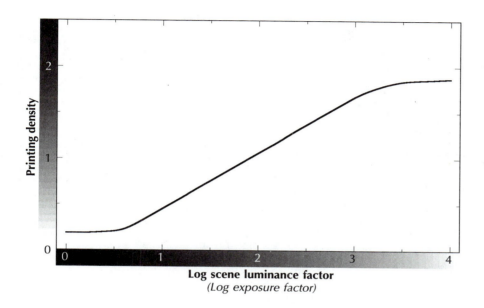

Figure G9
Printing-density grayscale of a representative motion-picture negative film. This grayscale is the basis for the values of Table G4.

A Method for Transforming Prototype CES Values to *FlashPix* NIFRGB Code Values

NIFRGB values, which are used in the *FlashPix* Format, specify color in terms of 8-bit *RGB* code values. The color represented by a set of NIFRGB values is that which would be formed if those code values were input to a specified reference monitor and if the resulting color stimulus produced by the monitor were viewed according to a specified set of encoding reference viewing conditions (Table G5).

The reference monitor is representative of those used on the majority of personal computers. It is defined in terms of a set of reference primaries and a characteristic curve relating nonlinear input signals to output relative intensities. The reference primaries are those defined in Recommendation ITU-R BT.709. The chromaticity coordinates of those primaries are given in Table G6.

Viewing flare	1.0%
Surround type	Average
Luminance level	80 cd/m²
Adaptive white	$x = 0.3127$, $y = 0.3290$

	Red	**Green**	**Blue**	**D_{65}**
x	0.6400	0.3000	0.1500	0.3127
y	0.3300	0.6000	0.0600	0.3290
z	0.0300	0.1000	0.7900	0.3583
u′	0.4507	0.1250	0.1754	0.1978
v′	0.5229	0.5625	0.1579	0.4683

The grayscale characteristic for the reference monitor (Fig. G10) was designed to meet three criteria. First, because NIFRGB code values are meant to be used directly as monitor code values, the characteristic had to be consistent with the characteristics of actual monitors. Second, the characteristic had to be such that its use produced images in which the effects of quantization were minimal. Third, for use in transformations, the characteristic had to have good mathematical reversibility.

The monitor characteristic is defined by the following equations relating nonlinear input signal values, $R'G'B'_{NIF}$, to output relative intensity values, RGB_{NIF}.

For $R'G'B'_{NIF} \geq 0.03929$:

$$R_{NIF} = \left(\frac{R'_{NIF} + 0.055}{1.055} \right)^{2.40}$$

$$G_{NIF} = \left(\frac{G'_{NIF} + 0.055}{1.055} \right)^{2.40} \qquad \{G34a\}$$

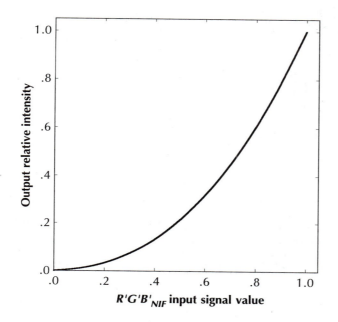

Figure G10
Characteristic for
the NIFRGB refer-
ence monitor. The
reference monitor
is representative of
those used on the
majority of per-
sonal computers.

$$B_{NIF} = \left(\frac{B'_{NIF} + 0.055}{1.055} \right)^{2.40}$$

For $R'G'B'_{NIF} < 0.03929$:

$$R_{NIF} = \frac{R'_{NIF}}{12.92}$$

$$G_{NIF} = \frac{G'_{NIF}}{12.92} \qquad \qquad \{G34b\}$$

$$B_{NIF} = \frac{B'_{NIF}}{12.92}$$

The first step in the transformation of prototype CES values to visually equivalent NIFRGB values is a conversion of CES code values to CIELAB $L*a*b*_{CES}$ values:

$$L^*_{CES} = \frac{CV_1}{2.10}$$

$$a^*_{CES} = CV_2 - 128 \qquad\qquad \{G35\}$$

$$b^*_{CES} = CV_3 - 128$$

The resulting CIELAB $L*a*b*_{CES}$ values then are converted to CIE XYZ_{CES} values. In the following calculations, the tristimulus values for the reference white are those of CIE Standard Illuminant D_{50} ($Xn_{CES} = 96.42$, $Yn_{CES} = 100.00$, and $Zn_{CES} = 82.49$).

$$Y_{CES} = Yn_{CES} \left(\frac{L^*_{CES} + 16}{116}\right)^3 \qquad\qquad \text{for } L^* > 8 \qquad \{G36\}$$

$$Y_{CES} = Yn_{CES} \left(\frac{L^*_{CES}}{903.3}\right) \qquad\qquad \text{for } L^* \le 8$$

$$f\left(\frac{Y_{CES}}{Yn_{CES}}\right) = \left(\frac{Y_{CES}}{Yn_{CES}}\right)^{(1/3)} \qquad\qquad \text{for } \frac{Y_{CES}}{Yn_{CES}} > 0.008856$$

$$f\left(\frac{Y_{CES}}{Yn_{CES}}\right) = 7.787 \left(\frac{Y_{CES}}{Yn_{CES}}\right) + \left(\frac{16}{116}\right) \qquad\qquad \text{for } \frac{Y_{CES}}{Yn_{CES}} \le 0.008856$$

$$f\left(\frac{X_{CES}}{Xn_{CES}}\right) = \left(\frac{a^*_{CES}}{500}\right) + f\left(\frac{Y_{CES}}{Yn_{CES}}\right)$$

$$f\left(\frac{Z_{CES}}{Zn_{CES}}\right) = f\left(\frac{X_{CES}}{Xn_{CES}}\right) - \left(\frac{b^*_{CES}}{200}\right)$$

$$X_{CES} = Xn_{CES} \, f\left(\frac{X_{CES}}{Xn_{CES}}\right)^3 \qquad \text{for } f\left(\frac{X_{CES}}{Xn_{CES}}\right) > 0.008856^{1/3}$$

$$X_{CES} = \frac{Xn_{CES}\left[f\left(\dfrac{X_{CES}}{Xn_{CES}}\right) - \left(\dfrac{16}{116}\right)\right]}{7.787} \qquad \text{for } f\left(\frac{X_{CES}}{Xn_{CES}}\right) \leq 0.008856^{1/3}$$

$$Z_{CES} = Zn_{CES} \, f\left(\frac{Z_{CES}}{Zn_{CES}}\right)^3 \qquad \text{for } f\left(\frac{Z_{CES}}{Zn_{CES}}\right) > 0.008856^{1/3}$$

$$Z_{CES} = \frac{Zn_{CES}\left[f\left(\dfrac{Z_{CES}}{Zn_{CES}}\right) - \left(\dfrac{16}{116}\right)\right]}{7.787} \qquad \text{for } f\left(\frac{Z_{CES}}{Zn_{CES}}\right) \leq 0.008856^{1/3}$$

The next step in the transformation is to convert the resulting XYZ_{CES} tristimulus values, which are based on D_{50} adaptive white chromaticity coordinates, to visually equivalent XYZ_{D65} tristimulus values, using the following von Kries chromatic adaptation matrix transformation:

$$\begin{bmatrix} X_{D_{65}} \\ Y_{D_{65}} \\ Z_{D_{65}} \end{bmatrix} = \begin{bmatrix} 0.9845 & -0.0547 & 0.0678 \\ -0.0060 & 1.0048 & 0.0012 \\ 0.0000 & 0.0000 & 1.3200 \end{bmatrix} \begin{bmatrix} X_{CES} \\ Y_{CES} \\ Z_{CES} \end{bmatrix} \qquad \{G37\}$$

The resulting XYZ_{D65} tristimulus values next are transformed to RGB_{NIF} tristimulus values:

$$\begin{bmatrix} R_{NIF} \\ G_{NIF} \\ B_{NIF} \end{bmatrix} = \begin{bmatrix} 3.2410 & -1.5374 & -0.4986 \\ -0.9692 & 1.8760 & 0.0416 \\ 0.0556 & -0.2040 & 1.0570 \end{bmatrix} \begin{bmatrix} \dfrac{X_{D_{65}}}{100} \\[2mm] \dfrac{Y_{D_{65}}}{100} \\[2mm] \dfrac{Z_{D_{65}}}{100} \end{bmatrix} \qquad \{G38\}$$

The resulting RGB_{NIF} tristimulus values, which represent reference monitor intensity values, are transformed to nonlinear values, $R'G'B'_{NIF}$, using equations that are the inverse of monitor characteristic given by Eqs. {G34}.

For $RGB_{NIF} \geq 0.00304$:

$$R'_{NIF} = 1.055 R_{NIF}^{(1/2.40)} - 0.055$$

$$G'_{NIF} = 1.055 G_{NIF}^{(1/2.40)} - 0.055 \qquad \{G39\}$$

$$B'_{NIF} = 1.055 B_{NIF}^{(1/2.40)} - 0.055$$

For $RGB_{NIF} < 0.00304$:

$$R'_{NIF} = 12.92 R_{NIF}$$

$$G'_{NIF} = 12.92 G_{NIF} \qquad \{G40\}$$

$$B'_{NIF} = 12.92 B_{NIF}$$

Finally, the resulting $R'G'B'_{NIF}$ values are converted to digital code values. For 24-bit (8 bits per channel) encoding, NIFRGB values are the nearest integers to the values determined from the following equations:

$$R_{NIFRGB} = 255 R'_{NIF}$$

$$G_{NIFRGB} = 255 G'_{NIF} \qquad \{G41\}$$

$$B_{NIFRGB} = 255 B'_{NIF}$$

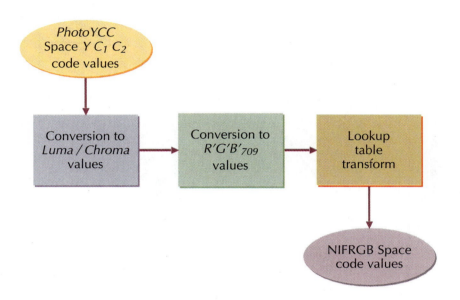

Figure G11
Relationship of
PhotoYCC Space
values to NIFRGB
values used in the
FlashPix Format.

A Method for Transforming *PhotoYCC* Space Values to NIFRGB Code Values

NIFRGB values, used in the *FlashPix* Format, are closely related to *Kodak PhotoYCC* Color Interchange Space values. The relationship is shown above in Fig. G11.

In the first step of the transformation of *PhotoYCC* Space values to NIFRGB values, luma and chroma values are computed from *PhotoYCC* Space Y, C_1, and C_2 digital code values. For 24-bit (8 bits per channel) encoding, the luma and chroma values are computed according to the following equations:

$$Luma = \left(\frac{1.402}{255}\right)Y$$

$$Chroma_1 = \frac{(C_1 - 156)}{111.40} \qquad \{G42\}$$

Figure G12

Graphical repre-
sentation of a
lookup table
for mapping
PhotoYCC Space
R'_{709}, G'_{709}, and
B'_{709} nonlinear
values to NIFRGB
code values. The
mapping prevents
clipping of high-
light information.

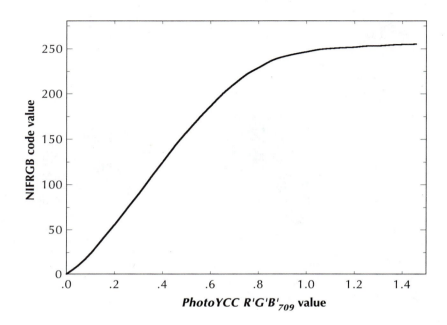

$$Chroma_2 = \frac{(C_2 - 137)}{135.64}$$

The resulting *Luma, Chroma$_1$,* and *Chroma$_2$* values are converted to nonlinear values, $R'G'B'_{709}$:

$$\begin{bmatrix} R'_{709} \\ G'_{709} \\ B'_{709} \end{bmatrix} = \begin{bmatrix} 1 & 0 & 1 \\ 1 & -0.194 & -0.509 \\ 1 & 1 & 0 \end{bmatrix} \begin{bmatrix} Luma \\ Chroma_1 \\ Chroma_2 \end{bmatrix} \qquad \{G43\}$$

The $R'G'B'_{709}$ nonlinear values are converted to NIFRGB values using the lookup table shown in Fig. G12 and listed in Table G7. The conversion scales and remaps the $R'G'B'_{709}$ values such that high-luminance information is not clipped. Note, however, that any negative $R'G'B'_{709}$ values are clipped at zero. The color gamut of NIFRGB encoding therefore is limited to that which can be produced on the reference monitor.

$R'G'B'_{709}$ Input value	NIFRGB Output value
≤0.00	0.00
0.05	10.15
0.10	23.44
0.15	39.17
0.20	55.23
0.25	72.35
0.30	89.13
0.35	107.06
0.40	124.35
0.45	141.63
0.50	157.24
0.55	172.15
0.60	186.07
0.65	199.58
0.70	210.65
0.75	221.07
0.80	228.59
0.85	236.00
0.90	240.79
0.95	243.94
1.00	246.41
1.05	248.92
1.10	250.17
1.15	251.04
1.20	251.64
1.25	252.88
1.30	253.07
1.35	254.03
1.40	254.61
≥1.402	255.00

Table G7

A lookup table for mapping R'_{709}, G'_{709} and B'_{709} values to NIFRGB code values.

Glossary

a b** diagram
A plot of $a*$ and $b*$ values of the 1976 CIE $L*a*b*$ (CIELAB) color space.

absorption
The transformation of radiant energy to a different form of energy by interaction with matter; retention of light without reflection or transmission.

achromatic
Perceived as having no hue; white, gray, or black.

adaptation
The process by which the visual mechanism adjusts to the conditions under which the eyes are exposed to radiant energy.

adaptive white
A color stimulus that an observer, adapted to a set of viewing conditions, would judge to be perfectly achromatic and to have a luminance factor of unity.

additive color
Color formed by the mixture of light from a set of primary light sources, generally red, green, and blue.

advanced colorimetry
Colorimetric measurement and numerical methods that include colorimetric adjustments for certain physical and perceptual factors determined according to perceptual experiments and/or models of the human visual system.

AgX
Silver halide; a light-sensitive crystalline compound used in conventional photographic materials.

average surround

An area, surrounding an image being viewed, that has a luminance factor of about 0.20 and chromaticity equal to that of the observer adaptive white; also called a normal surround.

bit

Contraction of *binary digit*; the smallest unit of information that a computer can store and process.

block dye

A theoretical dye having equal absorption of light at each wavelength within a given continuous range of wavelengths and no absorption at all other wavelengths of interest.

brightness

An attribute of a visual sensation according to which an area appears to exhibit more or less light.

brightness adaptation, general

The process by which the visual mechanism adjusts in response to the overall luminance level of the radiant energy to which the eyes are exposed.

brightness adaptation, lateral

A perceptual phenomenon wherein a stimulus appears more or less bright depending on the relative brightness of adjacent stimuli.

CCD

Abbreviation for *charge coupled device*; a solid-state sensor often used in digital still cameras and scanners to convert light into an electrical signal.

CCIR (Comité Consultatif Internationale des Radiocommunications)

Abbreviation for the *International Radio Consultive Committee*, an international television standardization organization, now ITU-R.

CCIR Recommendation 601

A document containing recommended specifications for digital component video, now referred to as Recommendation ITU-R BT.601, or more informally as Rec. 601.

CCIR Recommendation 709

A document containing recommended specifications for high-definition television signals, now referred to as Recommendation ITU-R BT.709, or more informally as Rec. 709.

CD-ROM

Abbreviation for *compact disc read-only memory*; a compact disc used for storing digital data for computer applications.

calibration

Procedure of correcting for any deviation from a standard.

CES

Abbreviation for *color encoding specification*.

characterization

Procedure of defining the color characteristics for a representative operating model of an input or output device.

charge coupled device (CCD)

A solid-state sensor often used in digital still cameras and scanners to convert light into an electrical signal.

chroma

1. The colorfulness of an area judged in proportion to the brightness of a similarly illuminated area that appears to be white; degree of departure of a color from a gray of the same lightness.
2. A color component of a color video signal.

chroma subsampling

A technique for compressing image information, generally for storage or transmission, in which luma (achromatic) information is retained at full spatial resolution while chroma (non-achromatic) information is reduced.

chromatic adaptation

The process by which the visual mechanism adjusts in response to the average chromaticity of the radiant energy to which the eyes are exposed.

chromaticity
The property of a color stimulus defined by its chromaticity coordinates, such as its CIE x, y, z values.

chromaticity coordinates
The ratio of each of a set of tristimulus values to their sum.

chromaticity diagram
A plane diagram in which points specified by chromaticity coordinates represent the chromaticities of color stimuli.

chrominance
The properties of a color other than its luminance.

CIE (Commission Internationale de l'Éclairage)
The *International Commission on Illumination*; the body responsible for international recommendations for photometry and colorimetry.

CIE colorimetry
Measurement of color stimuli according to the spectral responsivities of a CIE Standard Observer.

CIE 1931 Standard Colorimetric Observer
An ideal colorimetric observer with color-matching functions corresponding to a field of view subtending a 2° angle on the retina.

CIE tristimulus values
The values X, Y, and Z, determined according to the color-matching properties of the CIE 1931 Standard Colorimetric Observer.

CIELAB color space
A color space, defined in terms of L^*, a^*, and b^* coordinates, in which equal distances in the space represent approximately equal color differences.

CIELUV color space
A color space, defined in terms of L^*, u^*, and v^* coordinates, in which equal distances in the space represent approximately equal color differences.

CIEXYZ color space

A color space defined in terms of tristimulus values X, Y, and Z, which are determined according to the color-matching properties of the CIE Standard Colorimetric Observer.

CIS

Abbreviation for *color interchange standard*.

CMY/CMYK

Abbreviations for *cyan* (C), *magenta* (M), *yellow* (Y), and *black* (K) dyes or inks used in subtractive color imaging.

clipping

Condition where variation of an input signal produces no further variation of an output signal.

code value

A digital value produced by, or being provided to, an imaging device.

color encoding

The numerical specification of color information.

color-encoding data metric

The numerical units in which encoded color data are expressed.

color-encoding method

Measurement methods and signal-processing transformations that determine the meaning of encoded color values.

color encoding specification (CES)

A fully specified color-encoding scheme, defined by a color-encoding method and a color-encoding data metric, used for encoding color on an individual system. A complete CES also may include specifications for other factors, such as data compression method and data file format.

colorfulness

Attribute of a visual sensation according to which an area appears to exhibit more or less of its hue.

color gamut

The limits of the array of colors that can be captured by an image-capturing device, represented by a color-encoding data metric, or physically realized by an output device or medium.

colorant

A dye, pigment, ink, or other agent used to impart a color to a material.

colorimeter

Instrument that measures color stimuli in terms of tristimulus values according to responsivities prescribed for a standard observer.

colorimetric characteristics

Referring to characteristics, such as the color-reproduction characteristics of a device, medium, or system, as measured according to standard colorimetric techniques.

colorimetry

A branch of color science concerned with the measurement and specification of color stimuli; the science of color measurement.

colorimetry, standard

In this book, refers to colorimetric values determined according to current CIE recommended practices.

color interchange specification (CIS)

A fully specified color interchange scheme that includes a complete colorimetric specification, a defined data metric, and a defined set of reference viewing conditions. A complete CIS also may include specifications for other factors, such as data compression method and data file format.

colorist

An operator who adjusts the electronic signal processing in the transfer of photographic images to video.

color management

The use of appropriate hardware, software, and methodology to control and adjust color in an imaging system.

color-matching functions
The tristimulus values of a sequence of visible monochromatic stimuli of equal radiant power.

color primaries, additive
Independent light sources of different color (usually red, green, and blue) which may be combined to form various colors.

color primaries, subtractive
Colorants, each of which selectively absorbs light of one of the additive primaries. A cyan colorant absorbs red light, a magenta colorant absorbs green light, and a yellow colorant absorbs blue light.

color stimulus
Radiant energy such as that produced by an illuminant, by the reflection of light from a reflective object, or by the transmission of light through a transmissive object.

composite transform
A single signal-processing transform formed by the concatenation of a sequence of two or more individual transforms.

compositing
Merging portions of various images to form a single image.

compression
A process used to reduce the size of data files for storage or transmission.

concatenation
Process of combining a sequence of two or more individual signal-processing transforms to form a single equivalent transform.

cones
Photoreceptors in the retina that initiate the process of color vision.

contrast, objective
The degree of dissimilarity of a measured quantity, such as luminance, of two areas, expressed as a number computed by a specified formula.

contrast, subjective

The degree of dissimilarity in appearance of two parts of a field of view seen simultaneously or successively.

control voltage, CRT

Voltage signal used to modulate beam current, and thus light output, of a CRT.

corresponding colorimetric values

Colorimetric values for corresponding stimuli (see below).

corresponding stimuli

Pairs of color stimuli that look alike when one is viewed in one set of adaptation conditions, and the other is viewed in a different set.

coupler

An organic compound, used in most photographic media, which reacts with an oxidized developing agent to form a dye.

coupler, colored

A coupler (see above) that is itself colored.

cross-talk

Transfer of information from one color channel to another.

CRT

Abbreviation for *cathode ray tube*.

cyan

One of the subtractive primaries; a cyan colorant absorbs red light and reflects or transmits green and blue light.

DAC

Abbreviation for *digital-to-analog converter*.

dark surround

An area, surrounding an image being viewed, having a luminance much lower than that of the image itself.

dark-surround effect

A manifestation of lateral-brightness adaptation; an observer will perceive an image to have lower luminance contrast if that image is viewed in darker-surround conditions.

data metric

The numerical units in which a given set of data are expressed.

daylight

A mixture of skylight and direct sunlight.

daylight illuminant

An illuminant having the same, or nearly the same, relative spectral power distribution as a phase of daylight.

densitometer

A device for directly measuring transmission or reflection optical densities. For meaningful color measurements, the spectral responses of the densitometer must be specified.

densitometry

The measurement of optical density.

density, optical

The negative logarithm (base 10) of the reflectance factor or transmittance factor.

device-independent color

As defined by the authors, refers to techniques for numerically specifying and encoding color information in a way that is not restricted to either the luminance dynamic range or the color gamut achievable by physically realizable devices.

diffuse

Referring to light that is scattered, widely spread, not concentrated.

digital color encoding

The representation of color information in the form of digital values.

digital quantization
Conversion of continuous quantities to discrete digital values; the number of discrete values is determined by the number of bits that are used.

digitize
Convert analog signals or other continuous quantities to digital values.

display
An image presented to an observer; the process of presenting that image.

duplicate
A reproduction that is a one-to-one physical copy of an original. The spectral properties of the colorants of a duplicate are identical to those of the original.

dyes
Organic colorants used in silver-halide-based photographic media and in other imaging technologies.

dynamic range
Extent of minimum and maximum operational characteristics.

encoder and decoder circuits
Used in video systems to combine various signals into a composite signal and to subsequently extract the individual signals from the composite.

exposure
The quantity of radiant energy received per unit area; the quantity of radiant energy that is captured by a detector or that forms a detectable signal.

exposure factor
Ratio of exposure to that from a perfect diffuser that is illuminated identically.

field
That portion of the surface of a specimen that is illuminated by the illuminator or viewed by the receiver.

film terms
Input signal-processing transforms used on *Kodak Photo CD* System scanners to convert scanned values to *PhotoYCC* Space values.

film writer

An output device, used in hybrid color-imaging systems, which produces an image on a photographic film.

flare

Stray light; a non-imagewise addition or redistribution of light.

fluorescence

Process whereby incident radiant power at one wavelength is absorbed and immediately re-emitted at another (usually longer) wavelength.

gamma, photographic

The slope of the straight-line portion of a characteristic curve relating optical density to relative log exposure.

gamma, CRT

1. Exponent of a power-law equation relating CRT luminance to control-signal voltage.
2. The slope of the straight-line portion of a CRT characteristic curve relating log luminance to log voltage.

gamma correction

The use of signal processing in a video camera to complement the characteristics of a video display device such as a CRT.

gamut, color

The limits for a set of colors.

gamut boundary

Outermost surface of a color space defined by a particular color gamut.

gamut adjustment (or gamut mapping)

A method for replacing colorimetric values corresponding to colors that are not physically realizable by a considered output device or medium with substitute values that are attainable by that output. In some methods, values within the attainable gamut also are altered.

grayscale
A progression of achromatic colors from blacks to grays to white.

HDTV
An abbreviation for *high-definition television* system, a system having greater spatial resolution than that of current broadcast television systems.

hardcopy
General term referring to solid media such as paper or film base.

hue
Attribute of a visual sensation according to which an area appears to be similar to one, or to proportions of two, of the perceived colors red, yellow, green, and blue.

hybrid (color-imaging) system
A system which incorporates photographic and electronic imaging technologies.

ICC
Abbreviation for International Color Consortium, an industry group formed in 1993 to promote interoperability among color-imaging systems.

illuminant
A light, which may or may not be physically realizable as a source, defined in terms of its spectral power distribution.

illuminant sensitivity
Propensity for colors formed by a set of colorants to change in appearance as the spectral power distribution of the viewing illuminant is changed.

image dyes, image-forming dyes
Dyes, usually CMY or CMYK, that make up a displayable image.

independent primaries
Sets of light sources in which the chromaticities of each source can not be matched by any mixture of the remaining sources.

ink
A colored liquid or paste used in printing.

input

General term referring to imaging media, signals, or data to be put into a color-imaging system.

input compatibility

Expression used by the authors to describe the result of color encoding images such that encoded values completely and unambiguously specify the color of each pixel on a common basis, regardless of the disparity of the sources of the image data.

intensity

Flux per unit solid angle; used in this and other texts as a general term to indicate the amount of light.

interlayer effects

Chemical reactions that take place among the various layers of a photographic medium. These interactions are used for color signal processing.

ISO

Abbreviation for *International Standards Organization*.

isotropic

Independent of direction.

ITU

Abbreviation for *International Telecommunications Union;* the United Nations regulatory body covering all forms of communication. ITU-R (previously CCIR) deals with radio spectrum management issues and regulation.

latent image

A collection of latent-image sites (small clusters of metallic silver within silver halide crystals, formed by exposure of the crystals to light) in a photographic medium. During chemical processing, crystals with latent-image sites are developed to form metallic silver, while those without latent-image sites are not.

lateral brightness adaptation

A perceptual phenomenon wherein a stimulus appears more or less bright depending on the relative brightness of adjacent stimuli. (See dark surround.)

light

1. Electromagnetic radiant energy that is visually detectable by the normal human observer; radiant energy having wavelengths from about 380 nm to about 780 nm.
2. Adjective denoting high lightness.

lightness

The brightness of an area judged relative to the brightness of a similarly illuminated area that appears to be white or highly transmitting.

light source

A physically realizable emitter of visually detectable electromagnetic radiation, defined in terms of its spectral power distribution.

lookup table (LUT)

A computer memory device in which input values act as the address to the memory, which subsequently generates output values according to the data stored at the addressed locations.

luma

The achromatic component of a video signal.

luminance

A measure, of a luminous surface, that is an approximate correlate to the perception of brightness.

luminance contrast

Apparent rate of change from lighter to darker areas of an image. Luminance contrast approximately corresponds to grayscale photographic gamma.

luminance dynamic range

Extent of maximum and minimum luminance values, often expressed as a ratio, e.g., 1000:1, or as a logarithmic range, e.g., 3.0 log luminance.

luminance factor

Ratio of the luminance of a specimen to that of a perfect diffuser that is illuminated identically.

magenta
One of the subtractive primaries; a magenta colorant absorbs green light and reflects or transmits red and blue light.

metameric color stimuli
Spectrally different color stimuli that have the same tristimulus values.

metameric pair
Two spectrally different color stimuli that have the same tristimulus values.

metamerism, visual
Property of two specimens that match under a specified illuminator and to a specified observer and whose spectral reflectances or transmittances differ in the visible wavelengths.

metamerism, degree of
Reference to the extent to which matching stimuli are spectrally different. A pair of stimuli that match but have very different spectral characteristics are referred to as being highly metameric.

metamerism, instrument
Property of two specimens that measure identically according to the spectral responsivities of an instrument and whose spectral reflectances or transmittances differ in the wavelengths of those responsivities.

monitor white
Color stimulus produced by a monitor when maximum red, green, and blue code values are applied; measured values for that stimulus.

monochromatic
Electromagnetic radiation of one wavelength or of a very small range of wavelengths.

nanometer (nm)
Unit of length equal to 10^{-9} meter, commonly used for identifying wavelengths of the electromagnetic spectrum.

negative

A photographic medium, usually intended to be printed onto a second negative-working photographic medium, that forms a reversed image, i.e., higher exposure levels result in the formation of greater optical density.

neutral

Achromatic, without hue.

normal surround

An area, surrounding an image being viewed, that has a luminance factor of about 0.20 and chromaticity equal to that of the observer adaptive white; also called an average surround.

nm

Abbreviation for *nanometer*.

observer metamerism

The property of specimens having different spectral characteristics and having the same color when viewed by one observer, but different colors when viewed by a different observer under the same conditions.

opto-electronic transfer characteristic

Characteristic defining the relationship between exposure and output signal voltage for a video camera.

output

General term referring to images, signals, or data produced by color-imaging systems.

PCS

Abbreviation for *profile connection space*, a fully defined color space used for linking and/or concatenating a series of profiles.

perfect white

An ideal isotropic diffuser with a spectral reflectance factor or spectral transmittance factor equal to unity at each wavelength of interest.

phosphors

Materials, deposited on the screen of a cathode ray tube, which emit light when irradiated by the electron beam(s) of the tube.

***Photo CD* Player**

A device, similar to an audio compact disc player, which is used to display images from *Photo CD* Discs on conventional television receivers and monitors.

***Photo CD* System**

A hybrid color-imaging system, developed by Eastman Kodak Company, which produces compact discs of images by scanning and digitally encoding images from photographic media.

***PhotoYCC* Color Interchange Space**

The data metric of the *Kodak Photo* CD System, in which color data are encoded in terms of a luma value, Y, and two chroma values, C_1 and C_2.

photographic image-forming dyes

The cyan, magenta, and yellow dyes that are formed by the chemical processing of a photographic medium after exposure of that medium to light.

photon

A quantum of light or of other electromagnetic radiation.

pigment

Finely ground insoluble particles that, when dispersed in a liquid vehicle, give color to paints, printing inks, and other materials by reflecting and absorbing light.

PIW

Abbreviation for *Photo CD* Imaging Workstation. A system consisting of one or more input scanners, computers, monitors, and CD writers used for authoring *Photo CD* Discs.

pixel

Contraction of *picture element*; a single point sample of an image.

positive
A photographic medium, usually intended for direct viewing, in which higher levels of exposure result in the formation of less optical density.

power
Energy per unit time.

prepress
Term used to describe the process, or components of the process, of preparing information for printing after the writing and design concepts stages.

primaries
Basic colors used to make other colors by addition or subtraction.

principal subject area
The area of a scene that is metered or otherwise used in the determination of camera exposure.

printing density
Optical densities measured according to a set of effective spectral responsivities defined by the spectral power distribution of a printer light source and the spectral sensitivities of a print medium.

product-specific film terms
Input signal-processing transforms used in *Photo CD* Imaging Workstations to convert scanned values to *PhotoYCC* Space values. A product-specific film-term transform is based on the characteristics of the particular film being scanned. When product-specific film terms are used, differences among scanned films are minimized in the color encoding.

profile
A digital signal-processing transform, or collection of transforms, plus additional information concerning the transform(s), device, and data.

profile, abstract
A profile providing the information necessary to modify color values expressed in a profile connection space (PCS).

profile, destination
A profile providing the information necessary to convert color values expressed in a profile connection space (PCS) to output device values.

profile, source
A profile providing the information necessary to convert input device values to color values expressed in a profile connection space (PCS).

profile connection space (PCS)
A fully defined color space used for linking and/or concatenating a series of profiles.

psychological, signal processing
Modifier used in this book to refer to visual signal processing that includes higher-order mental and cognitive (interpretive) processes.

psychophysical, signal processing
Modifier used in this book to refer to visual signal processing that includes both physiological and mental processes.

purple boundary
On a CIE chromaticity diagram, the straight line connecting the red and blue ends of the spectrum locus.

quantization
Conversion of continuous quantities to discrete digital values; the number of discrete values is determined by the number of bits that are used.

Rec. 601
Informal name for *Recommendation ITU-R BT.601*, formerly known as CCIR Recommendation 601, a document containing recommended specifications for digital component video.

Rec. 709
Informal name for *Recommendation ITU-R BT.709*, formerly known as CCIR Recommendation 709, a document containing recommended specifications for high-definition television signals.

reference image-capturing device

A hypothetical reference device, defined in terms of spectral responsivities and opto-electronic transfer characteristics, which is associated with the color encoding used in the *Kodak Photo CD* System.

reflectance

Ratio of the reflected radiant or luminous flux to the incident flux under specified conditions of irradiation.

reflectance factor

The amount of radiation reflected by a medium relative to that reflected by a perfect diffuser.

retina

Layer on the back interior of the eyeball, containing various types of photo-receptive cells that are connected to the brain by means of the optic nerve.

relative colorimetry

Colorimetric values expressed relative to those of a reference white. In standard CIE calculations, the reference white is defined to be a *perfect* white. In "media-relative" colorimetry, the support of the particular medium being measured is defined as the reference white.

RGB

Abbreviation for *red, green,* and *blue*.

SBA

Abbreviation for *scene balance algorithm,* an algorithm that automatically adjusts the overall lightness and color balance of images.

SMPTE

Abbreviation for *Society of Motion Picture and Television Engineers*.

saturation

The colorfulness of an area judged in proportion to its brightness.

scanner

A device for forming image-bearing signals from two-dimensional images.

scene balance algorithm (SBA)
An algorithm that automatically adjusts the overall lightness and color balance of images.

sensitivity
Property of a detector that makes it responsive to radiant power.

signal processing
Chemical, electronic, or digital operations, such as linear and nonlinear amplification, by which original signals are altered and/or combined with other signals.

silver halide
A light-sensitive crystalline compound used in conventional chemical photographic media.

simulation
The use of one medium or system to imitate the appearance of another.

softcopy
Jargon for electronic displays such as CRTs.

source
1. A physically realizable light, the spectral power distribution of which can be experimentally determined.
2. An imaging-system term for *origin*.

spatial compression
A technique for reducing image information, generally for purposes of storage or transmission.

spectral
Adjective indicating that monochromatic concepts are being considered.

spectral power distribution
Power, or relative power, of electromagnetic radiation as a function of wavelength.

spectral reflectance
The fraction of the incident power reflected as a function of wavelength.

spectral reflection density

Reflection density as a function of wavelength; the negative logarithm of spectral reflectance.

spectral responsivity

The response of a detection system, such as a scanner or a densitometer, as a function of wavelength. Spectral responsivity is influenced by the spectral power distribution of the illuminant, the spectral filtration effects of various optical components, and the spectral sensitivity of the detector.

spectral sensitivity

The response of a detector to monochromatic stimuli of equal radiant power.

spectral transmittance

The fraction of the incident power transmitted as a function of wavelength.

spectral transmission density

Transmission density as a function of wavelength; the negative logarithm of spectral transmittance.

spectrum locus

On a chromaticity diagram, a line connecting the points representing the chromaticities of the spectrum colors.

specular

Referring to light that is reflected or transmitted with little or no scattering.

Standard Illuminants

Relative spectral power distributions defining illuminants for use in colorimetric computations.

Standard Colorimetric Observer

An ideal observer having visual response described according to a specified set of color-matching functions.

speed

Term used in photography to describe sensitivity to light. Higher speed means greater sensitivity to light; lower speed means lesser sensitivity to light.

Status A densitometer

Densitometer having spectral responsivities corresponding to those specified by the ISO for Status A densitometers. Status A densitometers are used for measurements of photographic and other types of hardcopy media that are meant to be viewed directly by an observer.

Status M densitometer

Densitometer having spectral responsivities corresponding to those specified by the ISO for Status M densitometers. Status M densitometers are used for measurements of photographic negative media.

stimulus, color

A spectral power distribution, such as that produced by an illuminant, by the reflection of light from a reflective object, or by the transmission of light through a transmissive object.

subsampling

Sampling within samples; a technique employed to compress digital image files.

subtractive color

Color formed by the subtraction of light by absorption, such as by cyan, magenta, and yellow (CMY) photographic dyes or by cyan, magenta, yellow, and black (CMYK) printing inks.

surface color

Color perceived as belonging to the surface of a specimen, without the specimen appearing to be self-luminous.

surround

The area surrounding an image being viewed.

surround effect

A manifestation of lateral-brightness adaptation; an observer will perceive an image as having lower or higher luminance contrast depending upon the average luminance of the surround relative to that of the image.

tags

In an image file or profile, descriptors of the underlying data.

telécine

An imaging system used to scan motion picture films to produce video signals for taping and television broadcast.

test target

A collection of color samples used in the evaluation of color-imaging systems, generally made up of spectrally nonselective neutral samples and samples of various colors.

thermal printer

An output device that uses heat to transfer dyes to produce images on reflection or transmission media.

transform

One or more signal processing operations, used in color-imaging systems incorporating digital signal processing.

transmittance

Ratio of the transmitted radiant or luminous flux to the incident flux under specified conditions of irradiation.

transmittance factor

The amount of radiation transmitted by a medium relative to that transmitted by a perfect transmitting diffuser.

transparency

An image formed on a clear or translucent base by means of a photographic, printing, or other process, which is viewed by transmitting light through the image.

trichromatic

Three-color.

trichromatic system

A system for specifying color stimuli in terms of tristimulus values based on matching colors by additive mixture of three suitably chosen reference color stimuli.

tristimulus values

The amounts of three stimuli, in a given trichromatic system, required to match a particular color stimulus.

tungsten lamp

An electric lamp having filaments of tungsten.

tungsten-halogen lamp

Lamp in which tungsten filaments operate in an atmosphere of low-pressure iodine (or other halogen) vapor.

uniform color space

Color space in which equal distances approximately represent equal color differences for stimuli having the same luminance.

universal film terms

Input signal-processing transforms used on *Photo CD* Imaging Workstations to convert scanned values to *PhotoYCC* Space values. A universal film-term transform is based on the characteristics of a reference film of the same basic type as that being scanned. When universal terms are used, differences of each scanned film from the reference film are reflected in the color encoding.

unwanted (spectral) absorption

Spectral absorptions of a colorant in portions of the spectrum where ideally there should be 100% transmission or reflection.

u', v' diagram

A uniform chromaticity diagram, introduced by the CIE in 1976, in which u' and v' chromaticity coordinates are used.

viewing conditions

Description of the characteristics of a viewing environment that physically alter a color stimulus or that affect an observer's perception of the stimulus.

viewing flare

Stray light present in an environment in which an image is viewed. The amount of viewing flare usually is expressed in terms of its amount relative to that of light reflected from, transmitted through, or produced by a white in the image.

visual density

Density measured according to a responsivity corresponding to the CIEXYZ $\bar{y}(\lambda)$ function.

visual neutral

A metameric match to a spectrally nonselective neutral viewed under identical conditions.

von Kries transformation

A chromatic adaptation transformation by which changes in chromatic adaptation are represented as adjustments of the sensitivities of the three cone systems.

wavelength

In a periodic wave, the distance between two points of corresponding phase in consecutive cycles.

white balance

The process of adjusting the RGB signals of a video camera such that equal signals are produced from an illuminated white object.

writer

General term for output devices that use photographic films or papers.

x, y diagram

A chromaticity diagram in which the x and y chromaticity coordinates of the CIE XYZ system are used.

yellow

One of the subtractive primaries; a yellow colorant absorbs blue light and reflects or transmits red and green light.

zeroing

Adjustment of an instrument such that a zero signal value would be obtained when an ideal reference specimen is measured. For example, reflection densitometers generally are adjusted such that a zero-density reading would be obtained if a perfect white diffuser were measured.

Recommended Reading

Colorimetry

Billmeyer, F. W., Jr., and Saltzman, M. *Principles of Color Technology*, Second Edition, Wiley, New York (1981).

CIE Publication 15.2, *Colorimetry*, Second Edition, CIE, Vienna (1986).

CIE *Standard on Colorimetric Observers*, CIE S002 (1986).

Hunt, R. W. G. *Measuring Color*, Second Edition, Ellis Horwood, Chichester, England, and Simon and Schuster, Englewood Cliffs, NJ (1991).

Judd, D. B., and Wyszecki, G. *Color in Business, Science, and Industry*, Wiley, New York (1975).

Wright, W. D. *The Measurement of Colour*, Fourth Edition, Hilger, Bristol, U.K. (1969).

Wyszecki, G., and Stiles, W. S. *Color Science*, Second Edition, Wiley, New York (1982).

Color and Vision

American Society for Testing and Materials, *ASTM Standards on Color and Appearance Measurement*, Fifth Edition, American Society for Testing and Materials, West Conshohocken, PA (1996).

Bartleson, C. J. "Measures of brightness and lightness," *Die Farbe* 28, Nr. 3/6 (1980).

Bartleson, C. J., and Breneman, E. J. "Brightness perception in complex fields," *J. Opt. Soc. Am.*, 57 (1977).

Braun, K. M., and Fairchild, M. D. "Evaluation of five color-appearance transforms across changes in viewing conditions and media," IS&T/SID 3rd Color Imaging Conference, Scottsdale, AZ (1995).

Breneman, E. J. "The effect of level of illuminance and relative surround luminance on the appearance of black-and-white photographs," *Photogr. Sci. and Eng.* Vol. 6 (1962).

Breneman, E. J. "Perceived saturation in stimuli viewed in light and dark surrounds," *J. Opt. Soc. Am.* 67(5), 657 (1977).

Breneman, E. J. "Corresponding chromaticities for different states of adaptation to complex visual fields," *J. Opt. Soc. Am.* A4(6) (1987).

Daniels, C. M. Master's Thesis, Rochester Institute of Technology, Rochester, NY (1996).

Estevez, O. Ph.D. Thesis, University of Amsterdam (1979).

Evans, R. M. *An Introduction to Color*, Wiley, New York (1948).

Evans, R. M. *Eye, Film, and Camera in Color Photography*, Wiley, New York (1959).

Evans, R. M. *The Perception of Color*, Wiley, New York (1974).

Fairchild, M. D. "Considering the surround in device-independent color imaging," *Color Res. and Appl.*, Vol. 20 (1995).

Fairchild, M. D. "Refinement of the RLAB color space," *Color Res. and Appl.*, Vol. 21 (1995).

Fairchild, M. D. *Color Appearance Models*, Addison Wesley Longman, Reading, MA (1998).

Fairchild, M. D., and Berns, R. S. "Image color appearance specification through extension of CIELAB," *Color Res. and Appl.*, Vol. 18 (1993).

Hunt, R. W. G. "Revised colour-appearance model for related and unrelated colors," *Color Res. and Appl.*, Vol. 16 (1991).

Hunt, R. W. G. "An improved predictor of colourfulness in a model of colour vision," *Color Res. and Appl.*, Vol. 19 (1994).

Hurvich, L. M. *Color Vision*, Sinauer Associates, Sunderland, MA (1981).

Jameson, D., and Hurvich, L. M. "Complexities of perceived brightness," *Science*, Vol. 133 (1961).

Nayatani, Y., Takahama, K., Sobagaki, H., and Hashimoto, K. "Color-appearance and chromatic-adaptation transform," *Color Res. Appl.*, Vol. 15 (1990).

Stevens, J. C., and Stevens, S. S. "Brightness functions: effects of adaptation," *J. Opt. Soc. Am.*, Vol. 53 (1963).

Color Science and Color Reproduction

Bartleson, C. J., and Breneman, E. J. "Brightness reproduction in the photographic process," *Photogr. Sci. and Eng.*, Vol. 11 (1967).

Bartleson, C. J., and Clapper, F. R. "The importance of viewing conditions in the appraisal of graphic reproductions," *Pr. Tech.* 136–144 (1967).

DeMarsh, L. E., and Giorgianni, E. J. "Color science for imaging systems," *Physics Today* (September 1989).

Hunt, R. W. G. *The Reproduction of Colour in Photography, Printing, and Television*, Fifth Edition, Fountain Press, Tolworth, U.K. (1995).

Pearson, M. L., and Yule, J. A. C. "Transformations of color mixture functions without negative portions," *Journal of Color and Appearance*, Vol. II, No. 1 (1973).

Pointer, M. R. "The gamut of real surface colors," *Color Res. Appl.*, Vol. 5 (1980).

von Kries, J. A. In "Handbuk der Physiologisches Optik," Vol. II, pp. 366–369. (W. Nagel, ed.) Leopold Voss, Hamburg (1911).

Wyszecki, G., and Stiles, W. S. *Color Science*, Second Edition, Wiley, New York (1982).

Yule, J. A. C. *Principles of Color Reproduction*, Wiley, New York (1967).

Photo CD System

Giorgianni, E. J., Johnson, S. E., Madden, T. E., and O'Such, W. R. *Fully Utilizing Photo CD Images*, Articles No. 1, 2, and 4, Eastman Kodak Company, Rochester, NY (1993).

Giorgianni, E. J., and Madden, T. E. "Color Encoding in the *Photo CD* System," *Color for Science, Art and Technology*, Elsevier Science Publishers B.V., Amsterdam, The Netherlands (1997).

"*KODAK Photo CD* System–A Planning Guide for Developers," Eastman Kodak Company, Rochester, NY (1991).

Video

CCIR Recommendation 709, "Basic Parameter Values for the HDTV Standard for the Studio and for International Programme Exchange," now Recommendation ITU-R BT.709.

CCIR Recommendation 601-1, "Encoding Parameters of Digital Television for Studios," now Recommendation ITU-R BT.601-1.

Poynton, C. A. *A Technical Introduction to Digital Video*, Wiley, New York (1996).

Sproson, W. N. *Color Science in Television and Display Systems*, Adam Hilger, Bristol, U.K. (1983).

Photography

Evans, R. M. *Eye, Film, and Camera in Color Photography*, Wiley, New York (1959).

Evans, R. M., Hanson, W. T., and Brewer, W. L. *Principles of Color Photography*, Wiley, New York (1953).

Mees, C. E. K., and James, T. H. *The Theory of the Photographic Process*, Fourth Edition, Macmillan, New York (1977).

Society of Motion Picture and Television Engineers, *Principles of Color Sensitometry*, Society of Motion Picture and Television Engineers, New York (1963).

Thomas, W. *S.P.S.E. Handbook of Photographic Science and Engineering*, Wiley, New York (1973).

Image Compression

Rabbani, M. *Digital Image Compression Techniques*, SPIE Optical Engineering Press, Bellingham, Washington (1991).

Index